CATALOGUE
OF THE ROMAN IMPERIAL COINS

in the Charles University Collection
(235–284 A. D.)

David Lužický

CHARLES UNIVERSITY IN PRAGUE • KAROLINUM PRESS 2026

KAROLINUM PRESS
Karolinum Press is a publishing department of Charles University
Ovocný trh 560/5, 116 36 Prague 1, Czech Republic
www.karolinum.cz, redakcenk@ruk.cuni.cz

Set and printed in the Czech Republic
Layout by DTP Karolinum
First edition

A catalogue record for this book is available from the National Library of the Czech Republic.

This work was supported by GA UK 257503 – Coins from the Period of Military Anarchy (in the numismatic collection of the Charles University).

ISBN 978-80-246-6145-2
ISBN 978-80-246-6156-8 (pdf)

The manuscript was reviewed by Jiří Militký (The Numismatic Department of the National Museum in Prague) and Martin Trefný (Jan Evangelista Purkyně University in Ústí nad Labem).

CONTENTS

For Vojtík

INTRODUCTION

The Institute for Greek and Latin studies has in its possession one of the largest public collections of Classical coins in the Czech Republic. Although this collection was being continually expanded from the middle of the 18th century,[1] it was not published until 1985. Only then, 287 Roman Republic coins were published by doc. PhDr. Václav Marek, CSc. in his book *The Roman Republican Coins in the Collection of the Charles University*. Although the original intention was to subsequently publish the entire collection, further work on the collection was only done in 2006, when, as part of the master's dissertation of the author, coins from the so-called Period of Military Anarchy, i.e., 235–284 A.D.,[2] were documented. This work was to be extended in the doctoral thesis of the author to catalogue the coins from the period of the First Tetrarchy, i.e., 284–305 A.D. Considering the relatively low number of coins representing this period, the catalogue was extended to 337 A.D.[3] Hence, 1,183 coins were selected and documented from the collection up to 2010. The first part of these is published here.

Federico Gambacorta followed upon this work in his *Catalogue of the Late Roman, Byzantine and Barbaric Coins in the Charles University Collection (364–1092)*, where a collection of 243 Late Classical coins was published in 2013. Further work on the collection should cover the period of 337–364 A.D., with which the documenting of the Late Imperial mints should be completed.

The main source, which was used in the process of cataloguing the collection of coins, is *The Roman Imperial Coinage (RIC)*. For this reason, the bibliography for the majority of coins features the RIC reference first. Considering the fact that some volumes of RIC are outdated, in our case particularly RIC 5.1 and 5.2., the coins were classified using some more recent literature, e.g., MIR, La Venéra, Monnaies de l'Empire Romain/Roman Imperial Coinage A.D. 268–276, The Cunetio Treasure, Normanby Hoard, etc.[4] For the coins in the presented catalogue where there was no more recent literature available and they could be determined only on the basis of RIC, these coins were assessed with respect to Pink's Aufbau.[5] A similar approach was applied with regard to the dating. The years of reign of particular rulers and members of their families were based on Kienast's tables.[6]

Among the 564 published coins we find many of those that feature minor variations from the RIC. These coins are marked at the end of the citation with the abbreviation var. – variant. We can specifically note the coins with catalogue number 11, 89, 120, 183, 339. As for the preservation and frequency of occurrence, the coins from the middle of the third century were typically minted using common metals and their preservation is average, sometimes below average. That is also the case with the coins catalogued here. The most frequent mintage is that of common metals,[7] which are often poorly preserved, sometimes hardly legible; silver coins are less frequent but mostly better preserved. In the presented catalogue there are no gold coins.

Last but not least, I would like to thank: my friend and colleague Mgr. Libor Grmela for the initial impulse which led to the cataloguing of the coins from the Period of Military Anarchy, to doc. PhDr. Václav Marek, CSc., for his patience and warm, welcoming and friendly attitude that accompanied me throughout my entire research on the collection, to my friend and colleague Dr. Federico Gambacorta Ph.D. not only for the photographs and other as-

1 Marek 1985, p. 7.

2 Work on this part of the catalogue was realised with the financial support of the Grant Agency of the Charles University in Prague No. 257503 – Coins from the Period of Military Anarchy (in the numismatic collection of the Charles University). Partial results were published in Lužický 2007 and Lužický 2008.

3 Work on this part of the catalogue was realised with the financial support of the Grant Agency of the Charles University No. 258140 – Coins of the Tetrarchy (in the numismatic collection of the Charles University). Partial results were published in Lužický 2012.

4 For more details, see Abbreviations and Bibliography.

5 For more details, see Bibliography.

6 Kienast 1996.

7 These coins were minted using an alloy of copper with another metal.

sistance, and to my colleagues from Vienna from the Institut für Numismatik und Geldgeschichte Universität Wien for their friendly attitude and help during my visits to their library. I am grateful to Ao. Univ.-Prof. i.R. Dr. Hubert Emmerig, M.A. (Institut für Numismatik und Geldgeschichte Universität Wien) and MMag. Dr. Alexander Ruske for valuable advice and consultations. I would like to especially thank my parents for their support of my studies and my wife Lenka for the great patience which she had with me when I was working on the collection.

NOTE ON THE CATALOGUE

The present catalogue of Roman Imperial coins includes 564 coins which were minted in the period of 235–284 A.D. Out of this number, it was possible to identify 65 coins in the inventory books of the old Czech collection.[8] The coins in the catalogue are ordered according to several criteria. Primarily, they are ordered based on their chronology, i.e., the minting emperors and members of their families. Secondarily, the ordering follows the geographic criterion, i.e., respects the location of the mint. The individual mints are ordered from west to east, i.e., from the mint in London to that in Rome and Cyzicus to Antiochia. Furthermore, the coins from individual mints are ordered by emissions, from the earliest to the latest. Wherever the collection features several coins of one emission and type, these coins are then ordered from the highest nominal value to the lowest. In short, the system is as follows: emperor – mint – emission – nominal value.

The measurements of coins are given in millimetres. The coins were measured on their axes on the twelfth and third hour; the weight is given in grams.

[8] These relate to the inventory numbers 15.03–953.

SYMBOLS AND ABBREVIATIONS

[]	reinstatement of letter(s) or word(s)
/	new line
–	division of text or legend
— — —//—	in field left, centre, right // in exergue
inv.	inverted
A.D.	*Anno Domini*
g.	grams
mm.	millimetres
h.	hours
inv. n.	inventory number
Obv.	obverse
Rev.	reverse
Lit.	literature
BMCRE	*Coins of the Roman Empire in the British Museum*
CUN	*The Cunetio Treasure*
LV	*Ripostiglio della Venèra: nuovo catalogo illustrato*
RIC temp	http://www.ric.mom.fr
MIR	*Moneta Imperii Romani*
NOR	*The Normanby Hoard and the other Roman Coin Hoards*
RIC	*The Roman Imperial Coinage*
Schulzki	*Die Antoninianprägung der gallischen Kaiser von Postumus bis Tetricus (AGK). Typenkatalog der regulären und nachgeprägten Münzen*

THE CATALOGUE

MAXIMINUS THRAX
(235 – 238 A.D.)

Roma

235 A.D.

Denarius
Obv. IMP MAXIMINVS PIVS AVG. Laureated bust of emperor in cuirass and paludamentum looking right, seen from rear.
Rev. FIDES MILITVM. Fides standing left holding vertical standard in each hand.
— — —//—
Lit.: MIR 27 Rom 2/9–3/A; RIC 4.2, p. 140, 7a; BMCRE 6, p. 222, 1

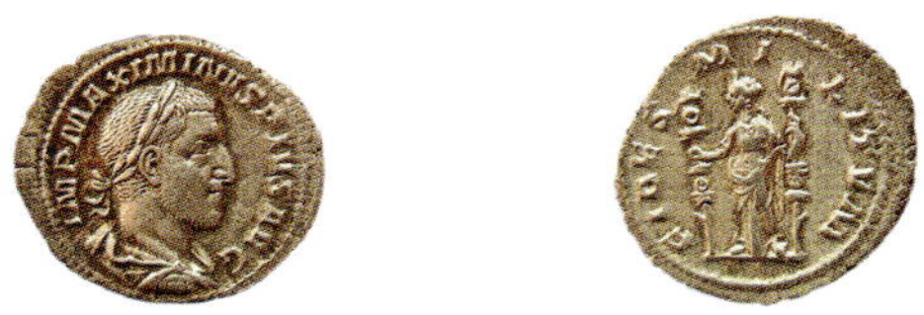

1. AR; 2,85 g.; 19,1 x 20,9 mm.; 1 h.; inv. n. 1353.
(Obv. IMP MAXIMINVS PIVS AVG; Rev. FIDES – MI-LITVM; — — —//—)

Denarius
Obv. IMP MAXIMINVS PIVS AVG. Laureated bust of emperor in cuirass and paludamentum looking right, seen from rear.
Rev. PROVIDENTIA AVG. Providentia standing left, holding baton in right hand and cornucopiae in left hand; at feet to left globe.
— — —//—
Lit.: MIR 27 Rom 2/11–3/A; RIC 4.2, p. 141, 13; BMCRE 6, p. 223, 15

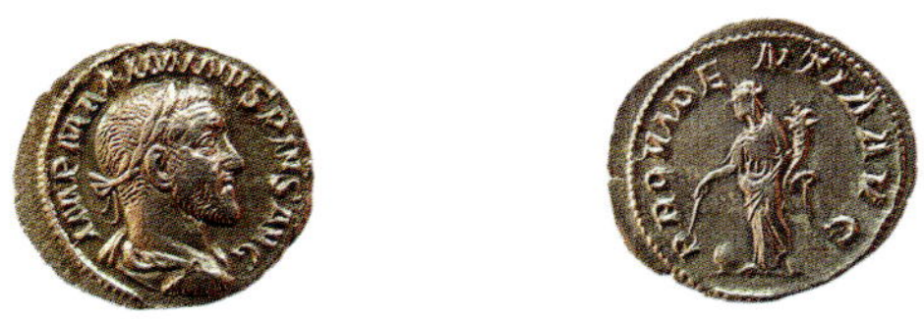

2. AR; 3,51 g.; 18,9 x 20,7 mm.; 12 h.; inv. n. 1354.
(Obv. IMP MAXIMINVS PIVS AVG; Rev. PROVIDE-NTIA AVG; — — —//—)

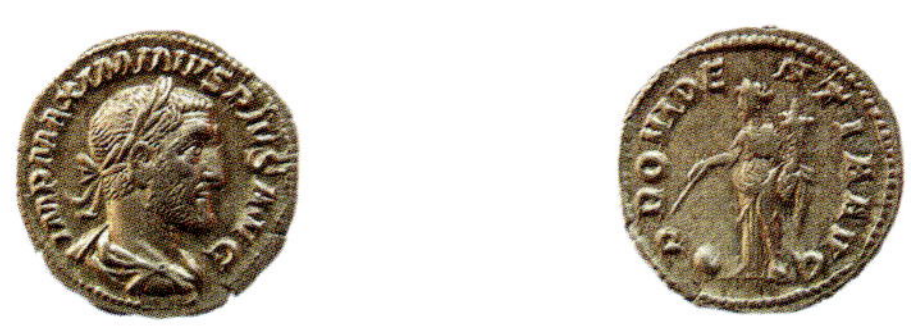

3. AR; 3,4 g.; 19,5 x 18,7 mm.; 12 h.; inv. n. 1355.
(Obv. IMP MAXIMINVS PIVS AVG; Rev. PROVIDE-NTIA AVG; — — —//—)

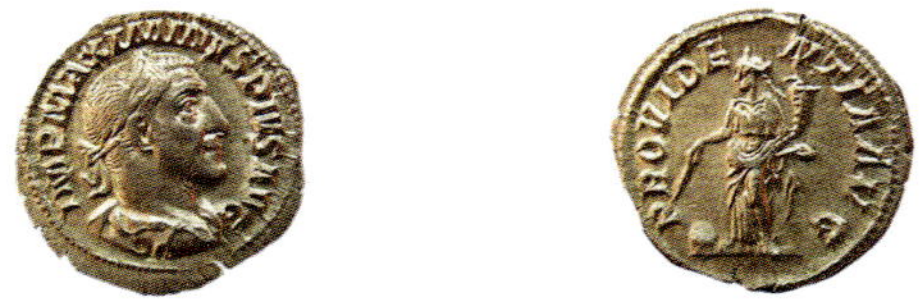

4. AR; 3,42 g.; 19,4 x 19,4 mm.; 12 h.; inv. n. 1356.
(Obv. IMP MAXIMINVS PIVS AVG; Rev. PROVIDE-NTIA AVG; — — —//—)

Denarius

Obv. IMP MAXIMINVS PIVS AVG. Laureated bust of emperor in cuirass and paludamentum looking right, seen from rear.

Rev. VICTORIA AVG. Victory walking right, holding wreath in right hand and palm in left hand.

— — —//—

Lit.: MIR 27 Rom 2/13–3/A; RIC 4.2, p. 141, 16; BMCRE 6, p. 224, 25

5. AR; 3,23 g.; 18,2 x 18,5 mm.; 12 h.; inv. n. 1357.
(Obv. IMP MAXIMINVS PIVS AVG; Rev. VICTO-RI-A AVG; — — —//—)

Denarius

Obv. IMP MAXIMINVS PIVS AVG. Laureated bust of emperor in cuirass and paludamentum looking right, seen from rear.

Rev. P M TR P P P. Emperor standing left between two standards, raising right hand, holding vertical spear in left hand.

— — —//—

Lit.: MIR 27 Rom 2/8–3/B; RIC 4.2, p. 138, 1; BMCRE 6, p. 223, 9

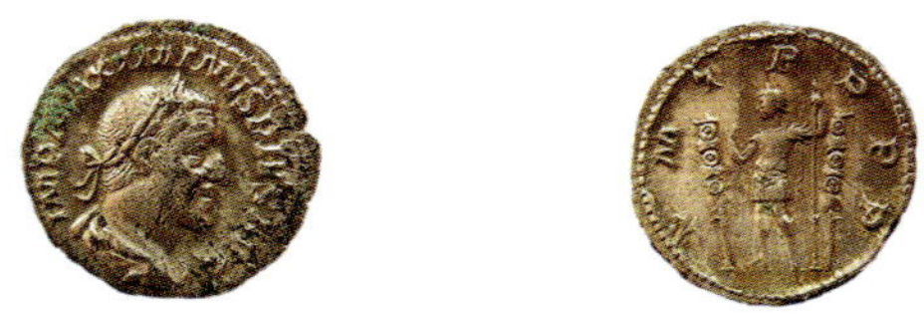

6. AR; 3,27 g.; 19,2 x 19,7 mm.; 1 h.; inv. n. 1358.
(Obv. IMP MAXIMINVS PIVS AVG; Rev. P M – TR – P – P P; — — —//—)

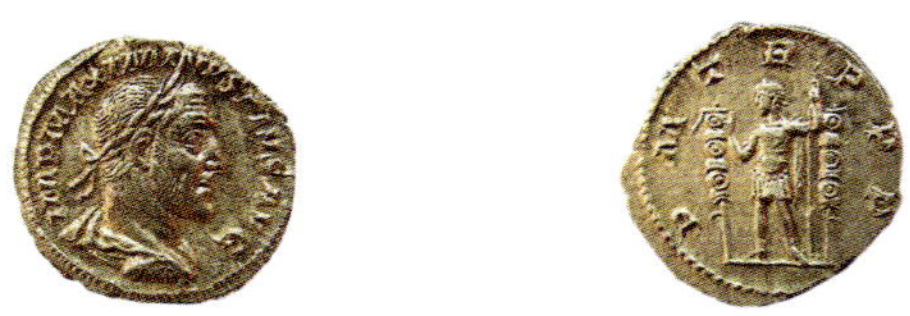

7. AR; 3,5 g.; 18,0 x 18,6 mm.; 1 h.; inv. n. 1359.
(Obv. IMP MAXIMINVS PIVS AVG; Rev. P M TR – P P P; — — —//—; Lit.: BMCRE 6, p. 223, 12)

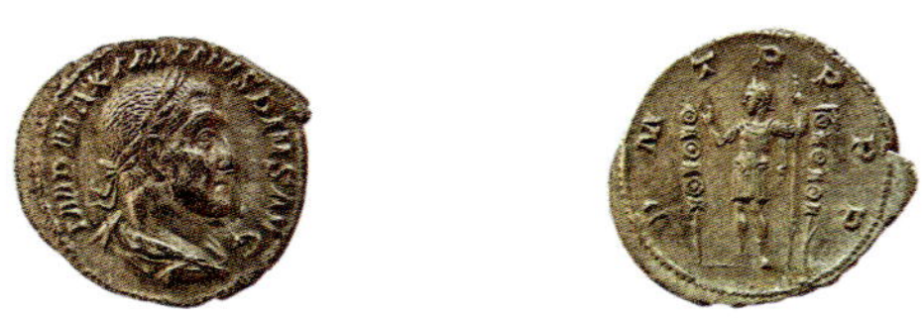

8. AR; 3,18 g.; 18,7 x 19,7 mm.; 7 h.; inv. n. 1360.
(Obv. IMP MAXIMINVS PIVS AVG; Rev. P M – TR P – P P; — — —//—; Lit.: BMCRE 6, p. 223, 11)

Sestertius
Obv. IMP MAXIMINVS PIVS AVG. Laureated bust of emperor in cuirass and paludamentum looking right, seen from rear.
Rev. FIDES MILITVM. Fides standing left holding vertical standard in each hand.
S — C//—
Lit.: MIR 27 Rom 2–3/9–5/B; RIC 4.2, p. 144, 43; BMCRE 6, p. 222, 2

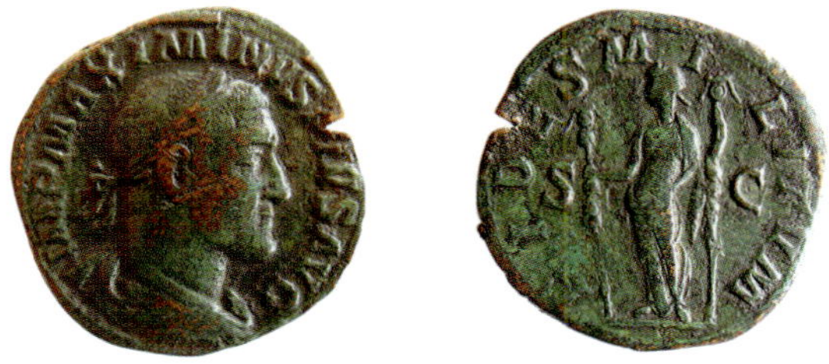

9. AE; 24,05 g.; 30,4 x 30,5 mm.; 1 h.; inv. n. 1361.
(Obv. IMP MAXIMINVS PIVS AVG; Rev. FIDES M-I-LITVM; S — C//—)

Denarius
Obv. IMP MAXIMINVS PIVS AVG. Laureated bust of emperor in cuirass and paludamentum looking right, seen from rear.
Rev. PAX AVGVSTI. Pax standing left, holding branch in right hand and transverse sceptre in left hand.
— — —//—
Lit.: MIR 27 Rom 2–3/10–3/B; RIC 4.2, p. 140, 12; BMCRE 6, p. 228, 70

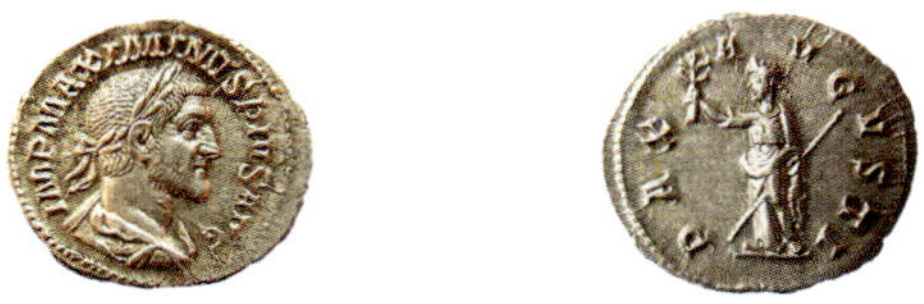

10. AR; 2,67 g.; 18,6 x 20,2 mm.; 12 h.; inv. n. 1362.
(Obv. IMP MAXIMINVS PIVS AVG; Rev. PAX – A-VGVSTI; — — —//—)

Sestertius
Obv. IMP MAXIMINVS PIVS AVG. Laureated bust of emperor in cuirass and paludamentum looking right, seen from rear.
Rev. PAX AVGVSTI. Pax standing left, holding branch in right hand and transverse sceptre in left hand.
S — C//—
Lit.: MIR 27 Rom 2–3/10–5/B; RIC 4.2, p. 145, 58; BMCRE 6, p. 228, 72 – 74

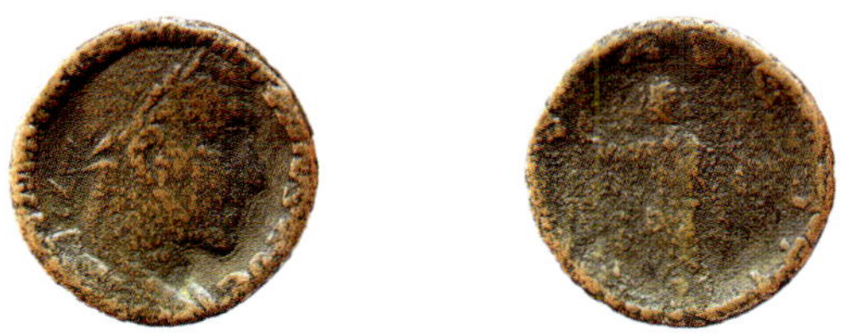

11.[9] AE; 14,42 g.; 24,6 x 23,9 mm.; 12 h.; inv. n. 1363.
(Obv. IMP MAXIMINVS PIVS AVG; Rev. [PAX] AVGVSTI; [S] — C//—)

9 Secondarily adjusted edge of the coin. For details, see Lužický 2012.

Denarius

Obv. MP MAXIMINVS PIVS AVG. Laureated bust of emperor in cuirass and paludamentum looking right, seen from rear.

Rev. PROVIDENTIA AVG. Providentia standing left, holding baton in right hand and cornucopiae in left hand; at feet to left globe.

— — —//—

Lit.: MIR 27 Rom 2–3/11–3/B; RIC 4.2, p. 141, 13; BMCRE 6, p. 230, 87

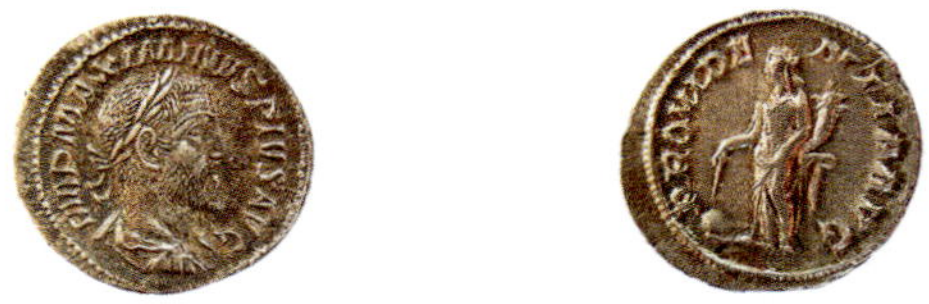

12. AR; 3,43 g.; 19,1 x 20,0 mm.; 1 h.; inv. n. 1364.
(Obv. IMP MAXIMINVS PIVS AVG; Rev. PROVIDE-NTIA AVG; — — —//—)

13. AR; 3,7 g.; 19,1 x 19,4 mm.; 6 h.; inv. n. 1365.
(Obv. IMP MAXIMINVS PIVS AVG; Rev. PROVIDENTIA AVG; — — —//—)

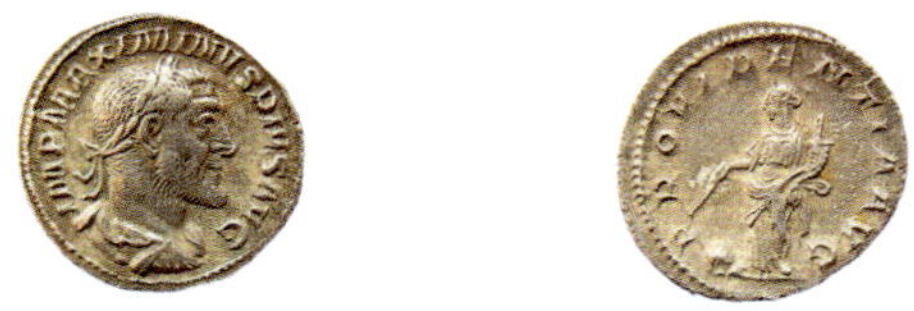

14. AR; 3,18 g.; 18,8 x 18,9 mm.; 6 h.; inv. n. 1366.
(Obv. IMP MAXIMINVS PIVS AVG; Rev. PROVIDENTIA AVG; — — —//—)

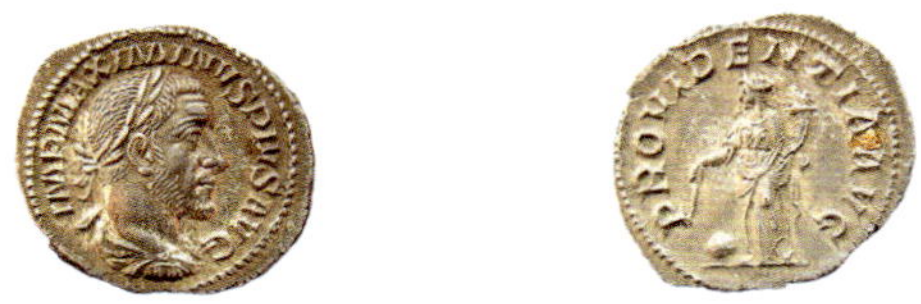

15. AR; 3,33 g.; 18,3 x 20,1 mm.; 6 h.; inv. n. 1367.
(Obv. IMP MAXIMINVS PIVS AVG; Rev. PROVIDENTIA AVG; — — —//—)

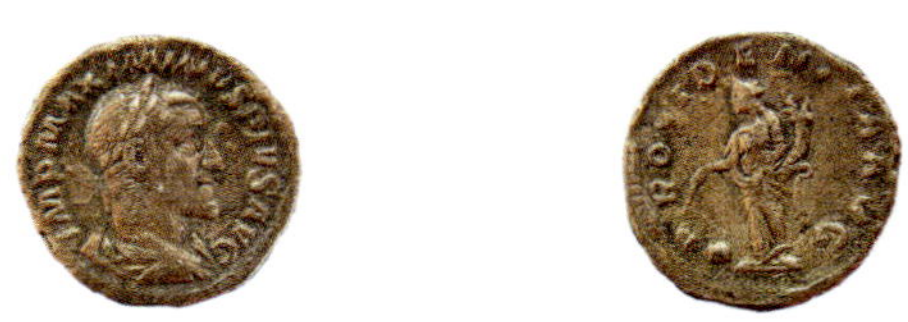

16. AR; 2,67 g.; 18,7 x 18,6 mm.; 7 h.; inv. n. 1368.
(Obv. IMP MAXIMINVS PIVS AVG; Rev. P-ROVIDENTIA AVG; — — —//—)

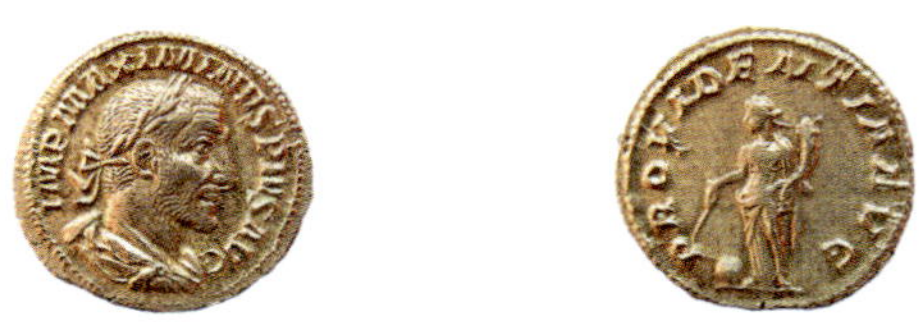

17. AR; 2,79 g.; 18,8 x 19,4 mm.; 12 h.; inv. n. 1369.
(Obv. IMP MAXIMINVS PIVS AVG; Rev. PROVIDENTIA AVG; — — —//—; Lit.: BMCRE 6, p. 230, 88)

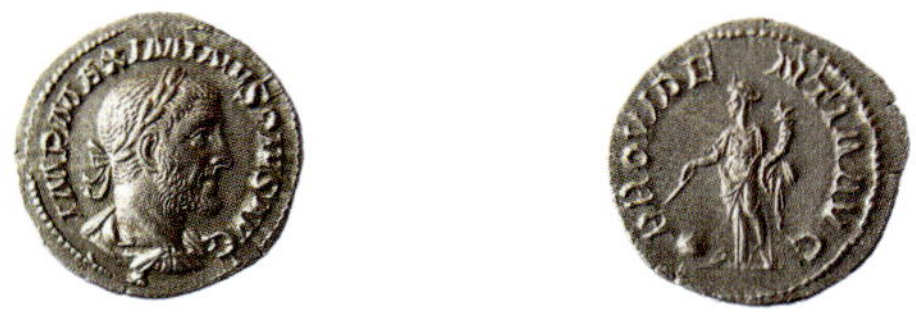

18. AR; 2,93 g.; 19,6 x 19,6 mm.; 12 h.; inv. n. 1370.
(Obv. IMP MAXIMINVS PIVS AVG; Rev. PROVIDE-NTIA AVG; — — —//—; Lit.: BMCRE 6, p. 230, 88)

Denarius

Obv. IMP MAXIMINVS PIVS AVG. Laureated bust of emperor in cuirass and paludamentum looking right, seen from rear.

Rev. SALVS AVGVSTI. Salus seated left, feeding snake rising from altar.

— — —//—

Lit.: MIR 27 Rom 2–3/12–3/B; RIC 4.2, p. 141, 14; BMCRE 6, p. 230, 99

19. AR; 3,14 g.; 19,8 x 18,7 mm.; 6 h.; inv. n. 1371.
(Obv. IMP MAXIMINVS PIVS AVG; Rev. SALVS AVGVSTI; — — —//—)

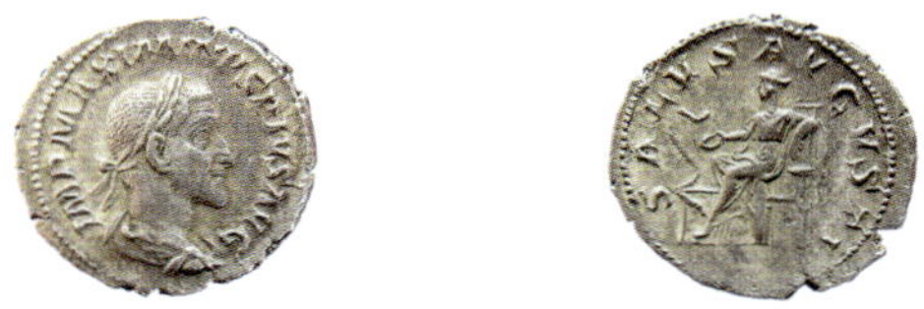

20. AR; 2,86 g.; 19,0 x 19,9 mm.; 6 h.; inv. n. 1372.
(Obv. IMP MAXIMINVS PIVS AVG; Rev. SALVS AVGVSTI; — — —//—)

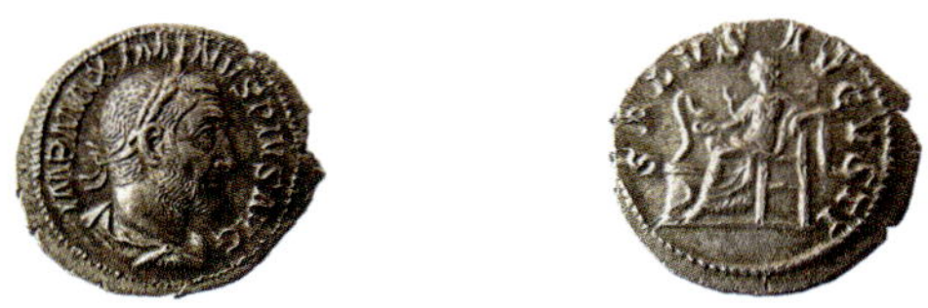

21. AR; 2,96 g.; 19,1 x 21,1 mm.; 6 h.; inv. n. 1373.
(Obv. IMP MAXIMINVS PIVS AVG; Rev. SALVS – AVGVSTI; — — —//—)

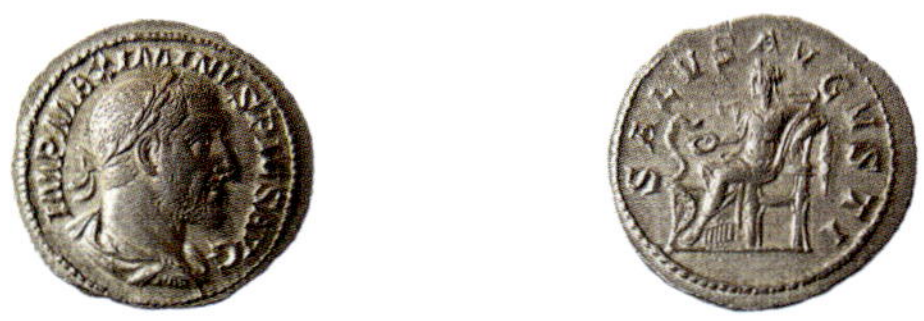

22. AR; 3,03 g.; 19,3 x 19,9 mm.; 6 h.; inv. n. 1374.
(Obv. IMP MAXIMINVS PIVS AVG; Rev. SALVS AVGVSTI; — — —//—)

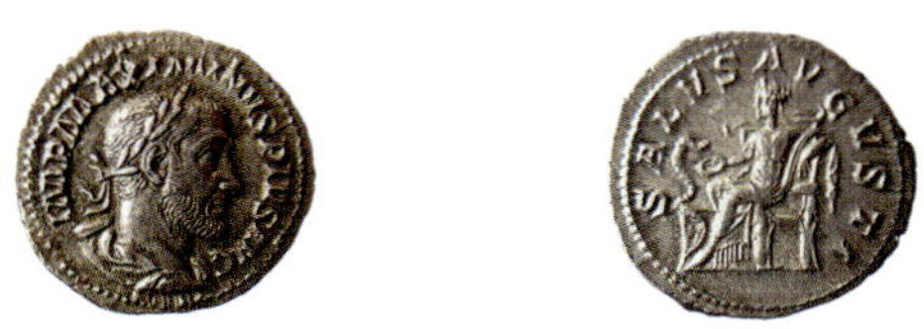

23. AR; 3,92 g.; 19,3 x 20,0 mm.; 6 h.; inv. n. 1375.
(Obv. IMP MAXIMINVS PIVS AVG; Rev. SALVS AVGVSTI; — — —//—)

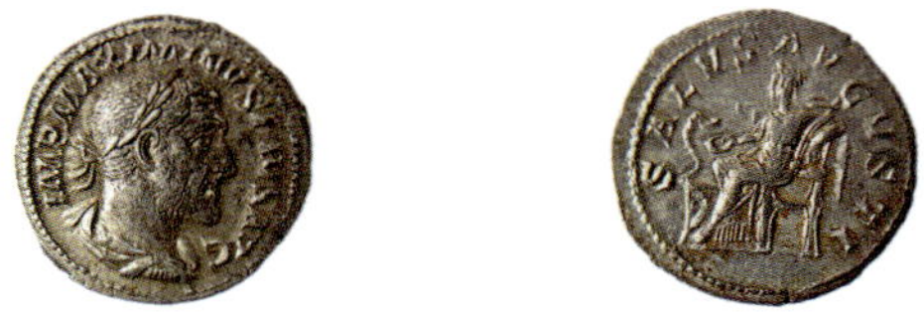

24. AR; 3,38 g.; 19,6 x 19,8 mm.; 6 h.; inv. n. 1376.
(Obv. IMP MAXIMINVS PIVS AVG; Rev. SALVS AVGVSTI; — — —//—)

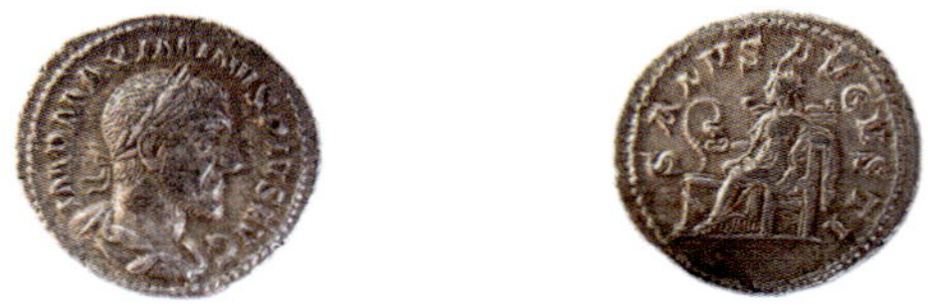

25. AR; 3,28 g.; 19,5 x 20,2 mm.; 6 h.; inv. n. 1377.
(Obv. IMP MAXIMINVS PIVS AVG; Rev. SALVS AVGVSTI; — — —//—)

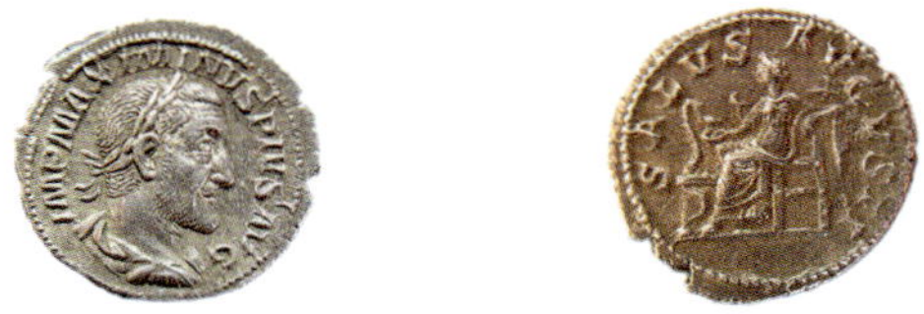

26. AR; 3,41 g.; 19,1 x 20,5 mm.; 7 h.; inv. n. 1378.
(Obv. IMP MAXIMINVS PIVS AVG; Rev. SALVS – AVGVSTI; — — —//—)

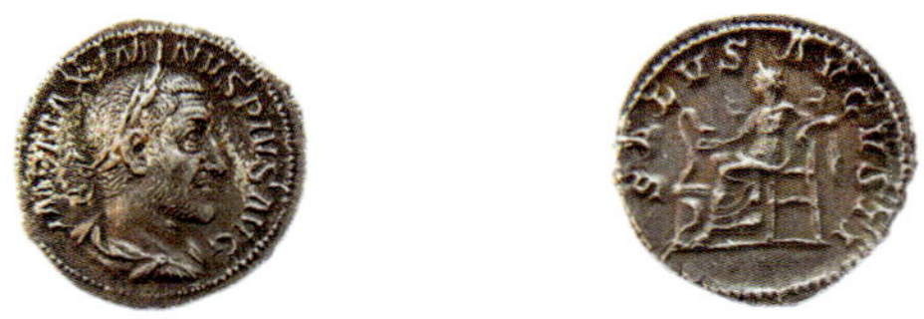

27. AR; 3,22 g.; 20,0 x 19,4 mm.; 7 h.; inv. n. 1379.
(Obv. IMP MAXIMINVS PIVS AVG; Rev. SALVS – AVGVSTI; — — —//—)

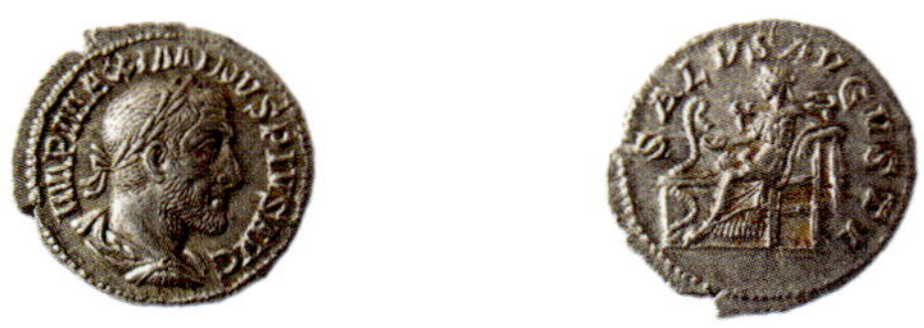

28. AR; 2,81 g.; 19,1 x 19,9 mm.; 7 h.; inv. n. 1380.
(Obv. IMP MAXIMINVS PIVS AVG; Rev. SALVS AVGVSTI; — — —//—)

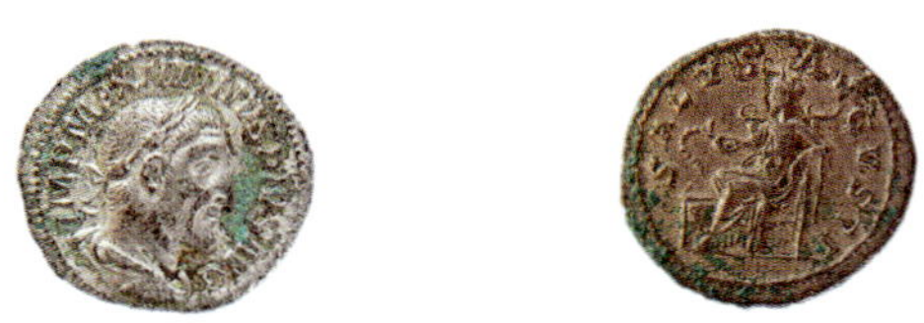

29. AR; 2,78 g.; 18,8 x 19,9 mm.; 7 h.; inv. n. 1381. (
Obv. IMP MAXIMINVS PIVS AVG; Rev. SALVS – AVGVSTI; — — —//—)

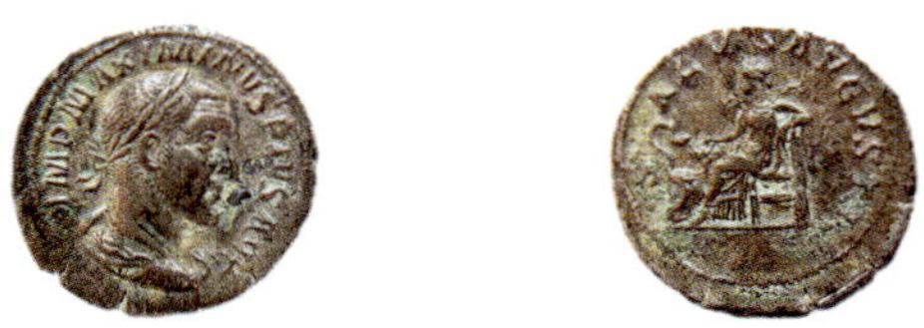

30. AR; 3,02 g.; 19,8 x 20,1 mm.; 12 h.; inv. n. 1382.
(Obv. IMP MAXIMINVS PIVS AVG; Rev. S-ALVS AVGVSTI; — — —//—)

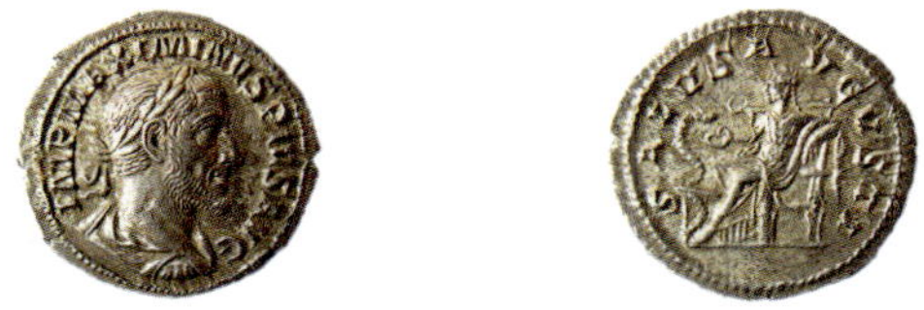

31. AR; 2,85 g.; 19,5 x 19,9 mm.; 12 h.; inv. n. 1383.
(Obv. IMP MAXIMINVS PIVS AVG; Rev. SALVS A-VGVSTI; — — —//—; Lit.: BMCRE 6, p. 224, 22)

Denarius
Obv. IMP MAXIMINVS PIVS AVG. Laureated bust of emperor in cuirass and paludamentum looking right, seen from rear.
Rev. VICTORIA AVG. Victory walking right, holding wreath in right hand and palm in left hand.
— — —//—
Lit.: MIR 27 Rom 2–3/13–3/B; RIC 4.2, p. 141, 16; BMCRE 6, p. 231, 106

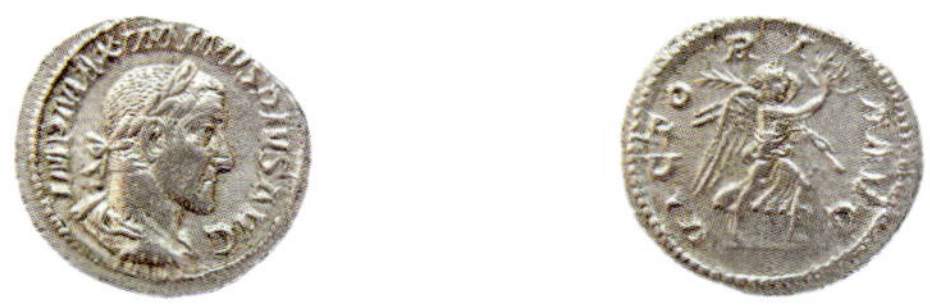

32. AR; 3,69 g.; 18,7 x 19,8 mm.; 1 h.; inv. n. 1384.
(Obv. IMP MAXIMINVS PIVS AVG; Rev. VICTO-RI-A AVG; — — —//—)

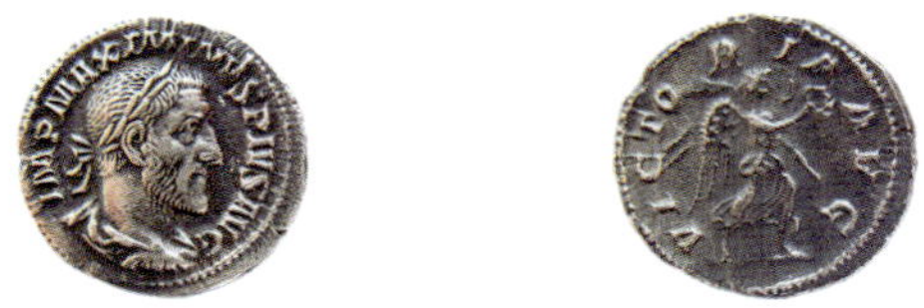

33. AR; 3,08 g.; 19,2 x 19,8 mm.; 5 h.; inv. n. 1385.
(Obv. IMP MAXIMINVS PIVS AVG; Rev. VICTO-R-IA – AVG; — — —//—; Lit.: BMCRE 6, p. 231, 105)

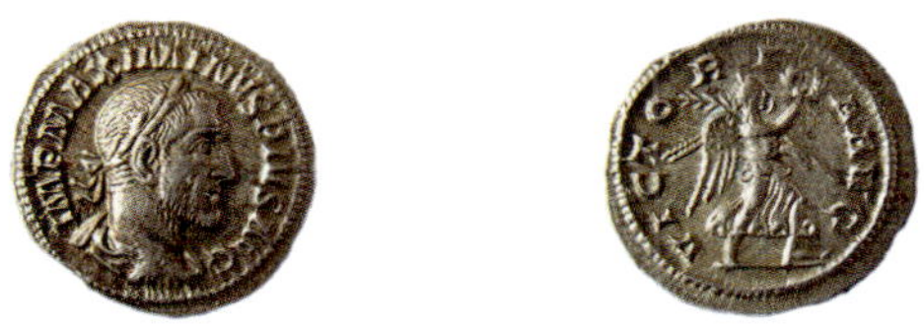

34. AR; 2,87 g.; 20,0 x 20,0 mm.; 6 h.; inv. n. 1386.
(Obv. IMP MAXIMINVS PIVS AVG; Rev. VICTO-R-I-A AVG; — — —//—; Lit.: BMCRE 6, p. 231, 105)

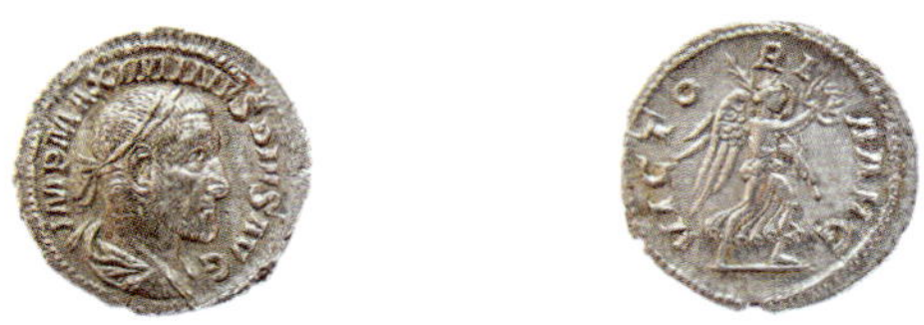

35. AR; 3,35 g.; 19,6 x 19,9 mm.; 12 h.; inv. n. 1387.
(Obv. IMP MAXIMINVS PIVS AVG; Rev. VICTO-RI-A AVG; — — —//—; Lit.: BMCRE 6, p. 231, 105)

236 A.D.

Sestertius
Obv. IMP MAXIMINVS PIVS AVG. Laureated bust of emperor in cuirass and paludamentum looking right, seen from rear.
Rev. SALVS AVGVSTI. Salus seated left, feeding snake rising from altar.
— — —//SC
Lit.: MIR 27 Rom 3/12–5/C; RIC 4.2, p. 145, 64; BMCRE 6, p. 231, 101

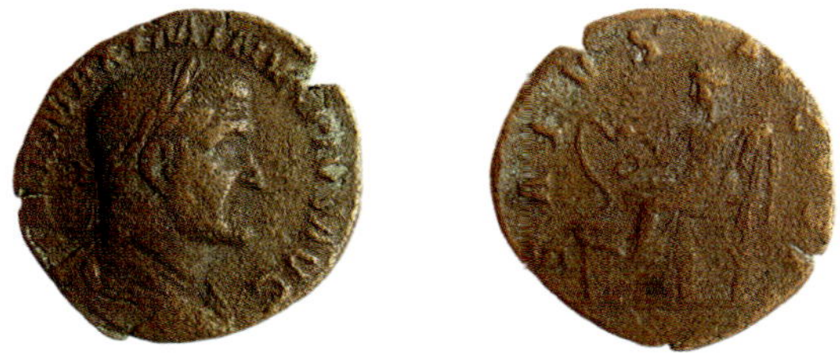

36. AE; 16,03 g.; 28,5 x 28,7 mm.; 12 h.; inv. n. 1388.
(Obv. IMP MAXIMINVS PIVS AVG; Rev. SALVS – AVGVSTI; — — —//SC)

Denarius

Obv. IMP MAXIMINVS PIVS AVG. Laureated bust of emperor in cuirass and paludamentum looking right, seen from rear.

Rev. P M TR P II COS P P. Emperor standing left between two standards, raising right hand, holding vertical spear in left hand.

— — —//—

Lit.: MIR 27 Rom 3/16–3/B; RIC 4.2, p. 139, 3; BMCRE 6, p. 229, 78

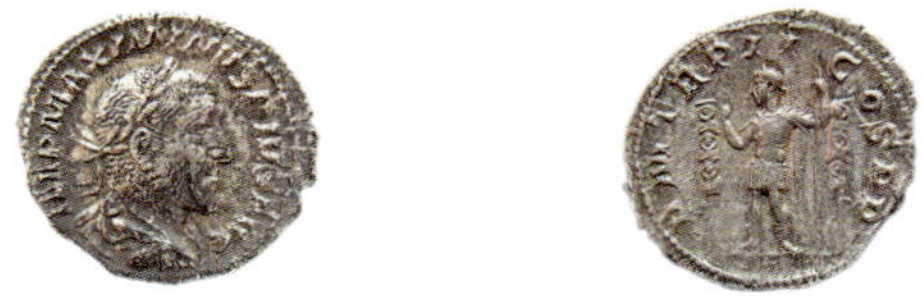

37. AR; 3,72 g.; 18,5 x 20,2 mm.; 1 h.; inv. n. 1389.
(Obv. IMP MAXIMINVS PIVS AVG; Rev. P M TR P II – COS P P; — — —//—)

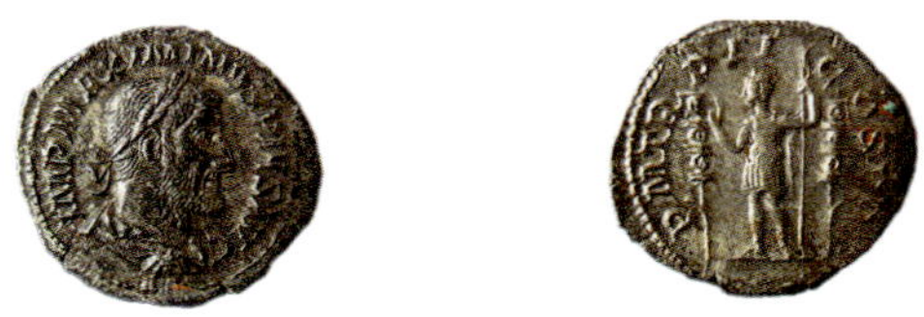

38. AR; 3,02 g.; 19,1 x 20,3 mm.; 6 h.; inv. n. 1390.
(Obv. IMP MAXIMINVS PIVS AVG; Rev. P M TR – P II – C-OS P P; — — —//—)

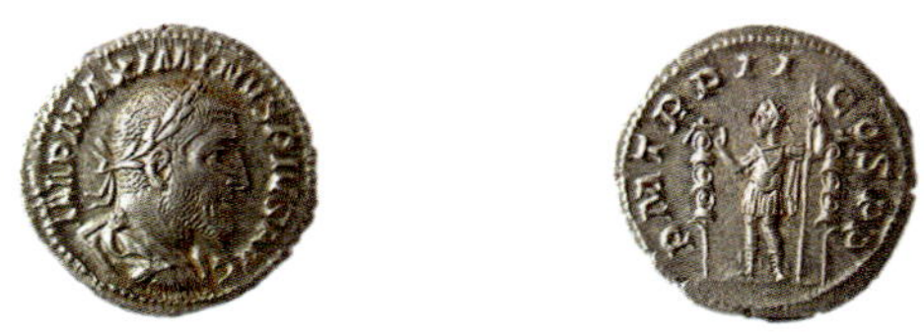

39. AR; 2,64 g.; 20,0 x 19,5 mm.; 6 h.; inv. n. 1391.
(Obv. IMP MAXIMINVS PIVS AVG; Rev. P M TR P II – COS P P; — — —//—; Lit.: BMCRE 6, p. 229, 79)

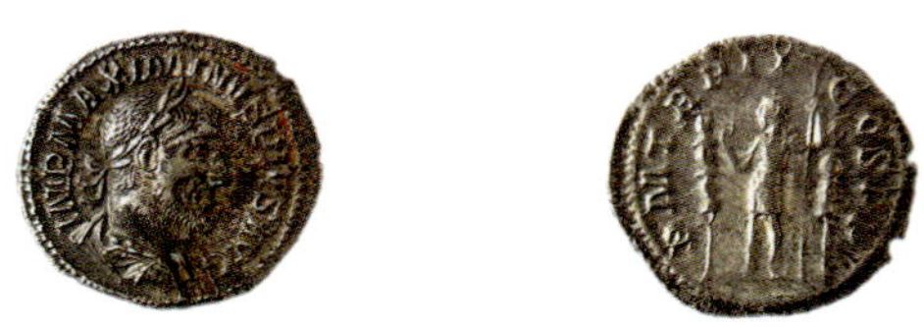

40. AR; 2,7 g.; 19,0 x 19,7 mm.; 7 h.; inv. n. 1392.
(Obv. IMP MAXIMINVS PIVS AVG; Rev. P M TR P II – COS P P; — — —//—)

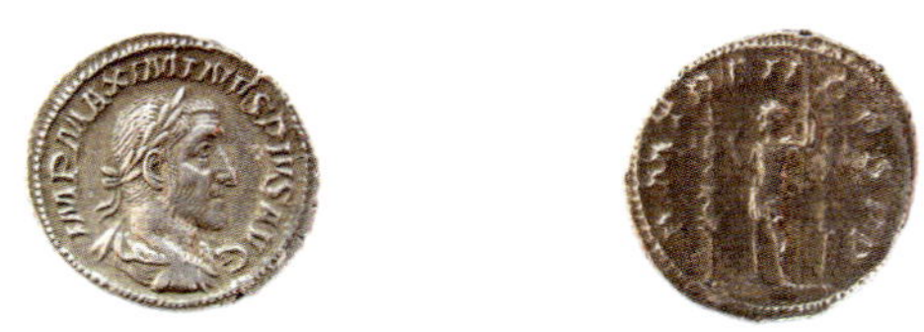

41. AR; 3,09 g.; 19,2 x 20,0 mm.; 7 h.; inv. n. 1393.
(Obv. IMP MAXIMINVS PIVS AVG; Rev. P M TR P II – COS P P; — — —//—; Lit.: BMCRE 6, p. 229, 79)

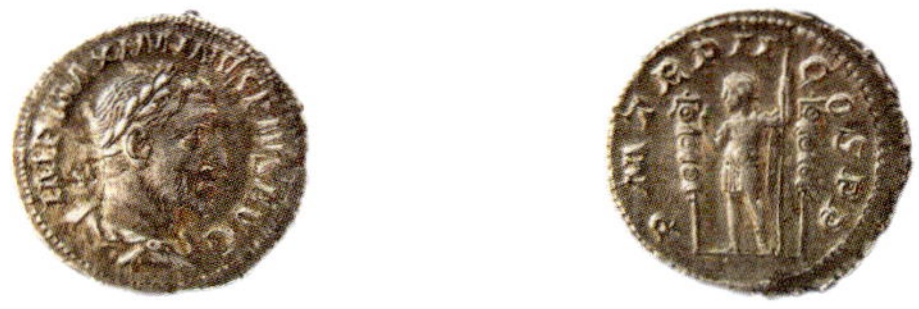

42. AR; 3,17 g.; 19,5 x 20,1 mm.; 7 h.; inv. n. 1394.
(Obv. IMP MAXIMINVS PIVS AVG; Rev. P M TR P II – COS P P; — — —//—; Lit.: BMCRE 6, p. 229, 79)

Sestertius
Obv. MP MAXIMINVS PIVS AVG. Laureated bust of emperor in cuirass and paludamentum looking right, seen from rear.
Rev. Illegible. Obscure.
— — —//—
Lit.: –

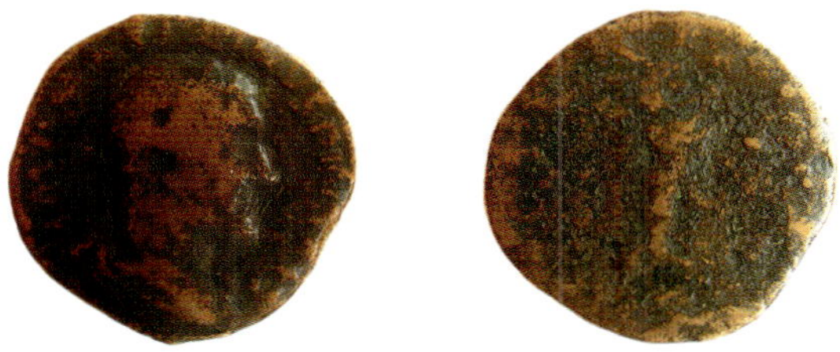

43. AE; 15,59 g.; 28,6 x 29,1 mm.; 1 h.; inv. n. 1395.
(Obv. IMP MAXIMINVS PIVS AVG; Rev. Illegible; — — —//—)

236 – 238 A.D.

Denarius
Obv. MAXIMINVS PIVS AVG GERM. Laureated bust of emperor in cuirass and paludamentum looking right, seen from rear.
Rev. FIDES MILITVM. Fides standing left, holding vertical standard in each hand.
— — —//—
Lit.: MIR 27 Rom 4–6/21–3/C; RIC 4.2, p. 141, 18a; BMCRE 6, p. 234, 137

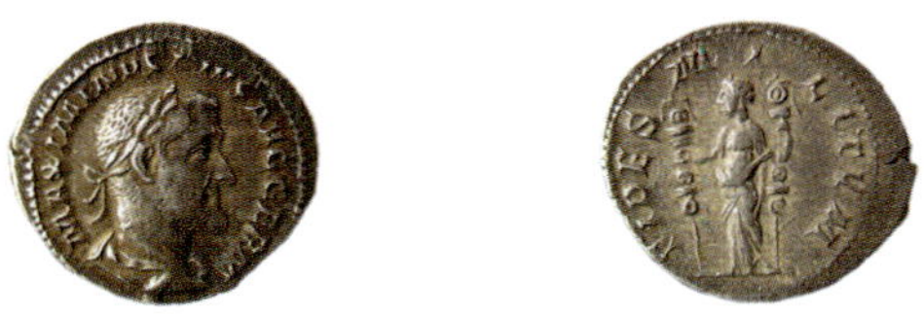

44. AR; 3,11 g.; 19,0 x 20,6 mm.; 12 h.; inv. n. 1396.
(Obv. MAXIMINVS PIVS AVG GERM; Rev. FIDES – MI-LITVM; — — —//—)

Sestertius
Obv. MAXIMINVS PIVS AVG GERM. Laureated bust of emperor in cuirass and paludamentum looking right, seen from rear.
Rev. FIDES MILITVM. Fides standing left, holding vertical standard in each hand.
S — C//—
Lit.: MIR 27 Rom 4–6/21–5/C; RIC 4.2, p. 146, 78; BMCRE 6, p. 234, 140

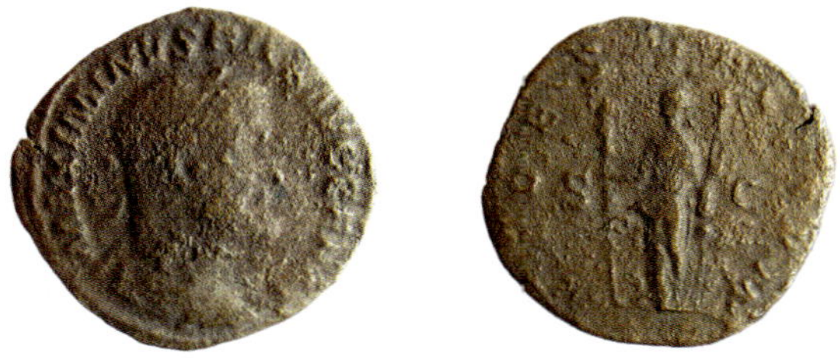

45. AE; 17,81 g.; 30,8 x 31,9 mm.; 1 h.; inv. n. 1397.
(Obv. MAXIMINVS PIVS AVG GERM; Rev. [F]IDES [M]I-[LIT]VM; S — C//—)

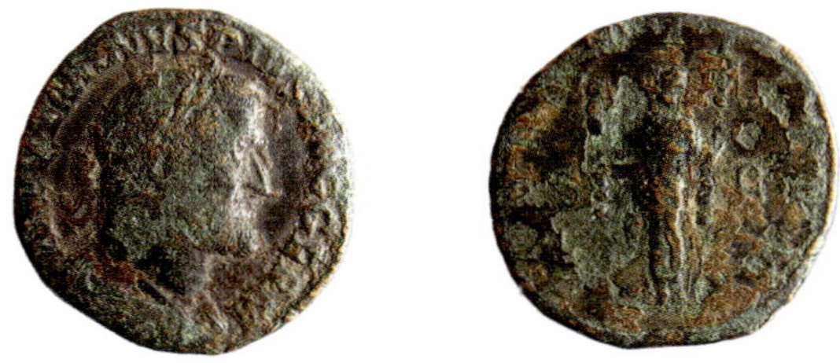

46. AE; 24,12 g.; 30,2 x 29,2 mm.; 12 h.; inv. n. 1398.
(Obv. MAXIMINVS PIVS AVG GERM; Rev. F[I]DES MILITVM; S — C//—; Lit.: BMCRE 6, p. 234, 139)

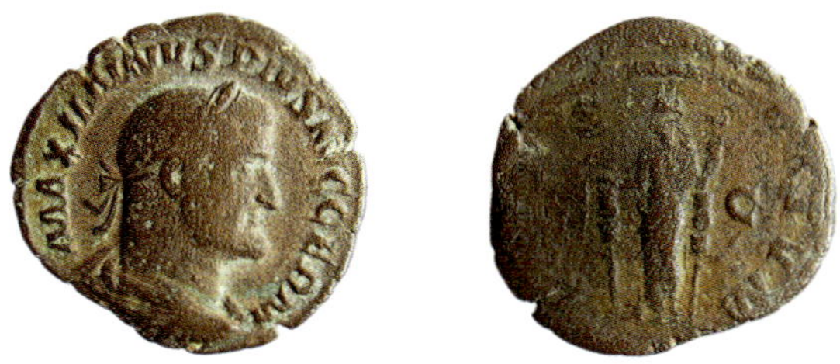

47. AE; 13,25 g.; 30,3 x 30,1 mm.; 12 h.; inv. n. 1399.
(Obv. MAXIMINVS PIVS AVG GERM; Rev. [FID]ES MI[LI]TVM; S — C//—)

Denarius
Obv. MAXIMINVS PIVS AVG GERM. Laureated bust of emperor in cuirass and paludamentum looking right, seen from rear.
Rev. PAX AVGVSTI. Pax standing left, holding branch in right hand and transverse sceptre in left hand.
— — —//—
Lit.: MIR 27 Rom 4–6/22–3/C; RIC 4.2, p. 141, 19; BMCRE 6, p. 234, 145

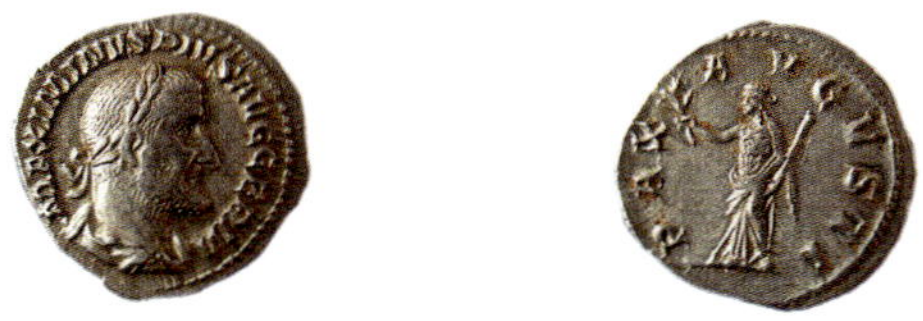

48. AR; 3,8 g.; 18,7 x 19,4 mm.; 12 h.; inv. n. 1400.
(Obv. MAXIMINVS PIVS AVG GERM; Rev. PAX – A-VGVSTI; — — —//—)

Sestertius
Obv. MAXIMINVS PIVS AVG GERM. Laureated bust of emperor in cuirass and paludamentum looking right, seen from rear.
Rev. PAX AVGVSTI. Pax standing left, holding branch in right hand and transverse sceptre in left hand.
S — C//—
Lit.: MIR 27 Rom 4–6/22–5/C; RIC 4.2, p. 146, 81; BMCRE 6, p. 235, 150

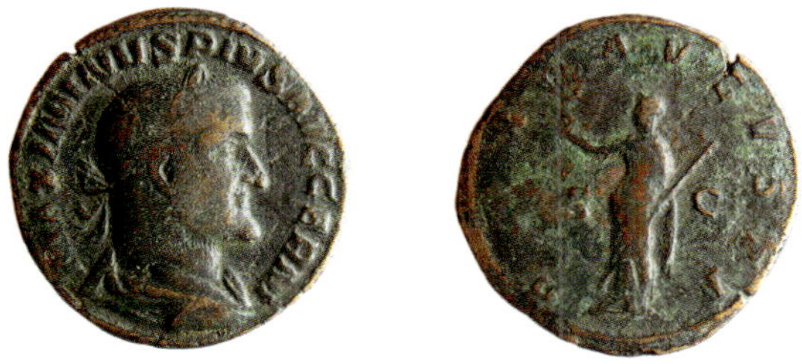

49. AE; 20,45 g.; 31,1 x 30,3 mm.; 12 h.; inv. n. 1401.
(Obv. MAXIMINVS PIVS AVG GERM; Rev. PAX – AVGVSTI; S — C//—)

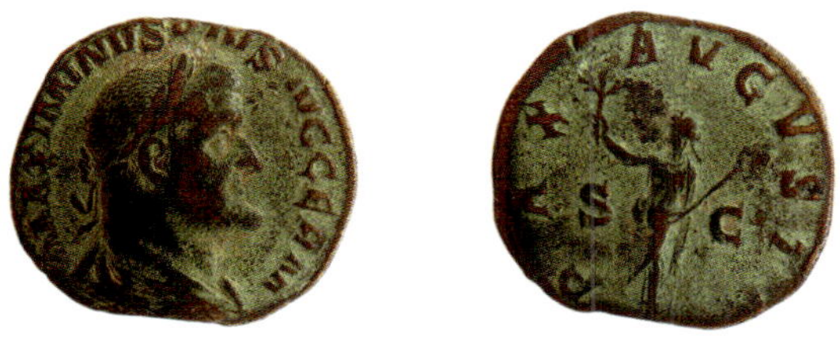

50. AE; 16,56 g.; 26,5 x 29,3 mm.; 12 h.; inv. n. 1402.
(Obv. MAXIMINVS PIVS AVG GERM; Rev. PAX – AVGVSTI; S — C//—; Lit.: BMCRE 6, p. 235, 151)

Denarius

Obv. MAXIMINVS PIVS AVG GERM. Laureated bust of emperor in cuirass and paludamentum looking right, seen from rear.

Rev. PROVIDENTIA AVG. Providentia standing left, holding baton in right hand and cornucopiae in left hand; at feet to left globe.

— — —//—

Lit.: MIR 27 Rom 4–6/23–3/C; RIC 4.2, p. 142, 20; BMCRE 6, p. 236, 170

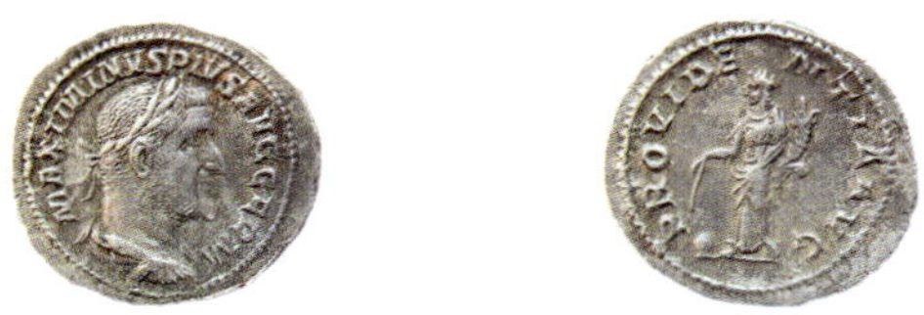

51. AR; 4,17 g.; 19,7 x 21,0 mm.; 6 h.; inv. n. 1403.
(Obv. MAXIMINVS PIVS AVG GERM; Rev. PROVIDE-NTIA AVG; — — —//—)

Sestertius

Obv. MAXIMINVS PIVS AVG GERM. Laureated bust of emperor in cuirass and paludamentum looking right, seen from rear.

Rev. VICTORIA GERMANICA. Victory standing left, holding wreath in right hand and palm in left hand; captive at feet to the left.

S — C//—

Lit.: MIR 27 Rom 4–6/27–5/C; RIC 4.2, p. 147, 90; BMCRE 6, p. 238, 191

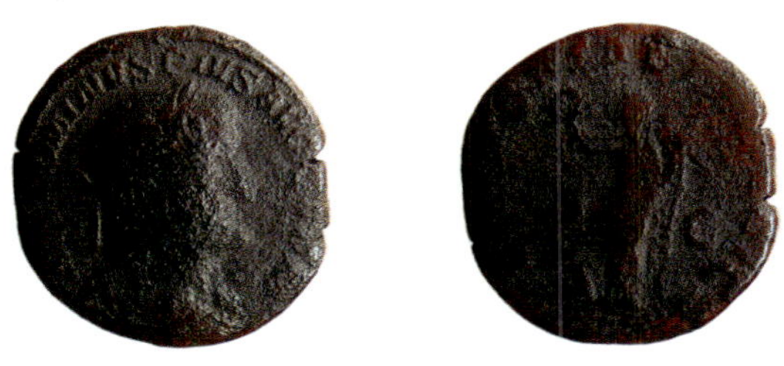

52. AE; 16,63 g.; 29,6 x 28,3 mm.; 6 h.; inv. n. 18.24.
(Obv. [MA]XIMINVS PIVS AVG [GER]M; Rev. V[IC]TORIA GE[RMA]NIC[A]; S — C//—)

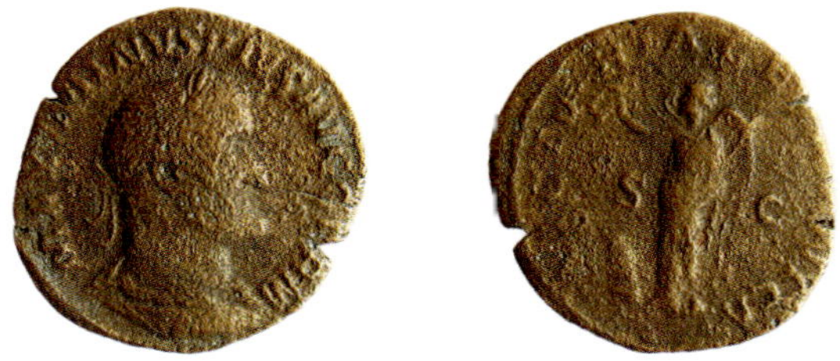

53. AE; 20,06 g.; 30,2 x 28,6 mm.; 12 h.; inv. n. 1404.
(Obv. MAXIMINVS PIVS AVG GERM; Rev. VICTO-RIA GE[RMA]NICA; S — C//—; Lit.: BMCRE 6, p. 238, 194)

237 A.D.

Denarius
Obv. MAXIMINVS PIVS AVG GERM. Laureated bust of emperor in cuirass and paludamentum looking right, seen from rear.
Rev. P M TR P III COS P P. Emperor standing left between two standards, raising right hand, holding vertical spear in left hand.
— — —//—
Lit.: MIR 27 Rom 5/28–3/C; RIC 4.2, p. 139, 5; BMCRE 6, p. 236, 163

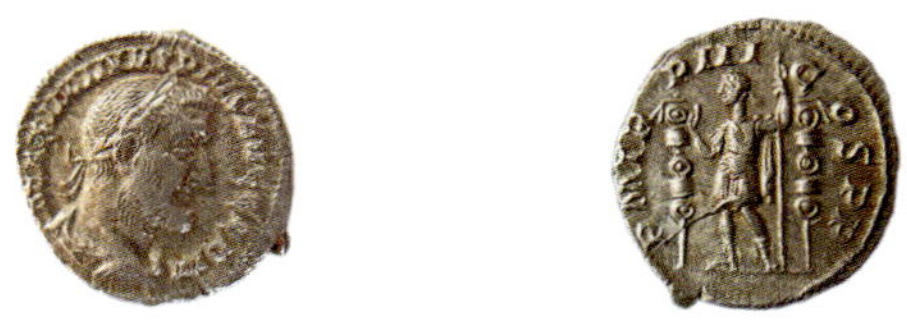

54. AR; 3,15 g.; 18,6 x 18,9 mm.; 1 h.; inv. n. 1405.
(Obv. MAXIMINVS PIVS AVG GERM; Rev. P M TR – P III – C-OS P P; — — —//—)

MAXIMUS
SON OF MAXIMINUS THRAX
(CAESAR 236 – 238 A.D.)

Roma

236 – 238 A.D.

Sestertius
Obv. MAXIMVS CAES GERM. Bust of emperor in paludamentum looking right, seen from rear.
Rev. PIETAS AVG. Sacrificial implements, variously arranged.
— — —//SC
Lit.: MIR 27 Rom 4–6/36–5; RIC 4.2, p. 156, Rome 11; BMCRE 6, p. 239, 204

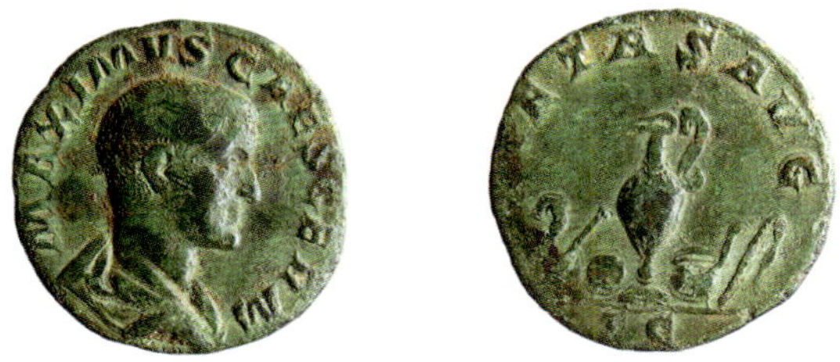

55. AE; 19,96 g.; 29,3 x 28,5 mm.; 1 h.; inv. n. 1406.
(Obv. MAXIMVS CAES GERM; Rev. PIETAS AVG; — — —//SC)

Sestertius
Obv. MAXIMVS CAES GERM. Bust of emperor in paludamentum looking right, seen from rear.
Rev. PRINCIPI IVVENTVTIS. Emperor standing left, holding baton in right hand and transverse spear in left hand; to right two standards.
S — C//—
Lit.: MIR 27 Rom 4–6/37–5; RIC 4.2, p. 156, Rome 13; BMCRE 6, p. 240, 213

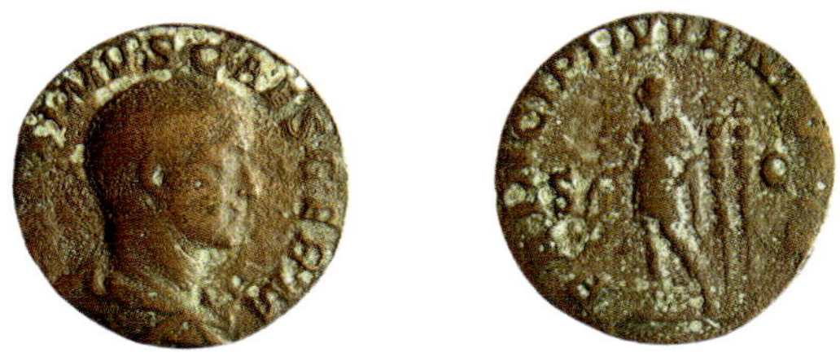

56. AE; 17,14 g.; 27,7 x 27,6 mm.; 12 h.; inv. n. 1407.
(Obv. MAXIMVS CAES GERM; Rev. PRINCIPI IVVENTVTIS; S — C//—)

BALBINUS
(238 A.D.)

Roma

238 A.D.

Denarius
Obv. IMP C D CAEL BALBINVS AVG. Laureated bust of emperor in cuirass and paludamentum looking right, seen from front.
Rev. PROVIDENTIA DEORVM. Providentia standing left, holding baton in right hand and cornucopiae in left hand; at feet to left globe.
— — —//—
Lit.: RIC 4.2, p. 170, Rome 7; BMCRE 6, p. 253, 33

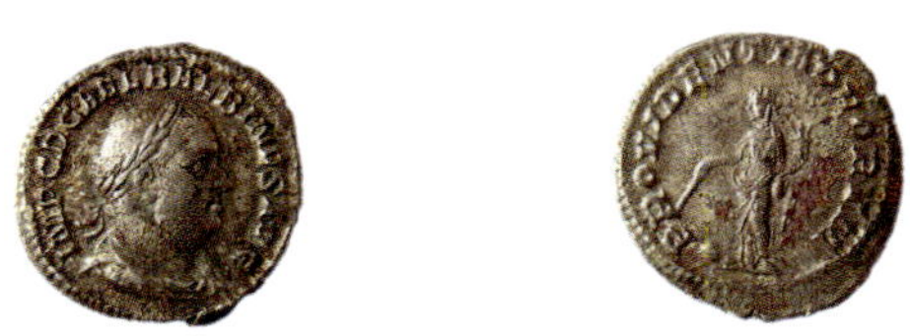

57. AR; 2,89 g.; 19,1 x 19,3 mm.; 6 h.; inv. n. 940.
(Obv. IMP C D CAEL BALBINVS AVG; Rev. PROVIDENTIA DEORVM; — — —//—)

Denarius

Obv. IMP C D CAEL BALBINVS AVG. Laureated bust of emperor in cuirass and paludamentum looking right, seen from front.

Rev. VICTORIA AVGG. Victory standing front, head turned left, holding wreath in right hand and palm in left hand.

— — —//—

Lit.: RIC 4.2, p. 170, Rome 8; BMCRE 6, p. 254, 37

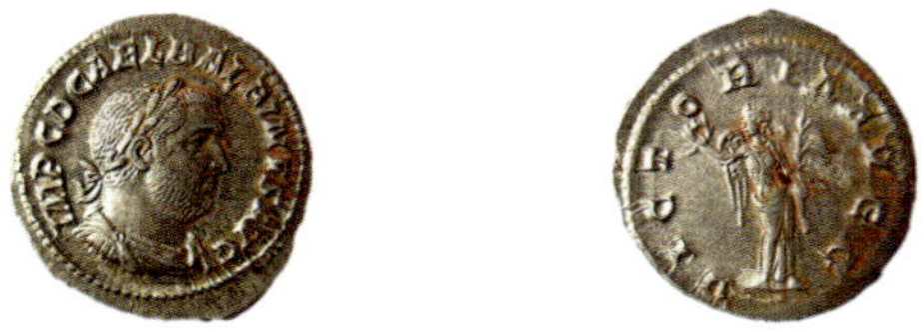

58. AR; 3,23 g.; 20,4 x 19,3 mm.; 7 h.; inv. n. 1408.
(Obv. IMP C D CAEL BALBINVS AVG; Rev. VICT-ORIA AVGG; — — —//—)

GORDIANUS III.
(238 – 244 A.D.)

Roma

238 A.D.

Antoninianus

Obv. IMP CAES M ANT GORDIANVS AVG. Radiated bust of emperor in cuirass and paludamentum looking right, seen from rear.

Rev. PAX AVGVSTI. Pax standing left, holding branch in right hand and transverse sceptre in left hand.

— — —//—

Lit. RIC 4.3, p. 16, Rome 3

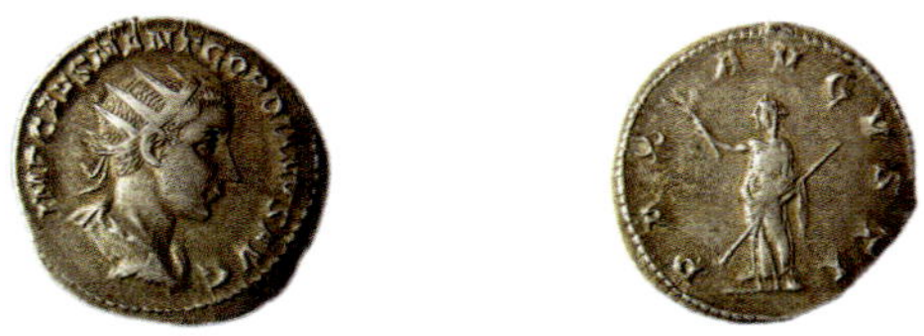

59. AR; 4,59 g.; 21,1 x 21,5 mm.; 6 h.; inv. n. 1409.
(Obv. IMP CAES M ANT GORDIANVS AVG; Rev. PAX – AVGVSTI; — — —//—)

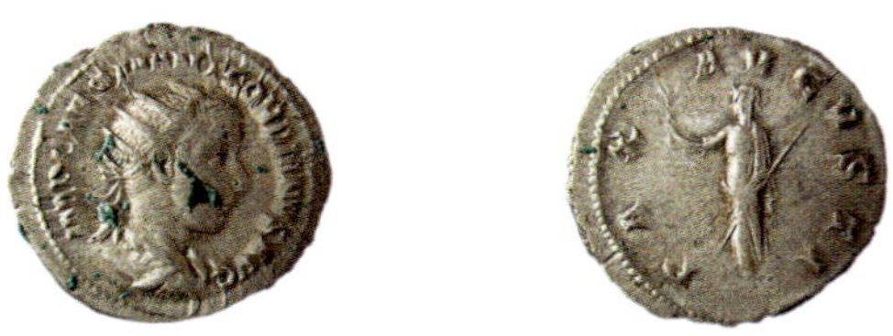

60. AR; 4,71 g.; 22,0 x 23,0 mm.; 7 h.; inv. n. 923.
(Obv. IMP CAES M ANT GORDIANVS AVG; Rev. PAX – AVGVSTI; — — —//—)

Antoninianus

Obv. IMP CAES M ANT GORDIANVS AVG. Radiated bust of emperor in cuirass and paludamentum looking right, seen from rear.

Rev. PROVIDENTIA AVG. Providentia standing left, holding globe in right hand and transverse sceptre in left hand.

— — —//—

Lit.: RIC 4.3, p. 16, Rome 4

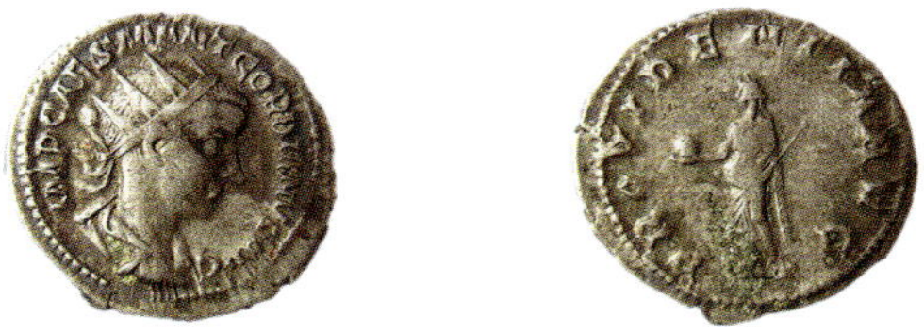

61. AR; 4,37 g.; 21,6 x 23,1 mm.; 11 h.; inv. n. 1410.
(Obv. IMP CAES M ANT GORDIANVS AVG; Rev. PROVIDENTIA AVG; — — —//—)

239 A.D.

Antoninianus

Obv. IMP CAES M ANT GORDIANVS AVG. Radiated bust of emperor in cuirass and paludamentum looking right, seen from rear.

Rev. LIBERALITAS AVG II. Liberalitas standing left, holding tessera in right hand and cornucopiae in left hand.

— — —//—

Lit.: RIC 4.3, p. 19, Rome 36

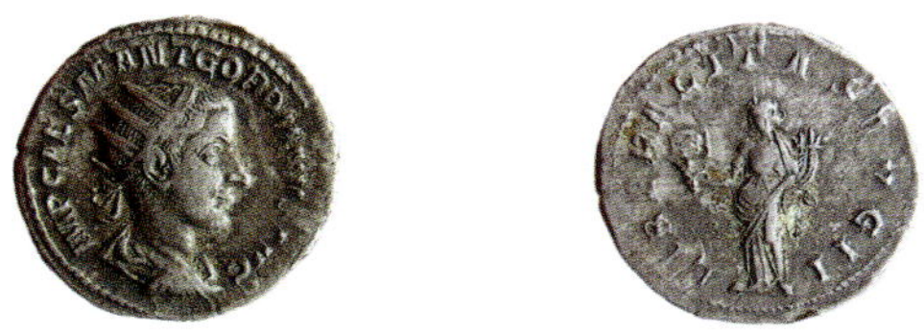

62. AR; 4,21 g.; 21,5 x 22,3 mm.; 1 h.; inv. n. 1411.
(Obv. IMP CAES M ANT GORDIANVS AVG; Rev. LIBERALITAS AVG II; — — —//—)

Antoninianus

Obv. IMP CAES M ANT GORDIANVS AVG. Radiated bust of emperor in cuirass and paludamentum looking right, seen from rear.

Rev. P M TR P II COS P P. Fides standing left, holding vertical standard in right hand and transverse sceptre in left hand.

— — —//—

Lit.: RIC 4.3, p. 17, Rome 15

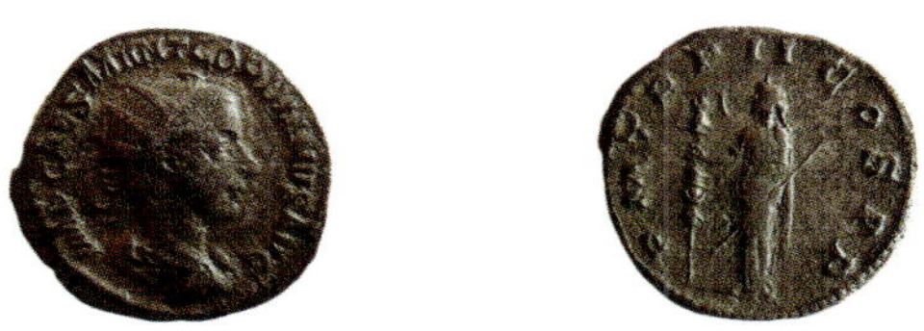

63. AR; 3,52 g.; 20,4 x 21,4 mm.; 6 h.; inv. n. 1412.
(Obv. IMP CAES M ANT GORDIANVS AVG; Rev. P M TR P II COS P P; — — —//—)

Antoninianus

Obv. IMP CAES M ANT GORDIANVS AVG. Radiated bust of emperor in cuirass and paludamentum looking right, seen from rear.

Rev. AEQVITAS AVG. Aequitas standing left, holding scales in right hand and cornucopiae in left hand.

— — —//—

Lit.: RIC 4.3, p. 19, Rome 34

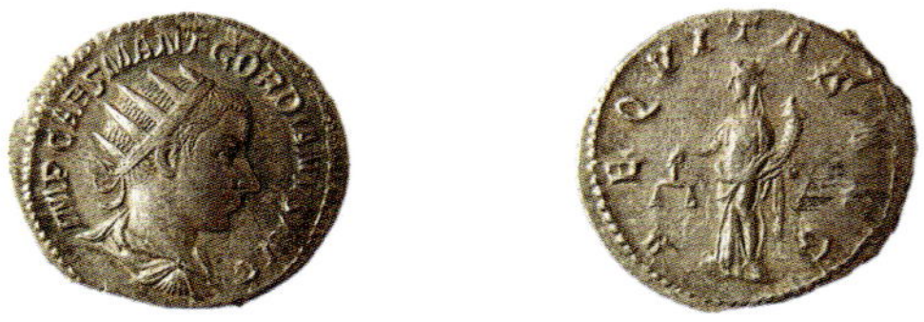

64. AR; 4,12 g.; 20,5 x 23,0 mm.; 1 h.; inv. n. 1413.
(Obv. IMP CAES M ANT GORDIANVS AVG; Rev. A-EQVITAS AVG; — — —//—)

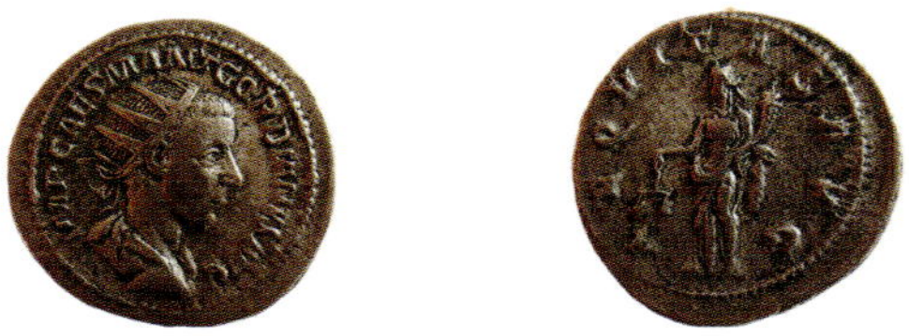

65. AR; 4,72 g.; 22,3 x 23,1 mm.; 1 h.; inv. n. 1414.
(Obv. IMP CAES M ANT GORDIANVS AVG; Rev. A-EQVITAS AVG; — — —//—)

Sestertius

Obv. IMP CAES GORDIANVS PIVS AVG. Laureated bust of emperor in cuirass and paludamentum looking right, seen from rear.

Rev. VIR-TV-S AVG. Virtus standing left, holding branch in right hand and vertical spear in left hand; shield rests against right foot.

S — C//—

Lit.: RIC 4.3, p. 46, Rome 281a

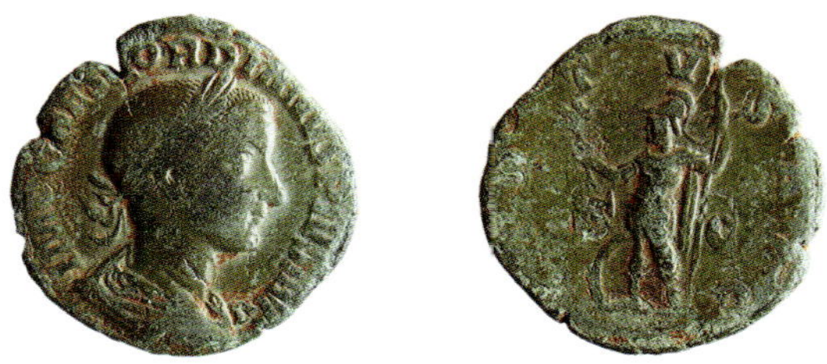

66. AE; 12,74 g.; 29,8 x 29,0 mm.; 12 h.; inv. n. 18.06.
(Obv. IMP CAES [G]ORDIANVS PIVS AVG; Rev. [V]IR-TV-S AVG; S — C//—)

As

Obv. MP GORDIANVS PIVS FEL AVG. Laureated bust of emperor in cuirass and paludamentum looking right, seen from rear.

Rev. AEQVITAS AVG. Aequitas standing left, holding scales in right hand and cornucopiae in left hand.

S — C//—

Lit.: RIC 4.3, p. 47, Rome 286b

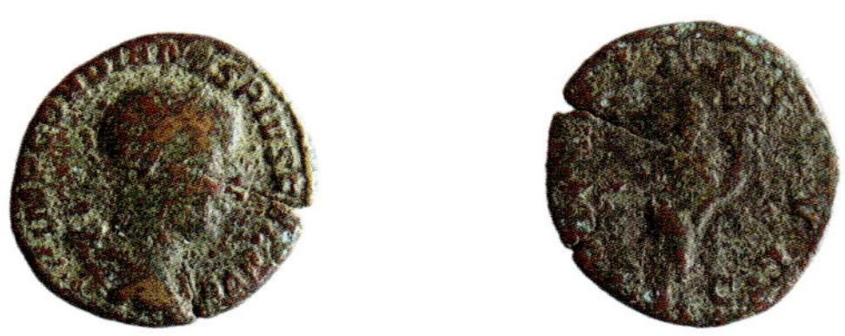

67. AE; 7,96 g.; 23,7 x 22,7 mm.; 11 h.; inv. n. 1415.
(Obv. IMP GORDIANVS PIVS FEL AVG; Rev. [AEQV]ITAS AVG; S — C//—)

Antoninianus[10]

Obv. IMP GORDIANVS PIVS FEL AVG. Radiated bust of emperor in cuirass and paludamentum looking right, seen from rear.

Rev. CONCORDIA (AVG/MILIT). Concordia seated left, holding patera in right hand and double cornucopiae in left hand.

— — —//—

Lit.: RIC 4.3, p. 22, Rome 64 or p. 23, Rome 65

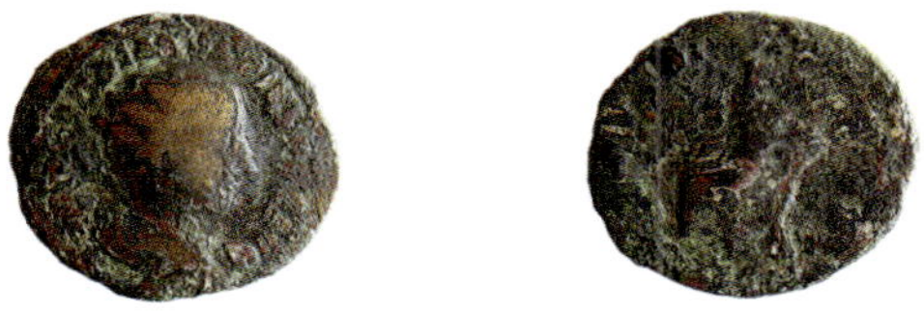

68. AE; 4,11 g.; 20,3 x 22,7 mm.; 7 h.; inv. n. 1416.
(Obv. IMP GORDIANVS PIVS FEL AVG; Rev. [CONCORDIA (AVG/MILIT)]; — — —//—)

Antoninianus

Obv. IMP GORDIANVS PIVS FEL AVG. Radiated bust of emperor in cuirass and paludamentum looking right, seen from rear.

Rev. ROMAE AETERNAE. Roma seated on shield left, holding Victoriola in right hand and long vertical sceptre in left hand.

— — —//—

Lit.: RIC 4.3, p. 23, Rome 70

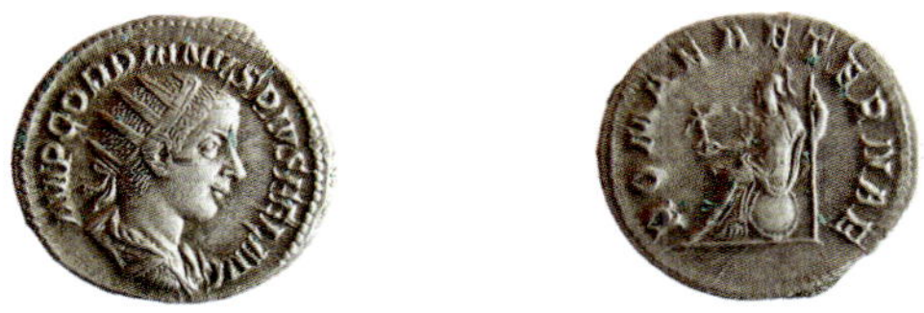

69. AR; 4,71 g.; 20,3 x 22,2 mm.; 6 h.; inv. n. 922.
(Obv. IMP GORDIANVS PIVS FEL AVG; Rev. ROMAE AETERNAE; — — —//—)

Antoninianus

Obv. IMP GORDIANVS PIVS FEL AVG. Radiated bust of emperor in cuirass and paludamentum looking right, seen from rear.

Rev. VIRTVS AVG. Virtus standing left, holding branch in right hand and vertical spear in left hand; shield rests against right foot.

— — —//—

Lit.: RIC 4.3, p. 23, Rome 71

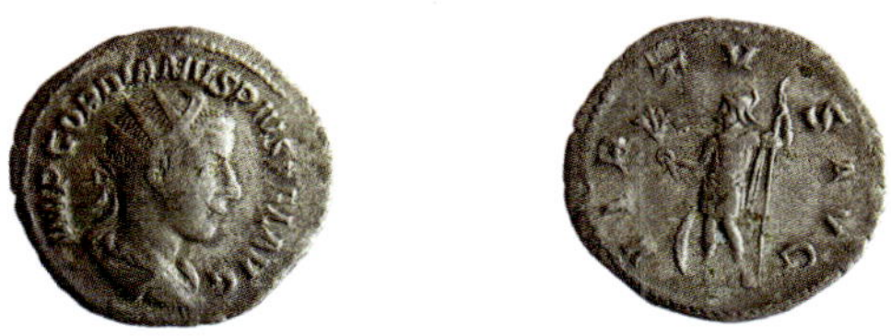

70. AR; 3,23 g.; 21,8 x 22,7 mm.; 6 h.; inv. n. 1417.
(Obv. IMP GORDIANVS PIVS FEL AVG; Rev. VIR-TV-S AVG; — — —//—)

[10] Suberate antoninian.

First half of 240 A.D.

Sestertius
Obv. IMP GORDIANVS PIVS FEL AVG. Laureated bust of emperor in cuirass and paludamentum looking right, seen from rear.
Rev. P M TR P III COS P P. Emperor seated left on curule chair, holding globe in right hand and transverse sceptre in left hand.
— — —//SC
Lit.: RIC 4.3, p. 47, Rome 294a

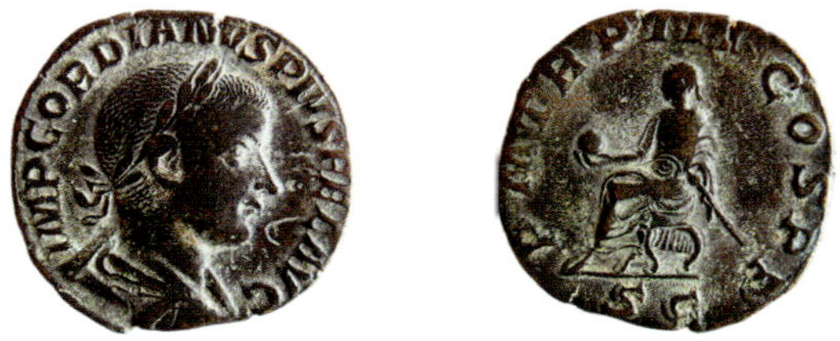

71. AE; 17,67 g.; 27,3 x 28,1 mm.; 12 h.; inv. n. 1418.
(Obv. IMP GORDIANVS PIVS FEL AVG; Rev. P M TR P III COS P P; — — —//—)

Sestertius
Obv. IMP GORDIANVS PIVS FEL AVG. Laureated bust of emperor in cuirass and paludamentum looking right, seen from rear.
Rev. PAX AETERNA. Pax walking left, holding branch in right hand and transverse sceptre in left hand.
S — C//—
Lit.: RIC 4.3, p. 50, Rome 319a

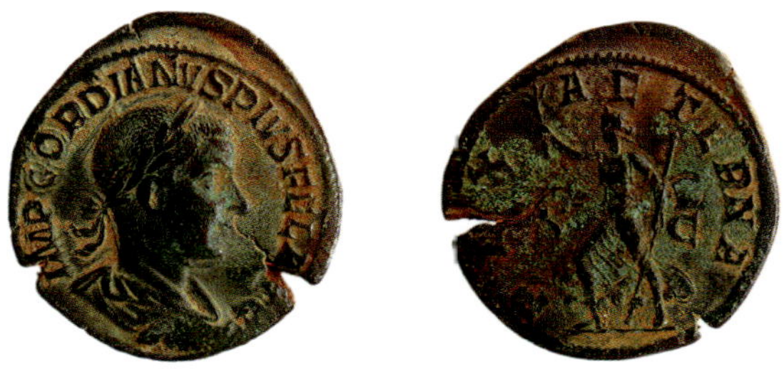

72. AE; 22,31 g.; 33,4 x 31,0 mm.; 11 h.; inv. n. 18.25.
(Obv. IMP GORDIANVS PIVS FEL A[V]G; Rev. PAX – AETERNA; S — C//—)

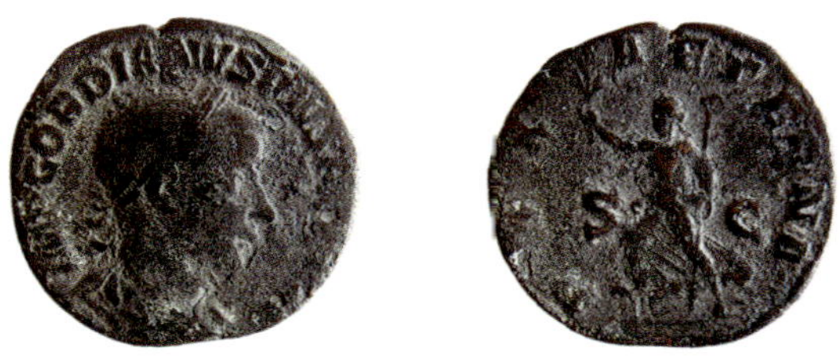

73. AE; 15,14 g.; 28,3 x 29,0 mm.; 12 h.; inv. n. 1419.
(Obv. IMP GORDIANVS PIVS F[EL AVG]; Rev. PAX – AETERNA; S — C//—)

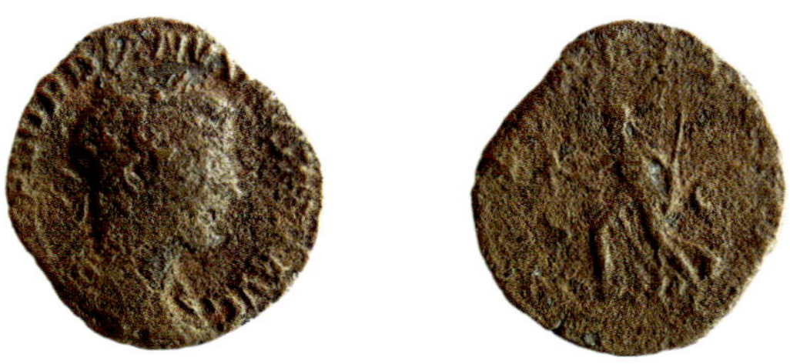

74. AE; 14,02 g.; 29,3 x 27,2 mm.; 12 h.; inv. n. 1420.
(Obv. [I]MP GORDIANVS PIVS FE[L] AVG; Rev. PAX – AET-[ERNA]; S — C//—)

Sestertius
Obv. IMP GORDIANVS PIVS FEL AVG. Laureated bust of emperor in cuirass and paludamentum looking right, seen from rear.
Rev. SECVRITAS AVG. Securitas seated left, holding sceptre in right hand and raising left hand to head.
— — —//SC
Lit.: RIC 4.3, p. 49, Rome 311a

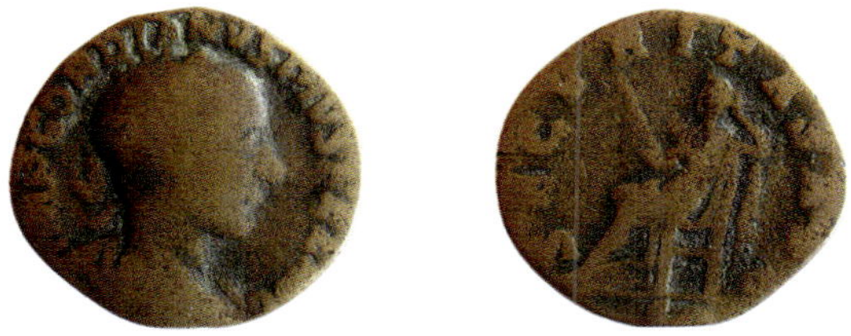

75. AE; 11,69 g.; 26,8 x 28,4 mm.; 1 h.; inv. n. 1421.
(Obv. [I]MP GORDIANVS PIVS FEL AVG; Rev. SECVRITAS A[V]G; — — —//SC)

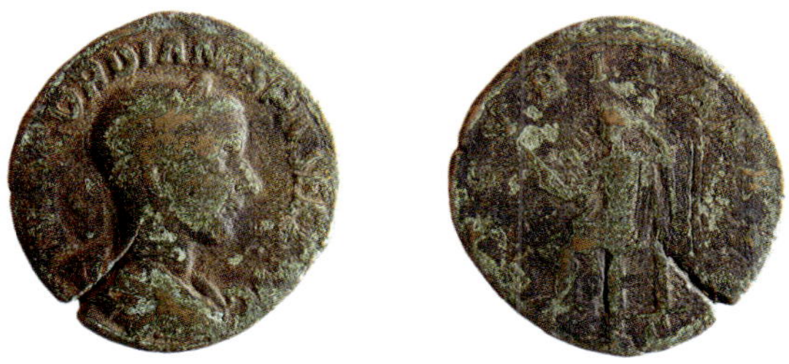

76. AE; 16,67 g.; 31,6 x 29,9 mm.; 12 h.; inv. n. 1422.
(Obv. [I]MP GORDIANVS PIVS FEL AVG; Rev. [S]ECVRITAS AV[G]; — — —//SC)

Second half of 240 A.D.

Antoninianus
Obv. IMP GORDIANVS PIVS FEL AVG. Radiated bust of emperor in cuirass and paludamentum looking right, seen from rear.
Rev. P M TR P III COS II P P. Apollo seated left, holding branch in right hand and resting left elbow on lyre.
— — —//—
Lit.: RIC 4.3, p. 25, Rome 87

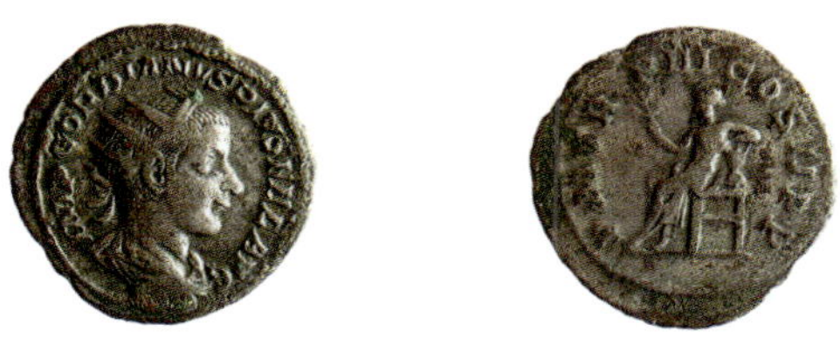

77. AR; 3,93 g.; 23,0 x 22,5 mm.; 12 h.; inv. n. 1423.
(Obv. IMP GORDIANVS PIVS FEL AVG; Rev. P M TR – P III COS II P P; — — —//—)

Antoninianus
Obv. IMP GORDIANVS PIVS FEL AVG. Radiated bust of emperor in cuirass and paludamentum looking right, seen from rear.
Rev. AETERNITATI AVG. Sol standing left, raising right hand, globe in left hand.
— — —//—
Lit.: RIC 4.3, p. 24, Rome 83

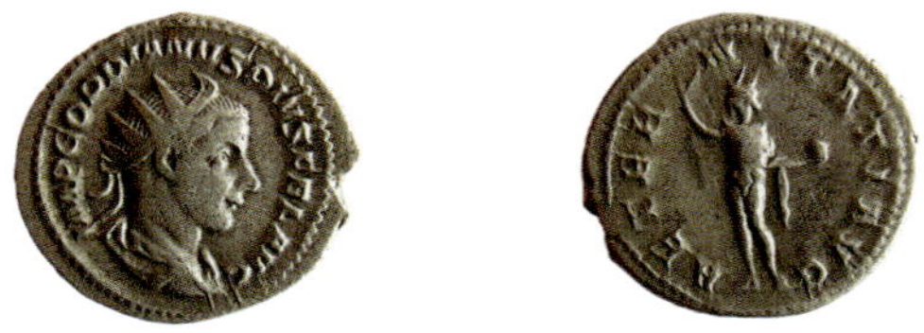

78. AR; 4,58 g.; 22,2 x 22,9 mm.; 12 h.; inv. n. 1424.
(Obv. IMP GORDIANVS PIVS FEL AVG; Rev. AETER-N-ITATI AVG; — — —//—)

Denarius
Obv. IMP GORDIANVS PIVS FEL AVG. Laureated bust of emperor in cuirass and paludamentum looking right, seen from rear.
Rev. AETERNITATI AVG. Sol standing right, head turned left, raising right hand, globe in left hand.
— — —//—
Lit.: RIC 4.3, p. 26, Rome 111

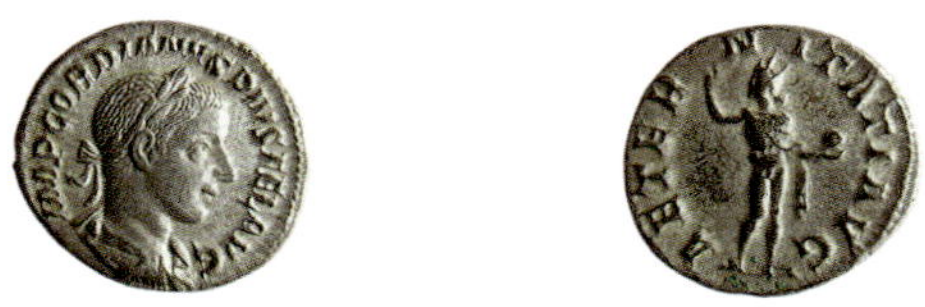

79. AR; 3,06 g.; 18,1 x 19,1 mm.; 12 h.; inv. n. 1425.
(Obv. IMP GORDIANVS PIVS FEL AVG; Rev. AETER-N-ITATI AVG; — — —//—)

Sestertius
Obv. IMP GORDIANVS PIVS FEL AVG. Laureated bust of emperor in cuirass and paludamentum looking right, seen from rear.
Rev. AETERNITATI AVG. Sol standing left, raising right hand, globe in left hand.
S — C//—
Lit.: RIC 4.3, p. 48, Rome 297a

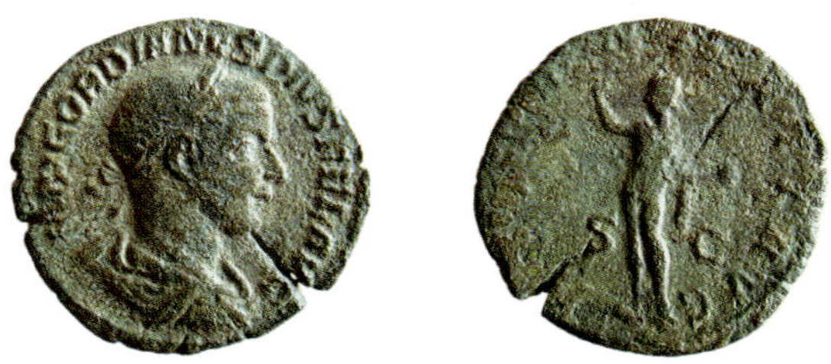

80. AE; 16,65 g.; 30,1 x 30,8 mm.; 12 h.; inv. n. 1426.
(Obv. IMP GORDIANVS PIVS FEL AVG; Rev. [AET]ER-N[IT]ATI AVG; S — C//—)

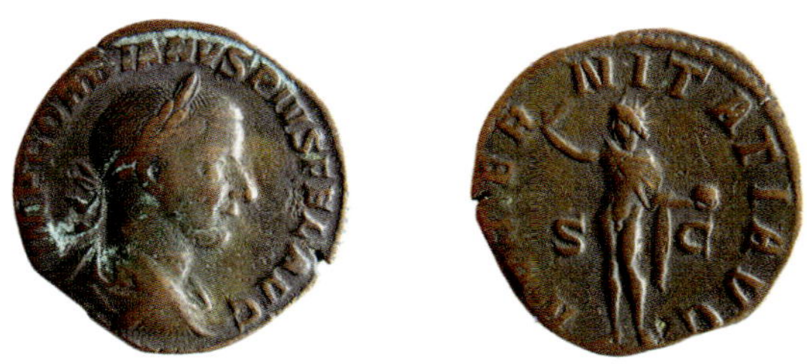

81. AE; 18,71 g.; 29,5 x 29,1 mm.; 11 h.; inv. n. 1427.
(Obv. IMP GORDIANVS PIVS FEL AVG; Rev. AETER-NITATI AVG; S — C//—)

As

Obv. IMP GORDIANVS PIVS FEL AVG. Laureated bust of emperor in cuirass and paludamentum looking right, seen from rear.

Rev. AETER-NITATI AVG. Sol standing right, head turned left, raising right hand, globe in left hand.

S — C//—

Lit.: RIC 4.3, p. 48, Rome 297b

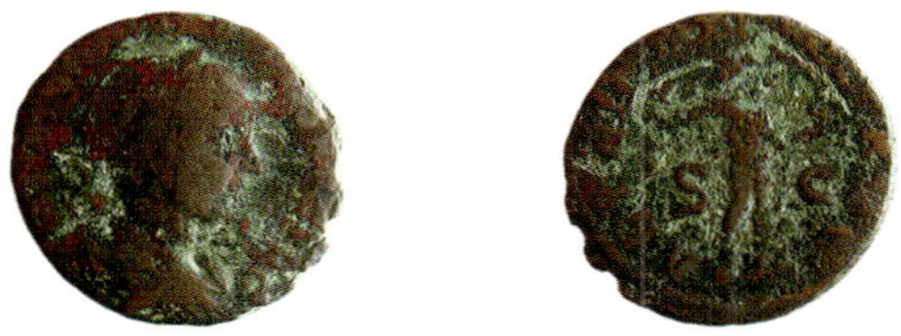

82. AE; 9,79 g.; 23,1 x 22,5 mm.; 12 h.; inv. n. 1428.
(Obv. [IMP GORDIANVS PIVS FEL A]VG; Rev. AETER-NI[TATI] A[V]G; S — C//—)

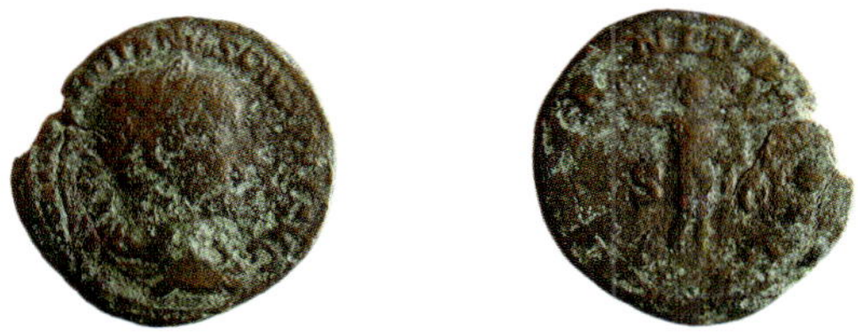

83. AE; 9,11 g.; 25,3 x 23,9 mm.; 12 h.; inv. n. 1429.
(Obv. I[MP GO]RDIANVS PIVS FEL AVG; Rev. AETER-NITAT[I] AVG; S — C//—)

Antoninianus

Obv. IMP GORDIANVS PIVS FEL AVG. Radiated bust of emperor in cuirass and paludamentum looking right, seen from rear.

Rev. LAETITIA AVG N. Laetitia standing left, holding wreath in right hand and anchor in left hand.

— — —//—

Lit.: RIC 4.3, p. 25, Rome 86

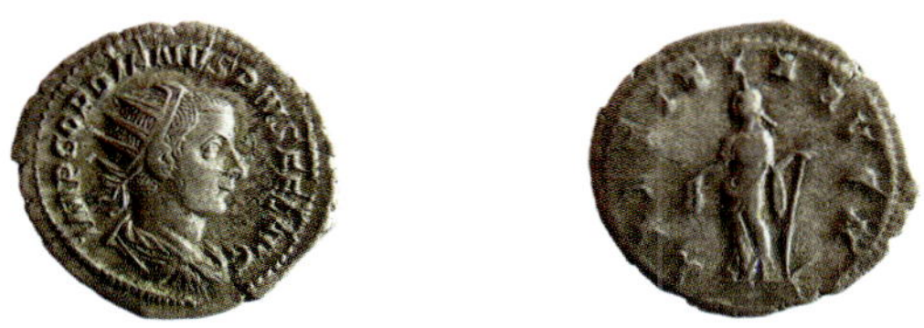

84. AR; 3,68 g.; 22,2 x 22,6 mm.; 5 h.; inv. n. 1430.
(Obv. IMP GORDIANVS PIVS FEL AVG; Rev. LAETITIA AVG N; — — —//—)

As

Obv. IMP GORDIANVS PIVS FEL AVG. Laureated bust of emperor in cuirass and paludamentum looking right, seen from rear.

Rev. LAETITIA AVG N. Laetitia standing left, holding wreath in right hand and anchor in left hand.

S — C//—

Lit.: RIC 4.3, p. 48, Rome 300b

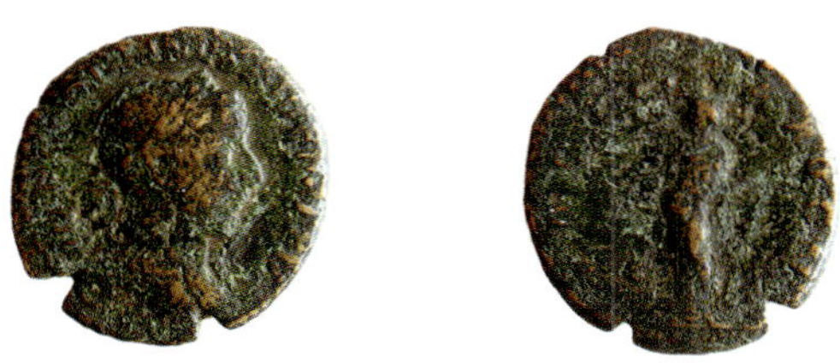

85. AE; 11,24 g.; 25,2 x 24,1 mm.; 12 h.; inv. n. 1431.
(Obv. IMP [GO]RDIANVS PIVS F[EL AVG]; Rev. LAE[TITIA] AVG N; S — C//—)

Antoninianus

Obv. IMP GORDIANVS PIVS FEL AVG. Radiated bust of emperor in cuirass and paludamentum looking right, seen from rear.

Rev. VIRTVTI AVGVSTI. Hercules standing right, hand resting on hip, left hand holding lion's skin and club which rests on rock.

— — —//—

Lit.: RIC 4.3, p. 25, Rome 95

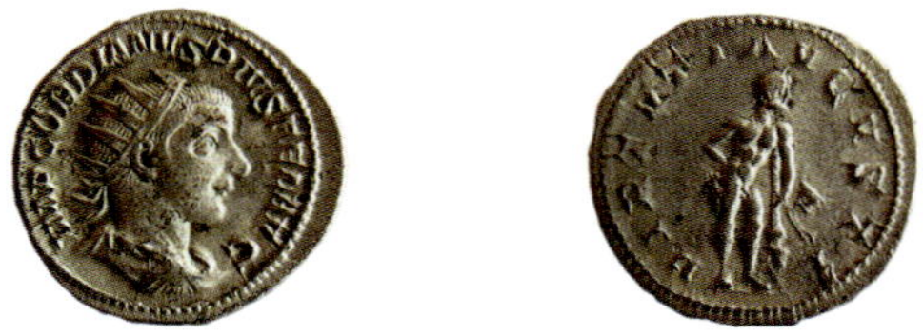

86. AR; 4,16 g.; 22,5 x 22,7 mm.; 8 h.; inv. n. 1432.
(Obv. IMP GORDIANVS PIVS FEL AVG; Rev. VIRTVTI AVGVSTI; — — —//—)

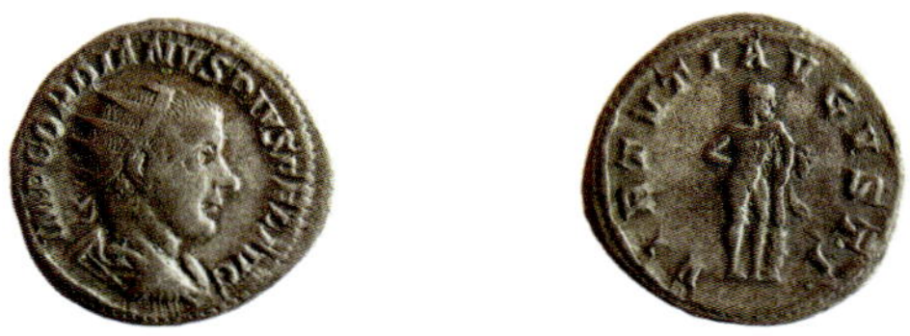

87. AR; 4,49 g.; 21,7 x 22,9 mm.; 12 h.; inv. n. 1433.
(Obv. IMP GORDIANVS PIVS FEL AVG; Rev. VIRTVTI AVGVSTI; — — —//—)

241 A.D.

Antoninianus

Obv. IMP GORDIANVS PIVS FEL AVG. Radiated bust of emperor in cuirass and paludamentum looking right, seen from rear.

Rev. LIBERALITAS AVG III. Liberalitas standing left, holding tessera in right hand and cornucopiae in left hand.

— — —//—

Lit.: RIC 4.3, p. 23, Rome 67

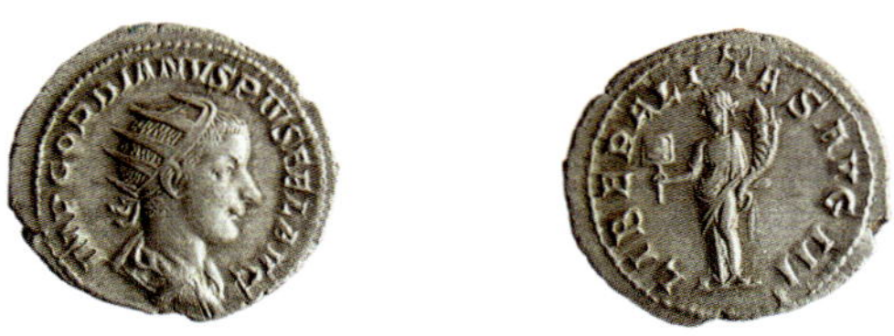

88. AR; 4,3 g.; 21,3 x 23,3 mm.; 12 h.; inv. n. 927.
(Obv. IMP GORDIANVS PIVS FEL AVG; Rev. LIBERALI-TAS AVG III; — — —//—)

Sestertius

Obv. IMP GORDIANVS PIVS FEL AVG. Laureated bust of emperor in cuirass and paludamentum looking right, seen from rear.

Rev. P M TR P IIII COS P P. Apollo seated left, holding branch in right hand and resting left elbow on lyre.

— — —//SC

Lit.: RIC 4.3, p. 48, Rome 302 var. [11]

[11] The wrong number of tribunates shown – engraver's error. For more details, see Lužický 2007.

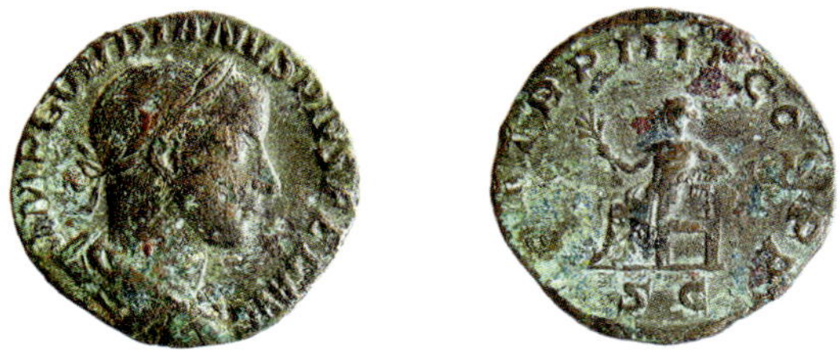

89. AE; 15,98 g.; 28,4 x 28,3 mm.; 12 h.; inv. n. 1434.
(Obv. IMP GORDIANVS PIVS FEL AVG; Rev. P M TR P IIII COS P P; — — —//SC)

Antoninianus
Obv. IMP GORDIANVS PIVS FEL AVG. Radiated bust of emperor in cuirass and paludamentum looking right, seen from rear.
Rev. P M TR P IIII COS II P P. Emperor standing left, holding transverse spear in right hand and globe in left hand.
— — —//—
Lit.: RIC 4.3, p. 25, Rome 92

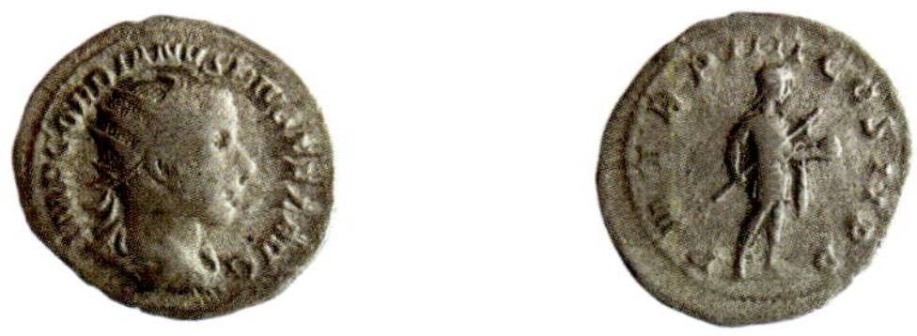

90. AR; 3,88 g.; 22,2 x 22,7 mm.; 1 h.; inv. n. 1435.
(Obv. IMP GORDIANVS PIVS FEL AVG; Rev. P M TR P IIII COS II P P; — — —//—)

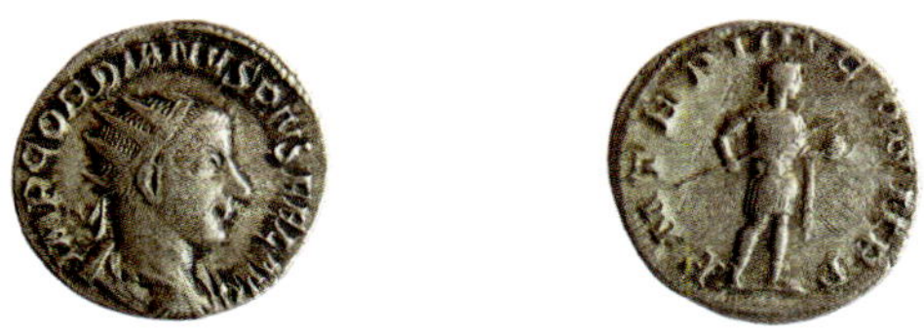

91. AR; 4,22 g.; 20,8 x 20,9 mm.; 6 h.; inv. n. 1436.
(Obv. IMP GORDIANVS PIVS FEL AVG; Rev. P M TR P IIII COS II P P; — — —//—)

Sestertius
Obv. IMP GORDIANVS PIVS FEL AVG. Laureated bust of emperor in cuirass and paludamentum looking right, seen from rear.
Rev. P M TR P IIII COS II P P. Emperor standing left, holding transverse spear in right hand and globe in left hand.
S — C//—
Lit.: RIC 4.3, p. 49, Rome 306a

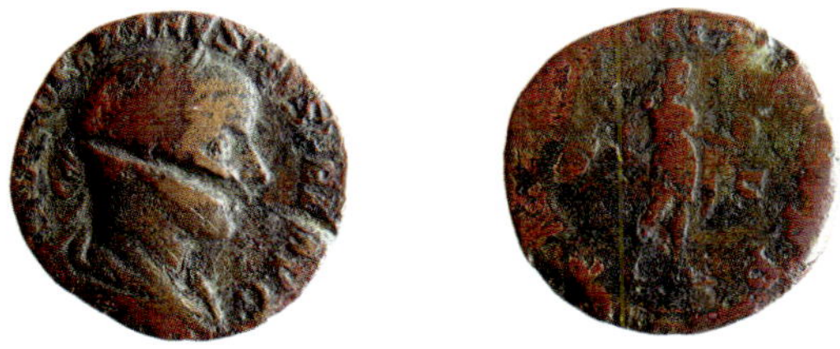

92. AE; 12,56 g.; 26,9 x 27,4 mm.; 6 h.; inv. n. 1437.
(Obv. IMP GORDIANVS PIVS FEL AVG; Rev. P M [TR P] IIII [COS] II P P; S — C//—)

Antoninianus

Obv. IMP GORDIANVS PIVS FEL AVG. Radiated bust of emperor in cuirass and paludamentum looking right, seen from rear.

Rev. IOVI STATORI. Jupiter standing front, head turned right, holding vertical sceptre in right hand and thunderbolt in left hand.

— — —//—

Lit.: RIC 4.3, p. 25, Rome 84

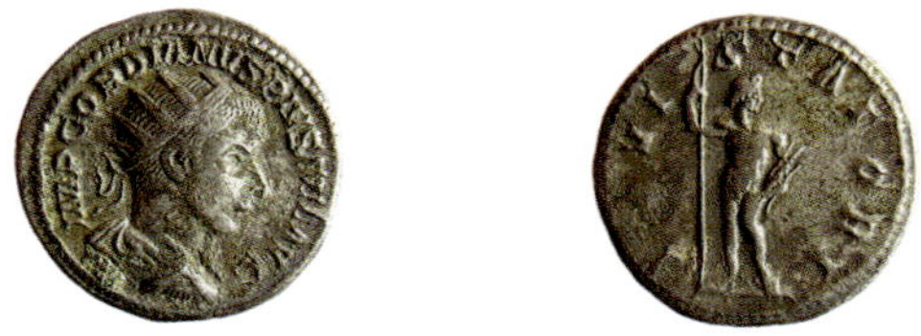

93. AR; 5,46 g.; 22,1 x 22,1 mm.; 1 h.; inv. n. 1438.
(Obv. IMP GORDIANVS PIVS FEL AVG; Rev. IOVI – STATORI; — — —//—)

Sestertius

Obv. IMP GORDIANVS PIVS FEL AVG. Laureated bust of emperor in cuirass and paludamentum looking right, seen from rear.

Rev. IOVI STATORI. Jupiter standing front, head turned right, holding vertical sceptre in right hand and thunderbolt in left hand.

S — C//—

Lit.: RIC 4.3, p. 48, Rome 298a

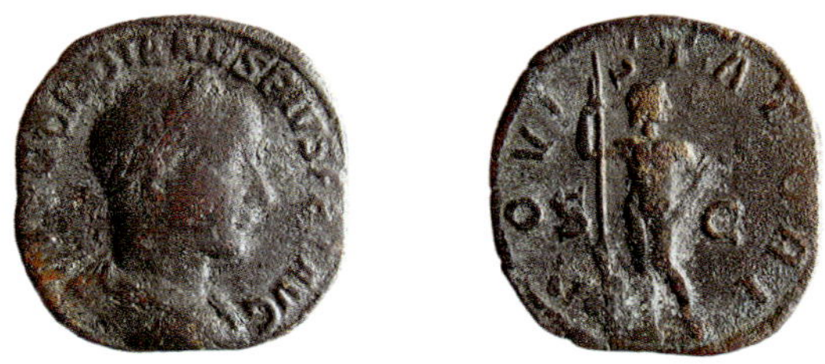

94. AE; 17,82 g.; 29,7 x 28,2 mm.; 12 h.; inv. n. 344.
(Obv. [IMP] GORDIANVS PIVS FEL AVG; Rev. IOVI – STATORI; S — C//—)

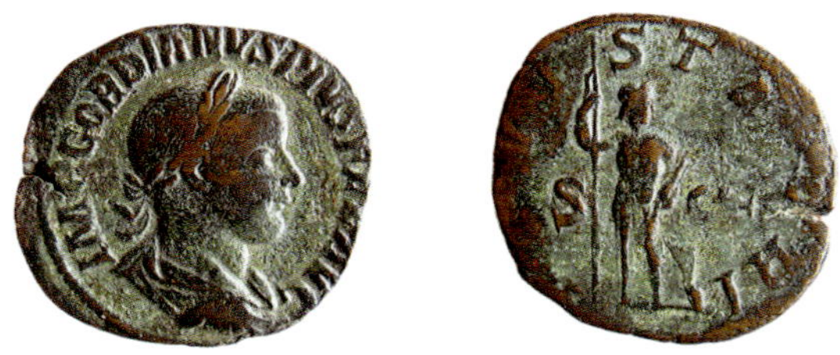

95. AE; 20,39 g.; 28,1 x 29,1 mm.; 12 h.; inv. n. 1439.
(Obv. IMP GORDIANVS PIVS FEL AVG; Rev. IOVI – STA[TO]RI; S — C//—)

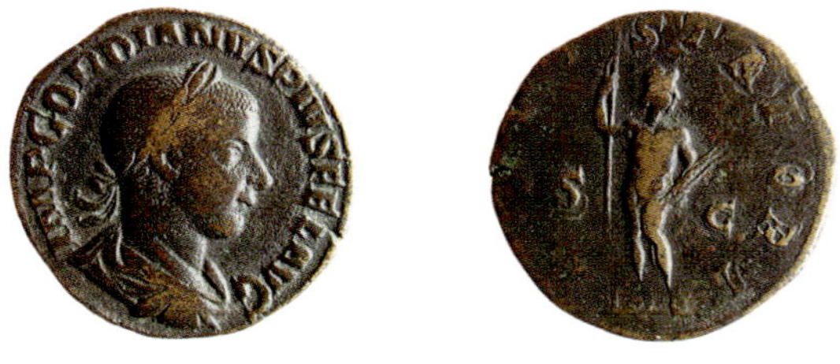

96. AE; 19,13 g.; 28,4 x 29,9 mm.; 12 h.; inv. n. 1440.
(Obv. IMP GORDIANVS PIVS FEL AVG; Rev. IOVI – STATORI; S — C//—)

As
Obv. IMP GORDIANVS PIVS FEL AVG. Laureated bust of emperor in cuirass and paludamentum looking right, seen from rear.
Rev. IOVI STATORI. Jupiter standing front, head turned right, holding vertical sceptre in right hand and thunderbolt in left hand.
S — C//—
Lit.: RIC 4.3, p. 48, Rome 298b

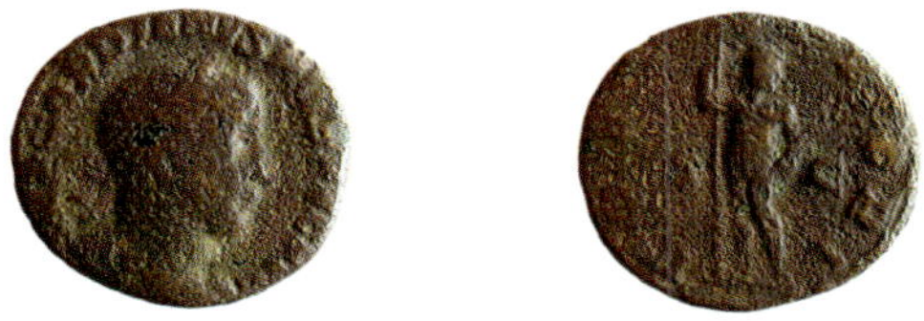

97. AE; 8,33 g.; 21,8 x 24,0 mm.; 12 h.; inv. n. 1441.
(Obv. [IMP] GORDIANVS PIVS FEL AVG; Rev. IOV[I STAT]ORI; S — C//—)

242 A.D.

Antoninianus
Obv. IMP GORDIANVS PIVS FEL AVG. Radiated bust of emperor in cuirass and paludamentum looking right, seen from rear.
Rev. P M TR P V COS II P P. Apollo seated left, holding branch in right hand and resting left elbow on lyre.
— — —//—
Lit.: RIC 4.3, p. 25, Rome 89

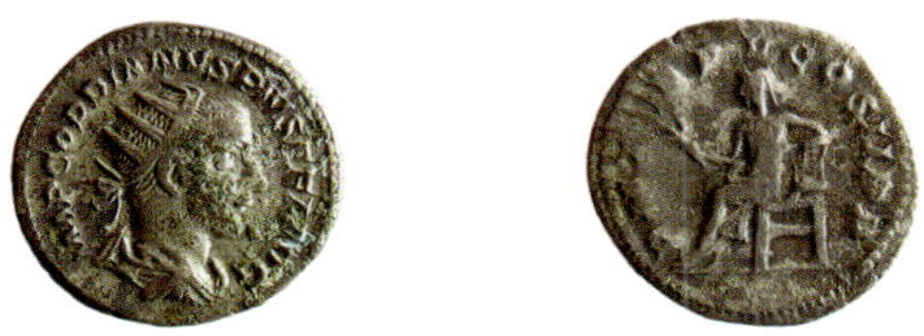

98. AR; 4,48 g.; 21,6 x 22,9 mm.; 11 h.; inv. n. 1442.
(Obv. IMP GORDIANVS PIVS FEL AVG; Rev. P M T-R P V COS II P P; — — —//—)

Sestertius
Obv. IMP GORDIANVS PIVS FEL AVG. Laureated bust of emperor in cuirass and paludamentum looking right, seen from rear.
Rev. P M TR P V COS II P P. Apollo seated left, holding branch in right hand and resting left elbow on lyre.
— — —//SC
Lit.: RIC 4.3, p. 48, Rome 303a

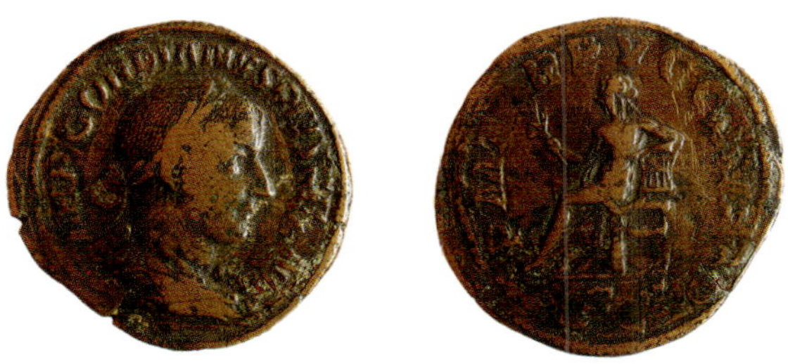

99. AE; 20,17 g.; 31,4 x 32,2 mm.; 1 h.; inv. n. 1443.
(Obv. IMP GORDIANVS PIVS FEL AVG; Rev. P M T-R P V COS II P P; — — —//SC)

Antoninianus

Obv. IMP GORDIANVS PIVS FEL AVG. Radiated bust of emperor in cuirass and paludamentum looking right, seen from rear.

Rev. P M TR P V COS II P P. Emperor standing left, holding transverse spear in right hand and globe in left hand.

— — —//—

Lit.: RIC 4.3, p. 25, Rome 93

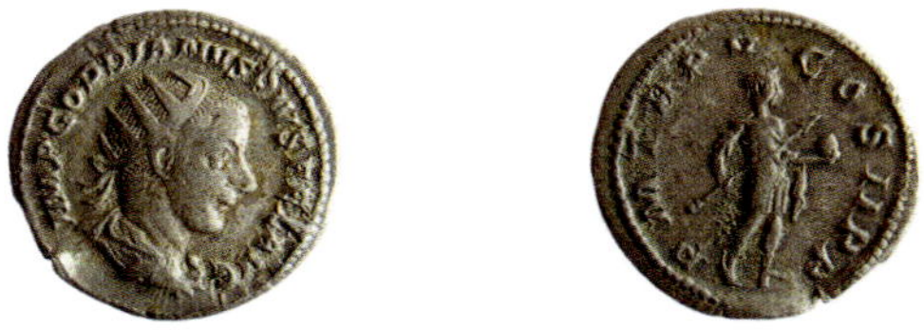

100. AR; 3,31 g.; 21,9 x 22,5 mm.; 12 h.; inv. n. 1444.
(Obv. IMP GORDIANVS PIVS FEL AVG; Rev. P M TR P V COS II P P; — — —//—)

Sestertius

Obv. IMP GORDIANVS PIVS FEL AVG. Laureated bust of emperor in cuirass and paludamentum looking right, seen from rear.

Rev. P M TR P V COS II P P. Emperor standing left, holding transverse spear in right hand and globe in left hand.

S — C//—

Lit.: RIC 4.3, p. 49, Rome 307a

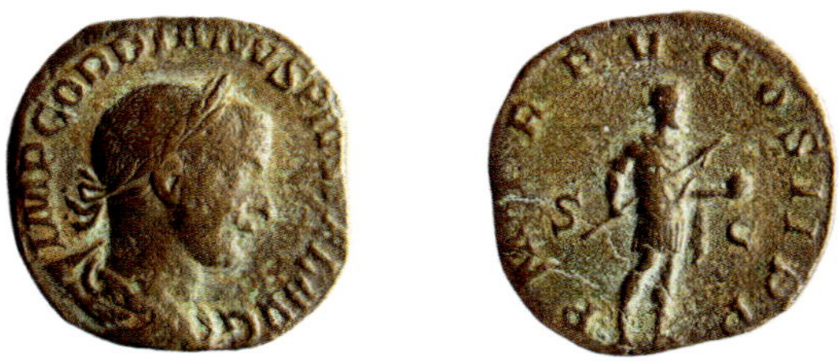

101. AE; 19,87 g.; 27,9 x 28,3 mm.; 1 h.; inv. n. 1445.
(Obv. IMP GORDIANVS PIVS FEL AVG; Rev. P M TR P V COS II P P; S — C//—)

Sestertius

Obv. IMP GORDIANVS PIVS FEL AVG. Laureated bust of emperor in cuirass and paludamentum looking right, seen from rear.

Rev. FORTVNA REDVX. Fortuna seated left, holding rudder in right hand and cornucopiae in left hand; wheel beneath seat.

— — —//SC

Lit.: RIC 4.3, p. 51, Rome 331a

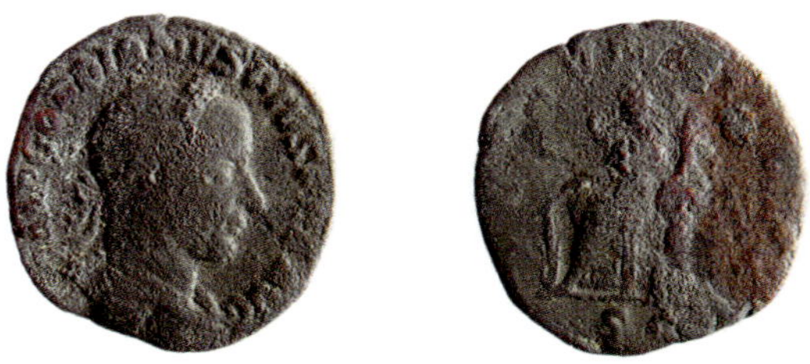

102. AE; 16,35 g.; 28,4 x 28,3 mm.; 12 h.; inv. n. 1446.
(Obv. IMP GORDIANVS PIVS [FEL] AVG; Rev. FO[RT]VNA [RED]VX; — — —//SC)

As
Obv. IMP GORDIANVS PIVS FEL AVG. Laureated bust of emperor in cuirass and paludamentum looking right, seen from rear.
Rev. FORTVNA REDVX. Fortuna seated left, holding rudder in right hand and cornucopiae in left hand; wheel beneath seat.
— — —//SC
Lit.: RIC 4.3, p. 51, Rome 331b

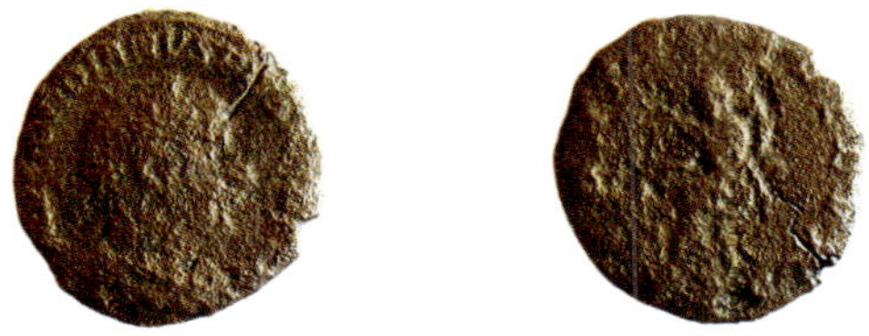

103. AE; 6,81 g.; 24,3 x 22,8 mm.; 7 h.; inv. n. 1447.
(Obv. [IMP G]ORDIANVS PIVS [FEL AVG]; Rev. [F]ORTV[NA] REDVX; — — —//[S]C)

Sestertius
Obv. IMP GORDIANVS PIVS FEL AVG. Laureated bust of emperor in cuirass and paludamentum looking right, seen from rear.
Rev. MARTEM PROPVGNATOREM. Mars walking right, holding transverse spear in right hand and shield in left hand.
S — C//—
Lit.: RIC 4.3, p. 52, Rome 333

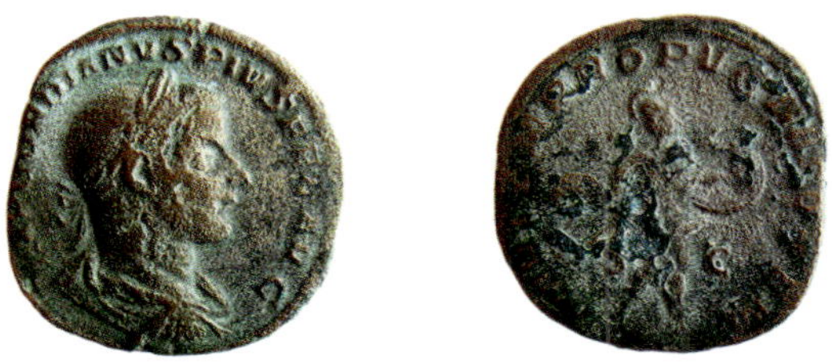

104. AE; 17,36 g.; 29,7 x 27,8 mm.; 12 h.; inv. n. 1448.
(Obv. IMP GORDIANVS PIVS FEL AVG; Rev. MARTEM PROPVGNATOREM; S — C//—)

Antoninianus
Obv. IMP GORDIANVS PIVS FEL AVG. Radiated bust of emperor in cuirass and paludamentum looking right, seen from rear.
Rev. VICTORIA AETERNA. Victory standing left, right hand leaning on shield, left hand holding palm; captive under shield
— — —//—
Lit.: RIC 4.3, p. 31, Rome 156

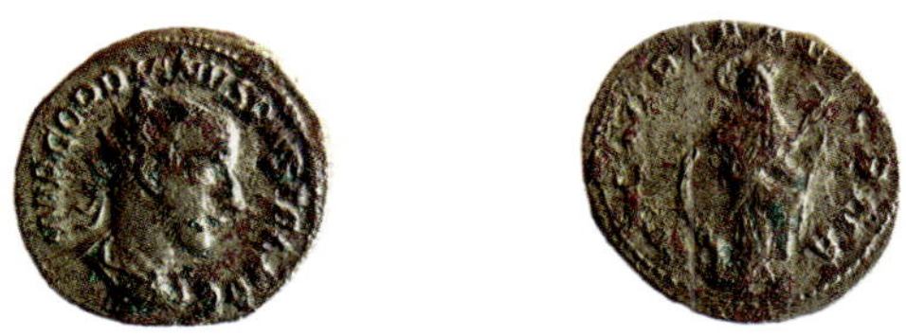

105. AR; 4,81 g.; 21,2 x 21,4 mm.; 6 h.; inv. n. 926.
(Obv. IMP GORDIANVS PIVS FEL AVG; Rev. VICTORIA AETERNA; — — —//—)

Sestertius

Obv. IMP GORDIANVS PIVS FEL AVG. Laureated bust of emperor in cuirass and paludamentum looking right, seen from rear.

Rev. VICTORIA AETERNA. Victory standing left, right hand leaning on shield, left hand holding palm; captive under shield.

S — C//—

Lit.: RIC 4.3, p. 52, Rome 338a

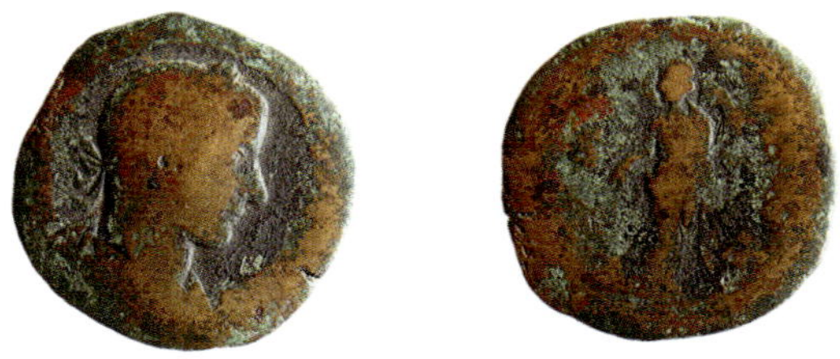

106. AE; 15,07 g.; 27,7 x 27,7 mm.; 1 h.; inv. n. 1449.
(Obv. [IMP GORDIANVS PIVS FEL AVG]; Rev. [VICTORIA AETERN]A; S — C//—)

243 A.D.

Antoninianus

Obv. IMP GORDIANVS PIVS FEL AVG. Radiated bust of emperor in cuirass and paludamentum looking right, seen from rear.

Rev. FORT REDVX. Fortuna seated left, holding rudder in right hand and cornucopiae in left hand; wheel beneath seat.

— — —//—

Lit.: RIC 4.3, p. 31, Rome 143

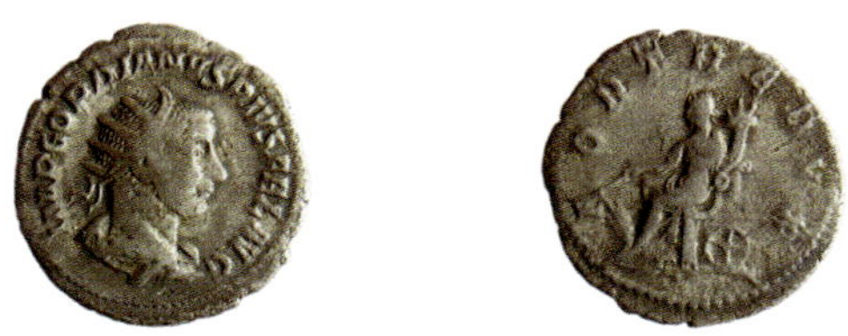

107. AR; 3,77 g.; 23,3 x 21,8 mm.; 1 h.; inv. n. 1450.
(Obv. IMP GORDIANVS PIVS FEL AVG; Rev. F-ORT REDVX; — — —//—)

As

Obv. IMP GORDIANVS PIVS FEL AVG. Laureated bust of emperor in cuirass and paludamentum looking right, seen from rear.

Rev. MARS PROPVGNAT. Mars walking right, holding transverse spear in right hand and shield in left hand.

S — C//—

Lit.: RIC 4.3, p. 52, Rome 332b

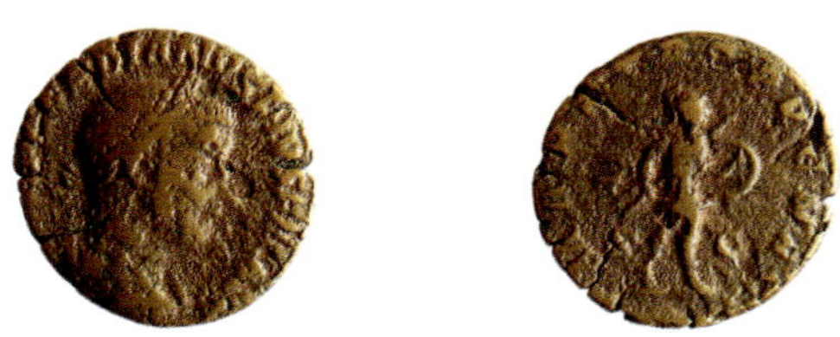

108. AE; 7,04 g.; 22,3 x 22,9 mm.; 6 h.; inv. n. 1451.
(Obv. [IMP] GORDIANVS PIVS FEL [AVG]; Rev. MAR[S P]ROPVGNAT; S — C//—)

Sestertius
Obv. IMP GORDIANVS PIVS FEL AVG. Laureated bust of emperor in cuirass and paludamentum looking right, seen from rear.
Rev. SECVRIT PERPET. Securitas standing front, legs crossed, head left, holding vertical sceptre in right hand and leaning on column with left elbow.
S — C//—
Lit.: RIC 4.3, p. 52, Rome 335a

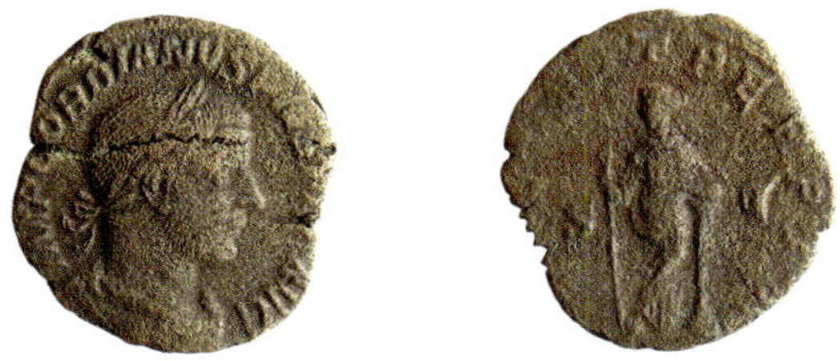

109. AE; 13,17 g.; 29,0 x 25,2 mm.; 1 h.; inv. n. 1452.
(Obv. IMP GORDIANVS PIVS FEL AVG; Rev. [SECVRI]T PERPE[T]; S — C//—)

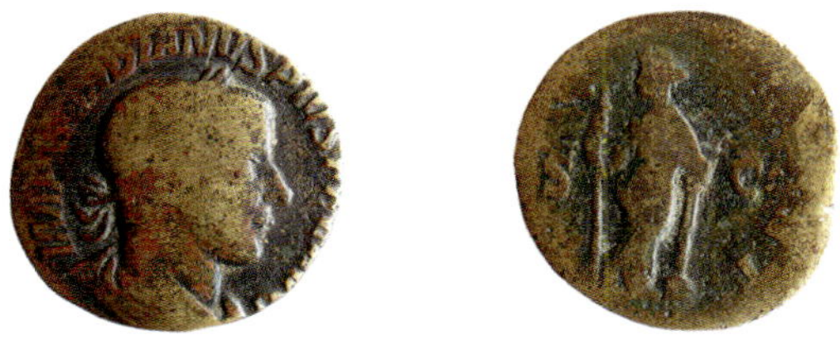

110. AE; 15 g.; 26,3 x 26,3 mm.; 12 h.; inv. n. 1453.
(Obv. IMP GORDIANVS PIVS FEL AVG; Rev. [SECVRIT PERP]ET; S — C//—)

Sestertius
Obv. IMP GORDIANVS PIVS FEL AVG. Laureated bust of emperor in cuirass and paludamentum looking right, seen from rear.
Rev. VICTORIA AETER. Victory standing left, right hand leaning on shield, left hand holding palm; captive under shield.
S — C//—
Lit.: RIC 4.3, p. 52, Rome 337a

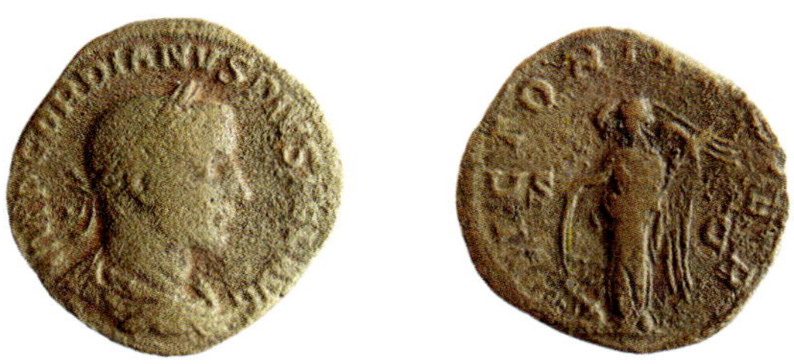

111. AE; 21,12 g.; 30,4 x 29,2 mm.; 1 h.; inv. n. 1454.
(Obv. IMP GORDIANVS PIVS FEL AVG; Rev. VICTORIA [AE]TE-R; S — C//—)

Antoninianus
Obv. IMP GORDIANVS PIVS FEL AVG. Radiated bust of emperor in cuirass and paludamentum looking right, seen from rear.
Rev. FELIC-IT TEMP. Felicitas standing left, holding long-handled vertical caduceus in right hand and cornucopiae in left hand.
— — —//—
Lit.: RIC 4.3, p. 30, Rome 140

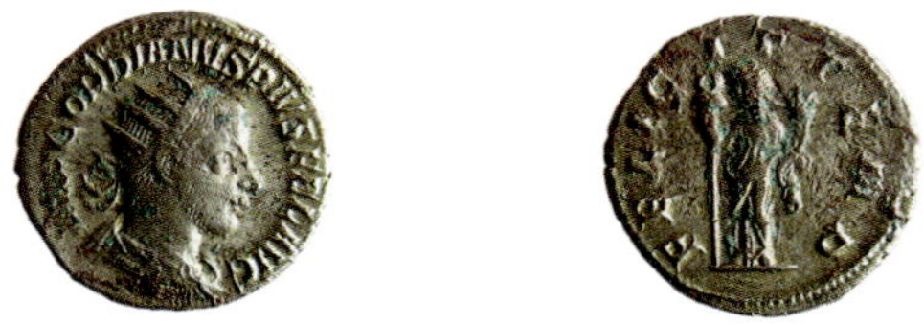

112. AR; 3,8 g.; 20,8 x 21,4 mm.; 6 h.; inv. n. 927.
(Obv. IMP GORDIANVS PIVS FEL AVG; Rev. FELIC-IT TEMP; — — —//—)

Antoninianus
Obv. IMP GORDIANVS PIVS FEL AVG. Radiated bust of emperor in cuirass and paludamentum looking right, seen from rear.
Rev. PROVID AVG. Providentia standing left, holding baton in right hand and vertical sceptre in left hand; at feet to left globe.
— — —//—
Lit.: RIC 4.3, p. 31, Rome 148

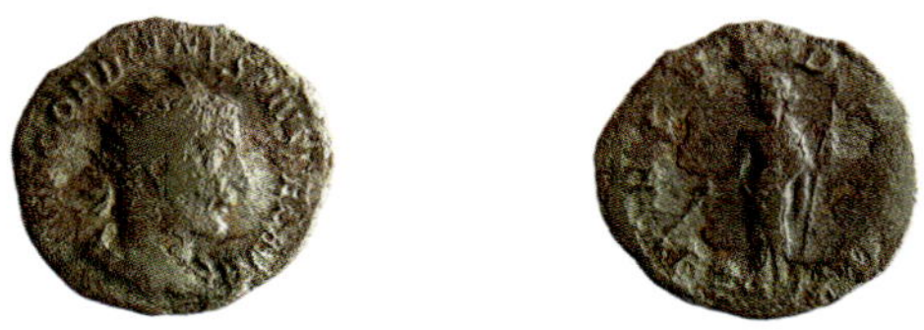

113. AR; 2,53 g.; 20,1 x 21,2 mm.; 1 h.; inv. n. 1455.
(Obv. [IMP] GORDIANVS PIVS FEL AVG; Rev. P-ROVID AVG; — — —//—)

Antoninianus
Obv. IMP GORDIANVS PIVS FEL AVG. Radiated bust of emperor in cuirass and paludamentum looking right, seen from rear.
Rev. SECVRIT PERP. Securitas standing front, legs crossed, head left, holding vertical sceptre in right hand and leaning on column with left elbow.
— — —//—
Lit.: RIC 4.3, p. 31, Rome 151

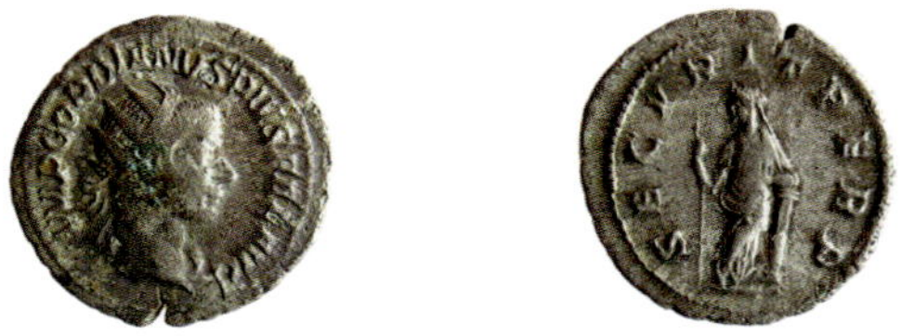

114. AR; 3,95 g.; 22,8 x 23,2 mm.; 6 h.; inv. n. 1456.
(Obv. IMP GORDIANVS PIVS FEL AVG; Rev. SECVRIT PERP; — — —//—)

Antoninianus
Obv. IMP GORDIANVS PIVS FEL AVG. Radiated bust of emperor in cuirass and paludamentum looking right, seen from rear.
Rev. VICTOR AETER. Victory standing left, right hand leaning on shield, left hand holding palm; captive under shield.
— — —//—
Lit.: RIC 4.3, p. 31, Rome 154

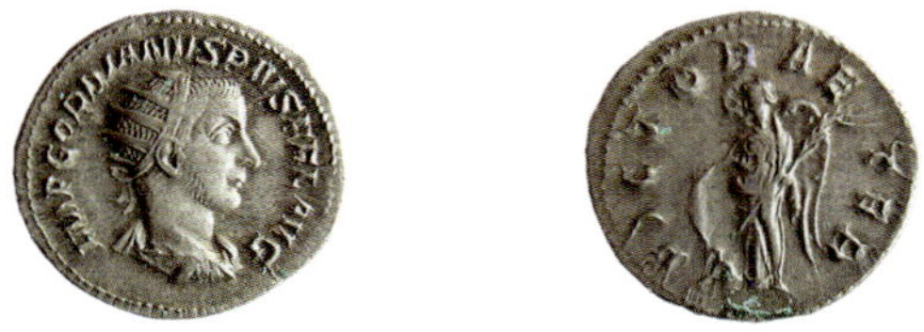

115. AR; 4,37 g.; 22,0 x 22,9 mm.; 6 h.; inv. n. 921.
(Obv. IMP GORDIANVS PIVS FEL AVG; Rev. VICTOR AE-TER; — — —//—)

Antiochia

242 – 244 A.D.

Antoninianus
Obv. IMP GORDIANVS PIVS FEL AVG. Radiated bust of emperor in cuirass looking right, seen from rear.
Rev. FORTVNA REDVX. Fortuna seated left, holding rudder in right hand and cornucopiae in left hand.
— — —//—
Lit.: RIC 4.3, p. 37, Antioch 210

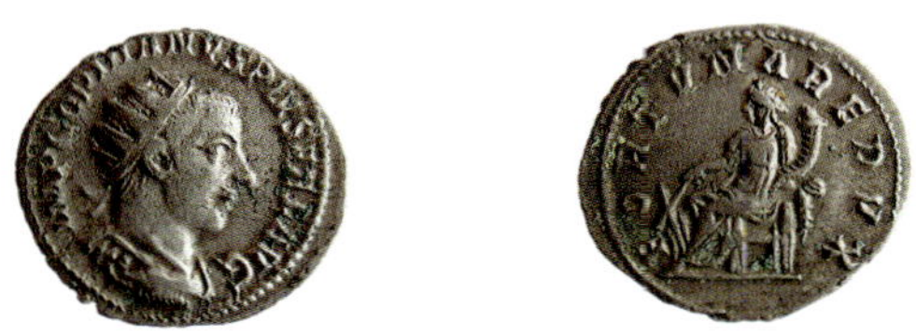

116. AR; 4,06 g.; 21,5 x 23,2 mm.; 6 h.; inv. n. 925.
(Obv. IMP GORDIANVS PIVS FEL AVG; Rev. F-ORTVNA REDVX; — — —//—)

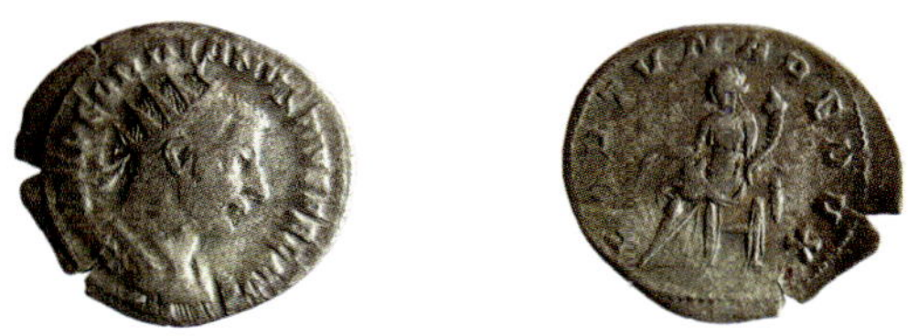

117. AR; 3,19 g.; 21,9 x 24,1 mm.; 12 h.; inv. n. 1457.
(Obv. IMP GORDIANVS PIVS FEL AVG; Rev. FORTVNA REDVX; — — —//—)

Antoninianus
Obv. IMP GORDIANVS PIVS FEL AVG. Radiated bust of emperor in cuirass looking right, seen from rear.
Rev. ORIENS AVG. Sol standing left, raising right hand, globe in left hand.
— — —//—
Lit.: RIC 4.3, p. 37, Antioch 213

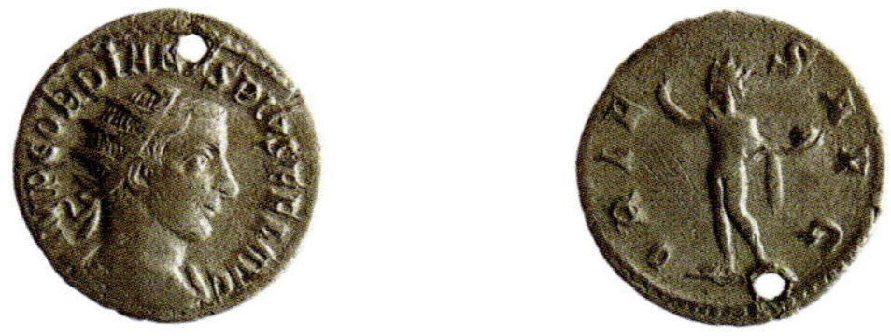

118. AR; 3,27 g.; 22,3 x 21,6 mm.; 6 h.; inv. n. 248.
(Obv. IMP GORDIAN[V]S PIVS FEL AVG; Rev. ORIE-[N]-S AVG; — — —//—)

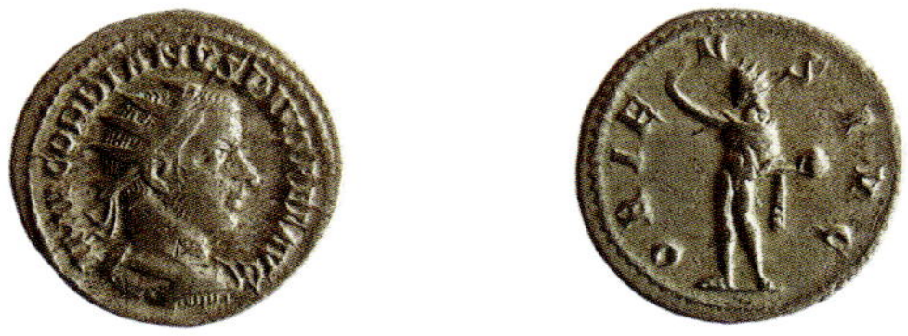

119. AR; 4,95 g.; 22,9 x 23,2 mm.; 7 h.; inv. n. 1458.
(Obv. IMP GORDIANVS PIVS FEL AVG; Rev. ORIE-N-S AVG; — — —//—)

Contemporary imitation

241 A.D.

Antoninianus
Obv. IMP CAES M ANT GORDIANVS AVG. Radiated bust of emperor in cuirass and paludamentum looking right, seen from rear.
Rev. LIBERALITAS AVG III. Liberalitas standing left, holding tessera in right hand and cornucopiae in left hand.
— — —//—
Lit.: RIC 4.3, -[12]

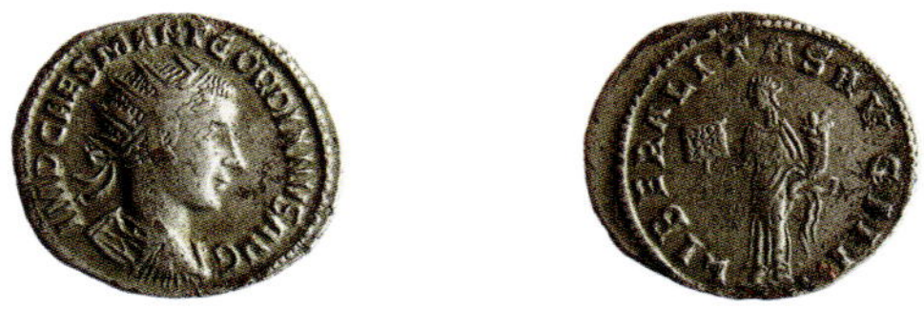

120. AR; 4,18 g.; 20,1 x 22,8 mm.; 6 h.; inv. n. 1459.
(Obv. IMP GORDIANVS PIVS FEL AVG; Rev. LIBERALITAS AVG III; — — —//—)

PHILIPPUS ARABS
(244 – 249 A.D.)

Roma

244 A.D.

Sestertius
Obv. IMP M IVL PHILIPPVS AVG. Laureated bust of emperor in cuirass and paludamentum looking right, seen from rear.
Rev. FIDES MILITVM. Fides standing left holding vertical standard in each hand.
S — C//—
Lit.: RIC 4.3, p. 90, Rome 172a

[12] Contemporary imitation, suberate antoninian, which combines avers die from 238–240 AD with reverse die from 241 AD. For more details, see Lužický 2007.

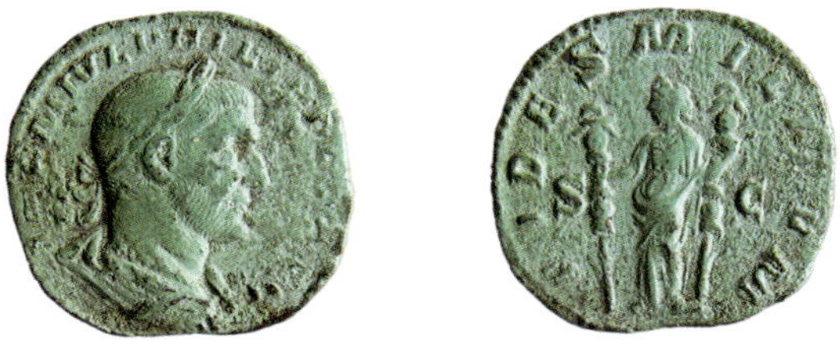

121. AE; 21,46 g.; 27,7 x 28,6 mm.; 12 h.; inv. n. 87.
(Obv. IMP M IVL PHILIPPVS AVG; Rev. FIDES MILITVM; S — C//—)

As
Obv. IMP M IVL PHILIPPVS AVG. Laureated bust of emperor in cuirass and paludamentum looking right, seen from rear.
Rev. FIDES MILITVM. Fides standing left, holding vertical vexilum in right hand and transverse standard in left hand.
S — C//—
Lit.: RIC 4.3, p. 90, Rome 173b var.[13]

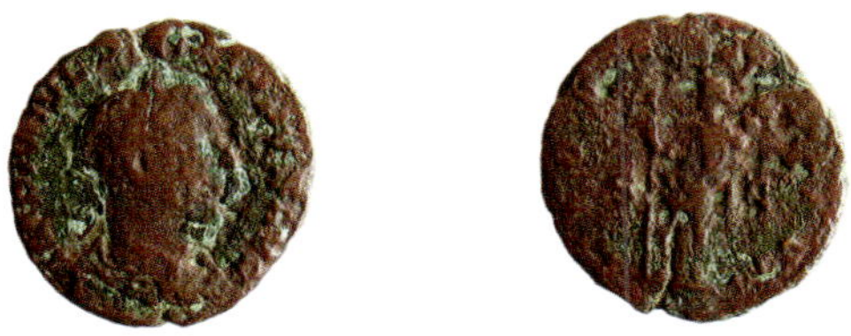

122. AE; 8,78 g.; 24,8 x 23,2 mm.; 6 h.; inv. n. 1460.
(Obv. IMP M IVL PHILIPPVS AVG; Rev. FIDES [MI]LITVM; S — C//—)

245 A.D.

Antoninianus
Obv. IMP M IVL PHILIPPVS AVG. Radiated bust of emperor in cuirass and paludamentum looking right, seen from rear.
Rev. LAETIT FVNDAT. Laetitia standing left, foot on prow, holding patera in right hand and rudder in left hand.
— — —//—
Lit.: RIC 4.3, p. 72, Rome 37b

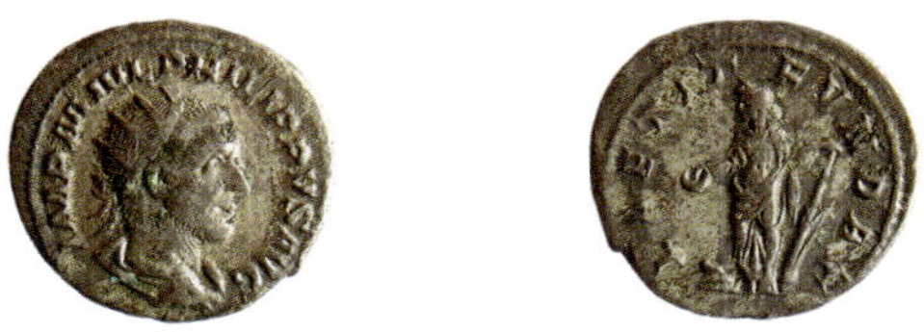

123. AR; 4,5 g.; 21,4 x 22,7 mm.; 12 h.; inv. n. 1461.
(Obv. IMP M IVL PHILIPPVS AVG; Rev. LAETIT – FVNDAT; — — —//—)

Sestertius
Obv. IMP M IVL PHILIPPVS AVG. Laureated bust of emperor in cuirass and paludamentum looking right, seen from rear.
Rev. LAET FVNDATA. Laetitia standing left, foot on prow, holding patera in right hand and rudder in left hand.
S — C//—
Lit.: RIC 4.3, p. 90, Rome 176a

[13] Similar revers with antoninianus RIC 4.3, p. 75, Rome 61 – from 247–249 AD with revers legend FIDES EXERCITVS.

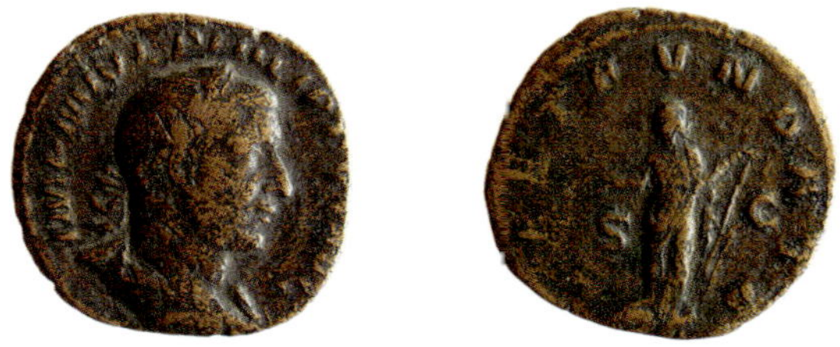

124. AE; 17,26 g.; 28,5 x 29,3 mm.; 12 h.; inv. n. 1462.
(Obv. IMP M IVL PHILIPPVS AVG; Rev. [L]AET FVNDATA; S — C//—)

Antoninianus
Obv. IMP M IVL PHILIPPVS AVG. Radiated bust of emperor in cuirass and paludamentum looking right, seen from rear.
Rev. SALVS AVG. Salus standing right, feeding snake held in right hand from patera held in left hand.
— — —//—
Lit.: RIC 4.3, p. 73, Rome 46b

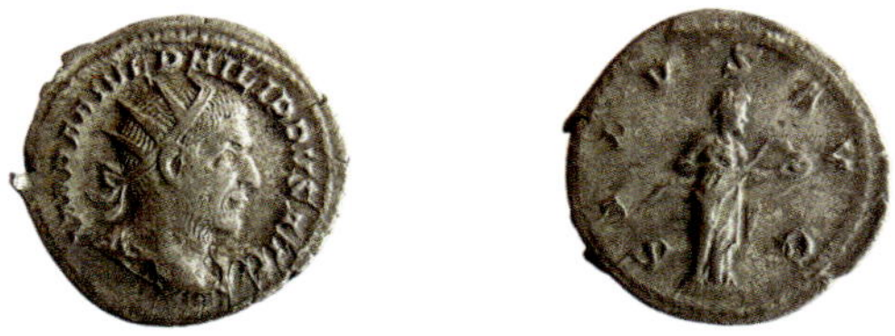

125. AR; 4,06 g.; 23,1 x 23,3 mm.; 6 h.; inv. n. 1463.
(Obv. IMP M IVL PHILIPPVS AVG; Rev. SALVS AVG; — — —//—)

246 A.D.

Sestertius
Obv. IMP M IVL PHILIPPVS AVG. Laureated bust of emperor in cuirass and paludamentum looking right, seen from rear.
Rev. P M TR P III COS P P. Felicitas standing left, holding long-handled vertical caduceus in right hand and cornucopiae in left hand.
S — C//—
Lit.: RIC 4.3, p. 88, Rome 153a

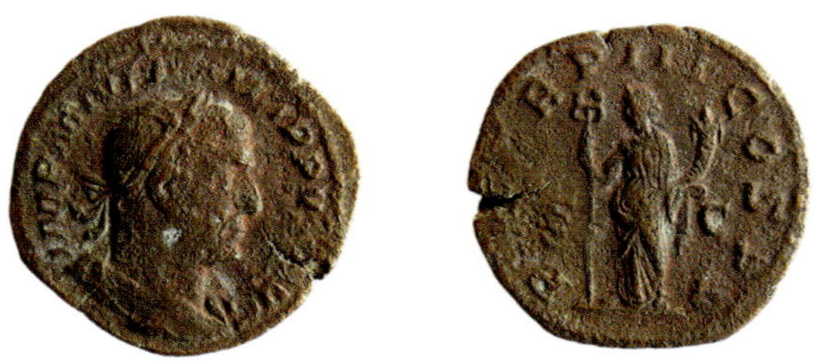

126. AE; 16,54 g.; 30,8 x 30,7 mm.; 11 h.; inv. n. 1464.
(Obv. IMP M IVL PHILIPPVS AVG; Rev. P M TR P III COS P P; S — C//—)

Sestertius

Obv. IMP (M IVL) PHILIPPVS AVG. Laureated bust of emperor in cuirass and paludamentum looking right, seen from rear.

Rev. P M TR P III(I) COS II P P. Felicitas standing left, holding long-handled vertical caduceus in right hand and cornucopiae in left hand.

S — C//—

Lit.: RIC 4.3, p. 87, Rome 150a or Rome 150c

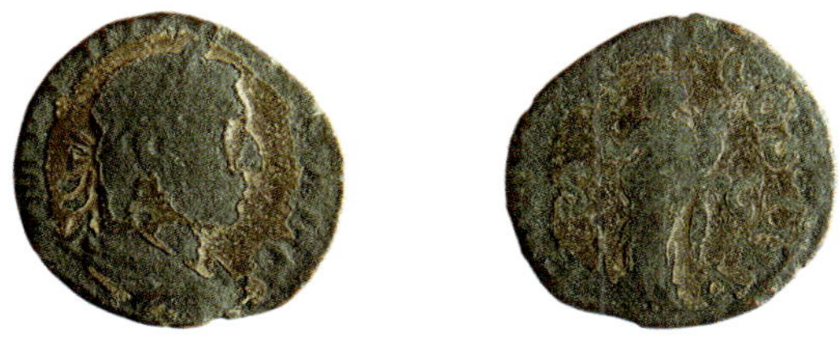

127. AE; 12,92 g.; 26,5 x 27,0 mm.; 12 h.; inv. n. 1465.
(Obv. IMP [(M IVL) PHILIPPVS] AVG; Rev. P [M TR P III(I)] COS II P P; S — C//—)

Antoninianus

Obv. IMP M IVL PHILIPPVS AVG. Radiated bust of emperor in cuirass and paludamentum looking right, seen from rear.

Rev. ADVENTVS AVGG. Emperor riding on horse left, rising right hand, holding transverse spear in left hand.

— — —//—

Lit.: RIC 4.3, p. 71, Rome 26b

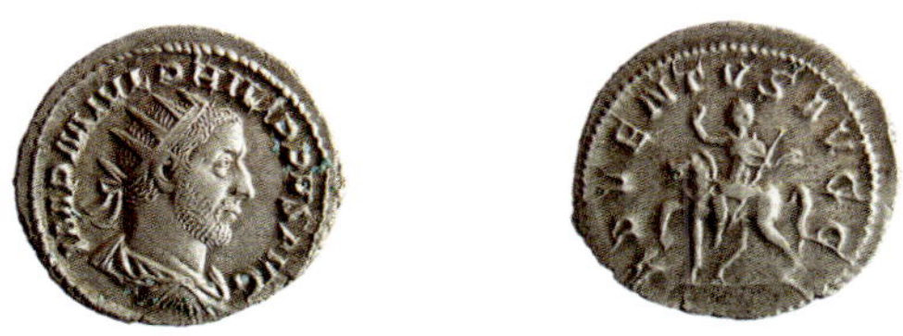

128. AR; 4,62 g.; 22,0 x 23,1 mm.; 1 h.; inv. n. 920.
(Obv. IMP M IVL PHILIPPVS AVG; Rev. ADVENTVS AVGG; — — —//—)

Antoninianus

Obv. IMP M IVL PHILIPPVS AVG. Radiated bust of emperor in cuirass and paludamentum looking right, seen from rear.

Rev. LIBERALITAS AVGG II. Liberalitas standing left, holding tessera in right hand and cornucopiae in left hand.

— — —//—

Lit.: RIC 4.3, p. 72, Rome 38b

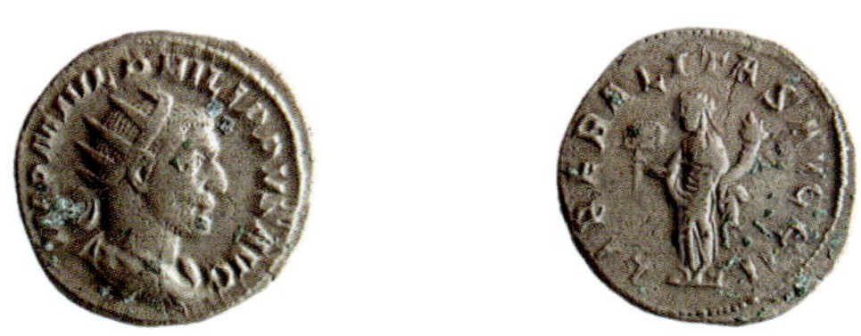

129. AR; 4,62 g.; 22,0 x 22,0 mm.; 6 h.; inv. n. 918.
(Obv. IMP M IVL PHILIPPVS AVG; Rev. LIBERALITAS AVGG II; — — —//—)

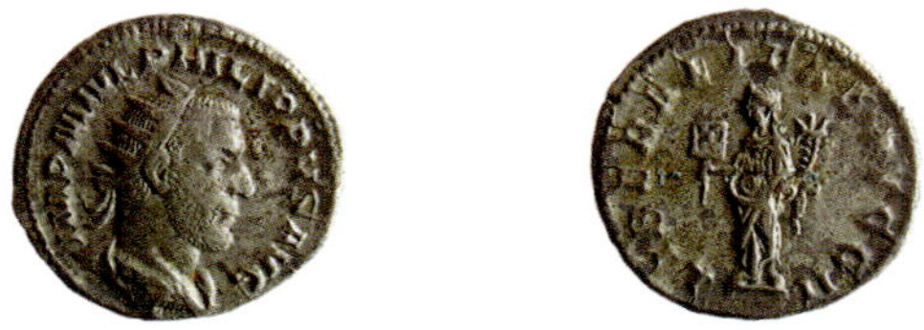

130. AR; 4,53 g.; 21,5 x 22,3 mm.; 6 h.; inv. n. 1466.
(Obv. IMP M IVL PHILIPPVS AVG; Rev. LIBERALITAS AVGG II; — — —//—)

Sestertius
Obv. IMP M IVL PHILIPPVS AVG. Laureated bust of emperor in cuirass and paludamentum looking right, seen from rear.
Rev. LIBERALITAS AVGG II. Liberalitas standing left, holding tessera in right hand and cornucopiae in left hand.
S — C//—
Lit.: RIC 4.3, p. 91, Rome 180a

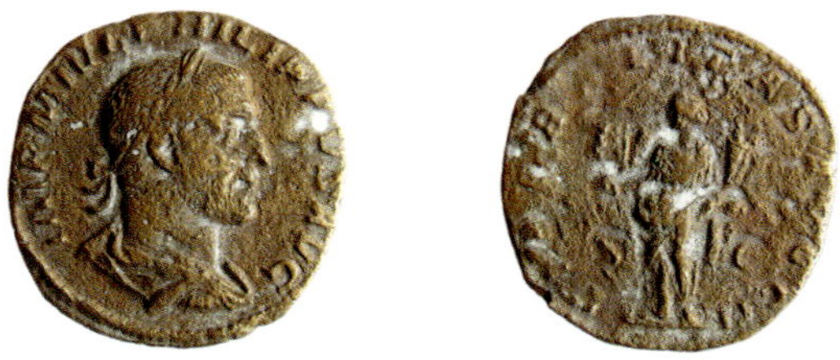

131. AE; 16,11 g.; 28,2 x 27,1 mm.; 12 h.; inv. n. 1467.
(Obv. IMP M IVL PHILIPPVS AVG; Rev. LIBERALITAS AVGG II; S — C//—)

Antoninianus
Obv. IMP M IVL PHILIPPVS AVG. Radiated bust of emperor in cuirass and paludamentum looking right, seen from rear.
Rev. AEQVITAS AVGG. Aequitas standing left, holding scales in right hand and cornucopiae in left hand.
— — —//—
Lit.: RIC 4.3, p. 71, Rome 27b

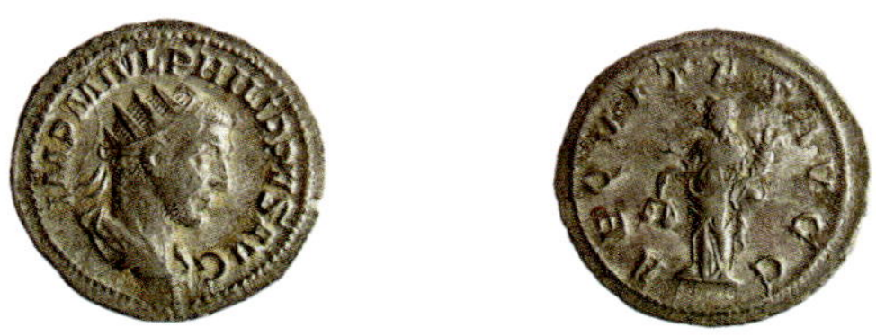

132. AR; 3,16 g.; 22,9 x 23,0 mm.; 6 h.; inv. n. 1468.
(Obv. IMP M IVL PHILIPPVS AVG; Rev. AEQVITAS AVGG; — — —//—)

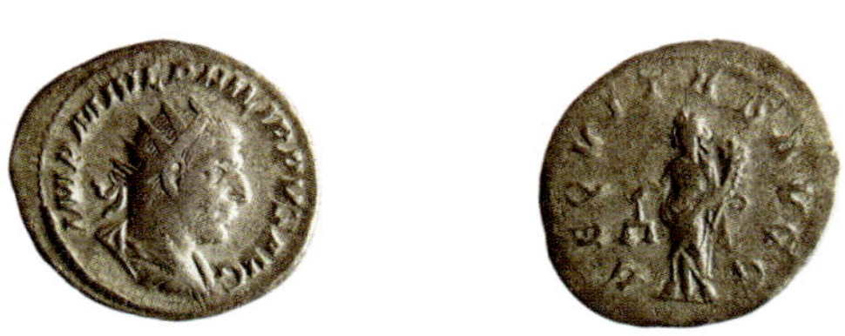

133. AR; 4,09 g.; 21,4 x 23,6 mm.; 8 h.; inv. n. 1469.
(Obv. IMP M IVL PHILIPPVS AVG; Rev. AEQVITAS AVGG; — — —//—)

Sestertius
Obv. IMP M IVL PHILIPPVS AVG. Laureated bust of emperor in cuirass and paludamentum looking right, seen from rear.
Rev. AEQVITAS AVGG. Aequitas standing left, holding scales in right hand and cornucopiae in left hand.
S — C//—
Lit.: RIC 4.3, p. 89, Rome 166a

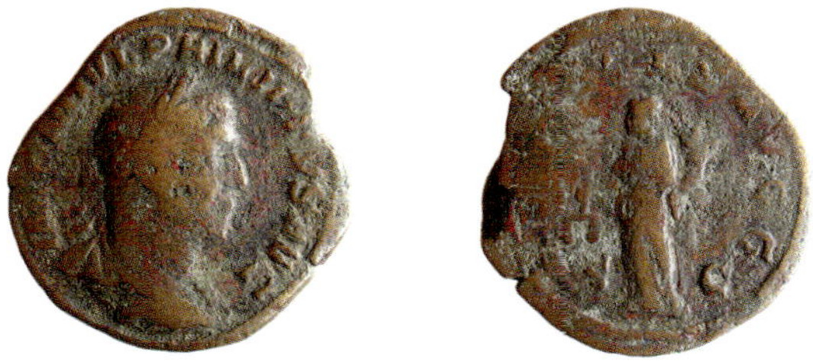

134. AE; 20,28 g.; 31,0 x 29,4 mm.; 12 h.; inv. n. 1470.
(Obv. IMP M IVL PHILIPPVS AVG; Rev. [A]EQ[VI]TAS AVGG; S — C//—)

Antoninianus
Obv. IMP M IVL PHILIPPVS AVG. Radiated bust of emperor in cuirass and paludamentum looking right, seen from rear.
Rev. ROMAE AETERNAE. Roma seated on shield left, holding Victoriola in right hand and long vertical spear in left hand.
— — —//—
Lit.: RIC 4.3, p. 73, Rome 44b

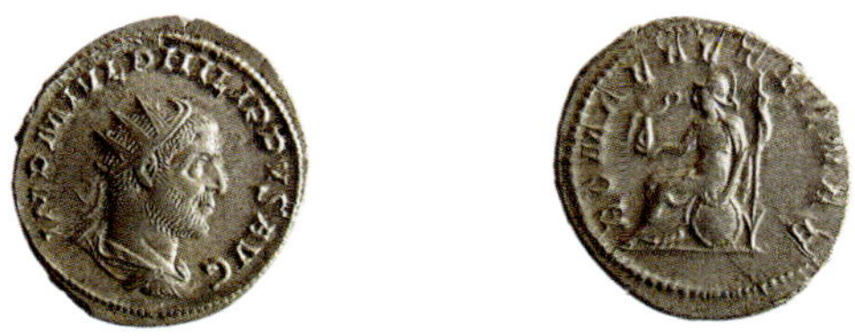

135. AR; 4,17 g.; 23,4 x 21,5 mm.; 1 h.; inv. n. 1471.
(Obv. IMP M IVL PHILIPPVS AVG; Rev. ROMAE AET-ERNAE; — — —//—)

Antoninianus
Obv. IMP PHILIPPVS AVG. Radiated bust of emperor in cuirass and paludamentum looking right, seen from rear.
Rev. FORTVNA REDVX. Fortuna seated left, holding rudder in right hand and cornucopiae in left hand; wheel beneath seat.
— — —//—
Lit.: RIC 4.3, p. 75, Rome 63b

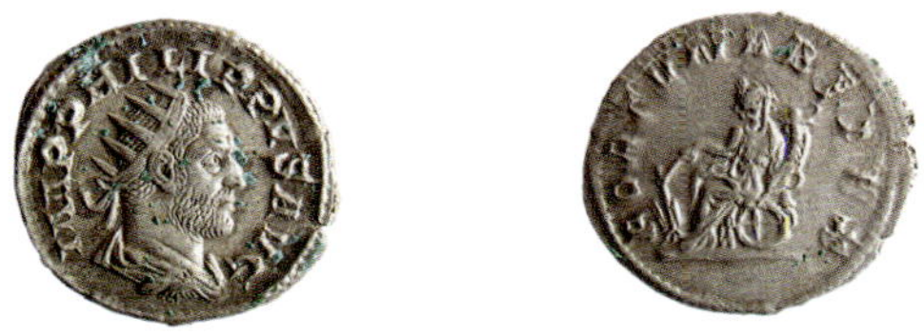

136. AR; 3,49 g.; 21,5 x 22,1 mm.; 6 h.; inv. n. 919.
(Obv. IMP PHILIPPVS AVG; Rev. FORTVNA REDVX; — — —//—)

Antoninianus
Obv. IMP PHILIPPVS AVG. Radiated bust of emperor in cuirass and paludamentum looking right, seen from rear.
Rev. AEQVITAS AVGG. Aequitas standing left, holding scales in right hand and cornucopiae in left hand.
— — —//—
Lit.: RIC 4.3, p. 75, Rome 57

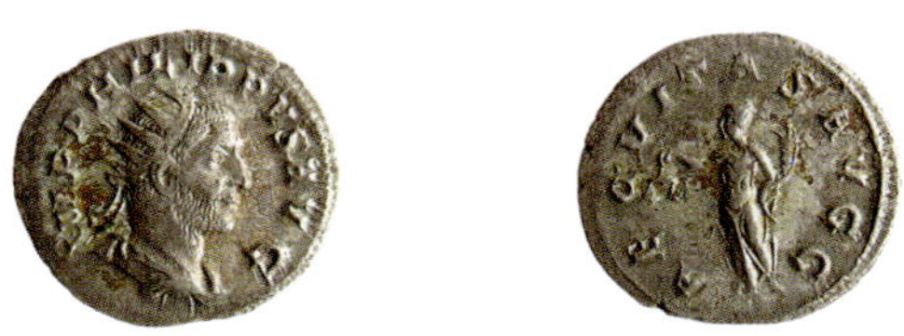

137. AR; 3,21 g.; 21,1 x 22,9 mm.; 6 h.; inv. n. 1472.
(Obv. IMP PHILIPPVS AVG; Rev. AEQVITAS AVGG; — — —//—)

Antoninianus
Obv. IMP PHILIPPVS AVG. Radiated bust of emperor in cuirass and paludamentum looking right, seen from rear.
Rev. ANNONA AVGG. Annona standing left, holding corn-ears over prow in right hand and cornucopiae in left hand.
— — —//—
Lit.: RIC 4.3, p. 75, Rome 59

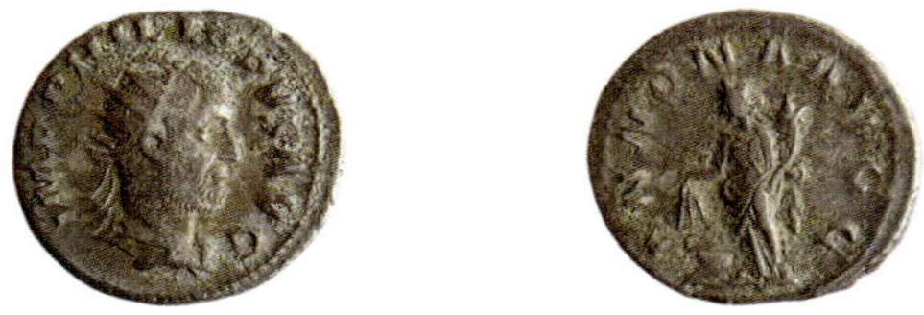

138. AR; 4,79 g.; 20,7 x 22,4 mm.; 6 h.; inv. n. 1473.
(Obv. IMP PHILIPPVS AVG; Rev. ANNONA AVGG; — — —//—)

248 A.D.

Antoninianus
Obv. IMP PHILIPPVS AVG. Radiated bust of emperor in cuirass and paludamentum looking right, seen from rear.
Rev. SAECVLVM NOVVM. Roma seated facing in hexastyle temple.
— — —//—
Lit.: RIC 4.3, p. 71, Rome 25b

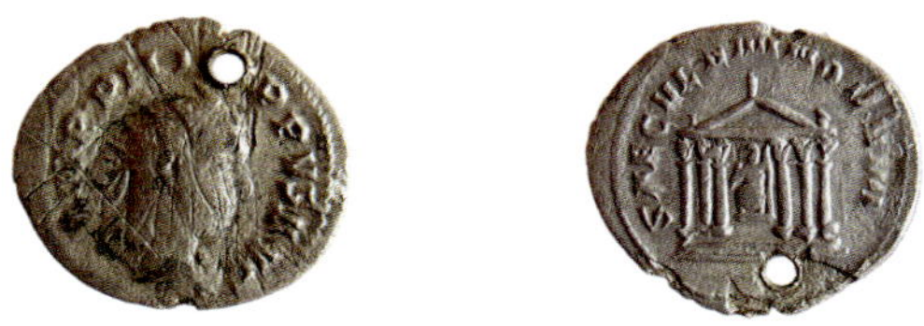

139. AR; 3,49 g.; 21,3 x 23,4 mm.; 6 h.; inv. n. 24.26.
(Obv. IMP PHI[LI]PPVS AVG; Rev. SAECVLVM NOVVM; — — —//—)

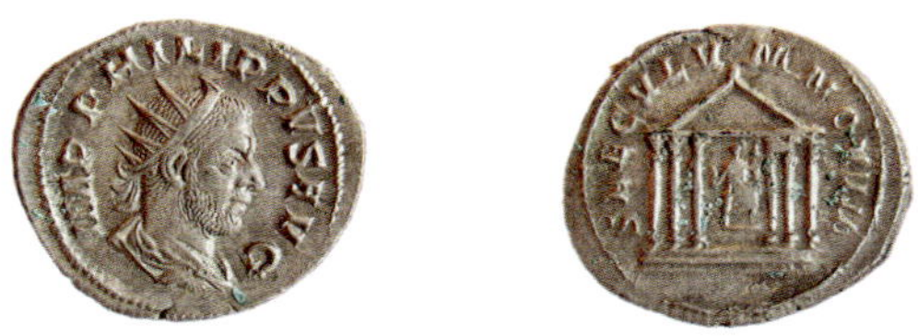

140. AR; 4,5 g.; 21,2 x 24,0 mm.; 6 h.; inv. n. 917.
(Obv. IMP PHILIPPVS AVG; Rev. SAECVLV-M NOVVM; — — —//—)

Sestertius
Obv. IMP M IVL PHILIPPVS AVG. Laureated bust of emperor in cuirass and paludamentum looking right, seen from rear.
Rev. SAECVLV-M NOVVM. Roma seated facing in octastyle temple.
— — —//SC
Lit.: RIC 4.3, p. 89, Rome 164

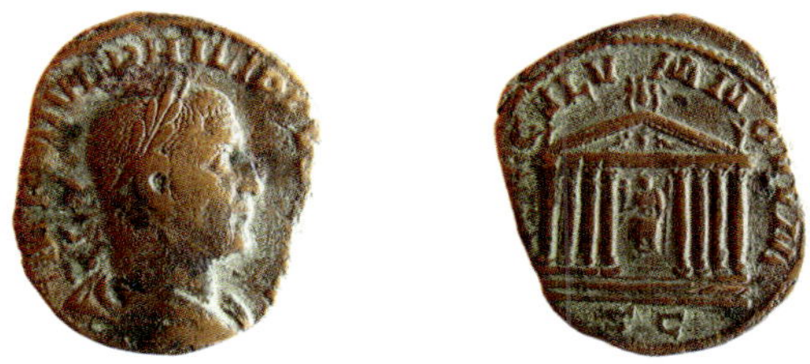

141. AE; 16,8 g.; 28,9 x 24,6 mm.; 12 h.; inv. n. 1474.
(Obv. IMP M IVL PHILIPPVS [AVG]; Rev. [SAE]CVLV-M NOVVM; — — —//SC)

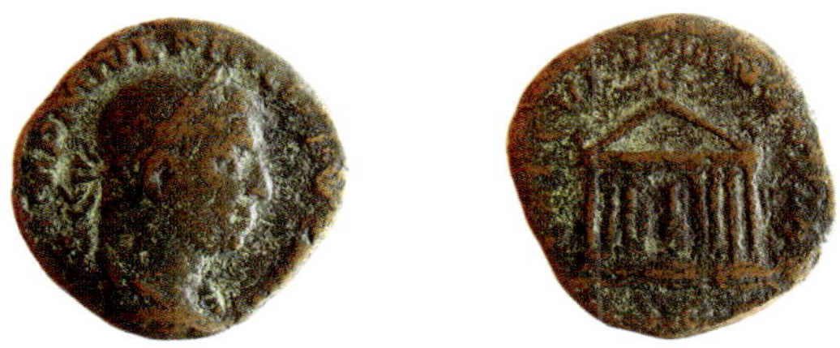

142. AE; 16,78 g.; 27,4 x 27,4 mm.; 12 h.; inv. n. 1475.
(Obv. IMP M IVL PHILIPPVS [AVG]; Rev. [S]AECVLVM NOVVM; — — —//SC)

Sestertius
Obv. IMP M IVL PHILIPPVS AVG. Laureated bust of emperor in cuirass and paludamentum looking right, seen from rear.
Rev. MILIARIVM SAECVLVM. Low column inscribed COS/III.
S — C//—
Lit.: RIC 4.3, p. 88, Rome 157a

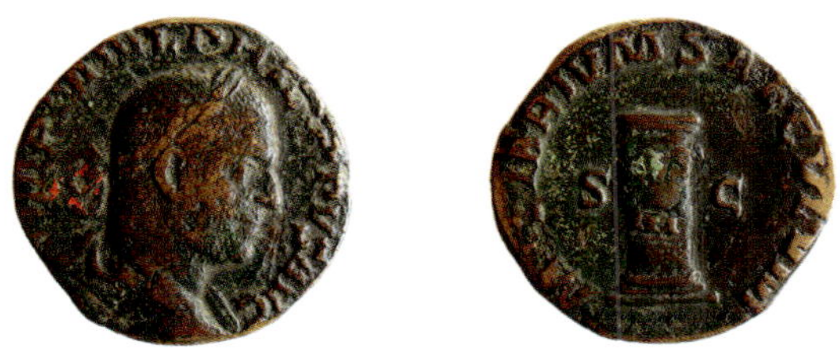

143. AE; 17,22 g.; 27,8 x 28,1 mm.; 1 h.; inv. n. 1476.
(Obv. IMP M IVL PHILIPPVS AVG; Rev. MILIARIVM SAECVLVM; COS/III; S — C//—)

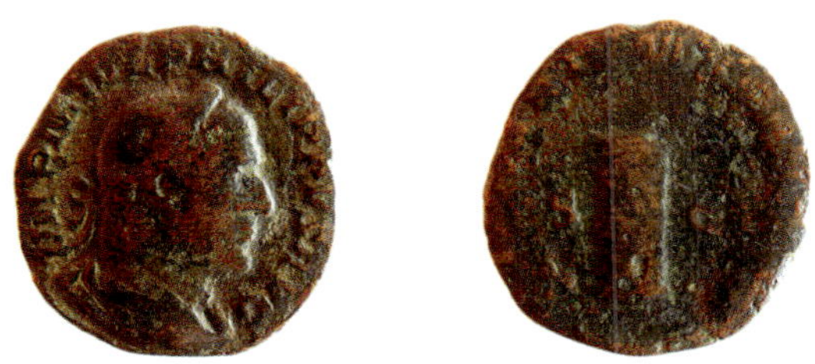

144. AE; 19,78 g.; 28,3 x 27,0 mm.; 12 h.; inv. n. 1477.
(Obv. IMP M IVL PHILIPPVS AVG; Rev. [MILI]ARIVM [SAECVLVM]; [COS/III]; S — C//—)

249 A.D.

Sestertius
Obv. IMP M IVL PHILIPPVS AVG. Laureated bust of emperor in cuirass and paludamentum looking right, seen from rear.
Rev. SAECVLARES AVGG. Stag walking right.
— — —//SC
Lit.: RIC 4.3, p. 89, Rome 160a

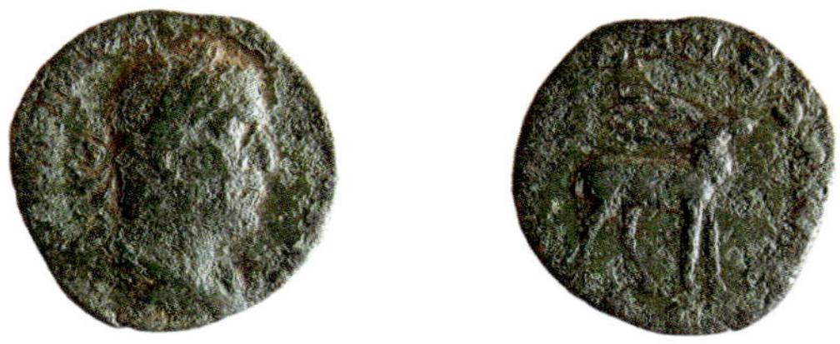

145. AE; 11,12 g.; 25,9 x 26,1 mm.; 1 h.; inv. n. 1478.
(Obv. IMP M [IVL PHILIPPVS AVG]; Rev. [SAECV]LARES [AVGG]; — — —//[S]C)

PHILIPPUS II.
SON OF PHILLIPUS ARABS
(CAESAR 244 – 247 A.D., AUGUSTUS 247 – 249 A.D.)

AS CAESAR

Roma

244 A.D.

Sestertius
Obv. M IVL PHILIPPVS CAES. Bust of emperor in paludamentum looking right, seen from rear.
Rev. PRINCIPI IVVENT. Emperor standing left, holding transverse spear in right hand and globe in left hand.
S — C//—
Lit.: RIC 4.3, p. 101, Rome 255a

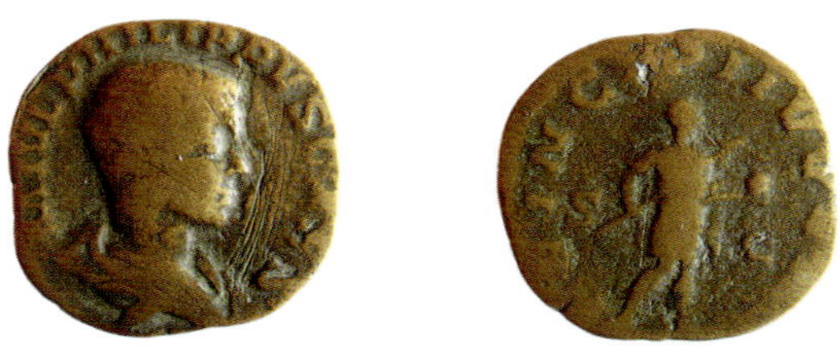

146. AE; 16,85 g.; 26,1 x 27,1 mm.; 1 h.; inv. n. 1479.
(Obv. M IVL PHILIPPVS CAES; Rev. PRINCIPI IVVE[NT]; S — C//—)

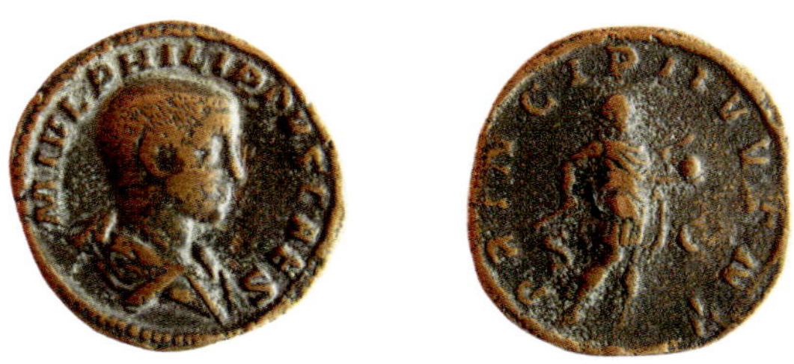

147. AE; 18,12 g.; 30,7 x 30.6 mm.; 1 h.; inv. n. 1480.
(Obv. M IVL PHILIPPVS CAES; Rev. PRINCIPI IVVENT; S — C//—)

Antoninianus
Obv. M IVL PHILIPPVS CAES. Radiated bust of emperor in cuirass and paludamentum looking right, seen from rear.
Rev. PIETAS AVGVSTOR. Sacrificial implements, variously arranged.
— — —//—
Lit.: RIC 4.3, p. 95, Rome 215

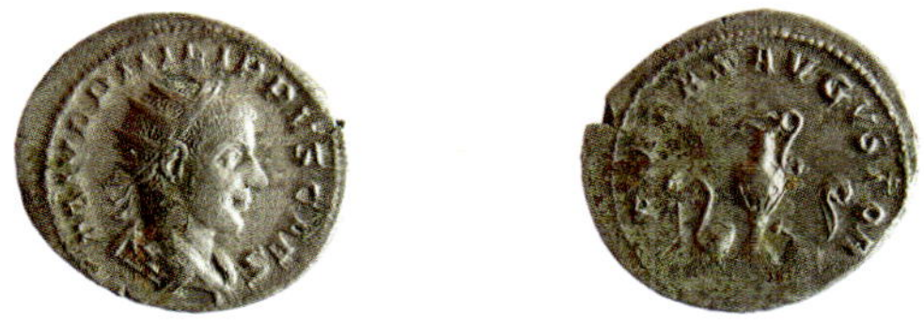

148. AR; 4,62 g.; 21,6 x 23,7 mm.; 1 h.; inv. n. 1481.
(Obv. M IVL PHILIPPVS CAES; Rev. PIETAS AVGVSTOR; — — —//—)

246 A.D.

Antoninianus
Obv. M IVL PHILIPPVS CAES. Radiated bust of emperor in cuirass and paludamentum looking right, seen from rear.
Rev. IOVI CONSERVAT. Jupiter standing front, head turned left, holding thunderbolt in right hand and vertical sceptre in left hand.
— — —//—
Lit.: RIC 4.3, p. 95, Rome 213

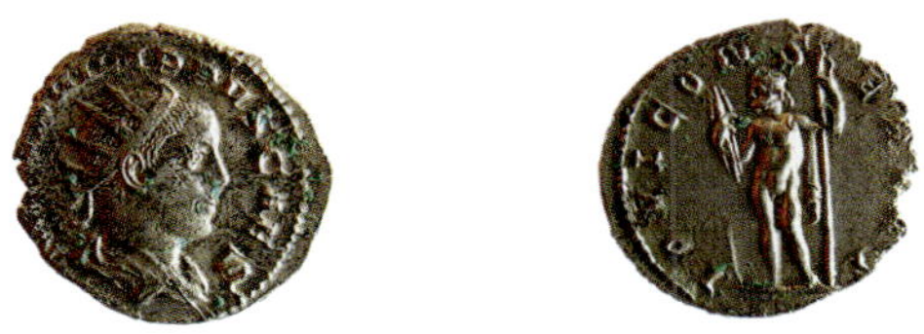

149. AR; 3,85 g.; 21,4 x 21,4 mm.; 12 h.; inv. n. 929.
(Obv. M [IVL] PHILIPPVS CAES; Rev. IOVI CO-N-S-ER[VA]T; — — —//—)

AS AUGUSTUS

Roma

247 A.D.

Antoninianus
Obv. IMP PHILIPPVS AVG. Radiated bust of emperor in cuirass and paludamentum looking right, seen from rear.
Rev. PAX AETERNA. Pax standing left, holding branch in right hand and transverse sceptre in left hand.
— — —//—
Lit.: RIC 4.3, p. 97, Rome 231c

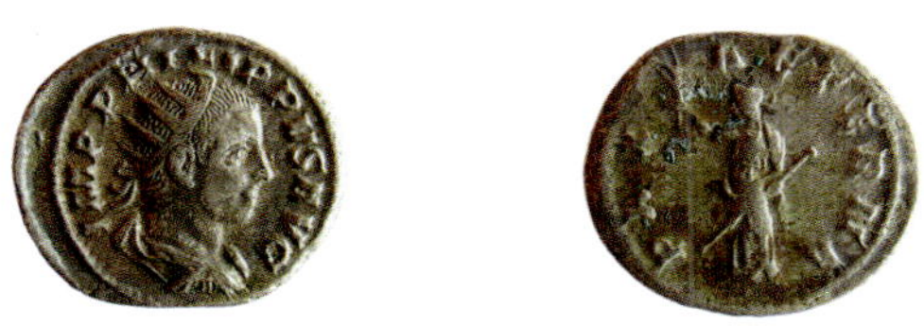

150. AR; 4,28 g.; 20,3 x 23,3 mm.; 6 h.; inv. n. 1482.
(Obv. IMP PHILIPPVS AVG; Rev. PAX – AETERNA; — — —//—)

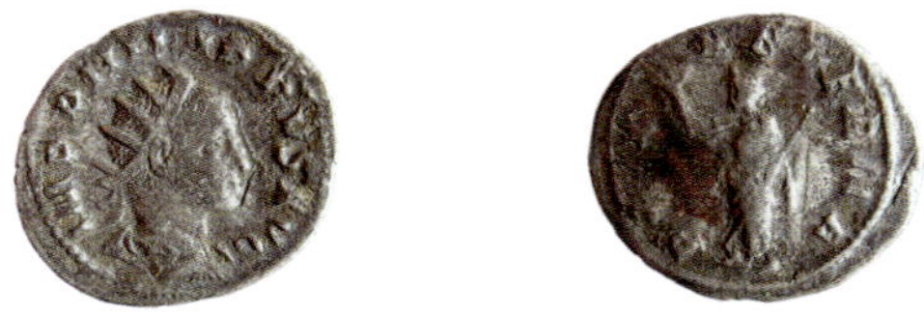

151. AR; 3,19 g.; 20,5 x 21,9 mm.; 7 h.; inv. n. 1483.
(Obv. IMP PHILIPPVS AVG; Rev. PAX – AETERNA; — — —//—)

248 A.D.

Antoninianus

Obv. IMP PHILIPPVS AVG. Radiated bust of emperor in cuirass and paludamentum looking right, seen from rear.

Rev. LIBERALITAS AVGG III. Two emperors seated on curule chairs left, first of them holding vertical sceptre.

— — —//—

Lit.: RIC 4.3, p. 97, Rome 230

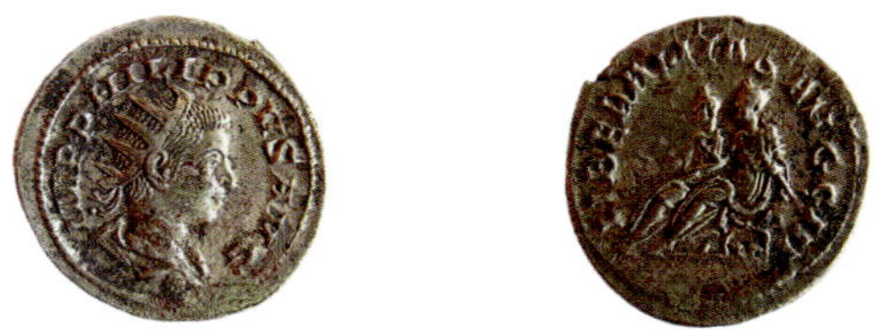

152. AR; 4,32 g.; 23,1 x 23,2 mm.; 6 h.; inv. n. 1484.
(Obv. IMP PHILIPPVS AVG; Rev. LIBERALITAS AVGG III; — — —//—)

249 A.D.

Antoninianus

Obv. IMP PHILIPPVS AVG. Radiated bust of emperor in cuirass and paludamentum looking right, seen from rear.

Rev. SAECVLARES AVGG. Goat walking left.

— — —//III

Lit.: RIC 4.3, p. 97, Rome 224

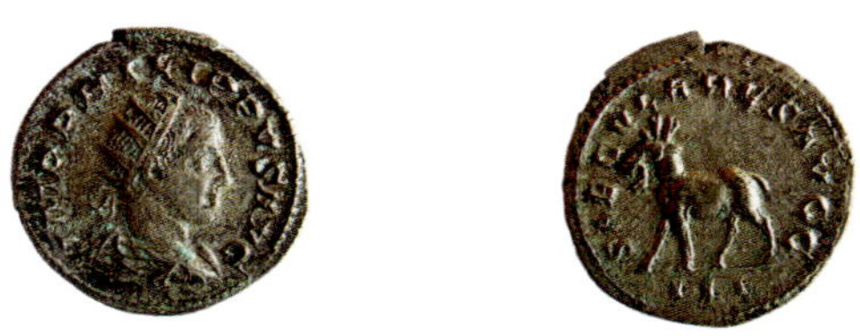

153. AR; 3,66 g.; 22,4 x 22,1 mm.; 1 h.; inv. n. 866.
(Obv. IMP PHILIPPVS AVG; Rev. SAECVLARES AVGG; — — —//III)

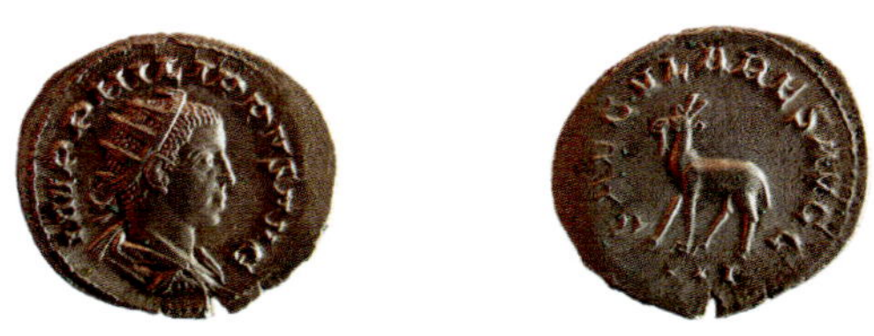

154. AR; 4,23 g.; 21,9 x 24,1 mm.; 1 h.; inv. n. 928.
(Obv. IMP PHILIPPVS AVG; Rev. SAECVLARES AVGG; — — —//III)

Antiochia

247 – 249 A.D.

Antoninianus
Obv. IMP M IVL PHILIPPVS AVG. Radiated bust of emperor in cuirass and paludamentum looking right, seen from rear.
Rev. FIDES EXERCITVS. Four standards, the second one from right side with eagle on top.
— — —//—
Lit.: RIC 4.3, p. 99, Antioch 248

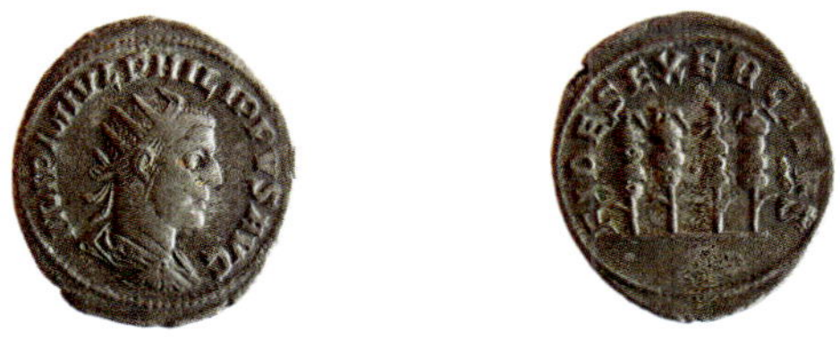

155. AR; 4,01 g.; 23,7 x 20,8 mm.; 6 h.; inv. n. 1485.
(Obv. IMP M IVL PHILIPPVS AVG; Rev. FIDES EXERCITVS; — — —//—)

OTACILIA SEVERA WIFE OF PHILIPPUS ARABS (AUGUSTA 244 – 249 A.D.)

Roma

244 A.D.

Antoninianus
Obv. MARCIA OTACIL SEVERA AVG. Diademed and draped bust of empress on crescent looking right.
Rev. PVDICITIA AVG. Veiled Pudicitia seated left, with right hand drawing veil and holding transverse sceptre in left hand.
— — —//—
Lit.: RIC 4.3, p. 83, Rome 123c

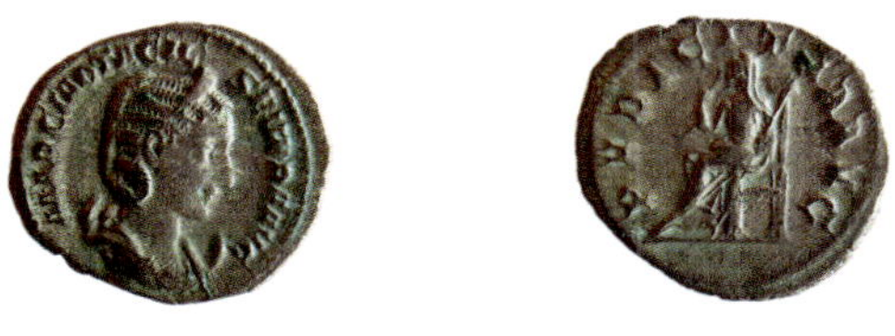

156. AR; 4,08 g.; 20,3 x 22,4 mm.; 6 h.; inv. n. 1486.
(Obv. MARCIA OTACIL – SEVERA AVG; Rev. PVDICI-TIA AVG; — — —//—)

Sestertius
Obv. MARCIA OTACIL SEVERA AVG. Diademed and draped bust of empress looking right.
Rev. PVDICITIA AVG. Veiled Pudicitia seated left, with right hand drawing veil and holding transverse sceptre in left hand.
— — —//SC
Lit.: RIC 4.3, p. 94, Rome 209a

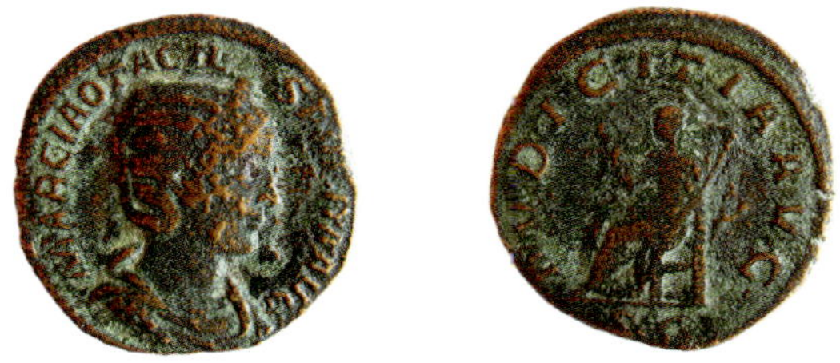

157. AE; 18,67 g.; 29,0 x 28,6 mm.; 12 h.; inv. n. 1487.
(Obv. MARCIA OTACIL – SEVERA AVG; Rev. PVDICITIA AVG; — — —//SC)

246 A.D.

Antoninianus
Obv. M OTACIL SEVERA AVG. Diademed and draped bust of empress on crescent looking right.
Rev. CONCORDIA AVGG. Concordia seated left, holding patera in right hand and double cornucopiae in left hand.
— — —//—
Lit.: RIC 4.3, p. 83, Rome 125c

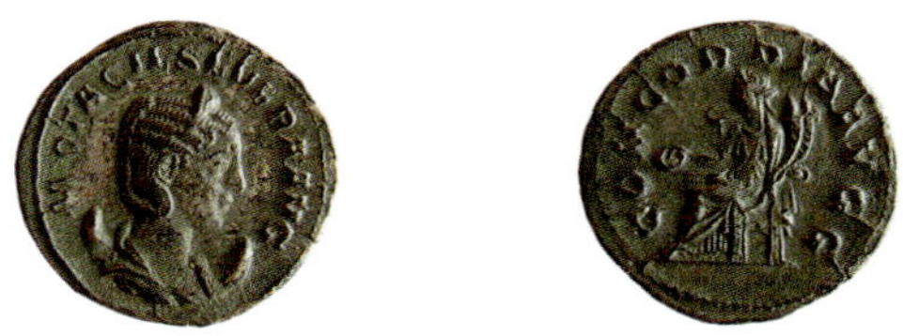

158. AR; 4,4 g.; 22,1 x 22,5 mm.; 6 h.; inv. n. 1488.
(Obv. M OTACIL SEVERA AVG; Rev. CONCOR-DIA AVGG; — — —//—)

Antoninianus
Obv. M OTACIL SEVERA AVG. Diademed and draped bust of empress on crescent looking right.
Rev. CONCORDIA AVGG. Concordia seated left, holding patera over altar in right hand and single cornucopiae in left hand.
— — —//—
Lit.: RIC 4.3, p. 83, Rome 126

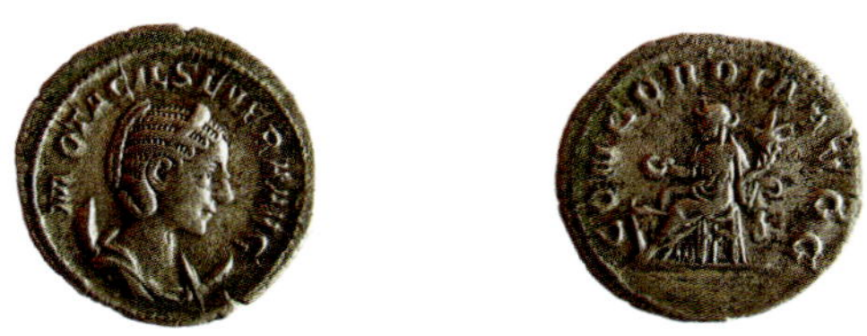

159. AR; 4,78 g.; 22,9 x 22,7 mm.; 5 h.; inv. n. 1489.
(Obv. M OTACIL SEVERA AVG; Rev. CONCORDIA AVGG; — — —//—)

Antoninianus
Obv. M OTACIL SEVERA AVG. Diademed and draped bust of empress on crescent looking right.
Rev. IVNO CONSERVAT. Juno standing left, holding patera in right hand and long vertical sceptre in left hand.
— — —//—
Lit.: RIC 4.3, p. 83, Rome 127

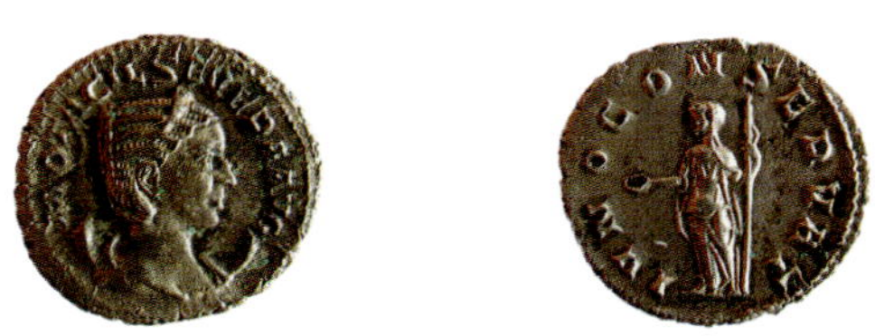

160. AR; 4,16 g.; 21,5 x 22,8 mm.; 7 h.; inv. n. 1490.
(Obv. M OTACIL SEVERA AVG; Rev. IVNO CONSERVAT; — — —//—)

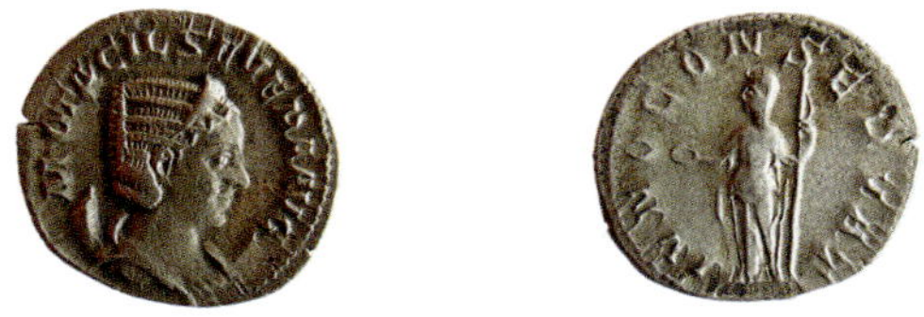

161. AR; 3,71 g.; 21,2 x 23,0 mm.; 12 h.; inv. n. 24.27.
(Obv. M OTACIL SEVERA AVG; Rev. IVNO CONS-ERVAT; — — —//—)

247 A.D.

Sestertius
Obv. OTACIL SEVERA AVG. Diademed and draped bust of empress looking right.
Rev. CONCORDIA AVGG. Concordia seated left, holding patera in right hand and double cornucopiae in left hand.
— — —//SC
Lit.: RIC 4.3, p. 94, Rome 203e

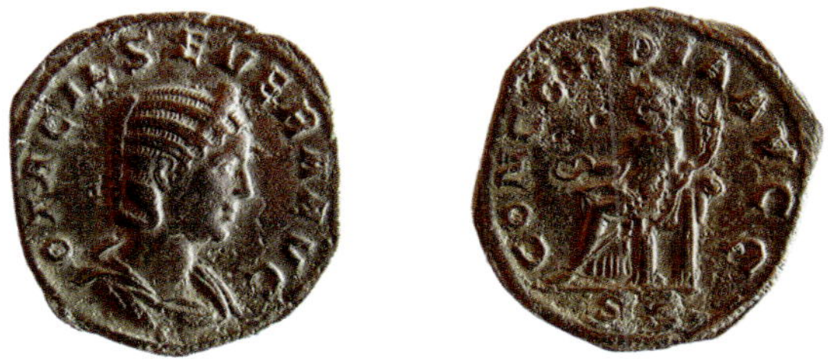

162. AE; 19,65 g.; 29,9 x 28,7 mm.; 12 h.; inv. n. 48.
(Obv. OTACIL SEVERA AVG; Rev. CONCORDIA AVGG; — — —//SC)

248 A.D.

Antoninianus
Obv. OTACIL SEVERA AVG. Diademed and draped bust of empress on crescent looking right.
Rev. PIETAS AVGVSTAE. Pietas standing left, with right hand raised and holding box in left hand.
— — —//—
Lit.: RIC 4.3, p. 84, Rome 130

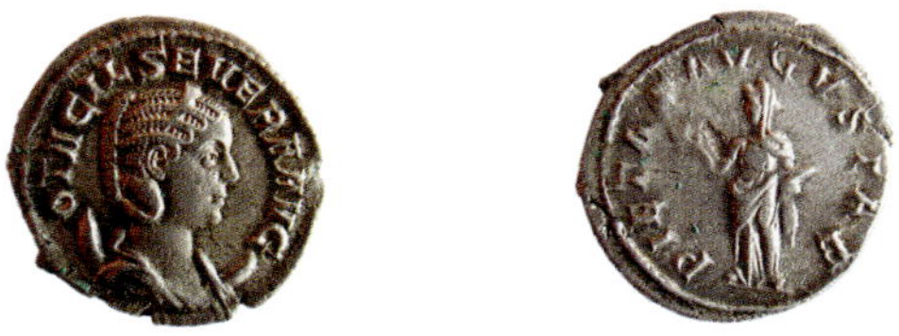

163. AR; 4,11 g.; 21,8 x 21,7 mm.; 6 h.; inv. n. 911.
(Obv. OTACIL SEVERA AVG; Rev. PIETAS AVGVSTAE; — — —//—)

Sestertius
Obv. MARCIA OTACIL SEVERA AVG. Diademed and draped bust of empress looking right.
Rev. PIETAS AVGVSTAE. Pietas standing left, with right hand raised and holding box in left hand.
S — C//—
Lit.: RIC 4.3, p. 94, Rome 208a

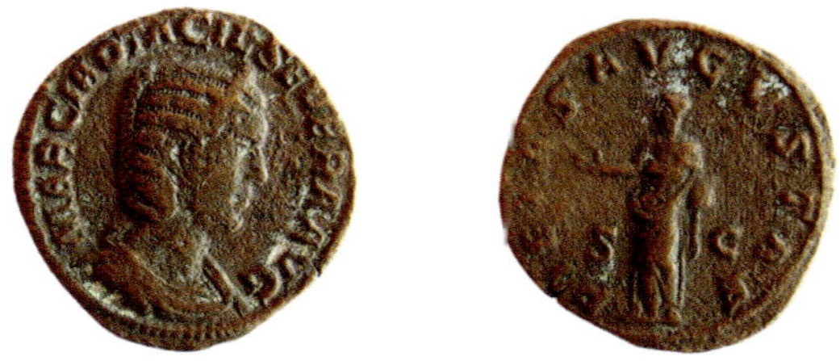

164. AE; 19,21 g.; 29,4 x 28,9 mm.; 1 h.; inv. n. 1491.
(Obv. MARCIA OTACIL SEVERA AVG; Rev. PIETAS AVGVSTAE; S — C//—)

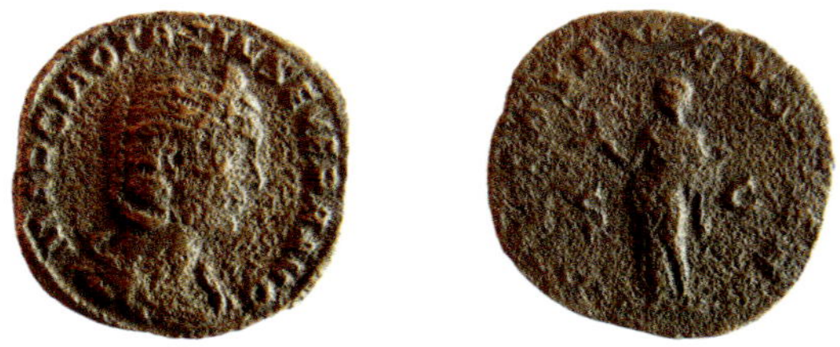

165. AE; 22,37 g.; 27,3 x 28,1 mm.; 12 h.; inv. n. 1492.
(Obv. MARCIA OTACIL SEVERA AVG; Rev. PIETAS AVGVSTAE; S — C//—)

Antoninianus
Obv. OTACIL SEVERA AVG. Diademed and draped bust of empress on crescent looking right.
Rev. PIETAS AVGG. Pietas standing left, with right hand sacrificing over altar to left and holding box in left hand.
Δ — —//—
Lit.: RIC 4.3, p. 82, Rome 115

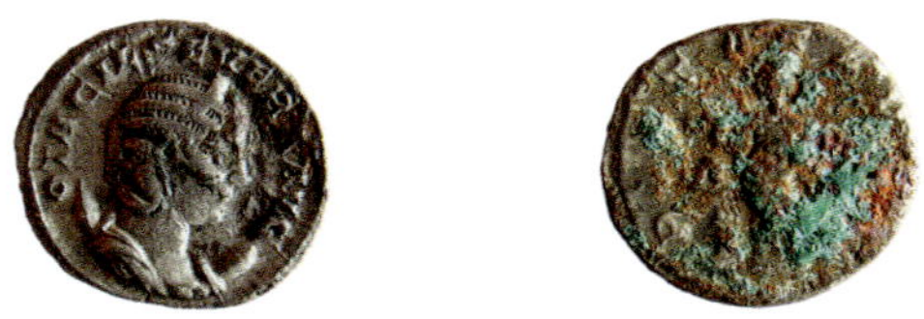

166. AR; 3,78 g.; 20,0 x 21,6 mm.; 6 h.; inv. n. 1493.
(Obv. OTACIL SEVERA AVG; Rev. PIETAS AV[GG]; Δ — —//—)

TRAIANUS DECIUS
(249 – 251 A.D.)

Roma

October 249 A.D.

Antoninianus
Obv. IMP C M Q TRAIANVS DECIVS AVG. Radiated bust of emperor in cuirass looking right, seen from rear.
Rev. ADVENTVS AVG. Emperor riding on horse left, raising right hand, holding transverse sceptre in left hand.
— — —//—
Lit.: RIC 4.3, p. 121, Rome 11b

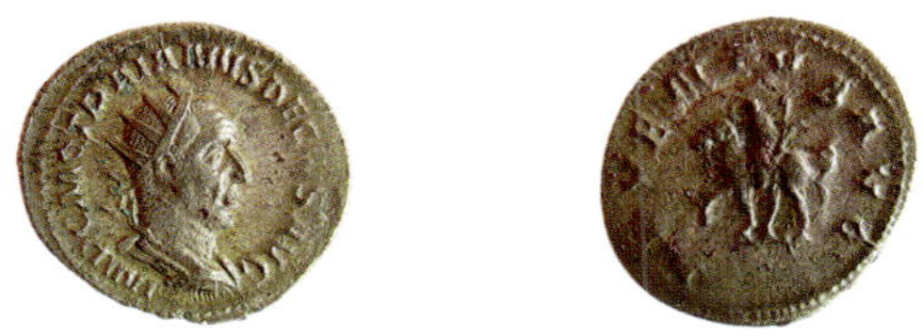

167. AR; 3,23 g.; 21,8 x 23,5 mm.; 1 h.; inv. n. 903.
(Obv. IMP C M Q TRAIANVS DECIVS AVG; Rev. ADVENTVS AVG; — — —//—)

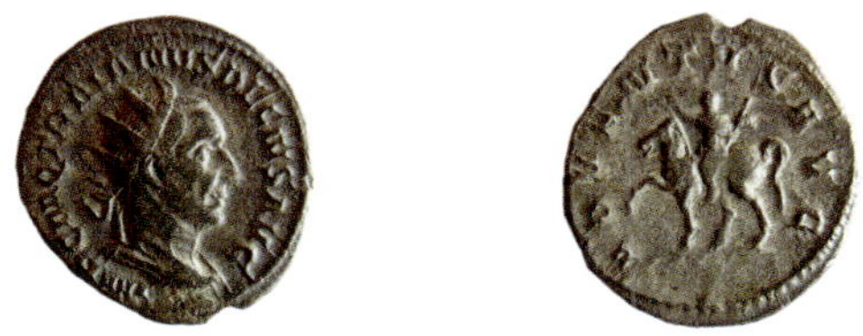

168. AR; 4,19 g.; 23,0 x 21,4 mm.; 6 h.; inv. n. 1494.
(Obv. IMP C M Q TRAIANVS DECIVS AVG; Rev. ADVENTVS AVG; — — —//—)

Antoninianus
Obv. IMP C M Q TRAIANVS DECIVS AVG. Radiated bust of emperor in cuirass looking right, seen from rear.
Rev. DACIA. Dacia standing left, holding long verical staff, surmounted by ass's head, in right hand.
— — —//—
Lit.: RIC 4.3, p. 121, Rome 12b

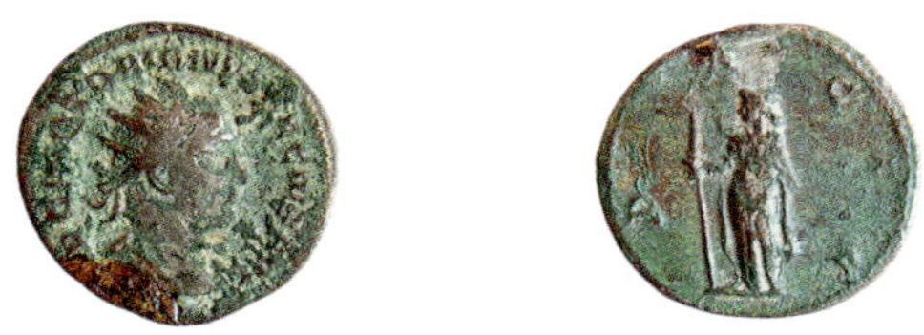

169. AR; 3,84 g.; 21,2 x 21,7 mm.; 5 h.; inv. n. 1495.
(Obv. [IM]P C M Q TRAIANVS DECIVS AV[G]; Rev. D-A-CIA; — — —//—)

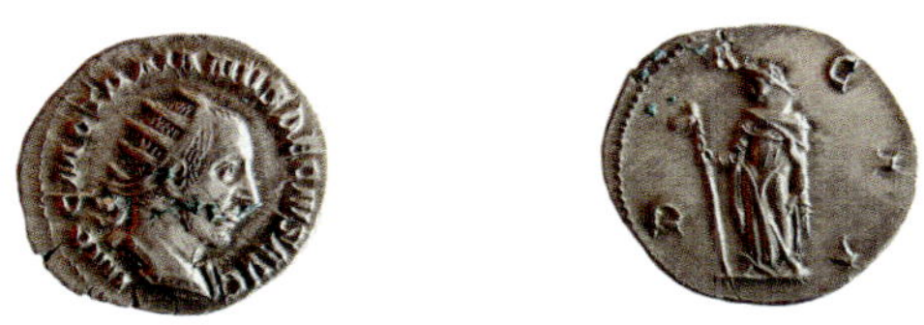

170. AR; 3,48 g.; 19,8 x 21,2 mm.; 6 h.; inv. n. 907.
(Obv. IMP C M Q TRAIANVS DECIVS AVG; Rev. D-A-CIA; — — —//—)

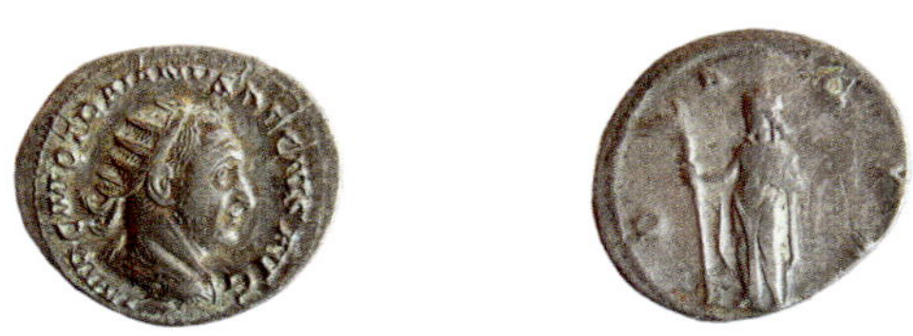

171. AR; 4,06 g.; 20,1 x 22,6 mm.; 7 h.; inv. n. 1496.
(Obv. IMP C M Q TRAIANVS DECIVS AVG; Rev. D-A-CIA; — — —//—)

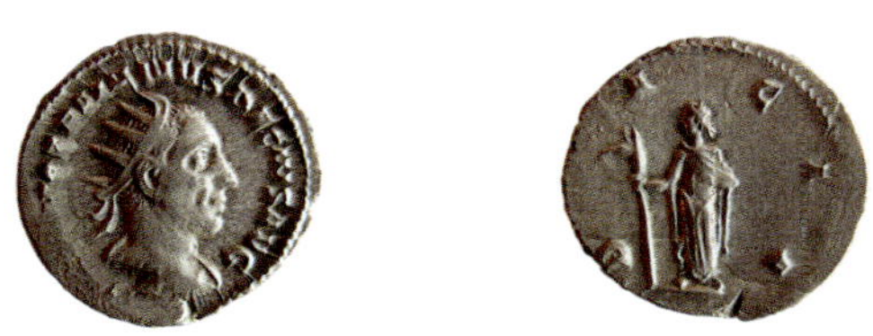

172. AR; 4,33 g.; 22,1 x 22,3 mm.; 12 h.; inv. n. 906.
(Obv. [IMP C M] Q TRAIANVS DECIVS AVG; Rev. D-A-CIA; — — —//—)

Antoninianus
Obv. IMP C M Q TRAIANVS DECIVS AVG. Radiated bust of emperor in cuirass looking right, seen from rear.
Rev. GENIVS EXERC ILLVRICIANI. Genius standing left, holding patera in right hand and cornucopiae in left hand; in ground to right standard.
— — —//—
Lit.: RIC 4.3, p. 122, Rome 16c

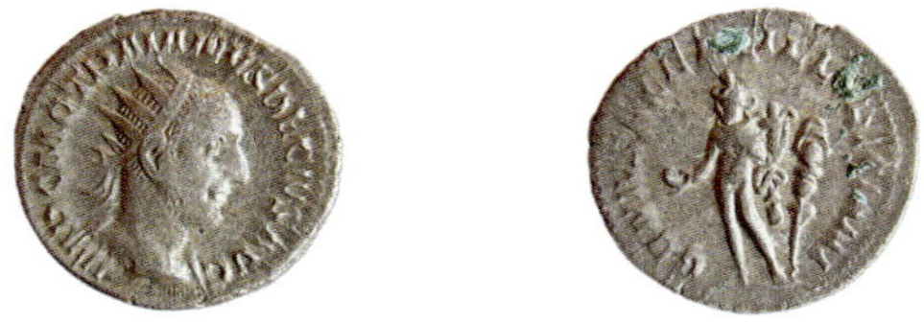

173. AR; 4,9 g.; 21,6 x 22,7 mm.; 12 h.; inv. n. 1497.
(Obv. IMP C M Q TRAIANVS DECIVS AVG; Rev. GENIVS EXERC ILL[V]RICIANI; — — —//—)

Antoninianus
Obv. IMP C M Q TRAIANVS DECIVS AVG. Radiated bust of emperor in cuirass looking right, seen from rear.
Rev. PANNONIAE. Two Pannoniae standing front, their heads turning right and left, away from each other; each holding standard, the one on right raising right hand.
— — —//—
Lit.: RIC 4.3, p. 122, Rome 21b

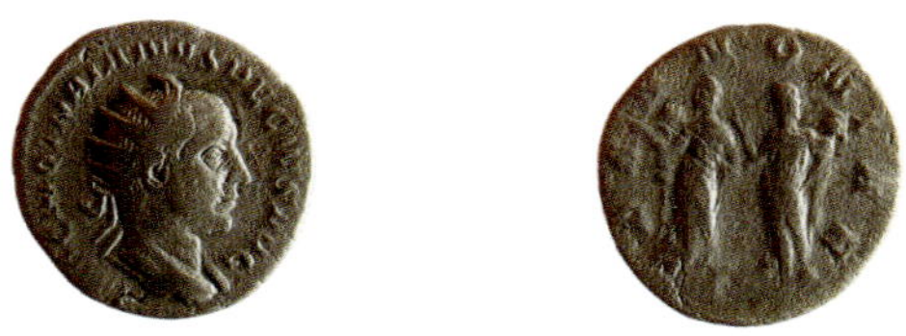

174. AR; 4,34 g.; 21,3 x 20,8 mm.; 12 h.; inv. n. 24.28.
(Obv. [IM]P C M Q TRAIANVS DECIVS AVG; Rev. PA-NNONIAE; — — —//—)

Antoninianus
Obv. IMP C M Q TRAIANVS DECIVS AVG. Radiated bust of emperor in cuirass looking right, seen from rear.
Rev. PANNONIAE. Two Pannoniae standing facing each other, clasping right hands in front of standard in centre.
— — —//—
Lit.: RIC 4.3, p. 123, Rome 26

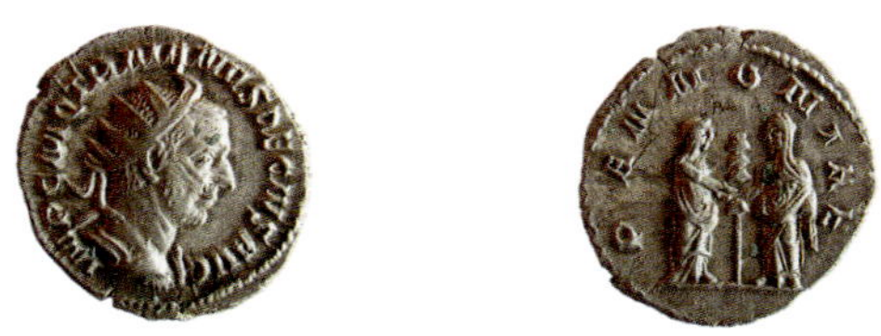

175. AR; 3,81 g.; 21,0 x 21,2 mm.; 7 h.; inv. n. 904.
(Obv. IMP C M Q TRAIANVS DECIVS AVG; Rev. PANNONIAE; — — —//—)

Antoninianus
Obv. IMP C M Q TRAIANVS DECIVS AVG. Radiated bust of emperor in cuirass looking right, seen from rear.
Rev. VICTORIA AVG. Victory walking left, holding wreath in right hand and palm in left hand.
— — —//—
Lit.: RIC 4.3, p. 123, Rome 29c

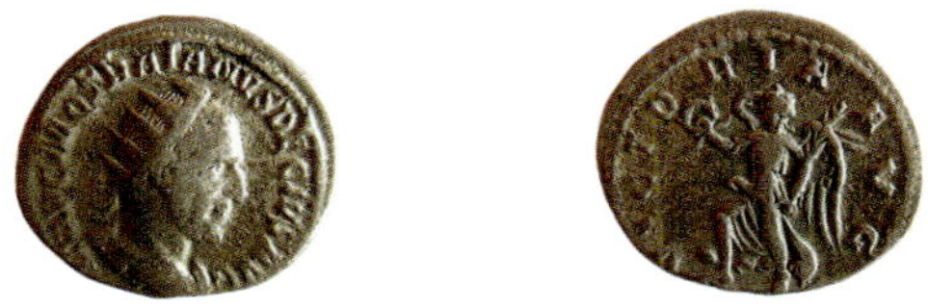

176. AR; 4,17 g.; 20,1 x 22,3 mm.; 12 h.; inv. n. 1498.
(Obv. IMP C M Q TRAIANVS DECIVS AVG; Rev. VICTO-RIA – AVG; — — —//—)

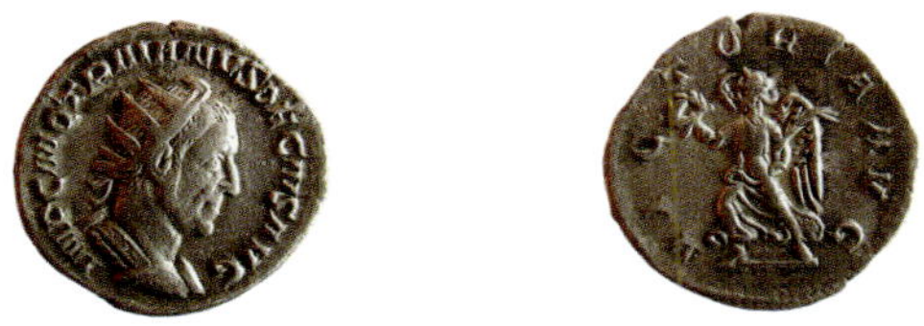

177. AR; 3,92 g.; 21,2 x 21,2 mm.; 12 h.; inv. n. 1499.
(Obv. IMP C M Q TRAIANVS DECIVS AVG; Rev. VIC-TORIA AVG; — — —//—)

Antoninianus
Obv. IMP C M Q TRAIANVS DECIVS AVG. Radiated bust of emperor in cuirass looking right, seen from rear.
Rev. GENIVS EXERCITVS ILLVRICIANI. Genius standing left, holding patera in right hand and cornucopiae in left hand; in ground to right standard.
— — —//—
Lit.: RIC 4.3, p. 122, Rome 18

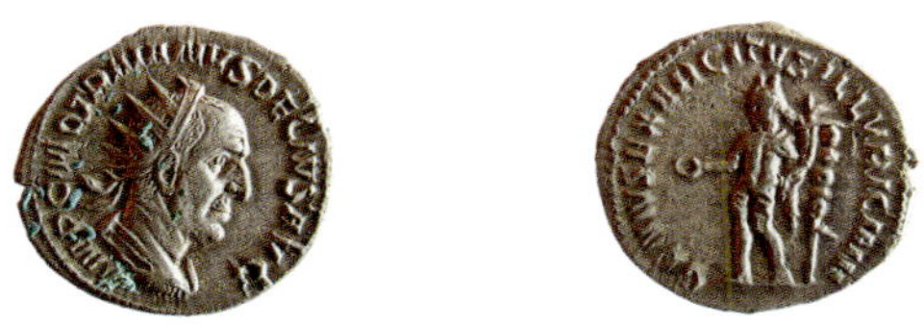

178. AR; 3,28 g.; 20,7 x 21,6 mm.; 1 h.; inv. n. 905.
(Obv. IMP C M Q TRAIANVS DECIVS AVG; Rev. GENIVS EXERCITVS ILLVRICIANI; — — —//—)

HERENNIUS ETRUSCUS SON OF TRAIANUS DECIUS (CAESAR 250 – 251 A.D., AUGUSTUS 251 A.D.)

AS CAESAR

Roma

Spring of 250 A.D.

Antoninianus
Obv. Q HER ETR MES DECIVS NOB C. Radiated bust of emperor in paludamentum looking right, seen from rear.
Rev. PRINCIPI IVVENTVTIS. Emperor standing left, holding buttom in right hand and transverse spear in left hand.
— — —//—
Lit.: RIC 4.3, p. 139, Rome 147c

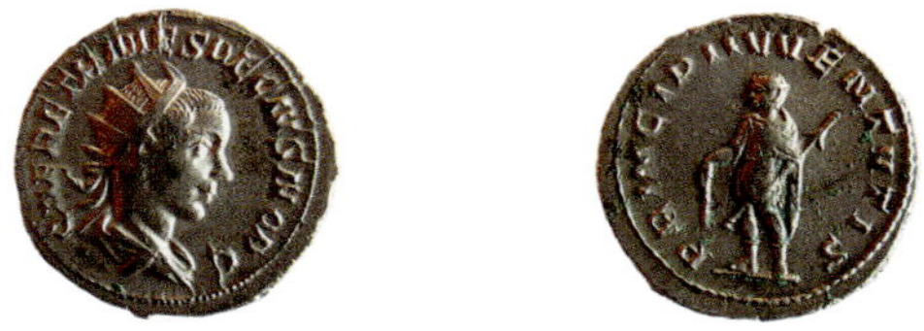

179. AR; 3,76 g.; 21,5 x 22,0 mm.; 12 h.; inv. n. 912.
(Obv. Q HER ETR MES DECIVS NOB C; Rev. PRINCIPI IVVENTVTIS; — — —//—)

Sestertius
Obv. Q HER ETR MES DECIVS NOB C. Bust of emperor in paludamentum looking right, seen from rear.
Rev. PRINCIPI IVVENTVTIS. Emperor standing left, holding baton in right hand and transverse spear in left hand.
S — C//—
Lit.: RIC 4.3, p. 143, Rome 171

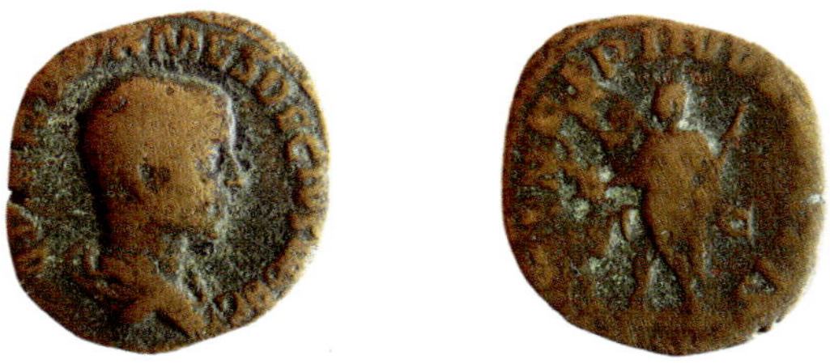

180. AE; 15,78 g.; 28,8 x 26,8 mm.; 12 h.; inv. n. 1500.
(Obv. Q HER [ET]R MES DECIVS NOB C; Rev. [PR]INCIPI IVVE[NTV]TIS; S — C//—)

Antoninianus
Obv. Q HER ETR MES DECIVS NOB C. Radiated bust of emperor in paludamentum looking right, seen from rear.
Rev. PIETAS AVGVSTORVM. Sacrificial implements, variously arranged.
— — —//—
Lit.: RIC 4.3, p. 139, Rome 143

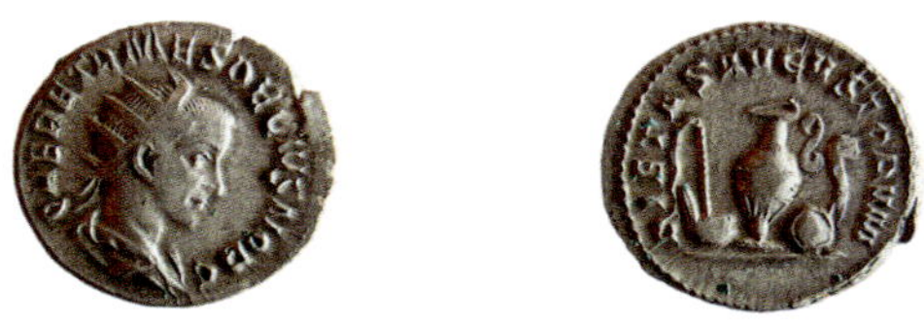

181. AR; 4,21 g.; 20,4 x 21,6 mm.; 6 h.; inv. n. 913.
(Obv. Q HER ETR MES DECIVS NOB C; Rev. PIETAS AVGVSTORVM; — — —//—)

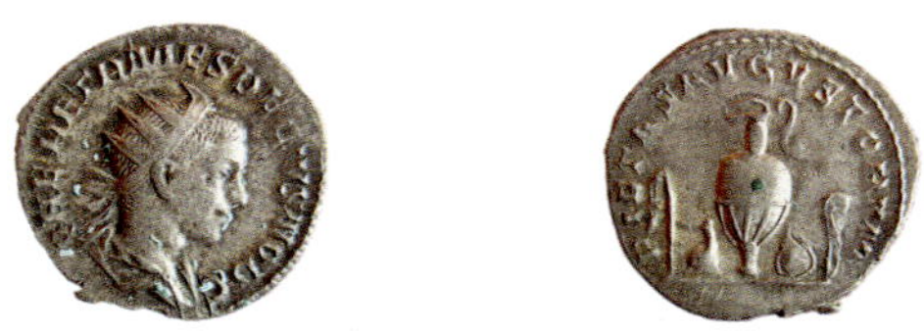

182. AR; 3,71 g.; 20,1 x 21,2 mm.; 12 h.; inv. n. 1501.
(Obv. Q HER ETR MES DECIVS NOB C; Rev. PIETAS AVGVSTORVM; — — —//—)

250 A.D.

Antoninianus[14]
Obv. Q HER ETR MES DECIVS NOB C. Radiated bust of emperor in paludamentum looking right, seen from rear.
Rev. PIETAS AVGG. Mercury standing left, holding purse in right hand and caduceus in left hand.
— — —//—
Lit.: RIC 4.3, p. 138, Rome 142b

[14] Overstrike of a denar of the Emperor Alexander Severus from 226–228 A.D. – for more details see Lužický 2008.

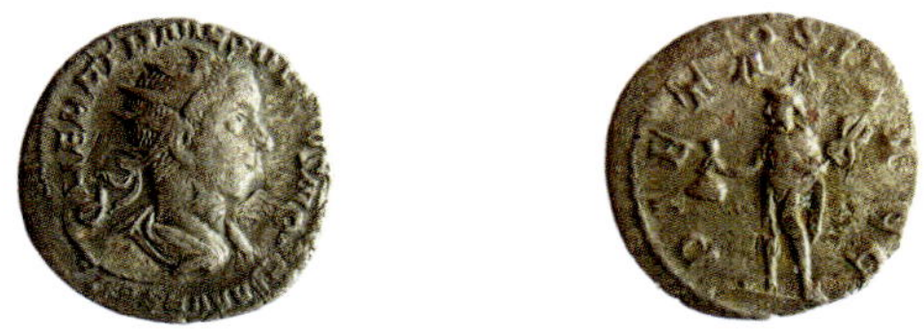

183. AR; 2,85 g.; 21,4 x 21,0 mm.; 6 h.; inv. n. 1502.
(Obv. Q HER ETR MES DE[C]IVS NO[B C]; Rev. PIETA[-S] AVGG; — — —//—)

Antoninianus
Obv. Q HER ETR MES DECIVS NOB C. Radiated bust of emperor in paludamentum looking right, seen from rear.
Rev. SPES PVBLICA. Spes walking left, holding flower in right hand and raising skirt with left hand.
— — —//—
Lit.: RIC 4.3, p. 139, Rome 149

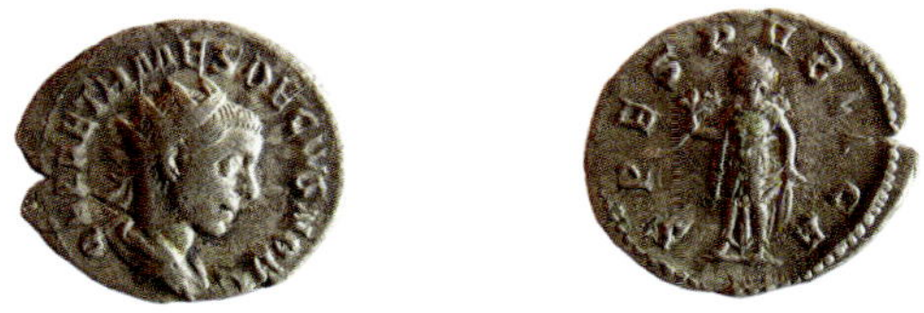

184. AR; 4,01 g.; 20,2 x 23,2 mm.; 1 h.; inv. n. 1503.
(Obv. Q HER ETR MES DECIVS NOB C; Rev. SPES P-VBLICA; — — —//—)

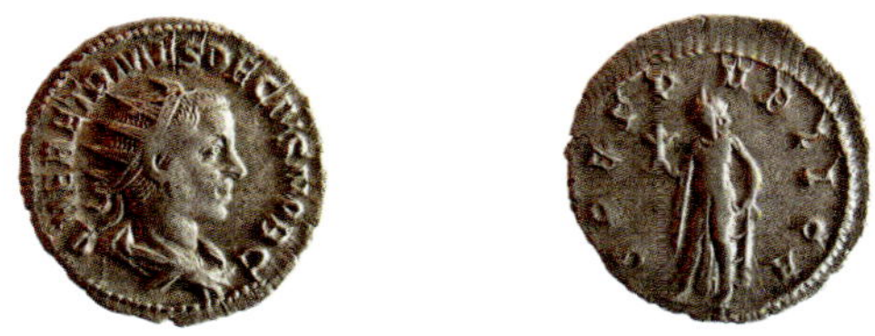

185. AR; 3,41 g.; 22,9 x 22,1 mm.; 1 h.; inv. n. 1504.
(Obv. Q HER ETR MES DECIVS NOB C; Rev. SPES P-VBLICA; — — —//—)

HOSTILIANUS SON OF TRAIANUS DECIUS (CAESAR 250 – 251 A.D., AUGUSTUS 251 A.D.)

AS CAESAR

Roma

250 A.D.

Antoninianus
Obv. C VALENS HOSTIL MES QVINTVS N C. Radiated bust of emperor in paludamentum looking right, seen from rear.
Rev. MARTI PROPVGNATORI. Mars walking right, holding transverse spear in right hand and shield in left hand.
— — —//—
Lit.: RIC 4.3, p. 144, Rome 177b

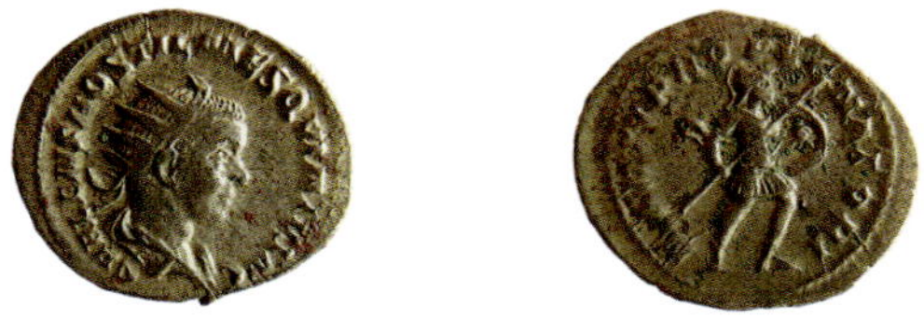

186. AR; 3,53 g.; 20,9 x 23,8 mm.; 5 h.; inv. n. 1505.
(Obv. C VALENS HOSTIL MES QVINTVS N C; Rev. MARTI PROPVG-NATORI; — — —//—)

HERENNIA ETRUSCILLA WIFE OF TRAIANUS DECIUS (AUGUSTA 249 – 251 A.D.)

Roma

250 A.D.

Antoninianus
Obv. HER ETRVSCILLA AVG. Diademed and draped bust of empress on crescent looking right.
Rev. PVDICITIA AVG. Veiled Pudicitia seated left, with right hand drawing veil and holding transverse sceptre in left hand.
— — —//—
Lit.: RIC 4.3, p. 127, Rome 59b

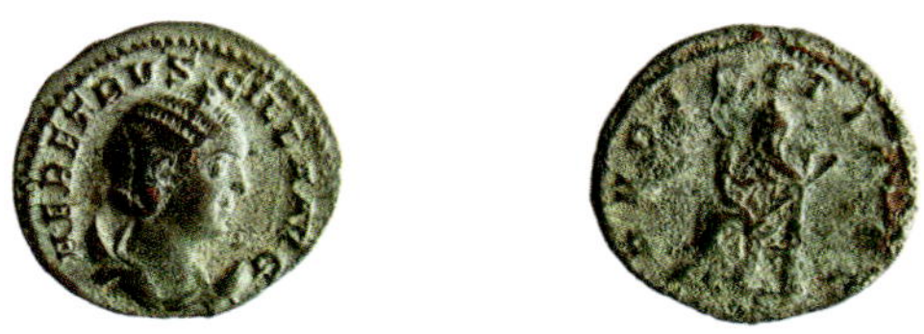

187. AR; 3,89 g.; 20,5 x 21,7 mm.; 1 h.; inv. n. 1506.
(Obv. HER ETRVS-CILLA AVG; Rev. PVDICITI[A AVG]; — — —//—)

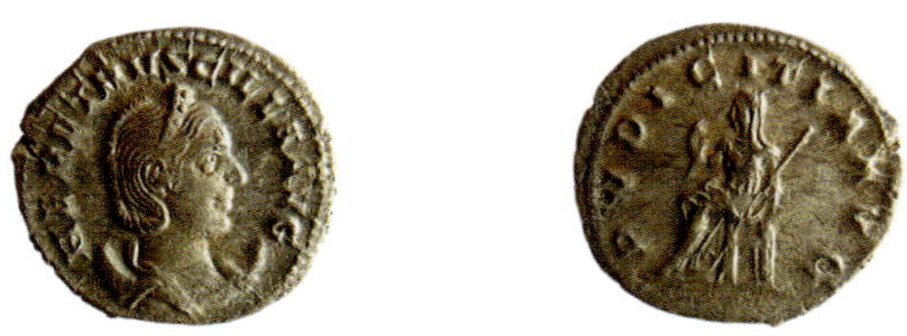

188. AR; 3,53 g.; 21,2 x 22,6 mm.; 12 h.; inv. n. 1507.
(Obv. HER ETRVSCILLA AVG; Rev. PVDICITIA AVG; — — —//—)

Sestertius
Obv. HERENNIA ETRVSCILLA AVG. Diademed and draped bust of empress looking right.
Rev. PVDICITIA AVG. Veiled Pudicitia seated left, with right hand drawing veil and holding transverse sceptre in left hand.
— — —//SC
Lit.: RIC 4.3, p. 137, Rome 136b

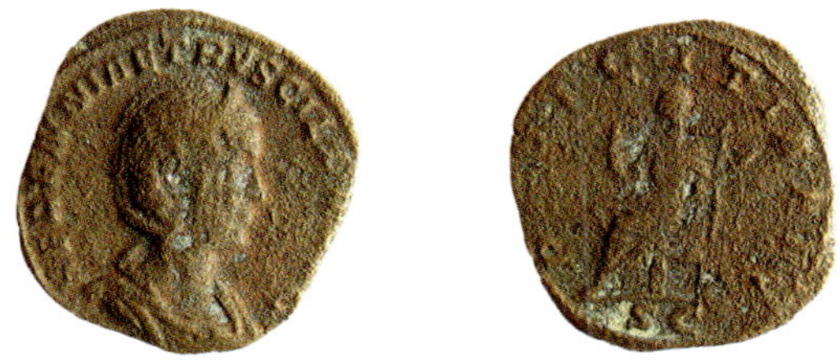

189. AE; 16,94 g.; 29,0 x 27,7 mm.; 12 h.; inv. n. 1508.
(Obv. HERENNIA ETRVSCILLA [AVG]; Rev. PVDICITIA AVG; — — —//SC)

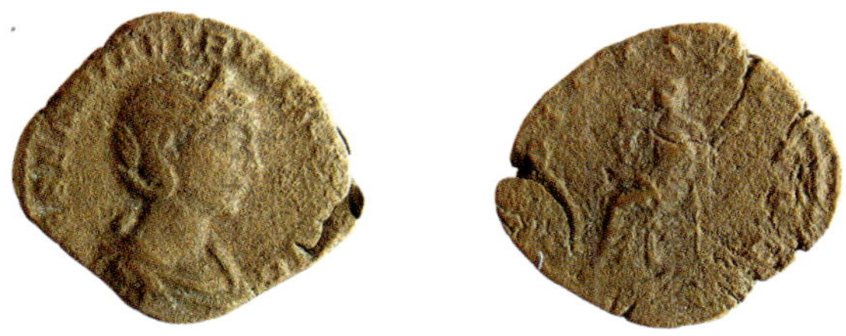

190. AE; 15,94 g.; 26,7 x 30,8 mm.; 12 h.; inv. n. 1509.
(Obv. [H]ERENNIA ETRVSC[ILLA AV]G; Rev. [PV]DICIT[IA] AVG; — — —//SC)

Antoninianus
Obv. HER ETRVSCILLA AVG. Diademed and draped bust of empress on crescent looking right.
Rev. PVDICITIA AVG. Veiled Pudicitia, standing left with right hand drawing veil and holding transverse sceptre in left hand.
— — —//—
Lit.: RIC 4.3, p. 127, Rome 58b

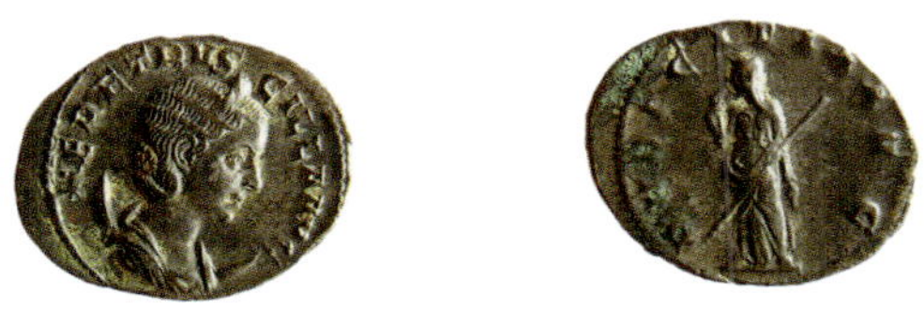

191. AR; 4,11 g.; 19,4 x 22,5 mm.; 6 h.; inv. n. 916.
(Obv. HER ETRVS-CILLA AVG; Rev. PVDICITIA AVG; — — —//—)

TREBONIANUS GALLUS
(251 – 253 A.D.)

Roma

2a emission, undated

Sestertius
Obv. IMP CAES C VIBIVS TREBONIANVS GALLVS AVG. Laureated bust of emperor in cuirass and paludamentum looking right, seen from rear.
Rev. FELICITAS PVBLICA. Felicitas standing left, holding caduceus in right hand and sceptre in left hand.
S — C//—
Lit.: RIC 4.3, p. 171, Rome 108a

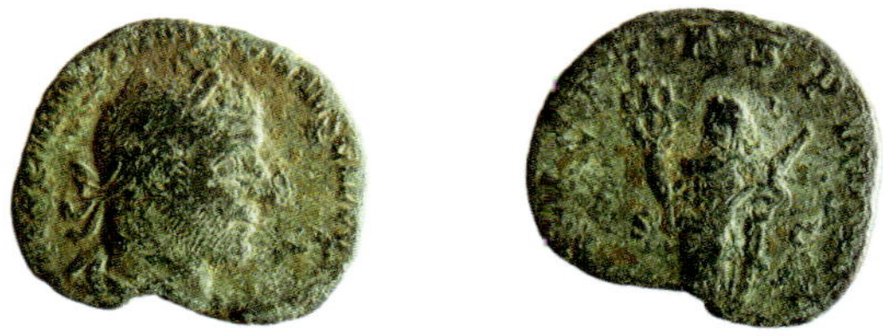

192. AE; 15,22 g.; 22,9 x 27,5 mm.; 12 h.; inv. n. 1510.
(Obv. [IMP C]AES C VIBIVS TREBONIANVS GALLV[S AVG]; Rev. [FEL]ICITAS PVB[LICA]; S — C//—)

Sestertius
Obv. IMP CAES C VIBIVS TREBONIANVS GALLVS AVG. Laureated bust of emperor in cuirass and paludamentum looking right, seen from rear.
Rev. IVNONI MARTIALI. Juno seated front in round distyle temple; peacock at her side.
S — C//—
Lit.: RIC 4.3, p. 171, Rome 110a

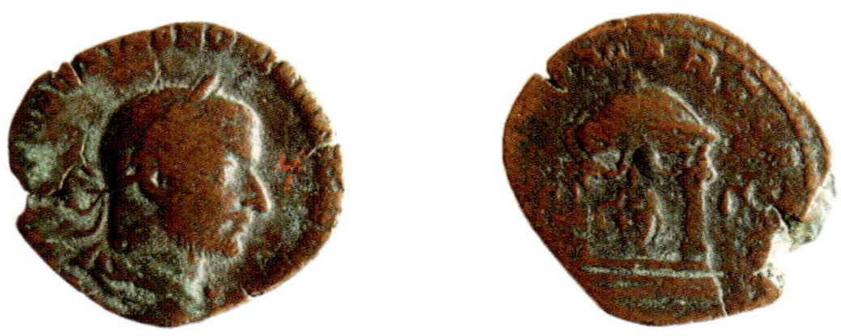

193. AE; 16,25 g.; 25,8 x 27,9 mm.; 11 h.; inv. n. 1511.
(Obv. [IMP CAES C V]IBIVS TREBONIANVS GALL[VS AVG]; Rev. [IVNONI] MARTIA[LI]; S — C//—)

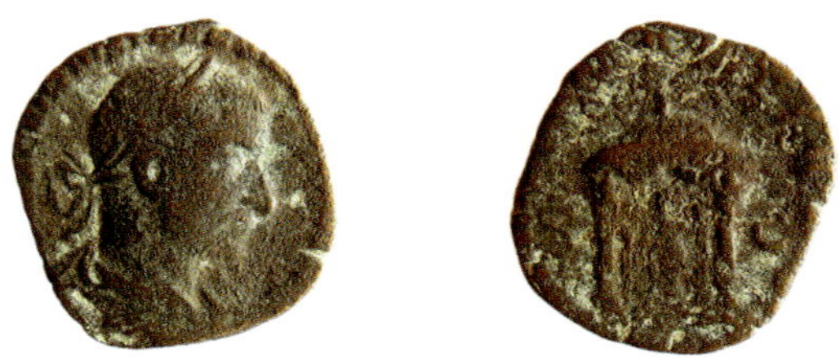

194. AE; 13,68 g.; 26,9 x 25,6 mm.; 12 h.; inv. n. 1512.
(Obv. [IMP CAE]S C VIBIVS TREBO[NIANVS GALLVS AVG]; Rev. [IVNONI] MARTI[ALI]; S — C//—)

2b emission, undated

Antoninianus
Obv. IMP CAE C VIB TREB GALLVS AVG. Radiated bust of emperor in cuirass and paludamentum looking right, seen from rear.
Rev. PIETAS AVGG. Pietas standing left, with both hands raised.
— — *//—
Lit.: CUN 354; RIC 4.3, p. 163, Rome 42

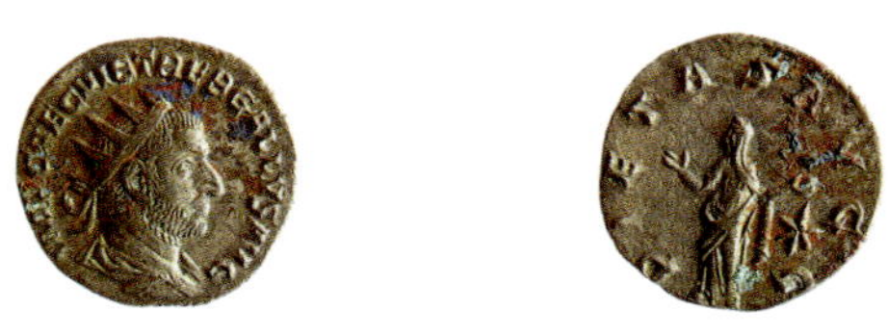

195. AR; 2,97 g.; 19,1 x 19,5 mm.; 11 h.; inv. n. 1513.
(Obv. IMP CAE C VIB TREB GALLVS AVG; Rev. PIETAS AVGG; — — *//—)

Roma – branch mint[15]

5th emission, undated

Antoninianus

Obv. IMP C C VIB TREB GALLVS AVG. Radiated bust of emperor in cuirass and paludamentum looking right, seen from rear.

Rev. IVNO MARTIALIS. Juno seated left, holding branch in right hand and long transverse sceptre in left hand.

— — —//—

Lit.: CUN 383; RIC 4.3, p. 166, Mediolanum 69

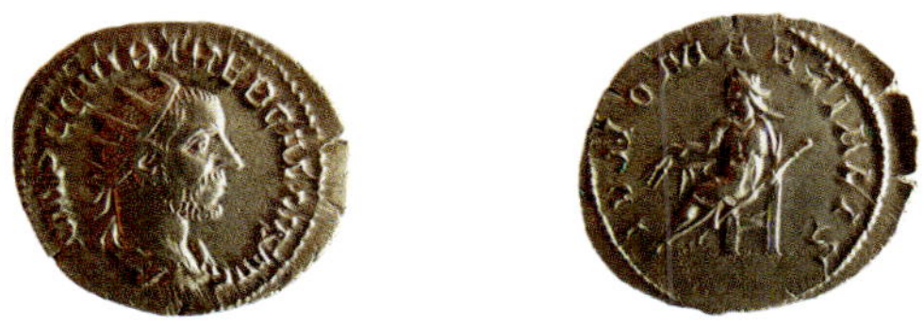

196. AR; 3,22 g.; 20,8 x 23,3 mm.; 6 h.; inv. n. 909.
(Obv. IMP C C VIB TREB GALLVS AVG; Rev. IVNO MARTIALIS; — — —//—)

Antoninianus

Obv. IMP C C VIB TREB GALLVS AVG. Radiated bust of emperor in cuirass and paludamentum looking right, seen from rear.

Rev. LIBERTAS PVBLICA. Libertas standing left, holding pileus in right hand and long transverse sceptre in left hand.

— — —//—

Lit.: CUN 384; RIC 4.3, p. 166, Mediolanum 70

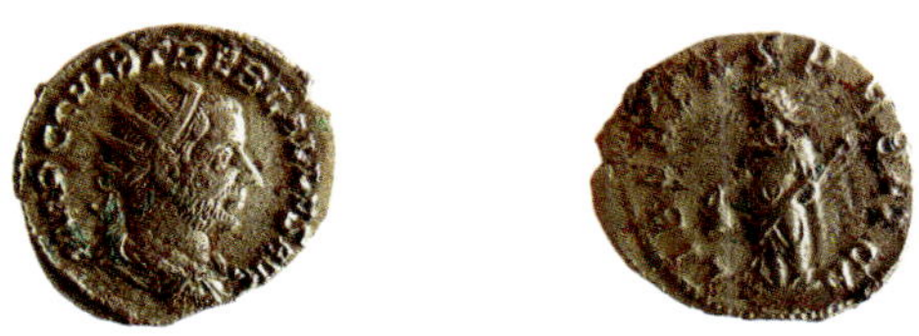

197. AR; 3,15 g.; 20,2 x 21,2 mm.; 12 h.; inv. n. 910.
(Obv. IMP C C VIB TREB GALLVS AVG; Rev. LIBERTAS PVBLICA; — — —//—)

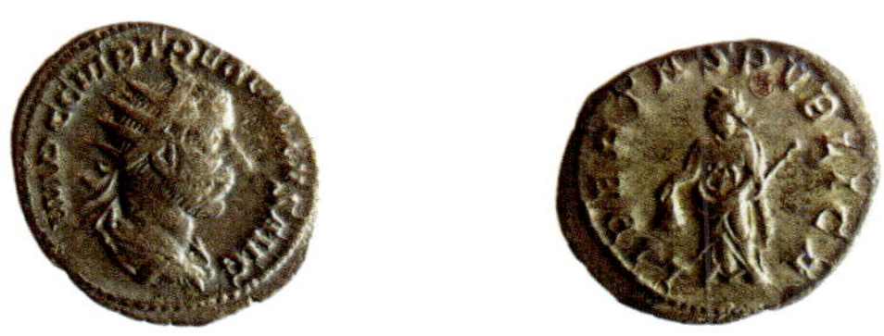

198. AR; 3,91 g.; 21,4 x 21,6 mm.; 12 h.; inv. n. 1514.
(Obv. IMP C C VIB TREB GALLVS AVG; Rev. LIBERTAS PVBLICA; — — —//—)

Antoninianus

Obv. IMP C C VIB TREB GALLVS AVG. Radiated bust of emperor in cuirass and paludamentum looking right, seen from rear.

Rev. PAX AETERNA. Pax standing left, holding branch in right hand and transverse sceptre in left hand.

— — —//—

Lit.: RIC 4.3, p. 166, Mediolanum 71

[15] Elks 1972, p. 111 – 115.

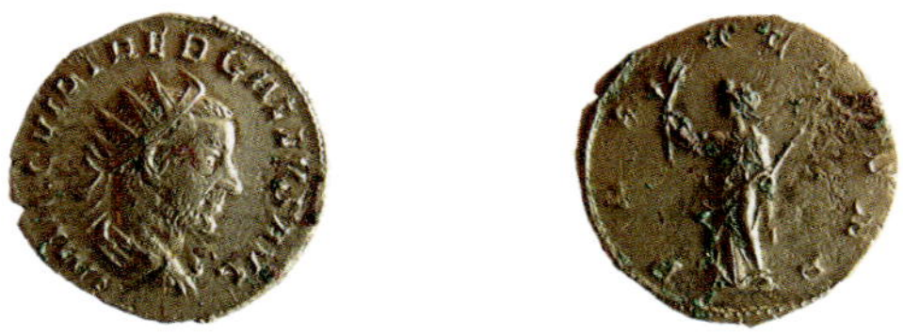

199. AR; 3,07 g.; 21,8 x 22,1 mm.; 6 h.; inv. n. 908.
(Obv. IMP C C VIB TREB GALLVS AVG; Rev. PAX – AETERNA; — — —//—)

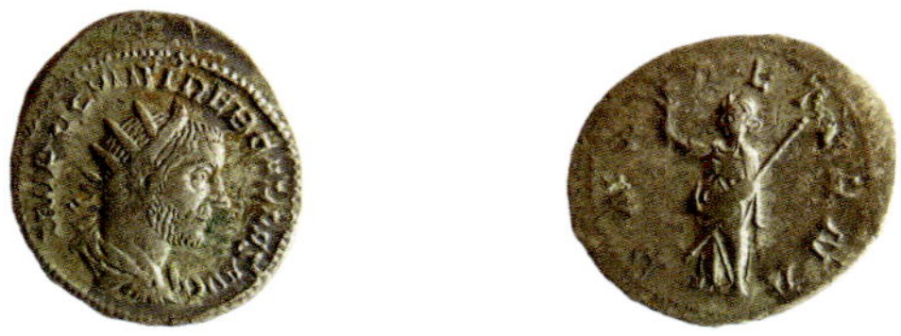

200. AR; 3,92 g.; 23,4 x 21,6 mm.; 11 h.; inv. n. 1515.
(Obv. IMP C C VIB TREB GALLVS AVG; Rev. PAX – AET-ERNA; — — —//—)

Antoninianus
Obv. IMP C C VIB TREB GALLVS AVG. Radiated bust of emperor in cuirass and paludamentum looking right, seen from rear.
Rev. PIETAS AVGG. Pietas standing left with both hands raised, at feet to left altar.
— — —//—
Lit.: RIC 4.3, p. 166, Mediolanum 72

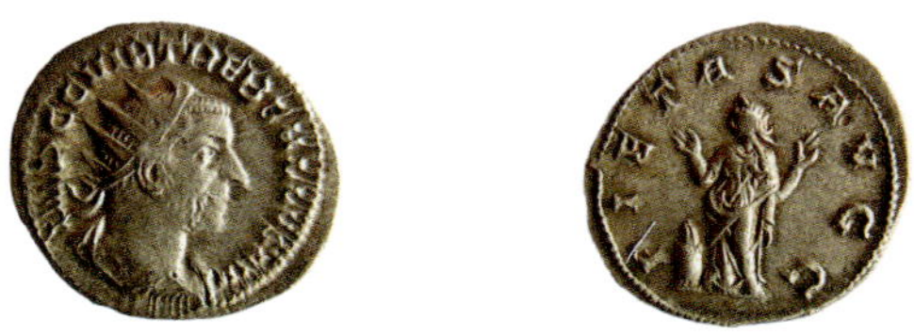

201. AR; 3,99 g.; 20,9 x 22,7 mm.; 1 h.; inv. n. 1516.
(Obv. IMP C C VIB TREB GALLVS AVG; Rev. PIETAS AVGG; — — —//—)

Antiochia

249 – 251 A.D.

Antoninianus
Obv. IMP C C VIB TREB GALLVS P F AVG. Radiated bust of emperor in cuirass and paludamentum looking right, seen from rear.
Rev. MARTEM PROPVGNATOREM. Mars walking right, holding transverse spear in right hand and shield in left hand.
— — —//—
Lit.: CUN 411; RIC 4.3, p. 168, Antioch 84

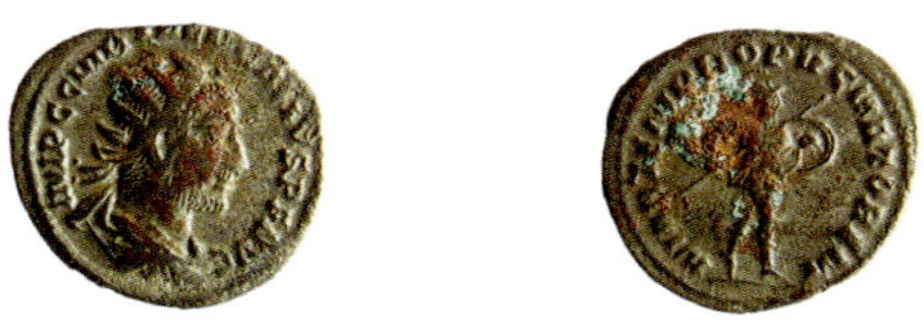

202. AR; 3,19 g.; 20,0 x 22,5 mm.; 1 h.; inv. n. 1517.
(Obv. IMP C C VIB TREB GALLVS P F AVG; Rev. MARTEM PROPVGNATOREM; — — —//—)

VOLUSIANUS
SON OF TREBONIANUS GALLUS
(CAESAR 251 A.D., AUGUSTUS 251 – 253 A.D.)

AS AUGUSTUS

Roma

2a emission, undated

Antoninianus
Obv. IMP CAE C VIB VOLVSIANO AVG. Radiated bust of emperor in cuirass and paludamentum looking right, seen from rear.
Rev. CONCORDIA AVGG. Concordia seated left, holding patera in right hand and double cornucopiae in left hand.
— — —//—
Lit.: CUN 347; RIC 4.3, p. 178, Rome 168

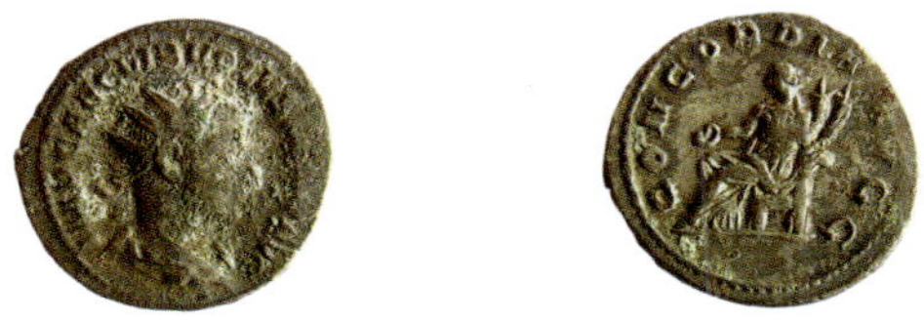

203. AR; 3,99 g.; 21,0 x 22,1 mm.; 6 h.; inv. n. 1518.
(Obv. IMP CAE C VIB VOLVS[IANO] AVG; Rev. CONCORDIA – AVGG; — — —//—)

2b emission, undated

Antoninianus
Obv. IMP CAE C VIB VOLVSIANO AVG. Radiated bust of emperor in cuirass and paludamentum looking right, seen from rear.
Rev. PAX AVGG. Pax standing left, holding branch in right hand and transverse sceptre in left hand.
— — *//—
Lit.: CUN 359; RIC 4.3, p. 178, Rome 180

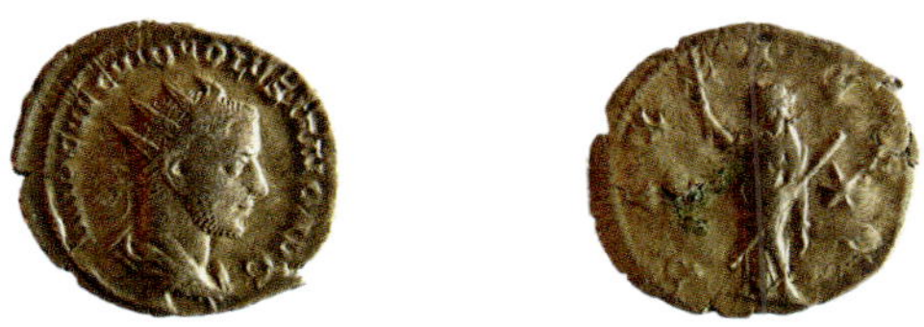

204. AR; 2,75 g.; 20,6 x 22,3 mm.; 6 h.; inv. n. 1519.
(Obv. IMP CAE C VIB VOLVSIANO AVG; Rev. PAX – AVGG; — — *//—)

3rd emission, undated

Antoninianus
Obv. IMP CAE C VIB VOLVSIANO AVG. Radiated bust of emperor in cuirass and paludamentum looking right, seen from rear.
Rev. PIETAS AVGG. Pietas standing left with both hands raised, at feet to left altar.
— — —//—
Lit.: CUN 369; RIC 4.3, p. 179, Rome 182

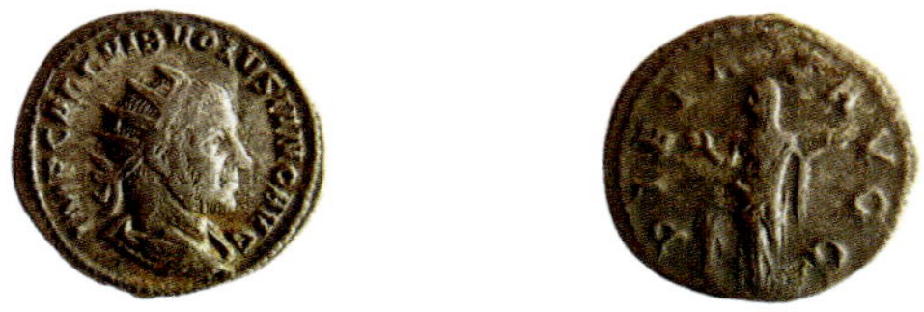

205. AR; 3,57 g.; 20,9 x 22,1 mm.; 6 h.; inv. n. 1520.
(Obv. IMP CAE C VIB VOLVSIANO AVG; Rev. PIETA-S AV-GG; — — —//—)

4th emission, undated

Antoninianus
Obv. IMP CAE C VIB VOLVSIANO AVG. Radiated bust of emperor in cuirass and paludamentum looking right, seen from rear.
Rev. AEQVITAS AVGG. Aequitas standing left, holding scales in right hand and cornucopiae in left hand.
— — —//—
Lit.: CUN 375; RIC 4.3, p. 178, Rome 166

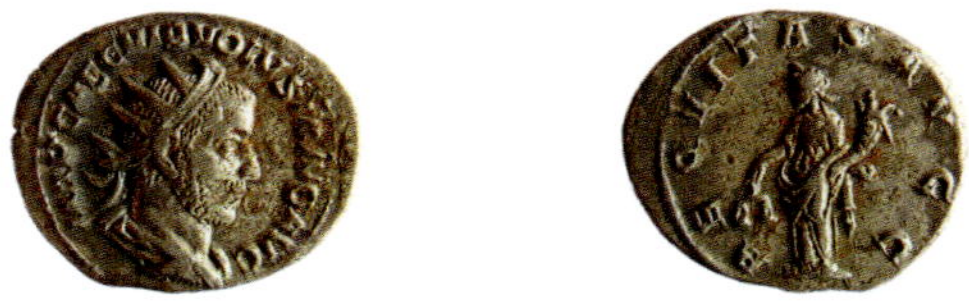

206. AR; 3,73 g.; 18,8 x 22,5 mm.; 12 h.; inv. n. 1521.
(Obv. IMP CAE C VIB VOLVSIANO AVG; Rev. AEQVITAS AVGG; — — —//—)

Roma – branch mint[16]

5th emission, undated

Antoninianus
Obv. IMP C C VIB VOLVSIANVS AVG. Radiated bust of emperor in cuirass and paludamentum looking right, seen from rear.
Rev. FELICITAS PVBL. Felicitas standing left, holding long-handled vertical caduceus in right hand and cornucopiae in left hand.
— — —//—
Lit.: RIC 4.3, p. 181, Mediolanum 205

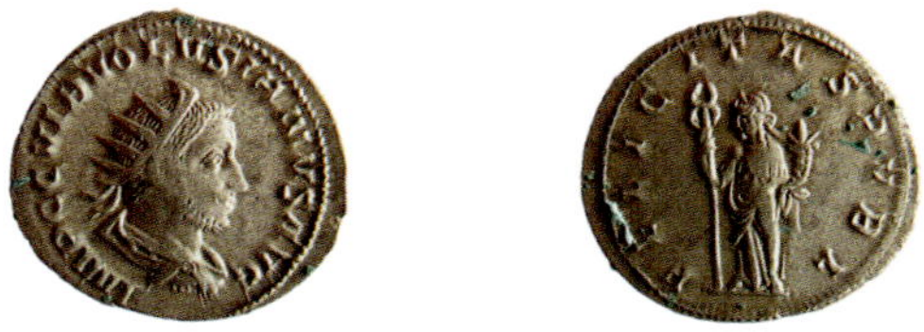

207. AR; 3,86 g.; 22,1 x 23,9 mm.; 12 h.; inv. n. 897.
(Obv. IMP C C VIB VOLVSIANVS AVG; Rev. FELICITAS PVBL; — — —//—)

Antoninianus
Obv. IMP C C VIB VOLVSIANVS AVG. Radiated bust of emperor in cuirass and paludamentum looking right, seen from rear.
Rev. VIRTVS AVGG. Mars standing right, holding vertical spear in right hand and shield which rests on ground in left hand.
— — —//—
Lit.: CUN 387; RIC 4.3, p. 181, Mediolanum 206

[16] Elks 1972, p. 111–115.

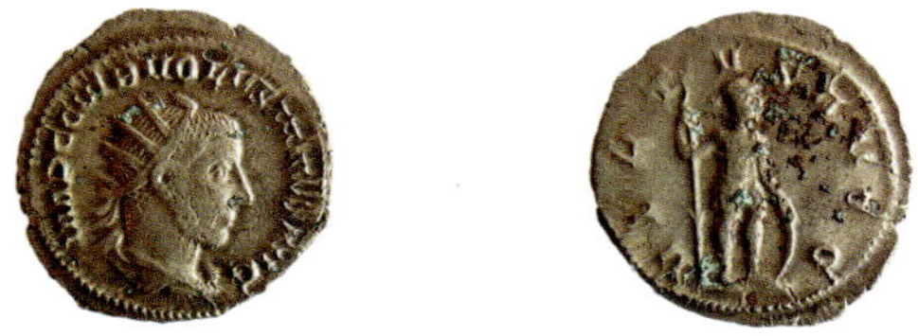

208. AR; 3,18 g.; 22,4 x 21,8 mm.; 12 h.; inv. n. 898.
(Obv. IMP C C VIB VOLVSIANVS AVG; Rev. VIRT-V-S AVGG; — — —//—)

VALERIANUS I.
(253 – 260 A.D.)

Colonia Agrippinensium

257 – 258 A.D.

Antoninianus
Obv. VALERIANVS • P • F • AVG. Radiated bust of emperor in cuirass and paludamentum looking right, seen from front.
Rev. ORIENS AVGG. Sol walking left, raising right hand, holding whip in left hand.
— — —//—
Lit.: MIR 36 Col 1d/868h; RIC 5.1, p. 39, Lugdunum 12

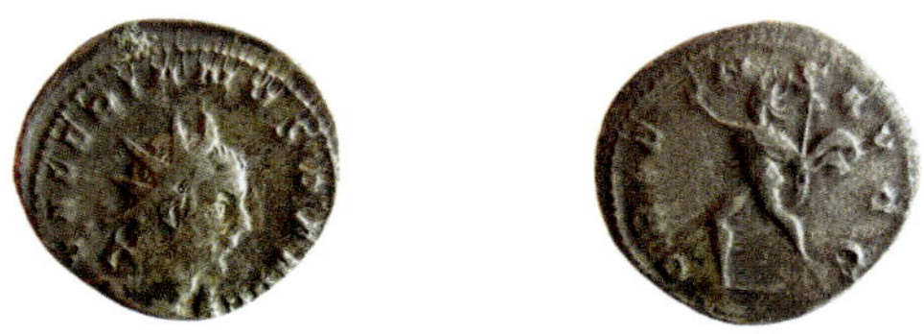

209. AR; 3,45 g.; 22,5 x 22,6 mm.; 12 h.; inv. n. 1522.
(Obv. VALERIANVS • P • F • AVG; Rev. ORIE-N-S AVGG; — — —//—)

Antoninianus
Obv. IMP VALERIANVS PIVS AVG. Radiated bust of emperor in cuirass and paludamentum looking right, seen from front.
Rev. SECVRIT PERPET. Securitas standing front, legs crossed, head left, holding vertical spear in right hand and leaning on column with left elbow.
— — —//—
Lit.: MIR 36 Col 1a/869a; RIC 5.1, p. 39, Lugdunum 17 var.[17]

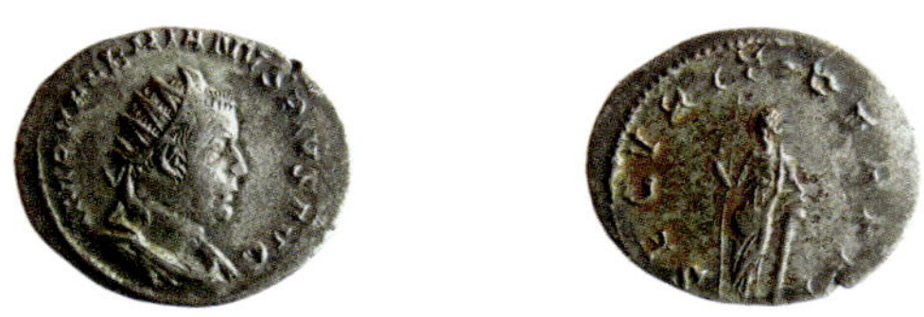

210. AR; 3,47 g.; 19,9 x 22,6 mm.; 6 h.; inv. n. 1523.
(Obv. IMP VALERIANVS PIVS AVG; Rev. SECVRIT PERPET; — — —//—)

[17] RIC 5.1, p. 39, Lugdunum 17 bust without cuirass, obverse legend SECVRIT PERP.

258 – 260 A.D.

Antoninianus
Obv. VALERIANVS • P • F • AVG. Radiated bust of emperor in cuirass and paludamentum looking right, seen from front.
Rev. ORIENS AVGG. Sol standing left, raising right hand, globe in left hand.
— — —//—
Lit.: MIR 36 Col 2/886c; RIC 5.1, p. 39, Lugdunum 13 var.[18]

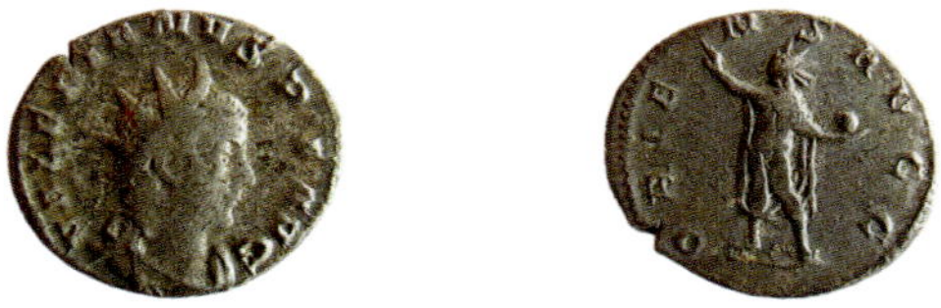

211. AR; 4,79 g.; 19,9 x 22,6 mm.; 6 h.; inv. n. 1524.
(Obv. VALERIANVS • P • F • AVG; Rev. ORIE-NS AVGG; — — —//—)

Roma

253 – 254 A.D.

Antoninianus
Obv. IMP C P LIC VALERIANVS AVG. Radiated bust of emperor in cuirass and paludamentum looking right, seen from front.
Rev. FIDES MILITVM. Fides standing left, holding vertical standard in each hand.
— — —//—
Lit.: MIR 36 Rom 1/22d; RIC 5.1, p. 45, Rome 89

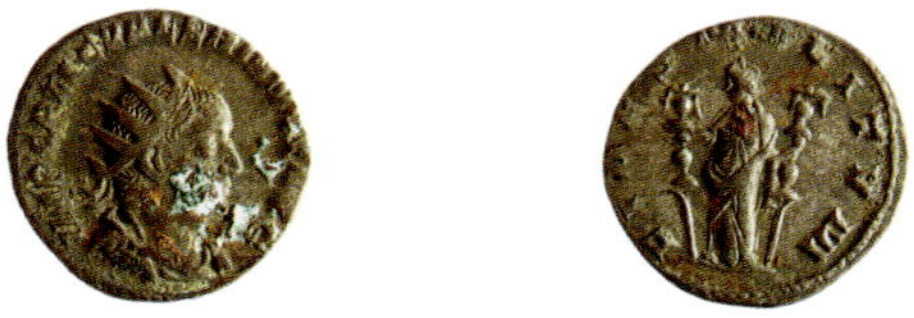

212. AR; 3,34 g.; 20,5 x 20,5 mm.; 12 h.; inv. n. 1525.
(Obv. IMP C P LIC VALERIANVS AVG; Rev. FIDES MILITVM; — — —//—)

Antoninianus
Obv. IMP C P LIC VALERIANVS AVG. Radiated bust of emperor in cuirass and paludamentum looking right, seen from front.
Rev. VICTORIA AVGG. Victory standing left, holding wreath in right hand and palm in left hand.
— — —//—
Lit.: MIR 36 Rom 1/30d; RIC 5.1, p. 48, Rome 125

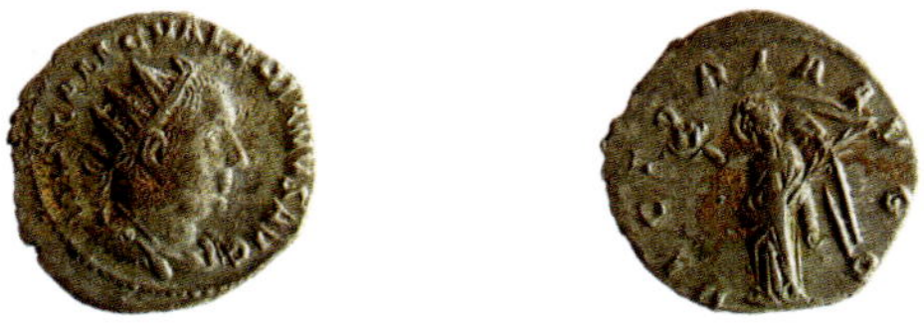

213. AR; 3,71 g.; 20,8 x 20,9 mm.; 5 h.; inv. n. 1526.
(Obv. IMP C P LIC VALERIANVS AVG; Rev. VICTORIA A-VGG; — — —//—)

[18] RIC 5.1, p. 39, Lugdunum 13 Sol walking left.

Sestertius
Obv. IMP C P LIC VALERIANVS AVG. Laureated bust of emperor in cuirass looking right, seen from front.
Rev. VICTORIA AVGG. Victory standing left, holding wreath in right hand and palm in left hand.
S — C//—
Lit.: MIR 36 Rom 1/30k; RIC 5.1, p. 52, Rome 177

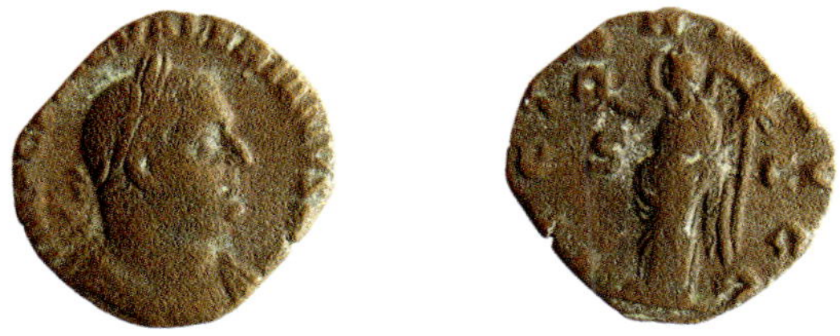

214. AE; 11,06 g.; 26,8 x 26,9 mm.; 12 h.; inv. n. 1527.
(Obv. IMP C P LIC VALERIANVS AVG; Rev. VICT-ORIA A-VGG; S — C//—)

Antoninianus
Obv. IMP C P LIC VALERIANVS AVG. Radiated bust of emperor in cuirass and paludamentum looking right, seen from front.
Rev. APOLINI CONSERVA. Apollo standing left, holding branch in right hand and lyre which rests on rock in left hand.
— — —//—
Lit.: MIR 36 Rom 1/42d; RIC 5.1, p. 44, Rome 71

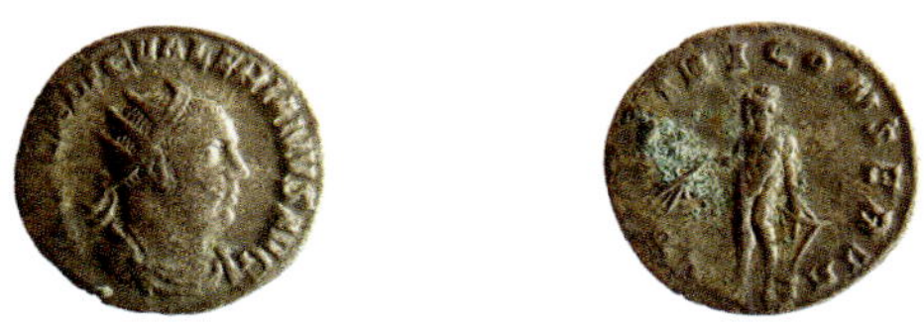

215. AR; 2,95 g.; 19,9 x 20,6 mm.; 6 h.; inv. n. 1528.
(Obv. IMP C P LIC VALERIANVS AVG; Rev. AP-OLINI CONSERVA; — — —//—)

Antoninianus
Obv. IMP C P LIC VALERIANVS AVG. Radiated bust of emperor in cuirass and paludamentum looking right, seen from front.
Rev. APOLINI PROPVG. Apollo standing right, aiming bow and arrow held in both hands; cloak flies out behind.
— — —//—
Lit.: MIR 36 Rom 1/44d; RIC 5.1, p. 45, Rome 74

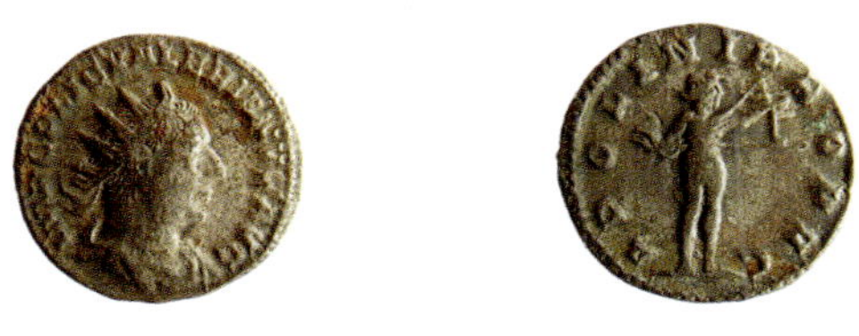

216. AR; 3,34 g.; 20,3 x 21,4 mm.; 6 h.; inv. n. 1529.
(Obv. IMP C P LIC VALERIANVS AVG; Rev. APOLINI PROPVG; — — —//—)

254 – 256 A.D.

Antoninianus
Obv. IMP C P LIC VALERIANVS P F AVG. Radiated bust of emperor in cuirass and paludamentum looking right, seen from front.
Rev. LIBERALITAS AVGG III. Liberalitas standing left, holding tessera in right hand and cornucopiae in left hand.
— — —//—
Lit.: MIR 36 Rom 2/69c; RIC 5.1, p. 46, Rome 104

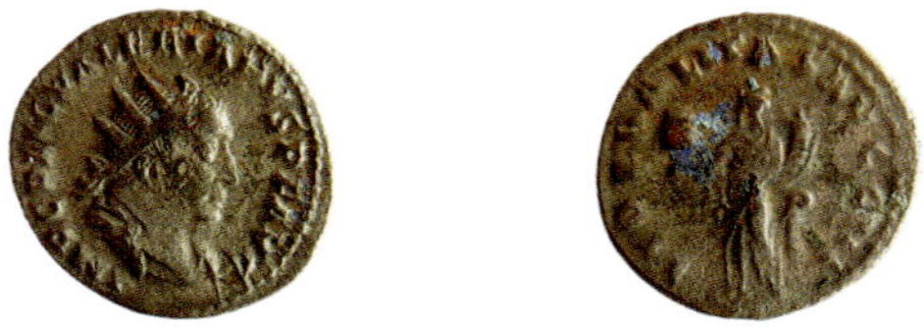

217. AR; 4,43 g.; 21,4 x 22,2 mm.; 12 h.; inv. n. 1530.
(Obv. IMP C P LIC VALERIANVS P F AVG; Rev. LIBERALITAS AVGG III; — — —//—)

Antoninianus

Obv. IMP C P LIC VALERIANVS P F AVG. Radiated bust of emperor in cuirass and paludamentum looking right, seen from front.

Rev. FELICITAS AVGG. Felicitas standing left, holding long-handled vertical caduceus in right hand and cornucopiae in left hand.

— — —//—

Lit.: MIR 36 Rom 2/73c; RIC 5.1, p. 87, Rome 74

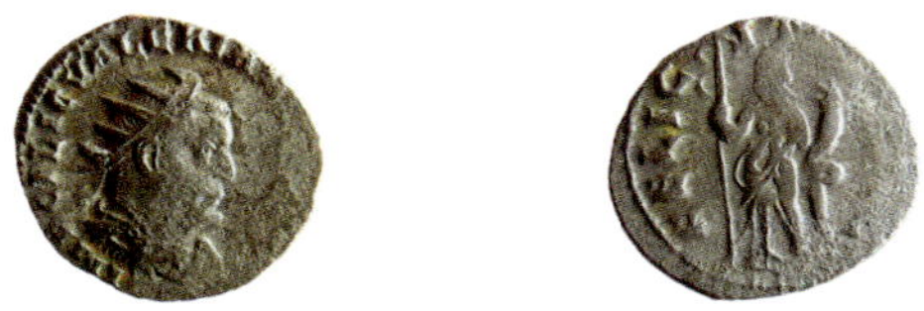

218. AR; 3,86 g.; 19,2 x 20,3 mm.; 6 h.; inv. n. 1531.
(Obv. IMP C P LIC VALERIA[NVS P F AVG]; Rev. FELIC-IT[AS AVGG]; — — —//—)

Antoninianus

Obv. IMP C P LIC VALERIANVS P F AVG. Radiated bust of emperor in cuirass and paludamentum looking right, seen from front.

Rev. ORIENS AVGG. Sol standing left, raising right hand, holding whip in left hand.

— — —//—

Lit.: MIR 36 Rom 2/75c; RIC 5.1, p. 47, Rome 106 var.[19]

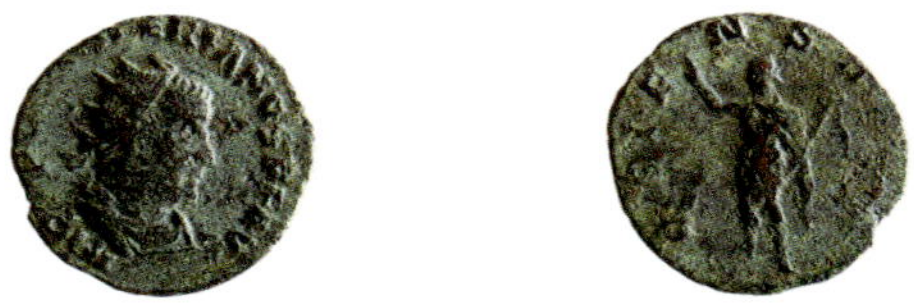

219. AE; 1,9 g.; 19,3 x 19,7 mm.; 12 h.; inv. n. 1532.
(Obv. IMP [C] P [LIC VA]LERIANVS P F AV[G]; Rev. ORIE-N-S A[VGG]; — — —//—)

256 A.D.

Antoninianus

Obv. IMP C P LIC VALERIANVS P F AVG. Radiated bust of emperor in cuirass and paludamentum looking right, seen from front.

Rev. ORIENS AVGG. Sol standing left, raising right hand, globe in left hand.

— — —//—

Lit.: MIR 36 Rom 3/108b; RIC 5.1, p. 47, Rome 106

[19] RIC 5.1, p. 47, Rome 106 bust without cuirass.

220. AE; 1,39 g.; 17,8 x 18,9 mm.; 11 h.; inv. n. 1533.
(Obv. [IMP C P] LIC VALERI[ANVS P F AVG]; Rev. [O]RI[ENS] AV[GG]; — — —//—)

Antoninianus
Obv. IMP C P LIC VALERIANVS P F AVG. Radiated bust of emperor in cuirass and paludamentum looking right, seen from front.
Rev. RESTITVTOR ORBIS. Emperor standing left, holding vertical sceptre in left hand, raising kneeling female with his right hand.
— — —//—
Lit.: MIR 36 Rom 3/111b; RIC 5.1, p. 47, Rome 117

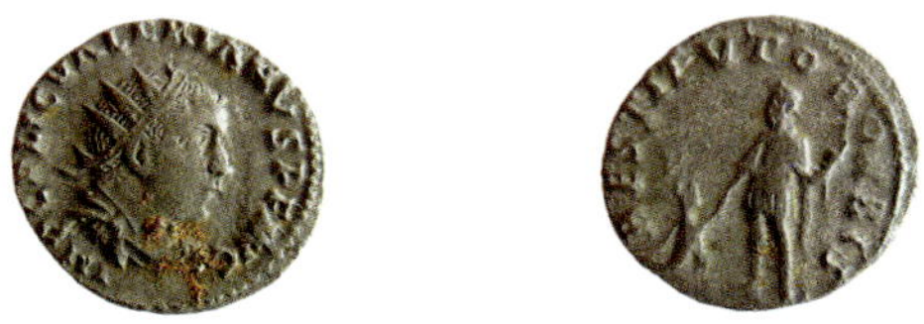

221. AR; 3,88 g.; 20,1 x 20,9 mm.; 6 h.; inv. n. 1534.
(Obv. IMP C P LIC VALERIANVS P F AVG; Rev. RESTITVTOR – ORBIS; — — —//—)

Viminacium

253 – 255 A.D.

Antoninianus
Obv. IMP P LIC VALERIANO AVG. Radiated bust of emperor in cuirass and paludamentum looking right, seen from rear.
Rev. VICTORIA GERMANICA. Victory standing left, right hand leaning on shield, left hand holding palm; captive under shield.
— — —//—
Lit.: MIR 36 Vim 1a/793d; RIC 5.1, p. 58, Mediolanum 264

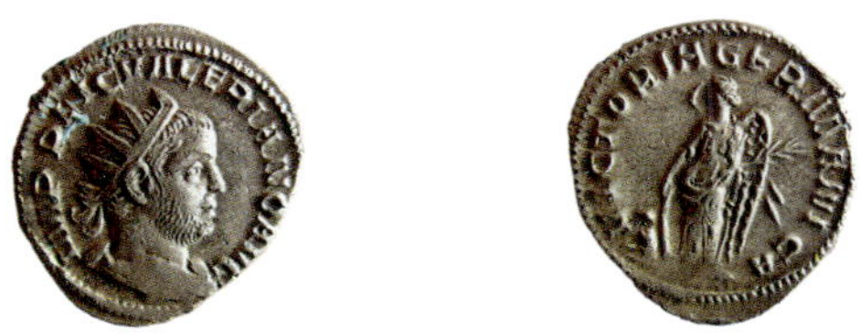

222. AR; 3,28 g.; 21,5 x 20,7 mm.; 12 h.; inv. n. 900.
(Obv. IMP P LIC VALERIANO AVG; Rev. VICTORIA GERMANICA; — — —//—)

Antoninianus
Obv. IMP VALERIANVS P AVG. Radiated bust of emperor in cuirass and paludamentum looking right, seen from rear.
Rev. FIDES MILITVM. Fides standing left with head turned right, holding vertical vexilum in right hand and transverse standard in left hand.
— — —//—
Lit.: MIR 36 Vim 2b/807d; RIC 5.1, p. 56, Mediolanum 241

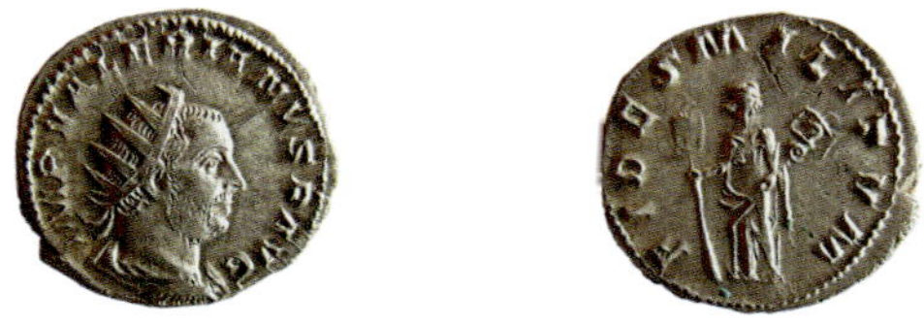

223. AR; 4,04 g.; 20,6 x 21,8 mm.; 12 h.; inv. n. 901.
(Obv. IMP VALERIANVS P AVG; Rev. FIDES MILITVM; — — —//—)

Antoninianus
Obv. IMP VALERIANVS P AVG. Radiated bust of emperor in cuirass and paludamentum looking right, seen from rear.
Rev. VIRTVS AVGG. Virtus standing left, holding Victory in right hand, shield and vertical spear in left hand.
— — —//—
Lit.: MIR 36 Vim 2b/811d; RIC 5.1, p. 58, Mediolanum 267 var.[20]

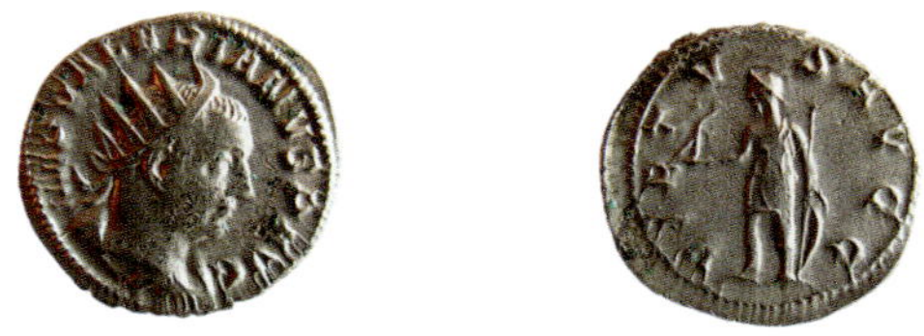

224. AR; 3,03 g.; 21,5 x 21,6 mm.; 6 h.; inv. n. 902.
(Obv. IMP VALERIANVS P AVG; Rev VIRT-V-S AVGG; — — —//—)

Antiochia

253 – 256 A.D.

Antoninianus
Obv. IMP C P LIC VALERIANVS AVG. Radiated bust of emperor in cuirass and paludamentum looking right, seen from front.
Rev. VICTORIA AVGG. Victory walking left, holding wreath in right hand and palm in left hand.
— — —//—
Lit.: MIR 36 Ant 1/1565a; RIC 5.1, –

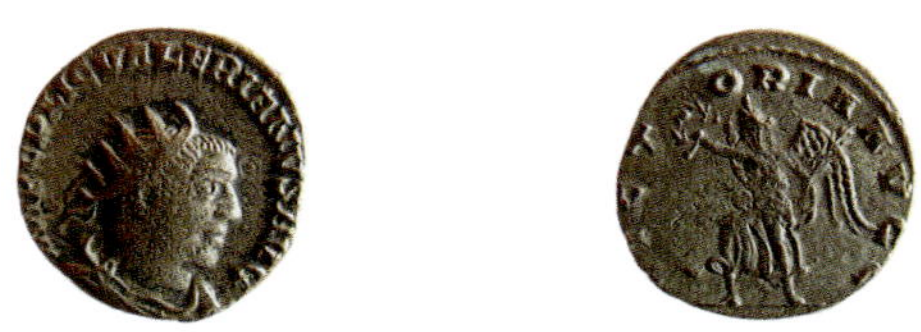

225. AR; 3,76 g.; 20,0 x 19,2 mm.; 12 h.; inv. n. 381.
(Obv. IMP C P LIC VALERIANVS AVG; Rev. VICT-ORIA AVGG; — — —//—)

257 – 260 A.D.

Antoninianus
Obv. IMP VALERIANVS AVG. Radiated bust of emperor in cuirass and paludamentum looking right, seen from front.
Rev. FELICITAS AVGG. Felicitas standing left, holding long-handled vertical caduceus in right hand and cornucopiae in left hand.
— — —//—
Lit.: MIR 36 Ant 5/1599a; RIC 5.1, p. 60, Antioch 283

[20] RIC 5.1, p. 58, Mediolanum 267 – Obverse legend IMP P LIC VALERIANO AVG.

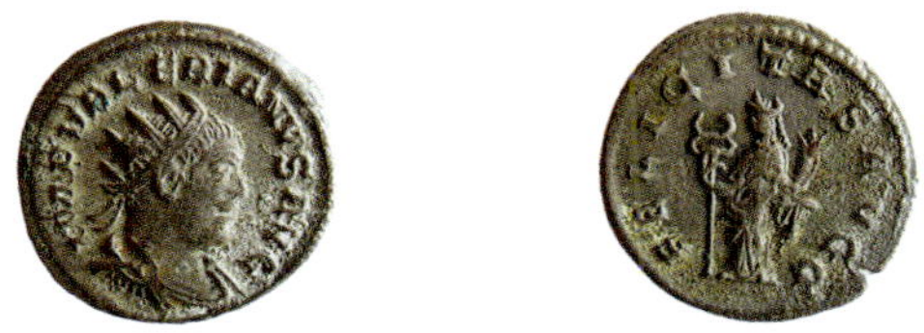

226. AR; 4,27 g.; 21,6 x 21,8 mm.; 6 h.; inv. n. 1535.
(Obv. IMP VALERIANVS AVG; Rev. FELICITAS AVGG; — — —//—)

Samosata

255 – 256 A.D.

Antoninianus
Obv. IMP C P LIC VALERIANVS AVG. Radiated bust of emperor in cuirass and paludamentum looking right, seen from front.
Rev. RESTITVT ORIENTIS. Emperor standing left, holding vertical spear in left hand, being crowned by female figure standing right, holding wreath in right hand.
— — —//—
Lit.: MIR 36 Sam 1/1677e; RIC 5.1, p. 60, Mint of Asia 286

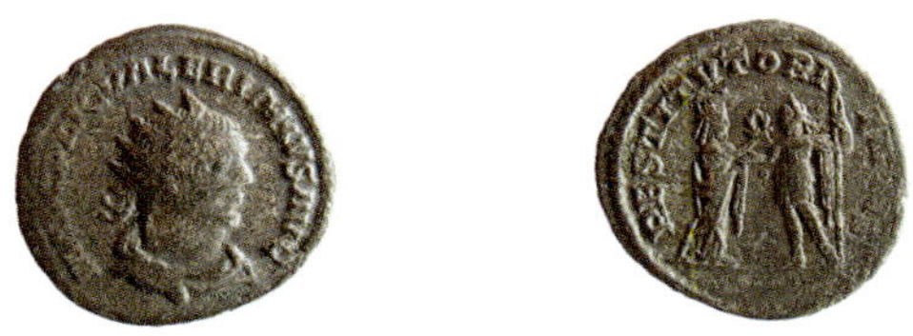

227. AR; 3,06 g.; 21,3 x 22,2 mm.; 12 h.; inv. n. 1536.
(Obv. IMP C P LIC VALERIANVS AVG; Rev. RESTITVT ORI-EN[T]IS; — — —//—)

Antoninianus
Obv. IMP C P LIC VALERIANVS AVG. Radiated bust of emperor in cuirass and paludamentum looking right, seen from front.
Rev. VIRTVS AVGG. Emperor standing right, holding vertical spear in right hand and globe in left hand, receiving Victory from emperor standing left, holding transverse spear in left hand.
— — —//—
Lit.: MIR 36 Sam 1/1681e; RIC 5.1, p. 60, Mint of Asia 292

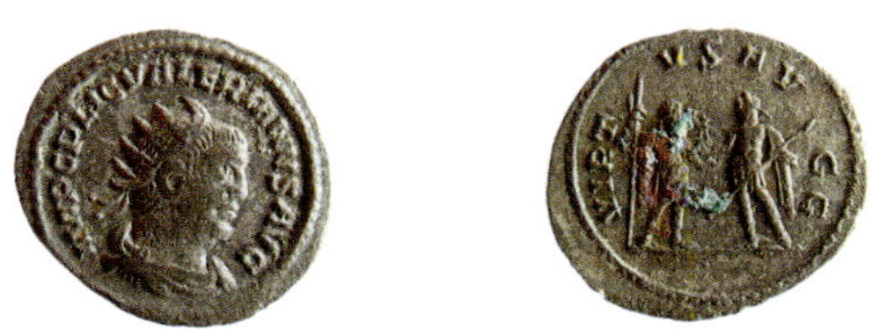

228. AR; 3,12 g.; 22,5 x 24,0 mm.; 12 h.; inv. n. 1537.
(Obv. IMP C P LIC VALERIANVS AVG; Rev. VIRT-VS AV-GG; — — —//—)

256 – 260 A.D.

Antoninianus
Obv. IMP C P LIC VALERIANVS P F AVG. Radiated bust of emperor in cuirass and paludamentum looking right, seen from front.
Rev. RESTITVT ORIENTIS. Emperor standing left, holding vertical spear in left hand, being crowned by female figure standing right, holding wreath in right hand.
— — —//—
Lit.: MIR 36 Sam 2/1685e; RIC 5.1, p. 60, Mint of Asia 287

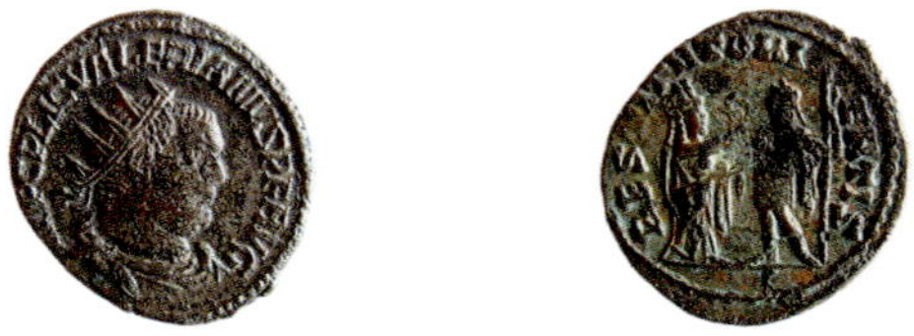

229. AR; 4,09 g.; 21,7 x 20,4 mm.; 6 h.; inv. n. 1538.
(Obv. IMP C P LIC VALERIANVS P F AVG; Rev. RESTITVT ORI-ENTIS; — — —//—)

MARINIANA
WIFE OF VALERIANUS I.

Roma

257 – 260 A.D.

Antoninianus
Obv. DIVAE MARINIANAE. Veiled bust of empress on crescent looking right.
Rev. CONSECRATIO. Peacock facing front, head turned right.
V — —//—
Lit.: MIR 36 Rom 4–5/225b; RIC 5.1, p. 64, Rome 4

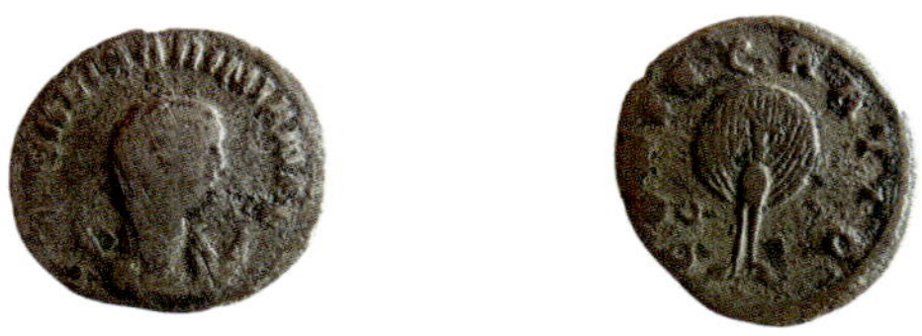

230. AR; 2,37 g.; 19,7 x 21,4 mm.; 10 h.; inv. n. 1539.
(Obv. DIVAE MARINIANAE; Rev. CONSECRATIO; V — —//—)

Viminacium

253 – 255 A.D.

Antoninianus
Obv. DIVAE MARINIANAE. Diademed and draped bust of empress on crescent looking right.
Rev. CONSECRATIO. Peacock flying right, carrying Empress who is seated left, with her right hand outstretched and holding sceptre in left hand.
— — —//—
Lit.: MIR 36 Vim 2b/849b; RIC 5.1, p. 64, Rome 6

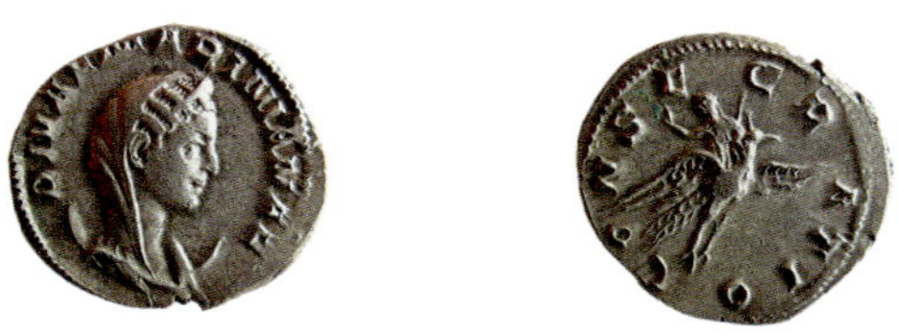

231. AR; 4,02 g.; 20,5 x 22,4 mm.; 3 h.; inv. n. 915.
(Obv. DIVAE MARINIANAE; Rev. CO-NS-E-CR-ATIO; — — —//—)

Antoninianus
Obv. DIVAE MARINIANAE. Veiled bust of empress on crescent looking right.
Rev. CONSECRATIO. Peacock flying right, carrying Empress who is seated left, with her right hand outstretched and holding sceptre in left hand.
— — —//—
Lit.: MIR 36 Vim 2c/850b; RIC 5.1, p. 64, Rome 6

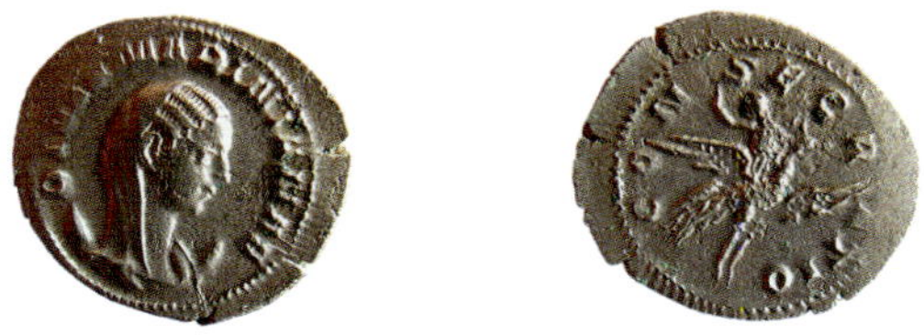

232. AR; 3,9 g.; 22,1 x 24,4 mm.; 12 h.; inv. n. 914.
(Obv. DIVAE MARINIANAE; Rev. CO-N-SECR-ATIO; — — —//—)

GALLIENUS SON OF VALERIANUS I. (253 – 268 A.D.)

Colonia Agrippinensium

257 – 258 A.D.

Antoninianus
Obv. GALLIENVS • P • F • AVG. Radiated bust of emperor in cuirass looking right, seen from front.
Rev. RESTIT • GALLIAR. Emperor standing left, holding vertical sceptre in left hand, raising kneeling female with his right hand.
— — —//—
Lit.: MIR 36 Col 1d/879l; RIC 5.1, p. 70, Lugdunum 29 var.[21]

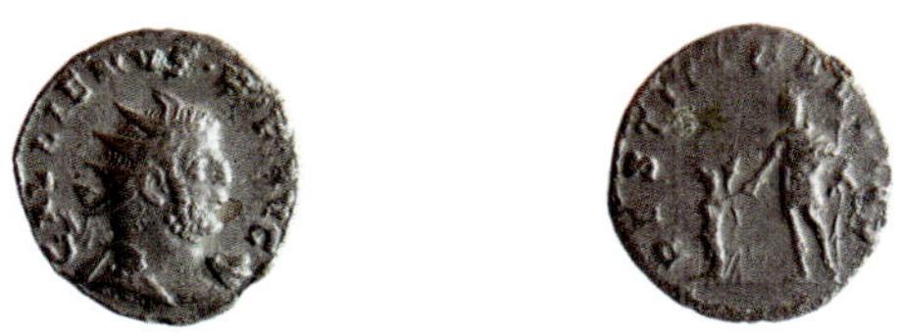

233. AR; 3,15 g.; 20,9 x 19,7 mm.; 6 h.; inv. n. 1540.
(Obv. GALLIENVS • P • F • AVG; Rev. RESTIT • GALLIAR; — — —//—)

Antoninianus
Obv. GALLIENVS • P • F • AVG. Radiated bust of emperor in cuirass looking right, seen from front.
Rev. VIRTVS AVGG. Emperor walking right, holding transverse spear in right hand and trophy in left hand.
— — —//—
Lit.: MIR 36 Col 1d/882l; RIC 5.1, p. 72, Lugdunum 56

[21] RIC 5.1, p. 70, Lugdunum 29 does not record radiated bust of emperor in cuirass in obverse; in reverse records emperor standing right instead of left.

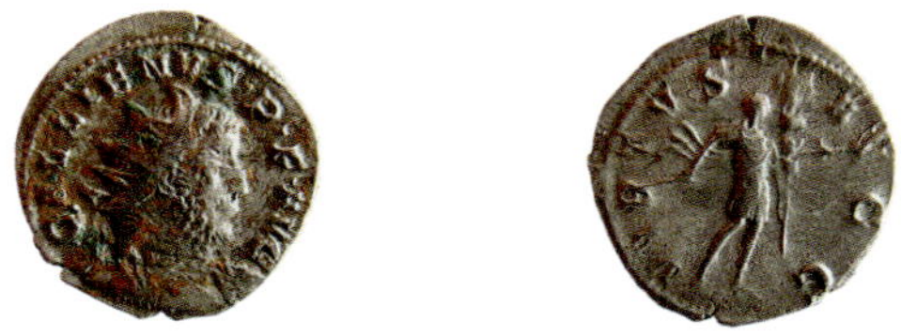

234. AR; 2,96 g.; 22,6 x 21,5 mm.; 12 h.; inv. n. 1541.
(Obv. GALLIENVS • P • F • AVG; Rev. VIRTVS – AVGG; — — —//—)

258 – 260 A.D.

Antoninianus
Obv. GALLIENVS • P • F • AVG. Radiated bust of emperor in cuirass looking right, seen from front.
Rev. VIRT GALLIENI AVG. Emperor walking right, holding transverse spear in right hand and shield in left hand; captive under left foot.
— — —//—
Lit.: MIR 36 Col 2/890h; RIC 5.1, p. 72, Lugdunum 54

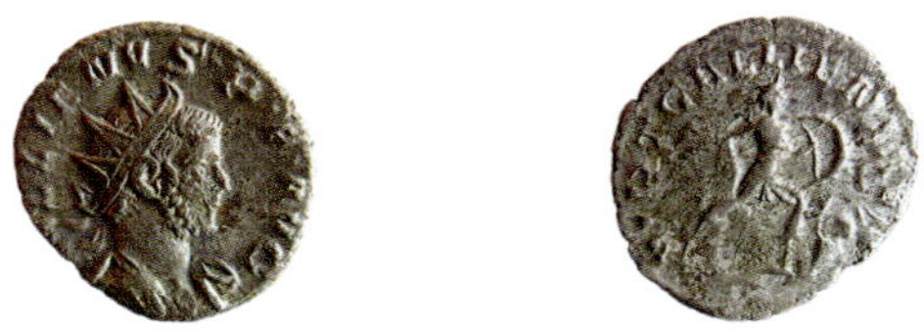

235. AR; 3,88 g.; 21,1 x 20,2 mm.; 12 h.; inv. n. 1542
(Obv. GALLIENVS • P • F • AVG; Rev. VIRT GALLIENI AVG; — — —//—)

Antoninianus
Obv. GALLIENVS • P • F • AVG. Radiated bust of emperor in cuirass looking left, with spear across right shoulder and shield in his left hand, seen from front.
Rev. VICT GERMANICA. Victory walking left, holding wreath in right hand and trophy in left hand, treading down enemy.
— — —//—
Lit.: MIR 36 Col 2/893i; RIC 5.1, p. 71, Lugdunum 44

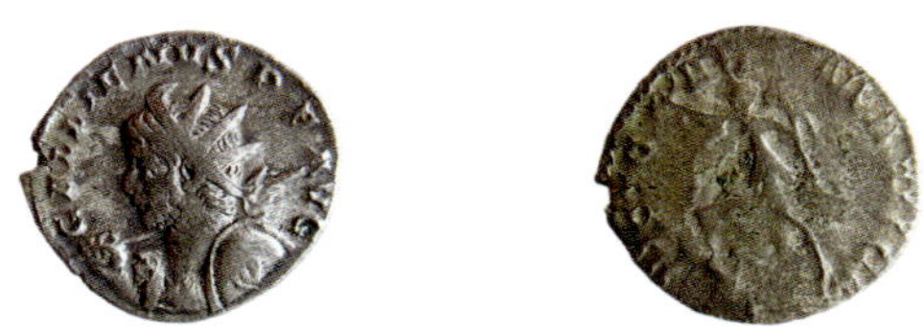

236. AR; 3,31 g.; 20,4 x 22,0 mm.; 6 h.; inv. n. 1543
(Obv. GALLIENVS • P • F • AVG; Rev. VICT G-ER-MANICA; — — —//—)

Mediolanum

258 – 259 A.D.

Antoninianus
Obv. IMP GALLIENVS AVG. Radiated bust of emperor in cuirass looking right, seen from front.
Rev. DIANA FELIX. Diana runnig right, with right hand drawing arrow from quiver which she has on her right shoulder and holding bow in left hand; at feet to right a small dog/stag running right.
— — —//—
Lit.: MIR 36 Med 1/920l; RIC 5.1, p. 98, Mediolanum 380

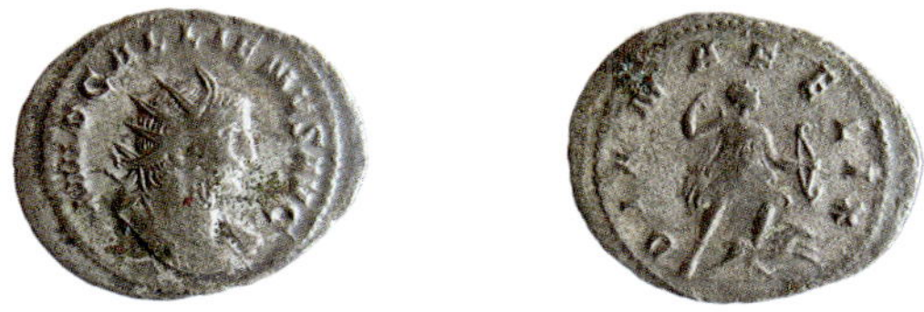

237. AR; 2,56 g.; 21,1 x 25,1 mm.; 6 h.; inv. n. 1544
(Obv. IMP GALLIENVS AVG; Rev. DIANA FELIX; — — —//—)

Antoninianus
Obv. IMP GALLIENVS AVG. Radiated bust of emperor in cuirass looking right, seen from front.
Rev. VICTORIA AVGG. Winged Victory between two shields holding unwound diadem in both hands.
— — —//—
Lit.: MIR 36 Med 1/921l; RIC 5.1, p. 99, Mediolanum 405

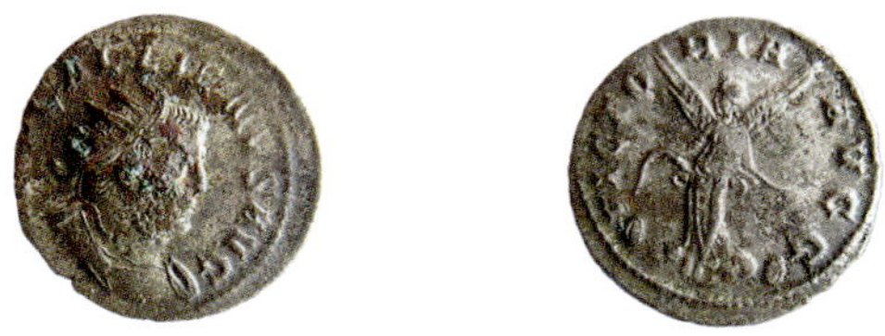

238. AR; 3,18 g.; 22,2 x 21,8 mm.; 12 h.; inv. n. 1545
(Obv. IMP GALLIENVS AVG; Rev. VICTO-RIA – AVGG; — — —//—)

262 A.D.

Antoninianus
Obv. GALLIENVS AVG. Radiated bust of emperor in cuirass looking right, seen from front.
Rev. PAX AVGVSTI. Pax walking left, holding branch in right hand and transverse sceptre in left hand.
— — —//—
Lit.: MIR 36 Med 3^1/1039p; RIC 5.1, p. 175, Mediolanum 502 var.[22]

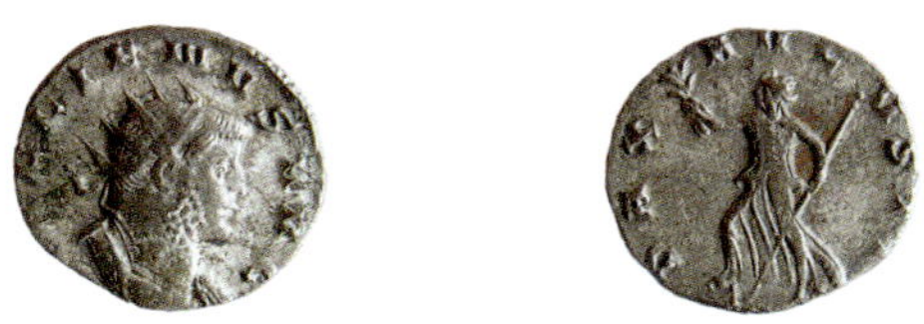

239. AR; 3,24 g.; 19,0 x 20,1 mm.; 12 h.; inv. n. 1546
(Obv. GALLIENVS AVG; Rev. PAX – AVG-VSTI; — — —//—)

263 – 264 A.D.

Antoninianus
Obv. GALLIENVS AVG. Radiated bust of emperor looking right with paludamentum on each shoulder.
Rev. LAETITIA AVG. Laetitia standing left, holding wreath in right hand and anchor in left hand.
— — —//—
Lit.: MIR 36 Med 4^1/1093k; RIC 5.1, p. 173, Mediolanum 489 var.[23]

[22] RIC 5.1, p. 175, Mediolanum 502 with S in field left on the reverse.
[23] RIC 5.1, p. 173, Mediolanum 489 without paludamentum in obverse and with officina mark in reverse.

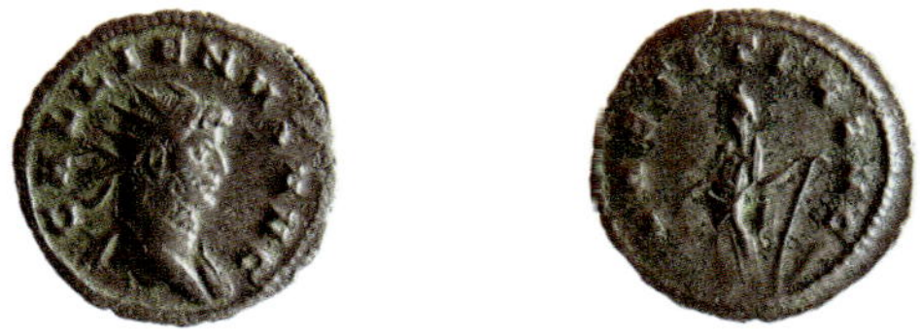

240. AE; 3,03 g.; 21,5 x 21,8 mm.; 12 h.; inv. n. 1547
(Obv. GALLIENVS AVG; Rev. LAETITIA AVG; — — —//—)

Antoninianus
Obv. IMP GALLIENVS P AVG. Radiated bust of emperor in paludamentum looking right, seen from front.
Rev. LAETI-TIA AVG. Laetitia standing left, holding wreath in right hand and anchor in left hand.
— — —//S
Lit.: MIR 36 Med 4^1/1119k; RIC 5.1, p. 173, Mediolanum 489 var.[24]

241. AE; 1,56 g.; 19,4 x 17,0 mm.; 12 h.; inv. n. 1548
(Obv. IMP GALLIENVS P AVG; Rev. LAETI-TIA AVG; — — —//S)

Antoninianus
Obv. GALLIENVS AVG. Radiated bust of emperor looking right.
Rev. ORIENS AVG. Sol standing left, raising right hand, globe in left hand.
— — —//—
Lit.: MIR 36 Med 4^2/1126m; RIC 5.1, p. 174, Mediolanum 495

242. AE; 2,25 g.; 18,4 x 19,2 mm.; 6 h.; inv. n. 1549
(Obv. GALLIENVS AVG; Rev. O[RIEN]S AVG; — — —//—)

Antoninianus
Obv. GALLIENVS AVG. Radiated bust of emperor looking right.
Rev. APOLLO CONSER. Apollo standing left, holding branch in right hand and mantle in left hand.
— — —//—
Lit.: MIR 36 Med 4^2/1171m; RIC 5.1, p. 172, Mediolanum 468

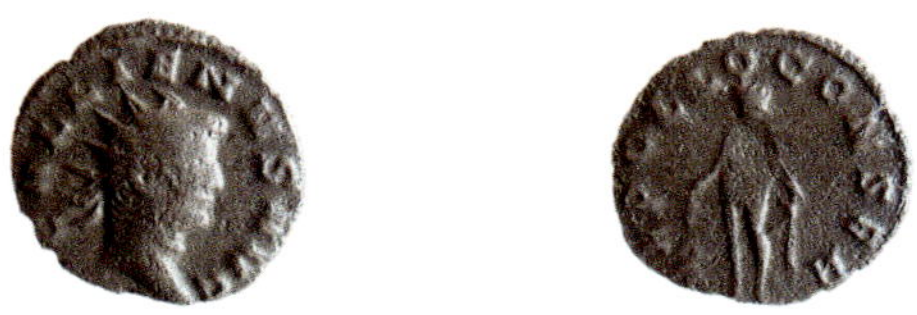

243. AE; 1,87 g.; 18,4 x 19,3 mm.; 12 h.; inv. n. 1550
(Obv. GALLIENVS AVG; Rev. APOLLO CONSER; — — —//—)

[24] RIC 5.1, p. 173, Mediolanum 489 without paludamentum in obverse and records legend GALLIENVS AVG.

264 – 265 A.D.

Antoninianus
Obv. GALLIENVS AVG. Radiated bust of emperor looking right.
Rev. IND-VLG AVG. Spes walking left, holding flower in right hand and raising skirt with left hand.
— — S//—
Lit.: MIR 36 Med 5/1201c; RIC 5.1, p. 173, Mediolanum 485 var.[25]

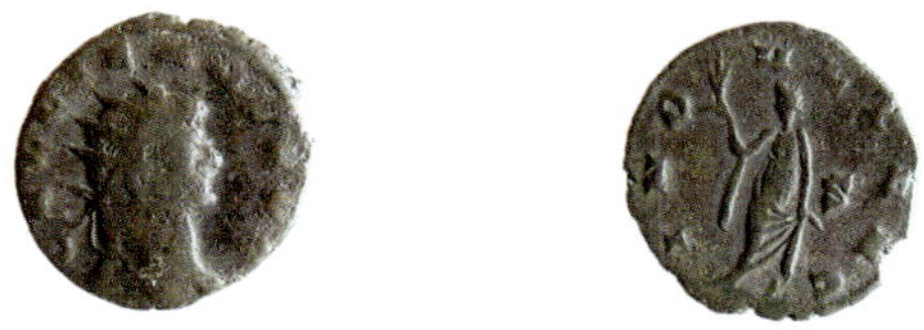

244. AE; 2,78 g.; 19,8 x 19,6 mm.; 6 h.; inv. n. 1551
(Obv. GALLIENVS AVG; Rev. IND-VLG AVG; — — S//—)

Antoninianus
Obv. GALLIENVS AVG. Radiated bust of emperor looking right with paludamentum on each shoulder.
Rev. ORIENS AVG. Sol standing left, raising right hand, holding whip in left hand.
— — —//P
Lit.: MIR 36 Med 5/1211g; RIC 5.1, p. 174, Mediolanum 494

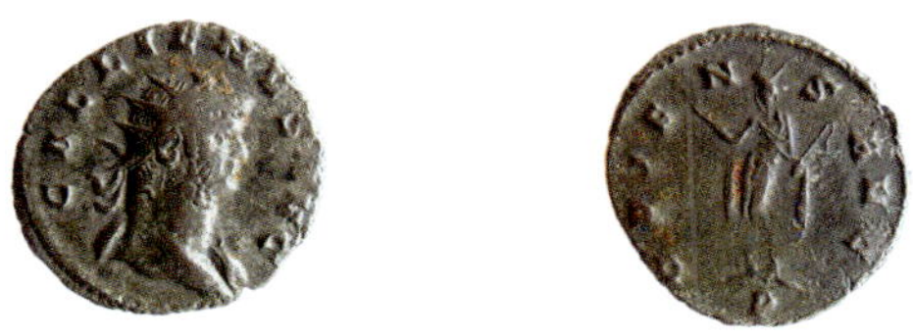

245. AE; 3,14 g.; 20,3 x 20,4 mm.; 6 h.; inv. n. 1552
(Obv. GALLIENVS AVG; Rev. ORIE-N-S – AVG; — — —//P)

End of 265 – 266 A.D.

Antoninianus
Obv. GALLIENVS AVG. Radiated bust of emperor looking right.
Rev. PIETAS AVG. Pietas standing left, with both hands raised, at feet to left altar.
— — —//—
Lit.: MIR 36 Med 6^1/1261f; RIC 5.1, p. 175, Mediolanum 507 var.[26]

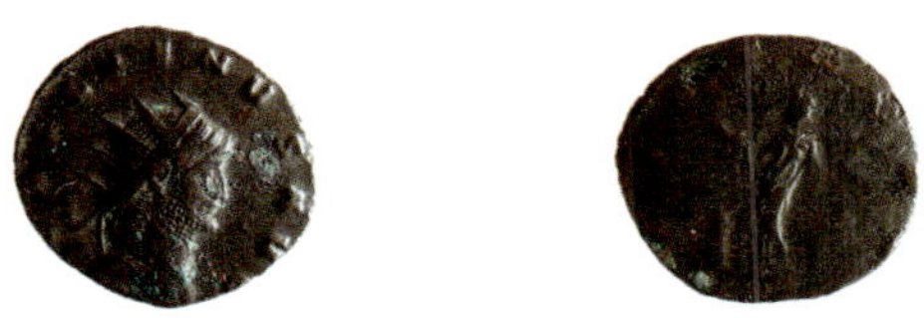

246. AE; 2,83 g.; 18,4 x 20,1 mm.; 12 h.; inv. n. 1553
(Obv. GALLIENVS AVG; Rev. PIETA[S] AV[G]; — — —//—)

[25] RIC 5.1, p. 173, Mediolanum 485 with officina mark in exerque.
[26] RIC 5.1, p. 175, Mediolanum 507 with officina mark in the field or in exerque.

266 – 268 A.D.

Antoninianus
Obv. GALLIENVS AVG. Radiated bust of emperor looking right.
Rev. SECVR TENPO (sic!). Securitas standing front, legs crossed, head left, holding vertical sceptre in right hand and leaning on column with left elbow.
— — —//MS
Lit.: MIR 36 Med 8/1372a; RIC 5.1, p. 176, Mediolanum 513 var.[27]

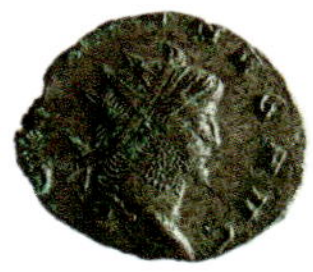 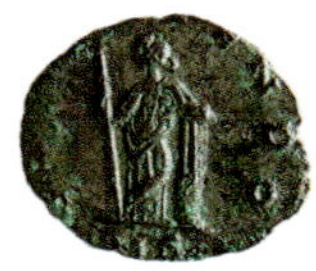

247. AE; 2,22 g.; 16,5 x 18,9 mm.; 12 h.; inv. n. 1554
(Obv. GALLIENVS AVG; Rev. S[ECVR T]ENPO; — — —//MS)

Roma

253 – 254 A.D.

Antoninianus
Obv. IMP C P LIC GALLIENVS AVG. Radiated bust of emperor in cuirass looking right, seen from front.
Rev. CONCORDIA EXERCIT. Concordia standing left, holding patera in right hand and single cornucopiae in left hand.
— — —//—
Lit.: MIR 36 Rom 1/15v; RIC 5.1, p. 80, Rome 132

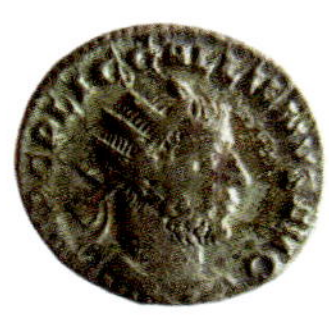 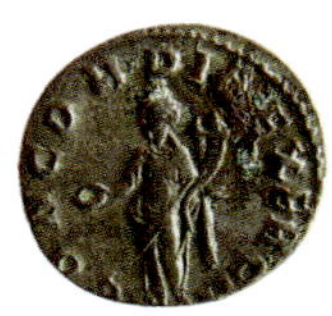

248. AR; 3,31 g.; 19,0 x 20,2 mm.; 12 h.; inv. n. 1555
(Obv. IMP C P LIC GALLIENVS AVG; Rev. CONCORDIA EXERCIT; — — —//—)

Antoninianus
Obv. IMP C P LIC GALLIENVS AVG. Radiated bust of emperor in cuirass looking right, seen from front.
Rev. VIRTVS AVGG. Virtus standing left, holding spear in right hand, leaning on shield set on ground.
— — —//—
Lit.: MIR 36 Rom 1/38v; RIC 5.1, p. 83, Rome 181

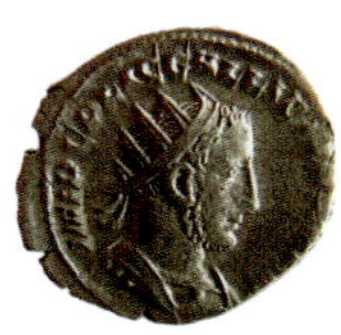 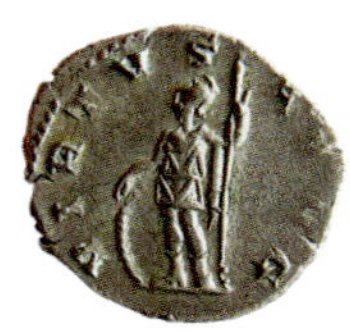

249. AR; 3,65 g.; 20,1 x 20,8 mm.; 6 h.; inv. n. 1556
(Obv. IMP C P LIC GALLIENVS [AVG]; Rev. VIRTVS – AVGG; — — —//—)

[27] RIC 5.1, p. 176, Mediolanum 513 records SECVR TEMPO.

254 – 256 A.D.

Antoninianus
Obv. IMP C P LIC GALLIENVS P F AVG. Radiated bust of emperor in cuirass looking right, seen from front.
Rev. LIBERALITAS AVGG. Liberalitas standing left, holding tessera in right hand and cornucopiae in left hand.
— — —//—
Lit.: MIR 36 Rom 2//66q; RIC 5.1, p. 81, Rome 148

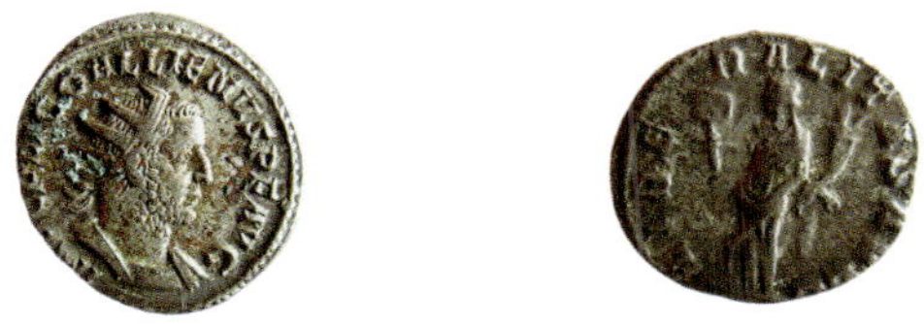

250. AR; 2,8 g.; 21,2 x 19,5 mm.; 5 h.; inv. n. 1557
(Obv. IMP C P LIC GALLIENVS P F AVG; Rev. LIBE-RALIT-AS AVGG; — — —//—)

Antoninianus
Obv. IMP C P LIC GALLIENVS P F AVG. Radiated bust of emperor in cuirass looking right, seen from front.
Rev. VICTORIA GERMANICA. Victory standing left, holding wreath in right hand and palm in left hand; at feet to left captive.
— — —//—
Lit.: MIR 36 Rom 2/80p; RIC 5.1, –

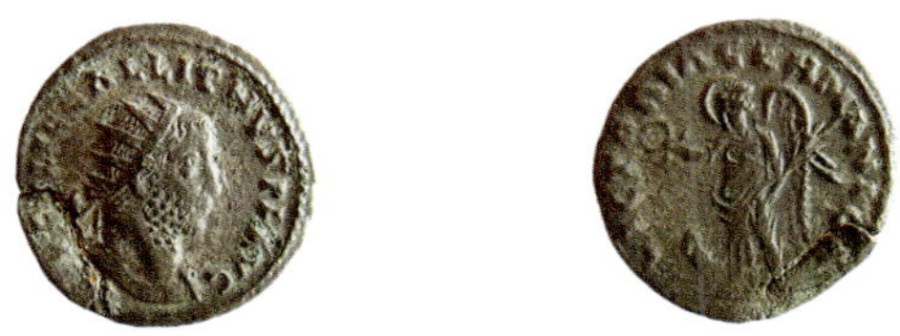

251. AR; 2,95 g.; 21,7 x 20,6 mm.; 12 h.; inv. n. 1558
(Obv. [IM]P C [P] LIC GALLIENVS P F AVG; Rev. VICTORIA GERMANICA; — — —//—)

260 – 261 A.D.

Antoninianus
Obv. GALLIENVS AVG. Radiated bust of emperor in cuirass and paludamentum looking right, seen from front.
Rev. VIRTVS AVG. Virtus standing left, holding globe in right hand and vertical spear in left hand.
P — —//—
Lit.: MIR 36 Rom 6^1/343m;[28] RIC 5.1, p. 158, Rome 317

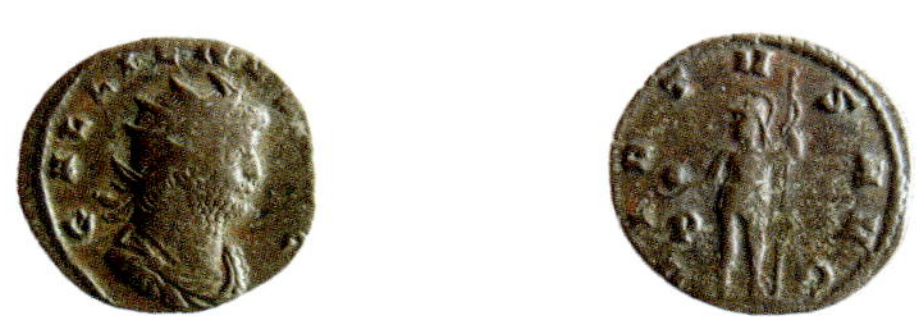

252. AE; 3,37 g.; 18,7 x 19,9 mm.; 6 h.; inv. n. 1559
(Obv. GALLIENVS AVG; Rev. VIRTV-S AVG; P — —//—)

Antoninianus
Obv. GALLIENVS AVG. Radiated bust of emperor in cuirass looking right, seen from front.
Rev. VIRTVS AVG. Virtus standing left, holding globe in right hand and vertical spear in left hand.
— — P//—
Lit.: MIR 36 Rom 6^1/344x; RIC 5.1, p. 158, Rome 317

[28] Unrecorded specimen to MIR 36; MIR records only plain bust or cuirassed bust.

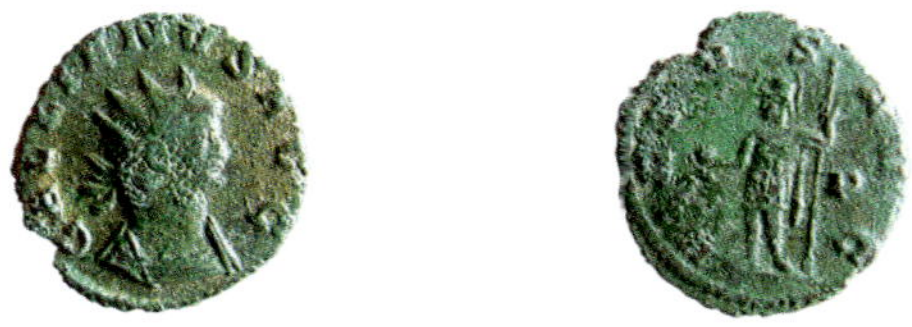

253. AE; 3,63 g.; 19,9 x 19,4 mm.; 6 h.; inv. n. 1560
(Obv. GALLIENVS AVG; Rev. VIRT-V-S – AV-G; — — P//—)

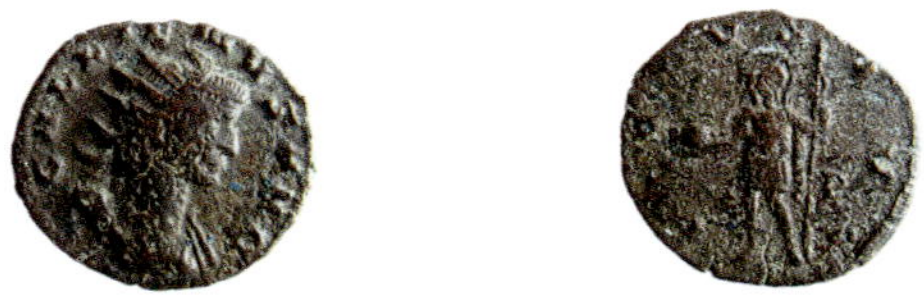

254. AE; 2,74 g.; 18,7 x 19,8 mm.; 12 h.; inv. n. 1561
(Obv. GALLIENVS AVG; Rev. VIRTVS – AVG; — — P//—)

Antoninianus
Obv. GALLIENVS AVG. Radiated bust of emperor in cuirass looking right, seen from front.
Rev. IOVI VLTORI. Jupiter walking left, head turned right, holding thunderbolt in right hand.
S — —//—
Lit.: MIR 36 Rom 6^1/348x; RIC 5.1, p. 150, Rome 221

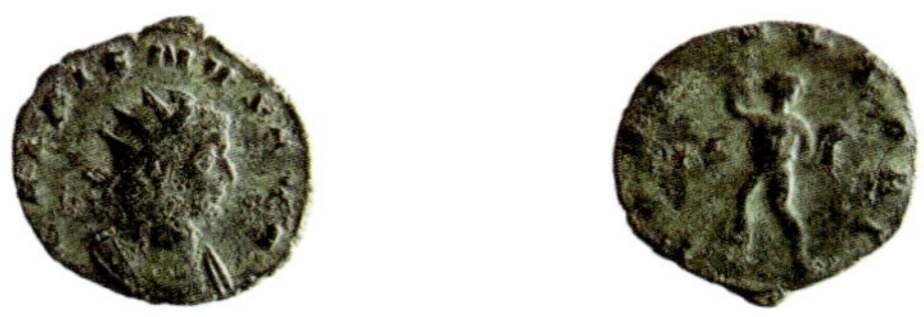

255. AE; 3,18 g.; 19,8 x 20,2 mm.; 6 h.; inv. n. 1562
(Obv. GALLIENVS AVG; Rev. IOVI – VLTORI; S — —//—)

Antoninianus
Obv. GALLIENVS AVG. Radiated bust of emperor looking right.
Rev. PAX AVG. Pax standing left, holding branch in right hand and transverse sceptre in left hand.
V — —//—
Lit.: MIR 36 Rom 6^1/366a ; RIC 5.1, p. 153, Rome 256 var.[29]

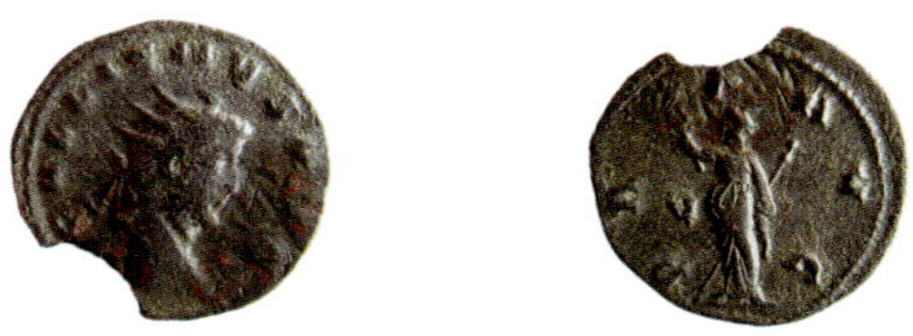

256. AE; 2,81 g.; 21,3 x 21,8 mm.; 6 h.; inv. n. 1563
(Obv. GALLIENVS AV[G]; Rev. PA-X AVG; V — —//—)

262 A.D.

Antoninianus
Obv. GALLIENVS AVG. Radiated bust of emperor looking right.
Rev. LIBERAL AVG. Liberalitas standing left, holding tessera in right hand and cornucopiae in left hand.
S — —//—
Lit.: MIR 36 Rom 7^1/470f; RIC 5.1, p. 151, Rome 227

[29] RIC 5.1, p. 153, Rome 256 records V right in field on the reverse.

257. AE; 1,96 g.; 16,5 x 16,5 mm.; 6 h.; inv. n. 1564
(Obv. [GALLIENVS AVG]; Rev. [LI]BE-RA-L [AVG]; S — —//—)

Antoninianus
Obv. GALLIENVS AVG. Radiated bust of emperor in cuirass looking right, seen from front.
Rev. AEQVITAS AVG. Aequitas standing left, holding scales in right hand and cornucopiae in left hand.
— — VI//—
Lit.: MIR 36 Rom 7^1/500q1; RIC 5.1, p. 144, Rome 159 var.[30]

258. AE; 3,16 g.; 18,6 x 18,2 mm.; 6 h.; inv. n. 1565
(Obv. GALLI[ENVS AV]G; Rev. AEQVITAS AVG; — — VI//—)

259. AE; 1,75 g.; 19,3 x 18,2 mm.; 12 h.; inv. n. 1566
(Obv. GALLIENVS AVG; Rev. AEQVI[TAS A]VG; — — VI//—)

264 – 267 A.D.

Antoninianus
Obv. GALLIENVS AVG. Radiated bust of emperor looking right.
Rev. MARTI PACIFERO. Mars standing left, holding branch in right hand, vertical spear and shield which rests on ground in left hand.
A — —//—
Lit.: MIR 36 Rom 9^1(1)/570a; RIC 5.1, p. 151, Rome 236

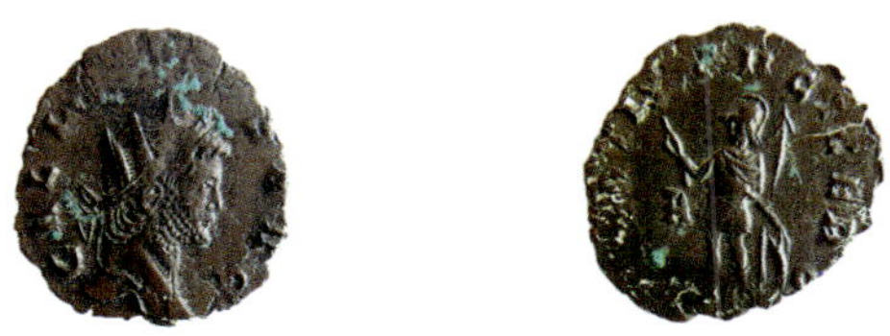

260. AE; 2 g.; 20,7 x 18,4 mm.; 6 h.; inv. n. 1567
(Obv. GALL[IENV]S AVG; Rev. [M]ARTI PACIFERO; A — —//—)

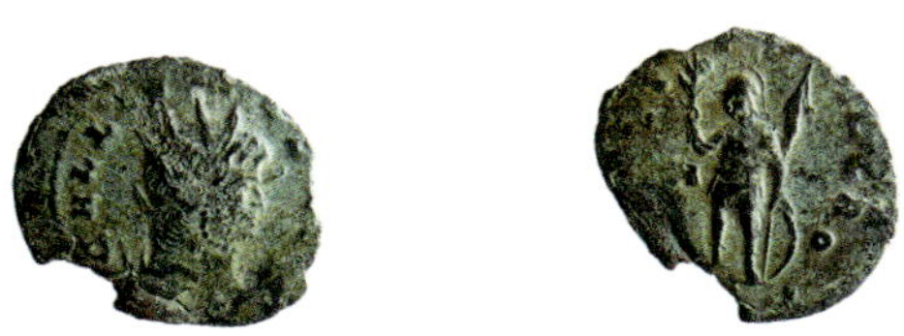

261. AE; 1,51 g.; 18,4 x 21,6 mm.; 11 h.; inv. n. 1568
(Obv. GALLI[ENV]S [AVG]; Rev. [MART]I – [PACI]F[E]RO; A — —//—)

30 RIC 5.1, p. 144, Rome 159 does not record VI in the field on the reverse.

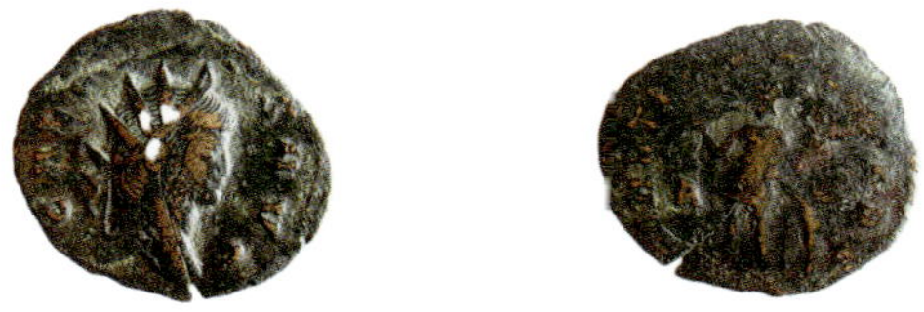

262. AE; 1,55 g.; 19,2 x 21,8 mm.; 12 h.; inv. n. 1569
(Obv. GALL[IENV]S AVG; Rev. MARTI – [PACIF]ERO; A — —//—)

263. AE; 2,18 g.; 17,8 x 19,1 mm.; 12 h.; inv. n. 1570
(Obv. GALLI[ENV]S AVG; Rev. M[ARTI PA]CIFERO; A — —//—)

Antoninianus
Obv. GALLIENVS AVG. Radiated bust of emperor looking right.
Rev. ABVNDANTIA AVG. Abundantia standing right, emptying cornucopiae.
B — —//—
Lit.: MIR 36 Rom 9^1(1)/574a; RIC 5.1, p. 144, Rome 157

264. AE; 2,33 g.; 18,1 x 18,4 mm.; 6 h.; inv. n. 1571
(Obv. GAL[LIENVS AV]G; Rev. [ABV]NDANTIA AVG; B — —//—)

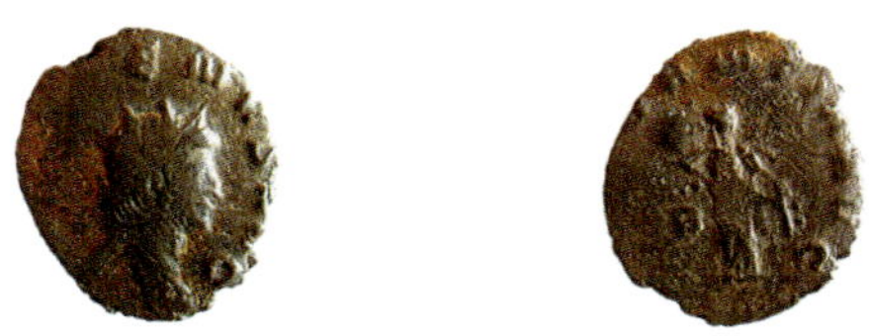

265. AE; 2,34 g.; 20,3 x 17,1 mm.; 6 h.; inv. n. 1572
(Obv. [GALLI]ENVS [AV]G; Rev. [ABVND]ANTIA AVG; B — —//—)

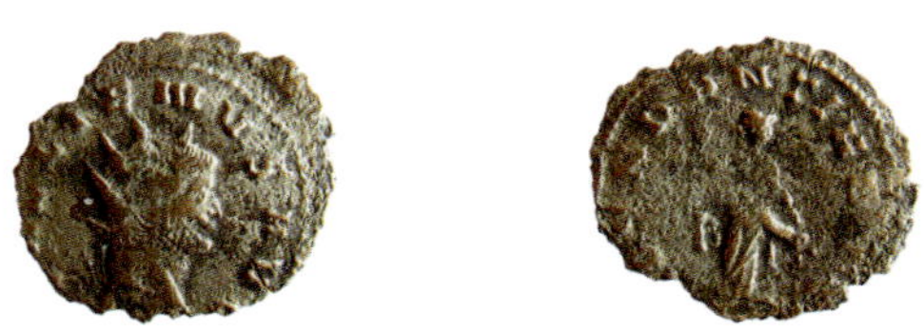

266. AE; 1,6 g.; 20,5 x 21,5 mm.; 7 h.; inv. n. 1573
(Obv. [G]ALLIENVS AVG; Rev. [A]BVNDANTIA AV[G]; B — —//—)

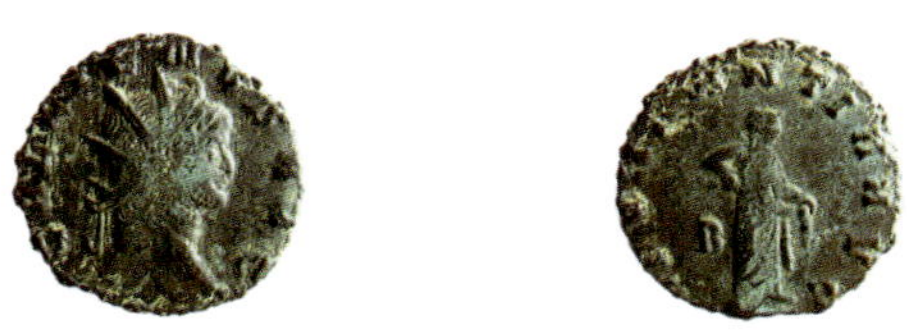

267. AE; 2,23 g.; 19,0 x 13,6 mm.; 12 h.; inv. n. 1574
(Obv. GALLIENVS AVG; Rev. ABVNDANTIA AVG; B — —//—)

Antoninianus
Obv. GALLIENVS AVG. Radiated bust of emperor looking right.
Rev. AETERNITAS AVG. Sol standing left, raising right hand, globe in left hand.
Γ — —//—
Lit.: MIR 36 Rom 9^1(1)/577a; RIC 5.1, p. 144, Rome 160

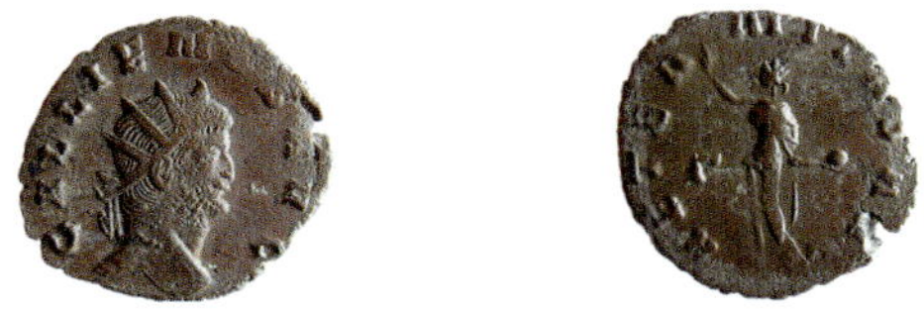

268. AE; 2,81 g.; 19,7 x 21,2 mm.; 6 h.; inv. n. 1575
(Obv. GALLIENVS AVG; Rev. AETER-NITAS AVG; Γ — —//—)

269. AE; 2,24 g.; 17,7 x 16,8 mm.; 7 h.; inv. n. 1576
(Obv. [GALLIENVS AVG]; Rev. [AETERNITA]S AVG; Γ — —//—)

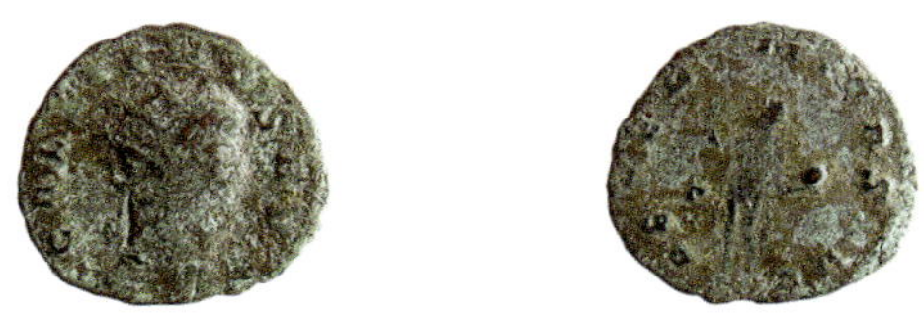

270. AE; 2,55 g.; 19,5 x 20,9 mm.; 12 h.; inv. n. 15.03
(Obv. GALLIENVS AVG; Rev. AETER-NITAS AVG; Γ — —//—)

Antoninianus
Obv. GALLIENVS AVG. Radiated bust of emperor in cuirass looking right, seen from front.
Rev. VBERITAS AVG. Uberitas standing left, holding purse in right hand and cornucopiae in left hand.
— — —//—
Lit.: MIR 36 Rom 9^1(1)/582w; RIC 5.1, p. 156, Rome 287 var.[31]

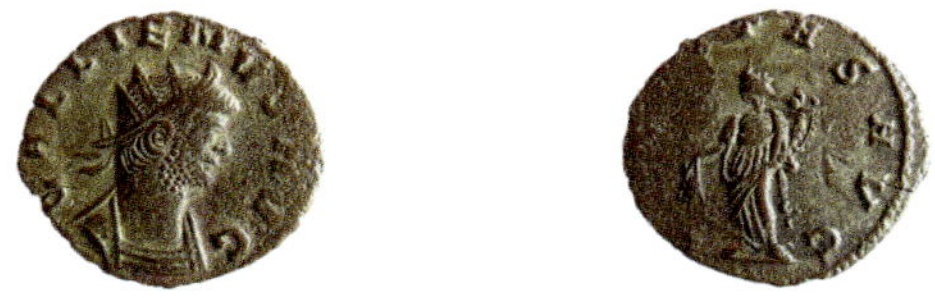

271. AE; 2,48 g.; 18,7 x 20,0 mm.; 12 h.; inv. n. 1577
(Obv. GALLIENVS AVG; Rev. V[BERI]TAS AVG; — — —//—)

Antoninianus
Obv. GALLIENVS AVG. Radiated bust of emperor looking right.
Rev. VBERITAS AVG. Uberitas standing left, holding purse in right hand and cornucopiae in left hand.
— — ε//—
Lit.: MIR 36 Rom 9^1(1)/583a; RIC 5.1, p. 156, Rome 287 var.[32]

[31] RIC 5.1, p. 156, Rome 287 records legend IMP GALLIENVS AVG in obverse.
[32] RIC 5.1, p. 156, Rome 287 records legend IMP GALLIENVS AVG in obverse and does not record ε in the field on the reverse.

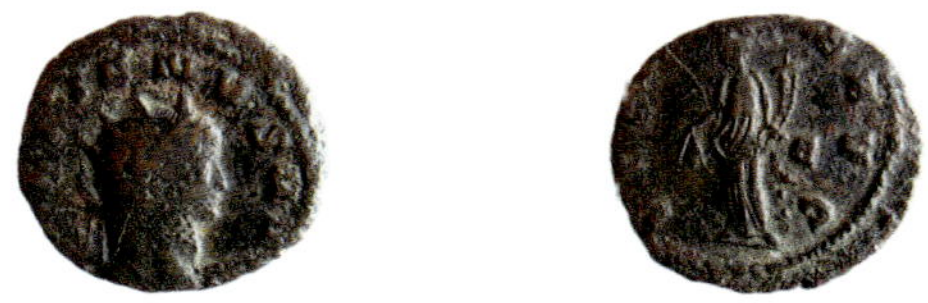

272. AE; 3,81 g.; 18,6 x 20,6 mm.; 6 h.; inv. n. 1578
(Obv. [G]ALLIENVS AV[G]; Rev. VBE[RITA]S AVG; — — ε//—)

273. AE; 2,34 g.; 17,9 x 18,5 mm.; 6 h.; inv. n. 1579
(Obv. GALLIENVS AVG; Rev. VBERITAS [AVG]; — — ε//—)

274. AE; 1,74 g.; 18,6 x 17,4 mm.; 12 h.; inv. n. 1580
(Obv. G[A]LLIENVS AVG; Rev. [VBER]ITAS AVG; — — ε//—)

Antoninianus
Obv. GALLIENVS AVG. Radiated bust of emperor looking right.
Rev. FORTVNA REDVX. Fortuna standing left, holding rudder in right hand and cornucopiae in left hand.
— — —//—
Lit.: MIR 36 Rom 9^1(1)/585a; RIC 5.1, p. 147, Rome 193 var.[33]

275. AE; 2,48 g.; 17,9 x 16,6 mm.; 11 h.; inv. n. 1581
(Obv. [GALLI]ENVS AVG; Rev. [FO]RTVNA RED[VX]; — — —//—)

Antoninianus
Obv. GALLIENVS AVG. Radiated bust of emperor looking right.
Rev. FORTVNA REDVX. Fortuna standing left, holding rudder in right hand and cornucopiae in left hand.
— — ς//—
Lit.: MIR 36 Rom 9^1(1)/586a; RIC 5.1, p. 147, Rome 193 var.[34]

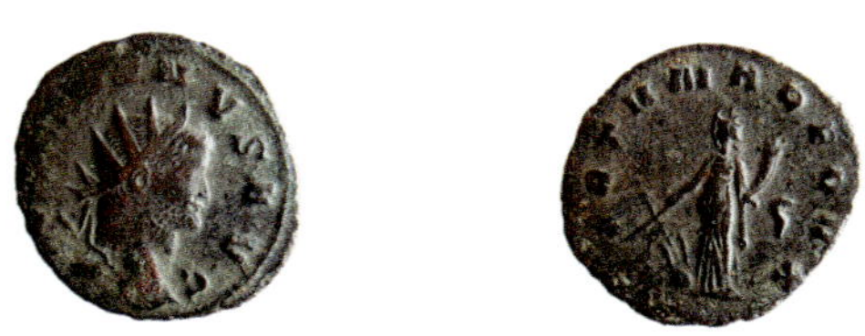

276. AE; 3,64 g.; 21,1 x 20,9 mm.; 6 h.; inv. n. 1582
(Obv. [GALLIE]NVS AVG; Rev. [FO]RTVNA REDVX; — — ς//—)

[33] RIC 5.1, p. 147, Rome 193 does not record radiated bust of emperor.
[34] RIC 5.1, p. 147, Rome 193 does not record radiated bust of emperor on the obverse and ς in field on the reverse.

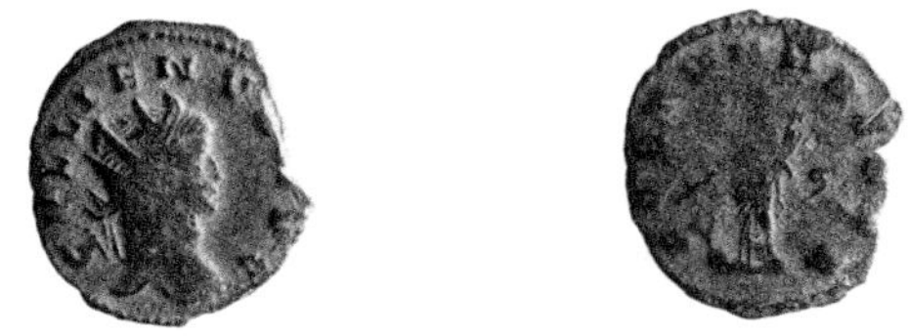

277. AE; 1,8 g.; 22,0 x 16,5 mm.; 6 h.; inv. n. 1583
(Obv. GALLIENVS [A]VG; Rev. FORTVNA REDVX; — — ς//—)

278. AE; 2,11 g.; 17,5 x 18,9 mm.; 6 h.; inv. n. 1584
(Obv. GALLIENVS AVG; Rev. FORTVNA REDVX; — — ς//—)

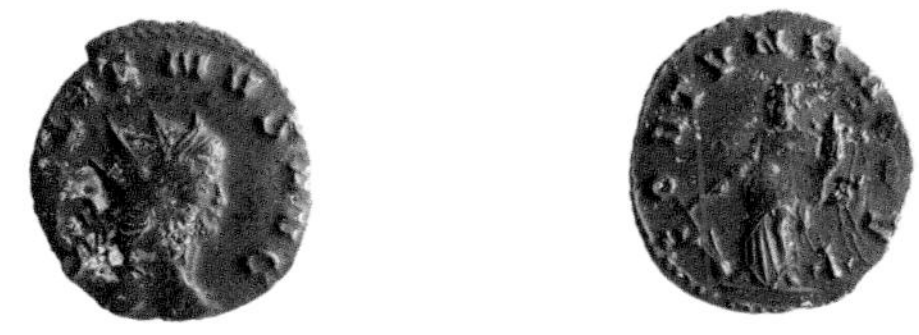

279. AE; 2,21 g.; 20,6 x 18,8 mm.; 12 h.; inv. n. 1585
(Obv. GALLIENVS AVG; Rev. F-ORTVNA R[ED]VX; — — ς//—)

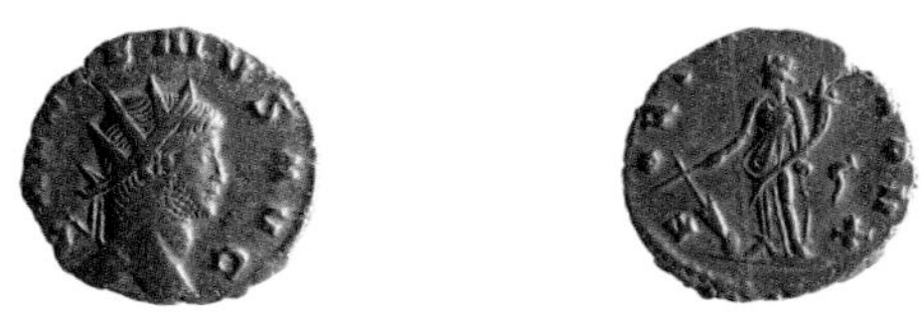

280. AE; 3 g.; 18,7 x 19,7 mm.; 12 h.; inv. n. 1586
(Obv. GALL[I]ENVS AVG; Rev. F-ORTV[NA R]EDVX; — — ς//—)

Antoninianus
Obv. GALLIENVS AVG. Radiated bust of emperor looking right.
Rev. VICTORIA AET. Victory standing left, holding wreath in right hand and palm in left hand.
Inv. Z — —//—
Lit.: MIR 36 Rom 9^1(1)/589a; RIC 5.1, p. 157, Rome 297 var.[35]

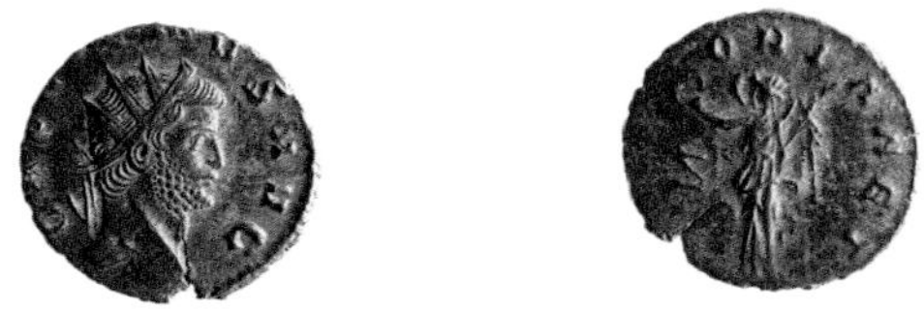

281. AE; 4,01 g.; 19,2 x 20,7 mm.; 11 h.; inv. n. 1587
(Obv. GALLIENVS AVG; Rev. VICT-ORI-A AET; Inv. Z — —//—)

Antoninianus
Obv. GALLIENVS AVG. Radiated bust of emperor looking right.
Rev. SECVRIT PERPET. Securitas standing front, legs crossed, head left, holding vertical sceptre in right hand and leaning on column with left elbow.
— — H//—
Lit.: MIR 36 Rom 9^1(1)/595a; RIC 5.1, p. 155, Rome 280

[35] RIC 5.1, p. 157, Rome 297 records Z on the reverse.

282. AE; 1,23 g.; 16,0 x 17,1 mm.; 1 h.; inv. n. 1588
(Obv. [GALLIENV]S AVG; Rev. SEC[VRIT P]ERPET; — — H//—)

283. AE; 2,67 g.; 18,5 x 18,1 mm.; 5 h.; inv. n. 1589
(Obv. GALLIENVS AVG; Rev. SECVR-IT PERPET; — — H//—)

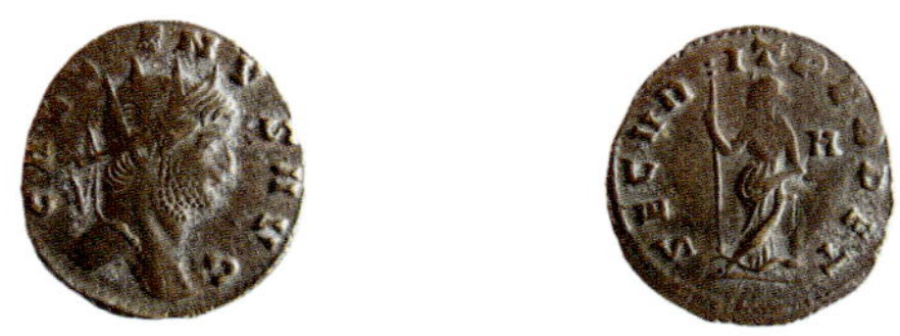

284. AE; 3,22 g.; 21,0 x 19,3 mm.; 12 h.; inv. n. 1590
(Obv. GALLIENVS AVG; Rev. SECVR-IT PERPET; — — H//—)

Antoninianus
Obv. GALLIENVS AVG. Radiated bust of emperor looking right.
Rev. FIDES MILITVM. Fides standing left, holding vertical standard in right hand and long vertical sceptre in left hand.
— — N//—
Lit.: MIR 36 Rom 9^1(1)/600a; RIC 5.1, p. 147, Rome 192a

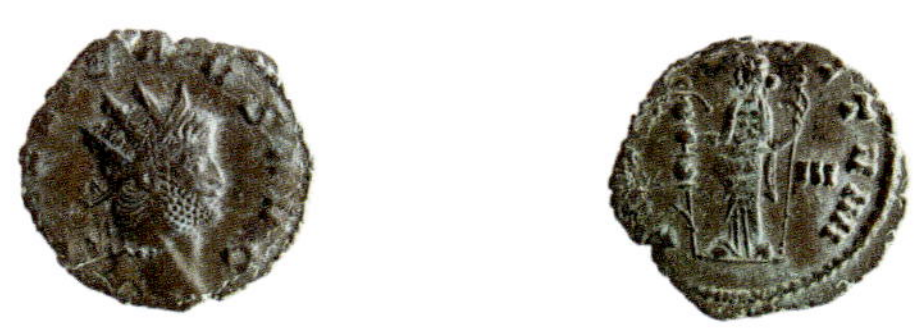

285. AE; 2,61 g.; 19,3 x 19,3 mm.; 4 h.; inv. n. 1591
(Obv. GALLIENVS AVG; Rev. FID[ES MI]LITVM; — — N//—)

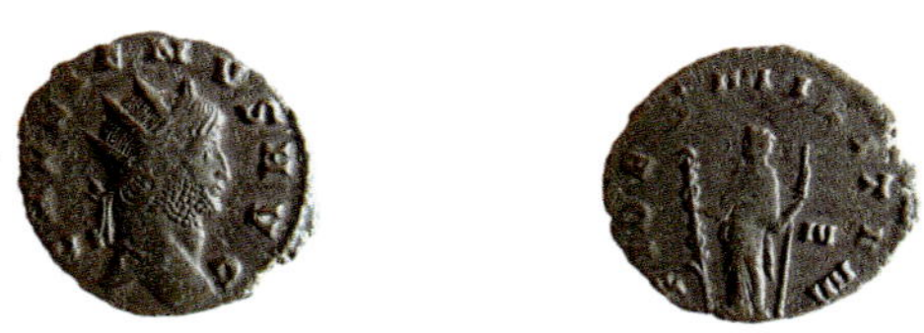

286. AE; 2,79 g.; 19,8 x 19,9 mm.; 6 h.; inv. n. 1592
(Obv. GALLIENVS AVG; Rev. FIDE-S MILITVM; — — N//—)

Antoninianus
Obv. GALLIENVS AVG. Radiated bust of emperor looking right.
Rev. PAX AVG. Pax standing left, holding branch in right hand and transverse sceptre in left hand.
— — Δ//—
Lit.: MIR 36 Rom 9^1(1)/604a; RIC 5.1, p. 153, Rome 256 var.[36]

[36] RIC 5.1, p. 153, Rome 256 does not record Δ right in field on the reverse.

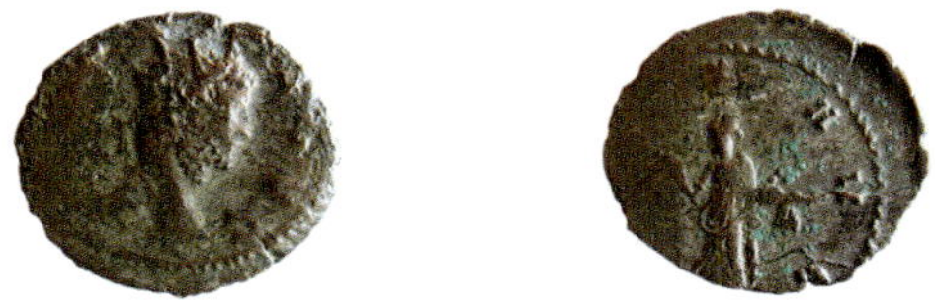

287. AE; 2,13 g.; 19,6 x 21,6 mm.; 6 h.; inv. n. 1593
(Obv. [GALLIENVS] AVG; Rev. [PA]X AVG; — — Δ//—)

Antoninianus
Obv. GALLIENVS AVG. Radiated bust of emperor looking right.
Rev. PAX AETERNA AVG. Pax standing left, holding branch in right hand and transverse sceptre in left hand.
Δ — —//—
Lit.: MIR 36 Rom 9[1](1)/609a; RIC 5.1, p. 153, Rome 253

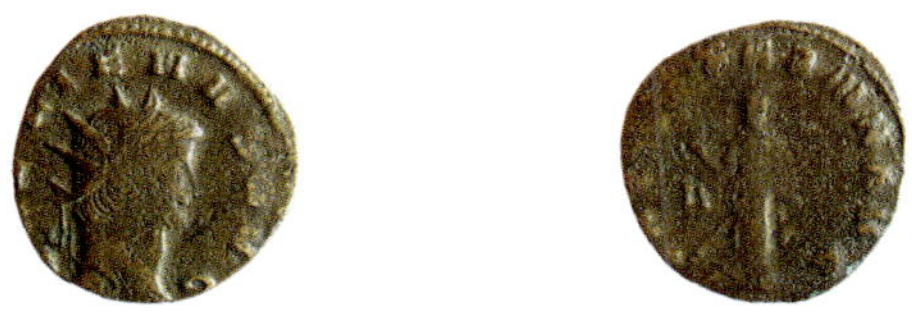

288. AE; 2,46 g.; 19,7 x 19,0 mm.; 12 h.; inv. n. 1594
(Obv. GALLIENVS AVG; Rev. PAX – AETERNA AVG; Δ — —//—)

Antoninianus
Obv. GALLIENVS AVG. Radiated bust of emperor looking right.
Rev. IOVIS STATOR. Jupiter standing front, head turned right, holding vertical sceptre in right hand and thunderbolt in left hand.
— — —//—
Lit.: MIR 36 Rom 9[1](1)/611a; RIC 5.1, p. 149, Rome 216

289. AE; 2,47 g.; 17,5 x 17,7 mm.; 6 h.; inv. n. 1595
(Obv. [GALLI]ENVS AVG; Rev. IOVIS – STATOR; — — —//—)

Antoninianus
Obv. GALLIENVS AVG. Radiated bust of emperor looking right.
Rev. IOVI CONSERVAT. Jupiter standing front, head turned left, holding thunderbolt in right hand and vertical sceptre in left hand.
N — —//—
Lit.: MIR 36 Rom 9[1](2)/625a; RIC 5.1, p. 149, Rome 210

290. AE; 2,22 g.; 16,5 x 19,1 mm.; 6 h.; inv. n. 1596
(Obv. GALLIE[NV]S [AVG]; Rev. IOVI C-O[NSERVAT]; N — —//—)

291. AE; 1,61 g.; 16,8 x 15,9 mm.; 6 h.; inv. n. 1597
(Obv. [GA]LLIENVS [AVG]; Rev. [IO]VI C-ONS-[ERVAT]; N — —//—)

Antoninianus
Obv. GALLIENVS AVG. Radiated bust of emperor looking right.
Rev. VIRTVS AVGVSTI. Virtus standing left, holding branch in right hand and vertical spear in left hand; right foot rests on helmet.
X — —//—
Lit.: MIR 36 Rom 9^{1}(2)/636a; RIC 5.1, p. 159, Rome 330 var.[37]

292. AE; 2,55 g.; 18,0 x 16,8 mm.; 7 h.; inv. n. 1598
(Obv. [GALL]IENVS AVG; Rev. [VIRTV]-S AVGVSTI; X — —//—)

Antoninianus
Obv. GALLIENVS AVG. Radiated bust of emperor looking right.
Rev. IOVI PROPVGNAT. Jupiter walking left, head turned right, holding thunderbolt in right hand.
XI — —//—
Lit.: MIR 36 Rom 9^{1}(2)/641a; RIC 5.1, p. 149, Rome 214

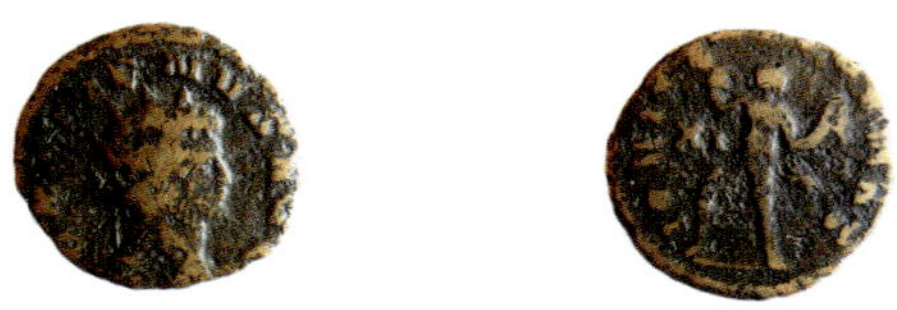

293. AE; 2,17 g.; 18,4 x 19,1 mm.; 6 h.; inv. n. 1599
(Obv. GALLIENVS AVG; Rev. IOVI PR[OP]VGNAT; XI — —//—)

Antoninianus
Obv. IMP GALLIENVS AVG. Radiated bust of emperor looking right.
Rev. PAX AETERNA AVG. Pax standing left, holding branch in right hand and transverse sceptre in left hand.
— — Δ//—
Lit.: MIR 36 Rom 9^{2}/679q1; RIC 5.1, p. 153, Rome 252 var.[38]

294. AE; 1,75 g.; 16,8 x 19,2 mm.; 12 h.; inv. n. 1600
(Obv. IMP GALLIENVS AVG; Rev. [PAX A]E – TERNA AVG; — — Δ//—)

[37] RIC 5.1, p. 159, Rome 330 records legend IMP CAES GALLIENVS AVG on the obverse.
[38] RIC 5.1, p. 153, Rome 252 does not record Δ right in field on the reverse.

267 – 268 A.D.

Antoninianus
Obv. GALLIENVS AVG. Radiated bust of emperor looking right.
Rev. SOLI CONS AVG. Pegasus flying right.
— — —//A
Lit.: MIR 36 Rom 10/712b; RIC 5.1, p. 155, Rome 283

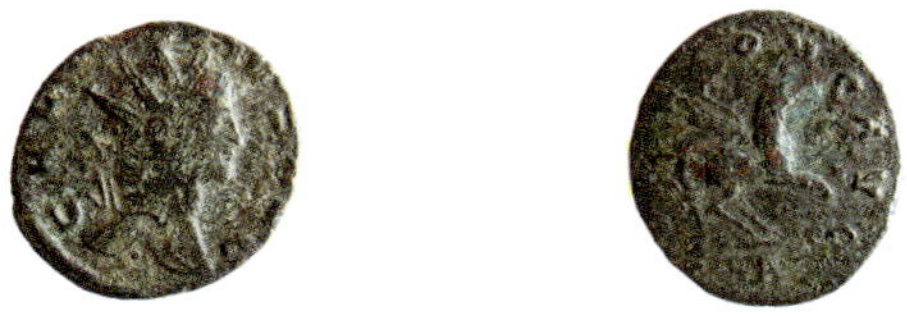

295. AE; 3,43 g.; 18,7 x 18,7 mm.; 11 h.; inv. n. 1601
(Obv. GALL[IEN]VS AVG; Rev. SOLI CONS AVG; — — —//A)

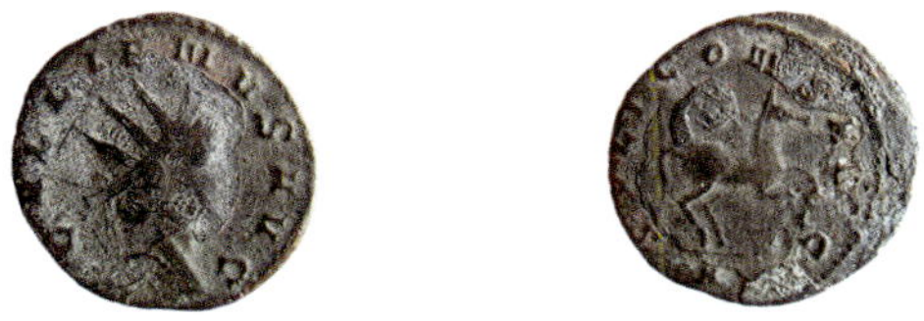

296. AE; 2,78 g.; 20,6 x 20,7 mm.; 12 h.; inv. n. 1602
(Obv. GALLIENVS AVG; Rev. SOLI CONS AV-G; — — —//A)

Antoninianus
Obv. GALLIENVS AVG. Radiated bust of emperor looking right.
Rev. LIBERO • P • CONS AVG. Lion walking left.
— — —//B
Lit.: MIR 36 Rom 10/713b; RIC 5.1, p. 151, Rome 230[39]

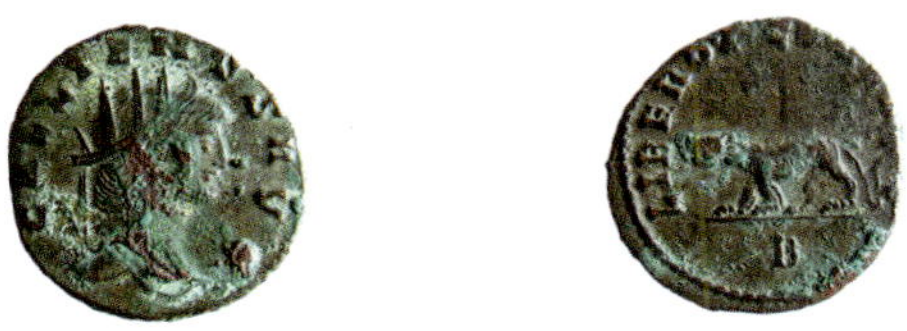

297. AE; 3,5 g.; 19,9 x 19,0 mm.; 12 h.; inv. n. 1603
(Obv. GALLIENVS AVG; Rev. LIBERO • P • CONS [AV]G; — — —//B)

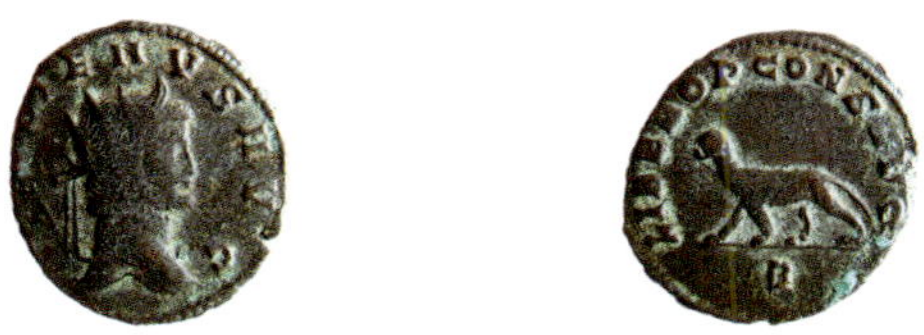

298.[40] AE; 3,56 g.; 21,0 x 18,3 mm.; 11 h.; inv. n. 1604
(Obv. G[A]LLIENVS AVG; Rev. LIBERO P CONS AVG; — — —//B)

Antoninianus
Obv. GALLIENVS AVG. Radiated bust of emperor looking right.
Rev. DIANAE CONS AVG. Antelope walking left.
— — —//Γ
Lit.: MIR 36 Rom 10/716b; RIC 5.1, p. 146, Rome 180 var.[41]

[39] RIC 5.1, p. 151, Rome 230 does not record dots in the legend on the reverse.
[40] This specimen is missing the dots in the legend on the reverse.
[41] RIC 5.1, p. 146, Rome 180 records obverse legend IMP GALLIENVS AVG.

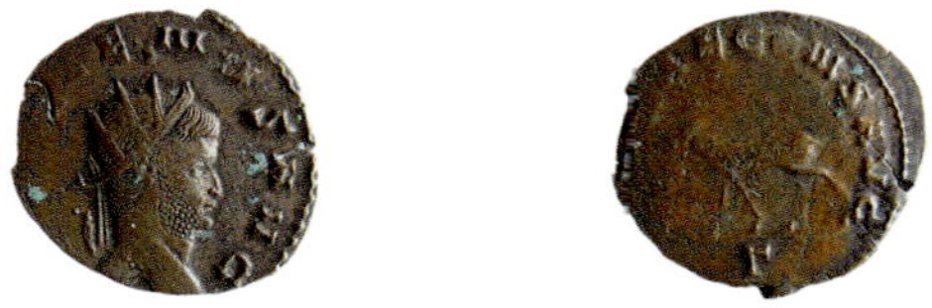

299. AE; 2,13 g.; 19,6 x 20,0 mm.; 5 h.; inv. n. 1605
(Obv. [GALLI]ENVS AVG; Rev. [DIAN]AE CONS AVG; — — —//Γ)

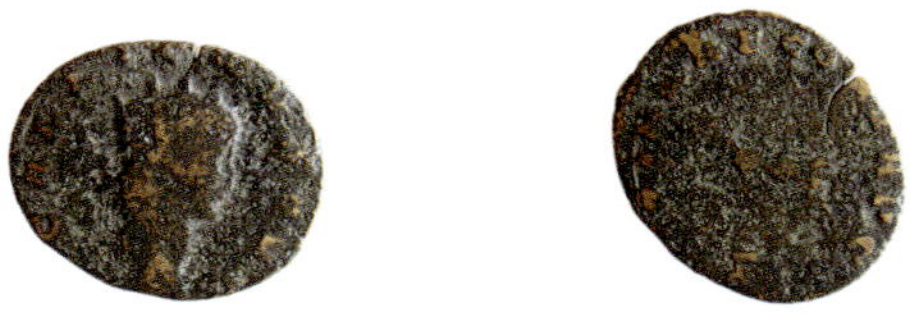

300. AE; 2,39 g.; 17,5 x 20,9 mm.; 11 h.; inv. n. 1606
(Obv. GALLIENVS AVG; Rev. DIANAE CONS AVG; — — —//Γ)

301. AE; 1,93 g.; 16,7 x 16,9 mm.; 12 h.; inv. n. 1607
(Obv. [GALL]IENVS AV[G]; Rev. DIAN-AE CONS [AVG]; — — —//[Γ])

302. AE; 2,09 g.; 18,2 x 17,9 mm.; 12 h.; inv. n. 1608
(Obv. [GALLIENV]S AVG; Rev. [D]IANAE CONS AVG; — — —//[Γ])

Antoninianus
Obv. IMP GALLIENVS AVG. Radiated bust of emperor looking right.
Rev. APOLLINI CONS AVG. Griffin walking left.
— — —//Δ
Lit.: MIR 36 Rom 10/718z; RIC 5.1, p. 145, Rome 165

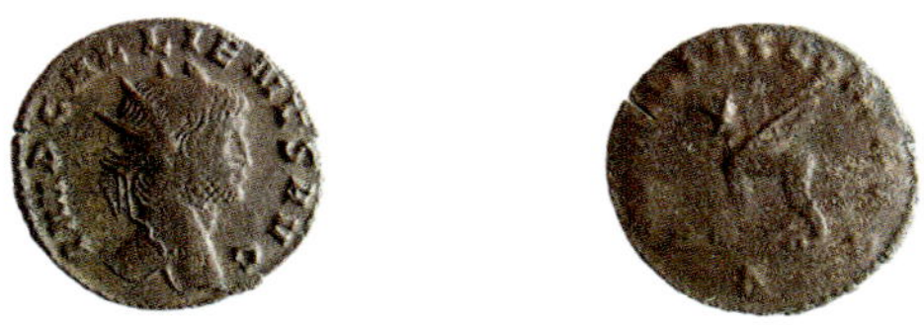

303. AE; 2,82 g.; 20,3 x 20,7 mm.; 10 h.; inv. n. 1609.
(Obv. IMP GALLIENVS AVG; Rev. APOLLINI CONS AVG; — — —//Δ)

Antoninianus
Obv. GALLIENVS AVG. Radiated bust of emperor looking right.
Rev. DIANAE CONS AVG. Doe walking right, head turned left.
— — —//ε
Lit.: MIR 36 Rom 10/728b; RIC 5.1, p. 146, Rome 177

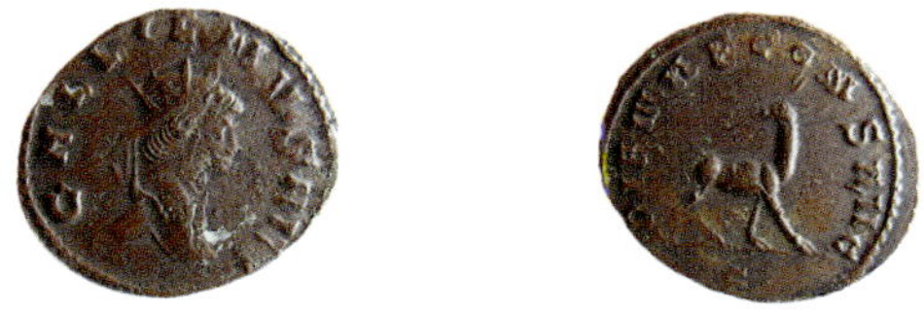

304. AE; 2,41 g.; 20,2 x 21,6 mm.; 12 h.; inv. n. 1610.
(Obv. GALLIENVS AVG; Rev. DIANAE CONS AVG; — — —//ε)

Antoninianus
Obv. IMP GALLIENVS AVG. Radiated bust of emperor looking right.
Rev. DIANAE CONS AVG. Doe walking right, head turned left.
— — —//•
Lit.: MIR 36 Rom 10/728z var.; RIC 5.1, p. 146, Rome 176

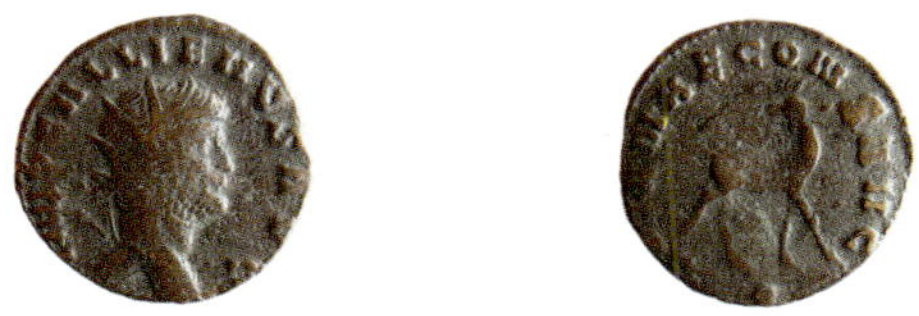

305.[42] AE; 3 g.; 19,6 x 19,7 mm.; 1 h.; inv. n. 1611.
(Obv. IMP GALLIENVS AVG; Rev. [D]IANAE CONS AVG; — — —//•)

Antoninianus
Obv. GALLIENVS AVG. Radiated bust of emperor looking right.
Rev. IOVI CONS AVG. Goat walking right.
— — —//ς
Lit.: MIR 36 Rom 10/731b; RIC 5.1, p. 149, Rome 207

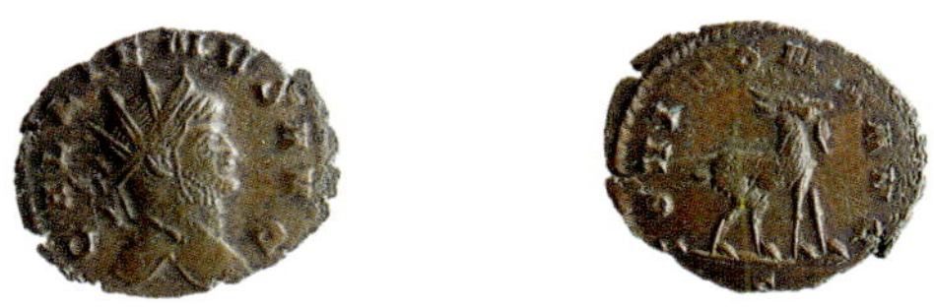

306. AE; 2,06 g.; 18,7 x 22,0 mm.; 6 h.; inv. n. 1612
(Obv. GALLIENVS AVG; Rev. IOVI CONS AVG; — — —//ς)

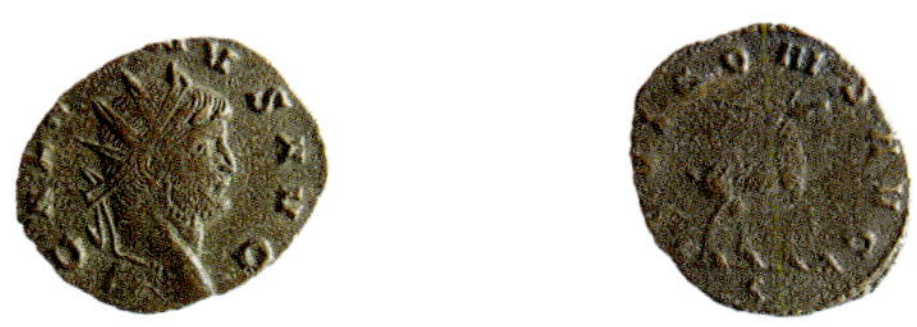

307. AE; 2,31 g.; 17,7 x 20,2 mm.; 10 h.; inv. n. 1613
(Obv. GALL[IE]NVS AVG; Rev. IOVI CONS AVG; — — —//ς)

Antoninianus
Obv. GALLIENVS AVG. Radiated bust of emperor looking right.
Rev. APOLLINI CONS AVG. Centaur walking left, holding globe in right hand and rudder over left shoulder.
— — —//Z
Lit.: MIR 36 Rom 10/733b; RIC 5.1, p. 145, Rome 164

---

42 • in the exerque on reverse could be the letter ε.

308. AE; 1,95 g.; 17,1 x 18,2 mm.; 4 h.; inv. n. 1614
(Obv. [G]ALLIENVS [AVG]; Rev. APOLLINI C[ONS AVG]; — — —//Z)

Antoninianus
Obv. GALLIENVS AVG. Radiated bust of emperor looking right.
Rev. APOLLINI CONS AVG. Centaur walking right, aiming bow and arrow held in both hands.
— — —//Z
Lit.: MIR 36 Rom 10/735b; RIC 5.1, p. 145, Rome 163

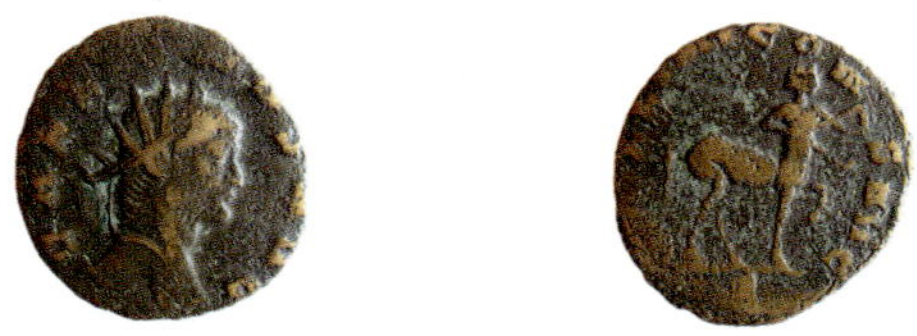

309. AE; 2,74 g.; 20,5 x 19,3 mm.; 6 h.; inv. n. 1615
(Obv. GALL[I]ENVS AVG; Rev. [APO]LLINI CON-S AVG; — — —//Z)

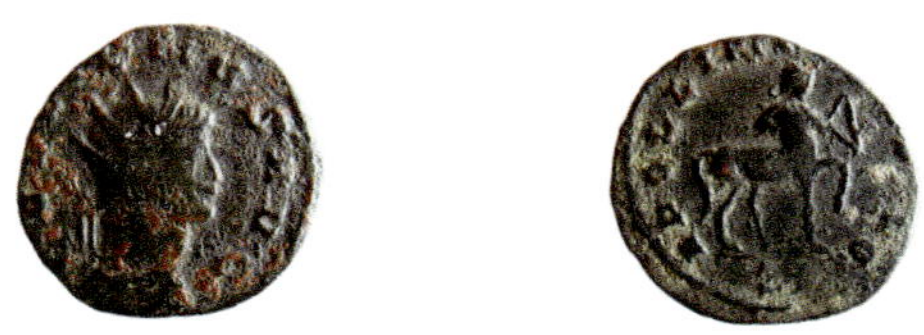

310. AE; 2,67 g.; 19,8 x 20,0 mm.; 12 h.; inv. n. 1616
(Obv. GALLIENVS AVG; Rev. APOLLINI [CON]S [A]VG; — — —//Z)

Antoninianus
Obv. IMP GALLIENVS AVG. Radiated bust of emperor looking right.
Rev. APOLLINI CONS AVG. Centaur walking right, aiming bow and arrow held in both hands.
— — —//Z
Lit.: MIR 36 Rom 10/735z; RIC 5.1, p. 145, Rome 163 var.[43]

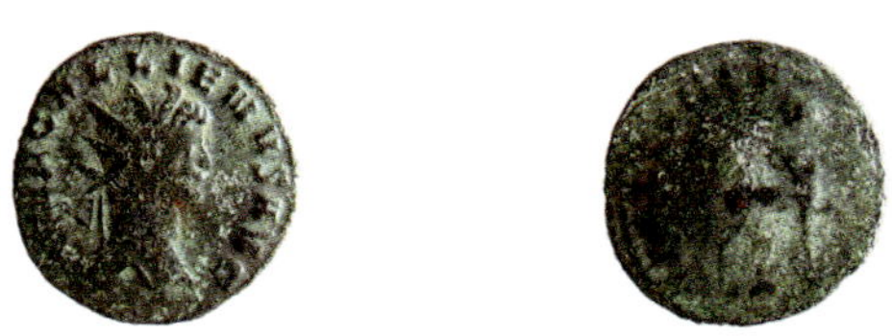

311. AE; 2,54 g.; 20,6 x 19,6 mm.; 6 h.; inv. n. 1617
(Obv. [IM]P GALLIENVS AVG; Rev. APOLLINI CO[NS AVG]; — — —//[Z])

Antoninianus
Obv. GALLIENVS AVG. Radiated bust of emperor looking right.
Rev. APOLLINI CONS AVG. Centaur walking left, holding globe in right hand and rudder over left shoulder.
— — —//H
Lit.: MIR 36 Rom 10/738b; RIC 5.1, p. 145, Rome 164

[43] RIC 5.1, p. 145, Rome 163 records obverse legend GALLIENVS AVG.

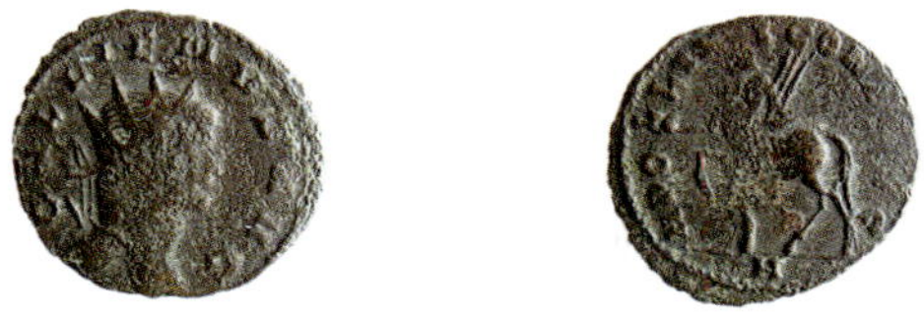

312. AE; 3,32 g.; 19,8 x 21,1 mm.; 7 h.; inv. n. 1618
(Obv. GALLIENVS AVG; Rev. APOLLIN-I CONS [AV]G; — — —//H)

313. AE; 3,06 g.; 19,3 x 18,5 mm.; 11 h.; inv. n. 1619
(Obv. [GAL]LIENVS AVG; Rev. [APO]LLINI CONS A[VG]; — — —//[H])

314. AE; 2,81 g.; 19,0 x 18,3 mm.; 12 h.; inv. n. 1620
(Obv. [GA]LLIENVS AVG; Rev. A[POL]LINI CONS A[VG]; — — —//H)

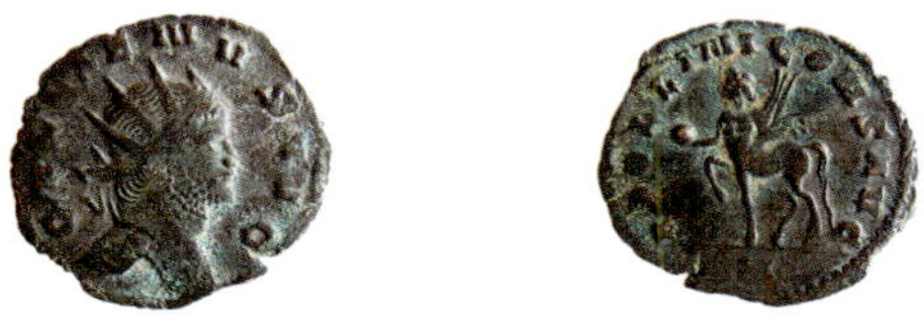

315. AE; 2,26 g.; 20,3 x 21,5 mm.; 12 h.; inv. n. 1621
(Obv. GALLIENVS AVG; Rev. APOLLINI CONS AVG; — — —//H)

Antoninianus
Obv. GALLIENVS AVG. Radiated bust of emperor looking right.
Rev. NEPTVNO CONS AVG. Hippocamp right.
— — —//N
Lit.: MIR 36 Rom 10/743b; RIC 5.1, p. 152, Rome 245

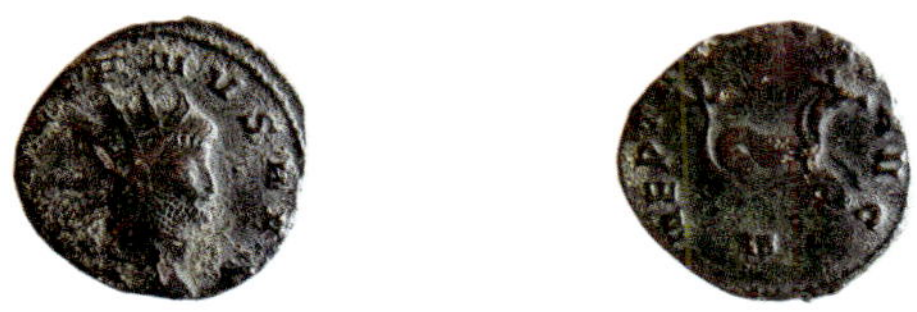

316. AE; 3,38 g.; 18,6 x 19,0 mm.; 6 h.; inv. n. 1622
(Obv. [GA]LLIENVS AVG; Rev. NEPTVNO CONS AVG; — — —//N)

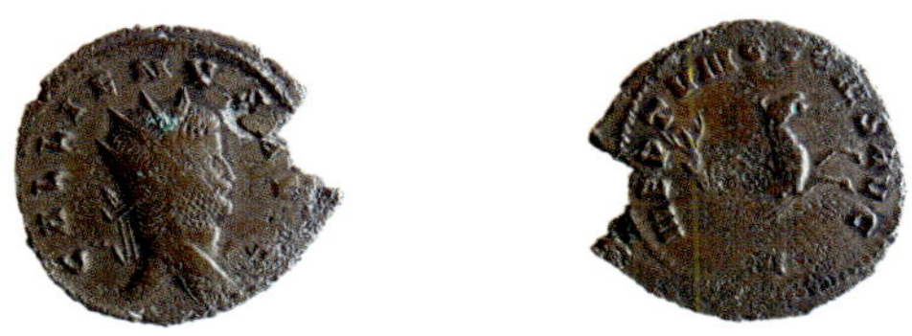

317. AE; 3,62 g.; 21,7 x 19,4 mm.; 12 h.; inv. n. 1623
(Obv. GALLIENVS AVG; Rev. NEPTVNO CONS AVG; — — —//N)

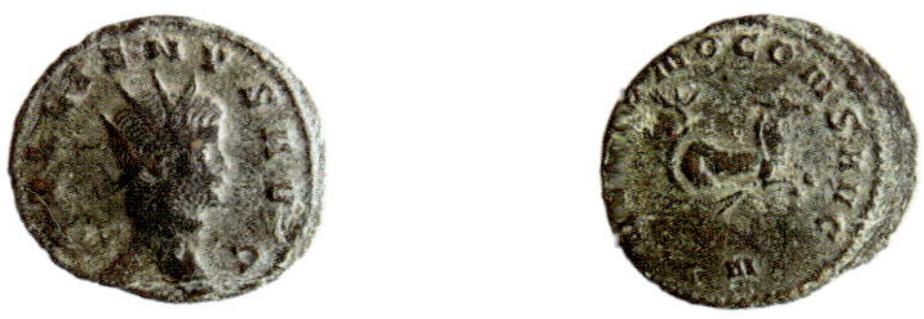

318. AE; 3,49 g.; 20,3 x 22,0 mm.; 12 h.; inv. n. 1624
(Obv. GALLIENVS AVG; Rev. NEPTVNO CONS AVG; — — —//N)

Antoninianus
Obv. GALLIENVS AVG. Radiated bust of emperor looking right.
Rev. DIANAE CONS AVG. Stag walking left.
— — —//X
Lit.: MIR 36 Rom 10/744b; RIC 5.1, p. 146, Rome 179

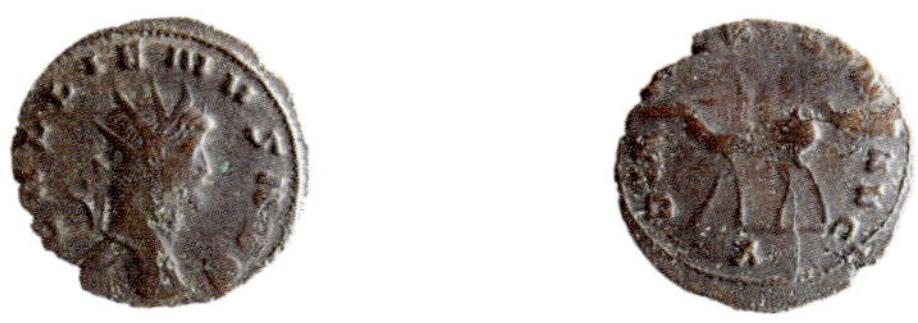

319. AE; 3,19 g.; 21,5 x 21,3 mm.; 6 h.; inv. n. 1625
(Obv. GALLIENVS AVG; Rev. DIA-[NAE] CONS AVG; — — —//X)

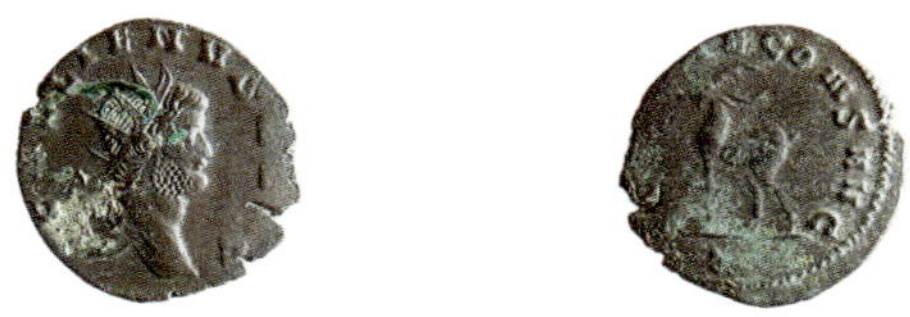

320. AE; 3,1 g.; 20,6 x 19,6 mm.; 12 h.; inv. n. 1626
(Obv. GALLIENVS AVG; Rev. [DIANA]E CONS AVG; — — —//X)

Antoninianus
Obv. GALLIENVS AVG. Radiated bust of emperor looking right.
Rev. DIANAE CONS AVG. Stag walking right.
— — —//X
Lit.: MIR 36 Rom 10/745b; RIC 5.1, p. 146, Rome 179

321. AE; 2,37 g.; 20,2 x 18,7 mm.; 12 h.; inv. n. 1627
(Obv. GALLIENVS A[VG]; Rev. DI[ANAE] C-ONS AVG; — — —//[X])

Antoninianus
Obv. GALLIENVS AVG. Radiated bust of emperor looking right.
Rev. DIANAE CONS AVG. Gazelle walking right.
— — —//XI
Lit.: MIR 36 Rom 10/747b; RIC 5.1, p. 146, Rome 181

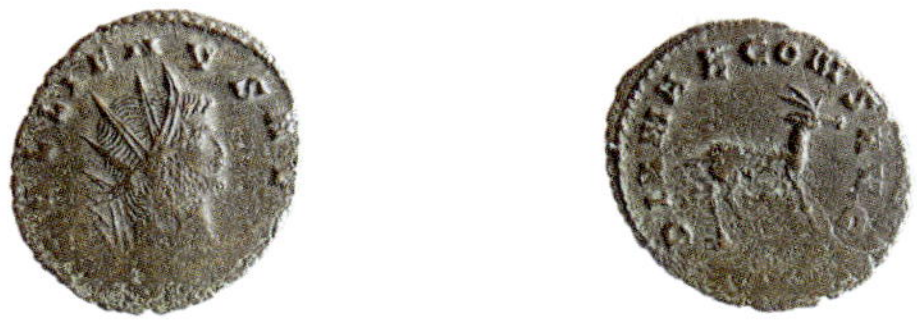

322. AE; 3,53 g.; 21,4 x 20,6 mm.; 12 h.; inv. n. 1628
(Obv. GALLIENVS AV[G]; Rev. DIANAE CONS AVG; — — —//[XI])

Antoninianus
Obv. IMP GALLIENVS AVG. Radiated bust of emperor looking right.
Rev. DIANAE CONS AVG. Gazelle walking right.
— — —//ε
Lit.: MIR 36 Rom 10/747z var.; RIC 5.1, p. 146, Rome 181 var.[44]

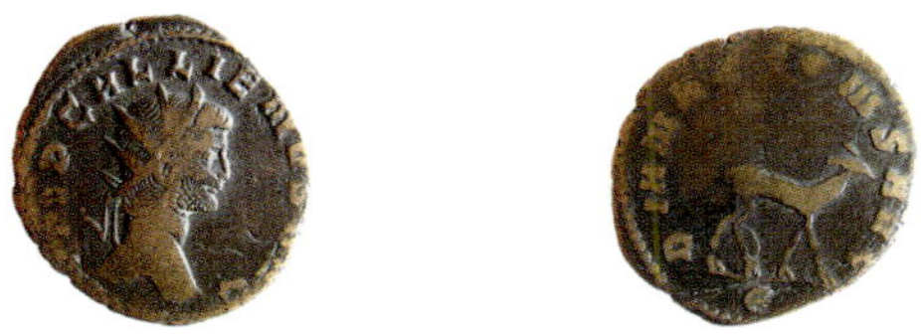

323. AE; 2,79 g.; 21,4 x 20,3 mm.; 6 h.; inv. n. 1629
(Obv. IMP GALLIENVS AVG; Rev. DIANAE CONS AVG; — — —//ε; MIR 36 Rom 10/747z var.)

Antoninianus
Obv. GALLIENVS AVG. Radiated bust of emperor looking right.
Rev. DIANAE CONS AVG. Gazelle walking left.
— — —//XII
Lit.: MIR 36 Rom 10/750b; RIC 5.1, p. 146, Rome 179

324. AE; 1,63 g.; 18,2 x 19,9 mm.; 6 h.; inv. n. 1630
(Obv. GALLIENVS AVG; Rev. DIANA[E CO]NS AVG; — — —//XII)

Antoninianus
Obv. GALLIENVS AVG. Radiated bust of emperor in cuirass looking right, seen from front.
Rev. DIANAE CONS AVG. Gazelle walking left.
— — —//XII
Lit.: MIR 36 Rom 10/750u; RIC 5.1, p. 146, Rome 181

325. AE; 2,09 g.; 17,8 x 18,5 mm.; 12 h.; inv. n. 1631
(Obv. GALLIENVS AVG; Rev. DIANAE CONS AVG; — — —//[XII])

[44] Nor MIR 36 Rom 10/747b, even RIC 5.1, p. 146, Rome 181 does not mention obverse legend IMP GALLIENVS AVG and ε in the reverse exerque.

Antoninianus
Obv. GALLIENVS AVG. Radiated bust of emperor looking right with paludamentum on each shoulder.
Rev. DIANAE CONS AVG. Gazelle walking right.
— — —//XII
Lit.: MIR 36 Rom 10/751e var.;[45] RIC 5.1, p. 146, Rome 181

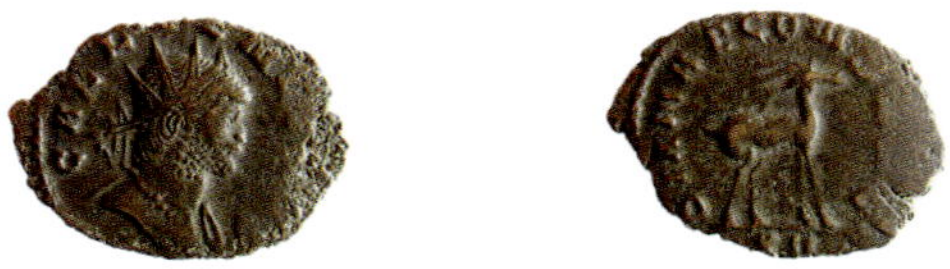

326. AE; 2,07 g.; 17,7 x 22,7 mm.; 6 h.; inv. n. 1632
(Obv. GALLIENVS [AV]G; Rev. DIANAE CONS AVG; — — —//XII)

Siscia

263 – 264 A.D.

Antoninianus
Obv. GALLIENVS AVG. Radiated bust of emperor looking right.
Rev. PROVIDEN AVG. Providentia standing left, holding baton in right hand and cornucopiae in left hand; at feet to left globe.
— — —//—
Lit.: MIR 36 Sis 1/1399i; RIC 5.1, p. 182, Siscia 580

327. AE; 2,97 g.; 18,9 x 19,5 mm.; 6 h.; inv. n. 1633
(Obv. GALLIENVS AVG; Rev. PROVIDEN AVG; — — —//—)

266 – 267 A.D.

Antoninianus
Obv. GALLIENVS AVG. Radiated bust of emperor looking right.
Rev. AEQVIT AVG. Aequitas standing left, holding scales in right hand and cornucopiae in left hand.
— — —//—
Lit.: MIR 36 Sis 3/1424i; RIC 5.1, p. 180, Siscia 553

328. AE; 3,16 g.; 18,4 x 18,9 mm.; 1 h.; inv. n. 1634
(Obv. GALLIENVS AVG; Rev. A-EQ[VIT] AVG; — — —//—)

[45] MIR does not have this type of depiction of emperor on the averse, it only mentions two variations – a plain bust looking right with one band on its shoulder and a bust in armour looking left, seen from the front, with one band on its shoulder, i.e., MIR Rom 10/751b or MIR Rom 10/751t.

329. AE; 3,63 g.; 19,4 x 19,6 mm.; 6 h.; inv. n. 1635
(Obv. GALLIENVS AVG; Rev. A-EQVIT AVG; — — —//—)

Antoninianus
Obv. GALLIENVS AVG. Radiated bust of emperor looking right.
Rev. PAX AVG. Pax standing left, holding branch in right hand and transverse sceptre in left hand.
— — —//—
Lit.: MIR 36 Sis 3/1441i; RIC 5.1, p. 182, Siscia 575

330. AE; 3,2 g.; 18,9 x 18,0 mm.; 12 h.; inv. n. 1636
(Obv. [GALLIE]NVS AVG; Rev. PA-X A-VG; — — —//—)

267 – 268 A.D.

Antoninianus
Obv. GALLIENVS AVG. Radiated bust of emperor looking right.
Rev. PROVI AVG. Providentia standing left, holding baton in right hand and cornucopiae in left hand; at feet to left globe.
— — —//—
Lit.: MIR 36 Sis 4/1461b; RIC 5.1, p. 182, Siscia 580

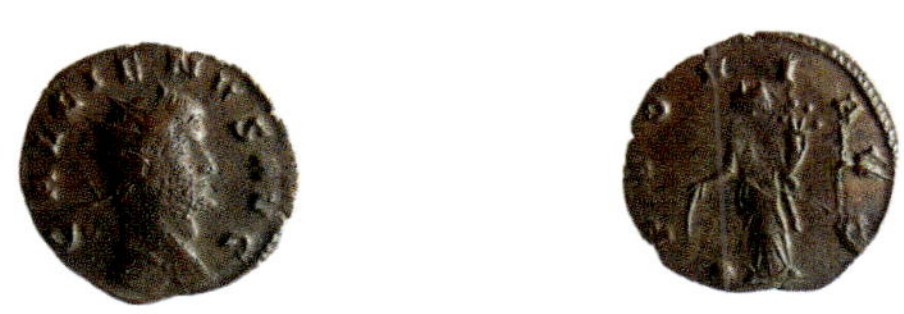

331. AE; 2,11 g.; 18,6 x 19,4 mm.; 12 h.; inv. n. 1637
(Obv. GALLIENVS AVG; Rev. PROV-I – AVG; — — —//—)

Antoninianus
Obv. GALLIENVS AVG. Radiated bust of emperor looking right.
Rev. PAX AVG. Pax standing left, holding branch in right hand and transverse sceptre in left hand.
S — I//—
Lit.: MIR 36 Sis 5/1472b; RIC 5.1, p. 182, Siscia 575

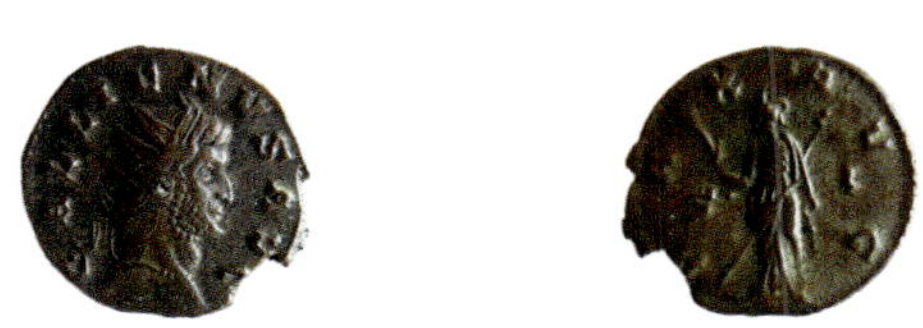

332. AE; 3,35 g.; 19,0 x 19,8 mm.; 12 h.; inv. n. 1638
(Obv. GALLIENVS AVG; Rev. PA-X – AVG; S — I//—)

Antoninianus
Obv. GALLIENVS AVG. Radiated bust of emperor looking right.
Rev. PROVI AVG. Providentia standing left, holding baton in right hand and cornucopiae in left hand; at feet to left globe.
II — —//—
Lit.: MIR 36 Sis 6/1476b var.; RIC 5.1, p. 182, Siscia 580 var.[46]

333. AE; 1,97 g.; 16,8 x 17,7 mm.; 6 h.; inv. n. 1639
(Obv. [GALLIENV]S AVG; Rev. [PROV]I AVG; II — —//—)

Antoninianus
Obv. GALLIENVS AVG. Radiated bust of emperor looking right.
Rev. SALVS AVG. Salus feeding snake rising from altar.
— — P//—
Lit.: MIR 36 Sis 9/1497b; RIC 5.1, p. 182, Siscia 581

334. AE; 4,28 g.; 18,1 x 19,7 mm.; 6 h.; inv. n. 1640
(Obv. [GALLIEN]VS AVG; Rev. [SA]LVS AVG; — — P//—)

Antiochia

253 – 256 A.D.

Antoninianus
Obv. IMP C P LIC GALLIENVS AVG. Radiated bust of emperor in cuirass and paludamentum looking right, seen from rear.
Rev. VICTORIA AVGG. Victory standing front, head turned left, holding wreath in right hand and palm in left hand.
— — —//—
Lit.: MIR 36 Ant 2/1574d; RIC 5.1, –

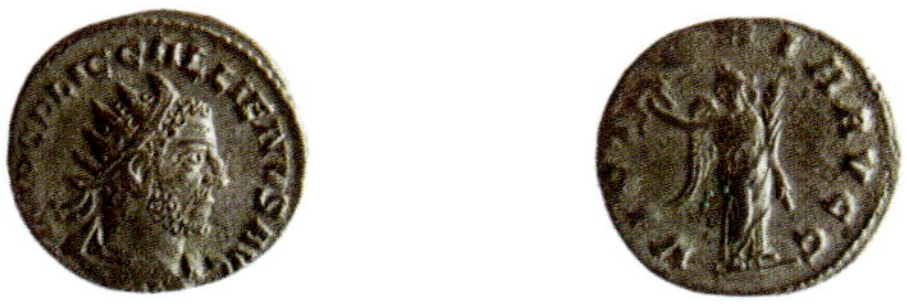

335. AE; 3,38 g.; 19,8 x 21,0 mm.; 6 h.; inv. n. 1641
(Obv. IMP C P LIC GALLIENVS AVG; Rev. VICT-ORIA AVGG; — — —//—)

[46] MIR 36 Sis 6/1476b describes II on the reverse only in the right segment. So does RIC 5.1, p. 182, Siscia 580.

257 – 260 A.D.

Antoninianus
Obv. IMP GALLIENVS AVG. Radiated bust of emperor in cuirass looking right, seen from front.
Rev. VICTORIA GERMAN. Emperor standing left, holding globe in right hand and vertical spear in left hand is crowned by Victory standing right, holding palm in left hand.
— — —//—
Lit.: MIR 36 Ant 5/1603b; RIC 5.1, p. 104, Mint of Asia 452 var.[47]

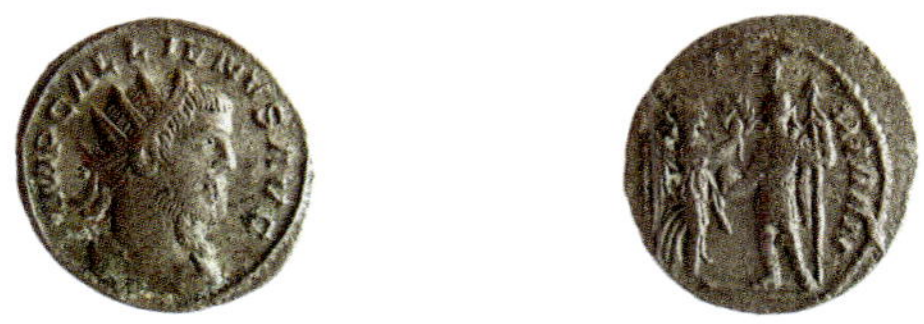

336. AE; 3,3 g.; 21,0 x 20,9 mm.; 7 h.; inv. n. 1642
(Obv. IMP GALLIENVS AVG; Rev. [VICT]OR[IA] GE-RMAN; — — —//—)

266 – 268 A.D.

Antoninianus
Obv. GALLIENVS AVG. Radiated bust of emperor in cuirass looking right, seen from front.
Rev. FORTVNA REDVX. Fortuna standing left, holding caduceus in right hand and cornucopiae in left hand.
— — —//VIIC•
Lit.: MIR 36 Ant 13a/1640b; RIC 5.1, p. 185, Mint of Asia 613

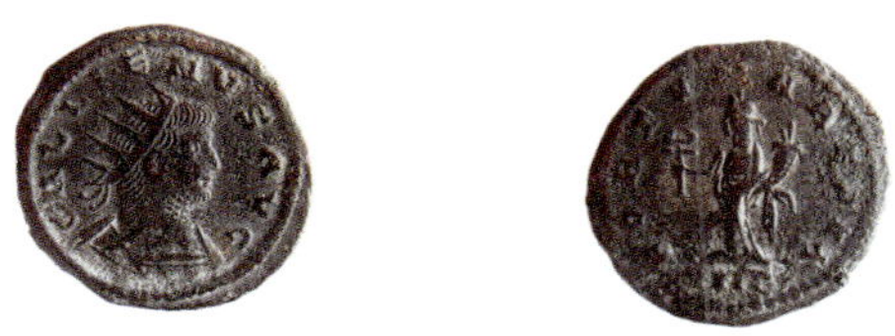

337. AE; 3,9 g.; 20,4 x 20,7 mm.; 12 h.; inv. n. 18.26
(Obv. GALLIENVS AVG; Rev. FORTVNA REDVX; — — —//[V]II[C•])

Samosata

256 – 260 A.D.

Antoninianus
Obv. IMP C P LIC GALLIENVS P F AVG. Radiated bust of emperor in cuirass and paludamentum looking right, seen from rear.
Rev. PIETAS AVGG. Emperor standing right, holding transverse sceptre in left hand, clasping right hand with another emperor, who stands left and holds transverse sword in left hand; between them altar.
— — —//—
Lit.: MIR 36 Sam 2/1684m; RIC 5.1, p. 103, Mint of Asia 446 var.[48]

[47] RIC V.I, S. 104, mint of Asia 452 records S * on the reverse.
[48] RIC V.I, S. 103, mint of Asia 446 records different mint marks in the reverse field.

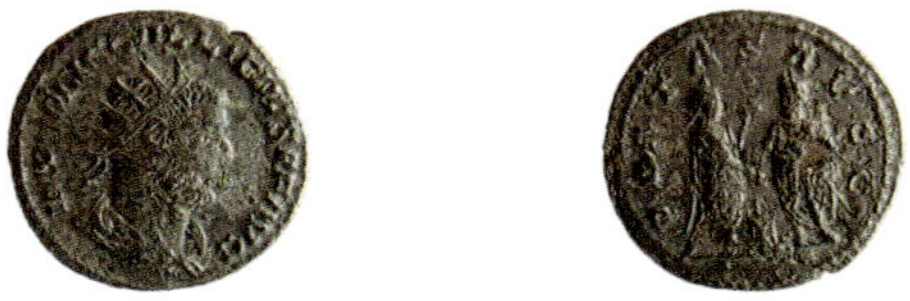

338. AE; 3,74 g.; 20,0 x 21,0 mm.; 12 h.; inv. n. 1643
(Obv. IMP C P LIC GALLIENVS P F AVG; Rev. PIETAS AVGG; — — —//—)

VALERIANUS II.
SON OF GALLIENUS
(CAESAR 255 – 258 A.D.)

Colonia Agrippinensium

Mid 258 A.D.

Antoninianus
Obv. DIVO VALERIANO CAES. Radiated bust of emperor in paludamentum looking right, seen from rear.
Rev. PIETAS AVG(G). Sacrificial implements, variously arranged.
— — —//—
Lit.: MIR 36 Col 1/908e var.; RIC 5.1, p. 116, Lugdunum 48e var.

339.[49] AR; 2,57 g.; 17,4 x 19,1 mm.; 6 h.; inv. n. 1644
(Obv. DIVO V[ALER]IANO C[AES]; Rev. [PI]ETAS AVG[(G)]; — — —//—)

Roma

254 – 260 A.D.

Antoninianus
Obv. P C L VALERIANVS NOB CAES. Radiated bust of emperor in cuirass and paludamentum looking right, seen from rear.
Rev. PIETAS AVGG. Sacrificial implements, variously arranged.
— — —//—
Lit.: MIR 36 Rom 2–5/248k; RIC 5.1, p. 118, Rome 20

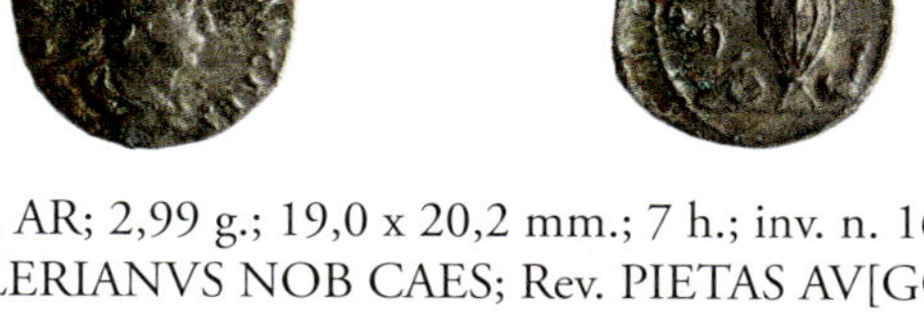

340. AR; 2,99 g.; 19,0 x 20,2 mm.; 7 h.; inv. n. 1645
(Obv. [P C] L VALERIANVS NOB CAES; Rev. PIETAS AV[GG]; — — —//—)

[49] A hybrid coinage – for more details see Lužický 2007, p. 141–150.

SALONINA
WIFE OF GALLIENUS
(AUGUSTA 254 – 268 A.D.)

Colonia Agrippinensium

257 – 258 A.D.

Antoninianus
Obv. SALONINA AVG. Diademed and draped bust of empress on crescent looking right.
Rev. VENVS FELIX. Venus seated left, holding apple in right hand and transverse sceptre in left hand; to left small person.
— — —//—
Lit.: MIR 36 Col 1/898c; RIC 5.1, p. 108, Lugdunum 7

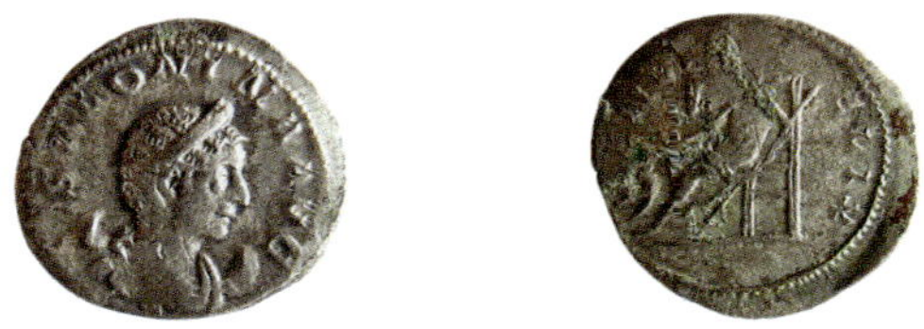

341. AR; 3,1 g.; 22,1 x 23,2 mm.; 6 h.; inv. n. 1646
(Obv. SALONINA AVG; Rev. VENV-S [F]-ELIX; — — —//—)

Mediolanum

263 – 264 A.D.

Antoninianus
Obv. SALONINA AVG. Diademed and draped bust of empress on crescent looking right.
Rev. VESTA. Vesta standing left, holding patera in right hand and sceptre in left hand.
— — —//—
Lit.: MIR 36 Med 4^2/1174dd2; RIC 5.1, p. 198, Mediolanum 68

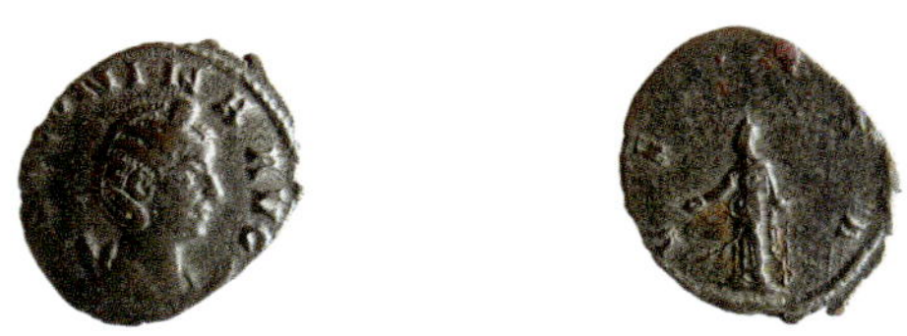

342. AE; 2,01 g.; 20,7 x 19,7 mm.; 6 h.; inv. n. 1647
(Obv. SALONINA AVG; Rev. VESTA; — — —//—)

Roma

253 – 257 A.D.

Antoninianus
Obv. SALONINA AVG. Diademed and draped bust of empress on crescent looking right.
Rev. IVNO REGINA. Juno standing left, holding patera in right hand and long vertical sceptre in left hand.
— — —//—
Lit.: MIR 36 Rom 1–4/227b; RIC 5.1, p. 111, Rome 29

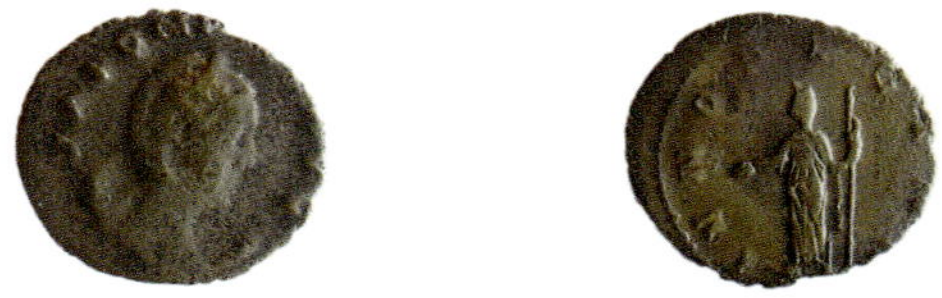

343. AE; 2,8 g.; 18,8 x 20,8 mm.; 6 h.; inv. n. 1648
(Obv. SALONI[NA] AVG; Rev. IVNO REGINA; — — —//—)

344. AE; 1,88 g.; 18,0 x 19,8 mm.; 7 h.; inv. n. 1649
(Obv. SALONINA AVG; Rev. IVNO REGINA; — — —//—)

345. AE; 2,7 g.; 17,5 x 16,0 mm.; 11 h.; inv. n. 1650
(Obv. SALONIN[A AVG]; Rev. [IVNO RE]GINA; — — —//—)

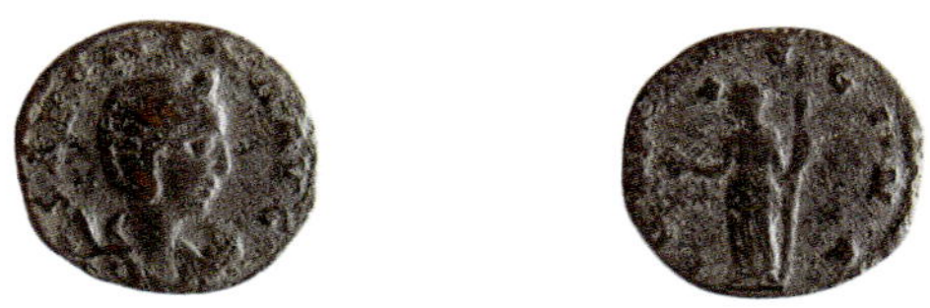

346. AE; 2,51 g.; 19,1 x 21,0 mm.; 12 h.; inv. n. 18.27
(Obv. SALONINA AVG; Rev. IV[NO R]EGINA; — — —//—)

254 – 257 A.D.

Antoninianus
Obv. SALONINA AVG. Diademed and draped bust of empress on crescent looking right.
Rev. PIETAS AVGG. Pietas seated left, right arm outstretched to two small children who stand at Pietas's feet, to left, looking up to her; Pietas holds long vertical sceptre in left hand.
— — —//—
Lit.: MIR 36 Rom 2–4/229b; RIC 5.1, p. 111, Rome 35 var.[50]

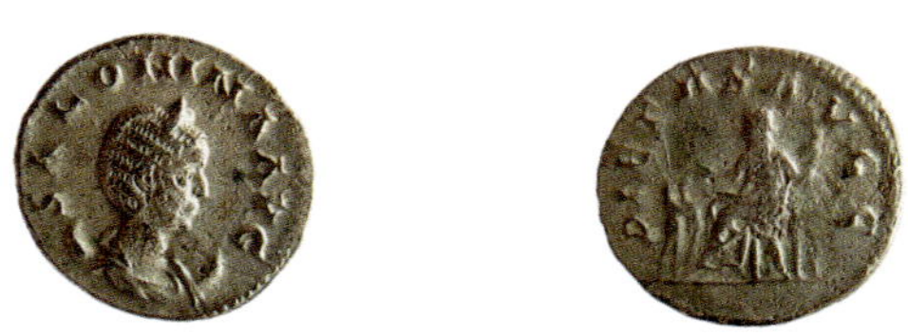

347. AR; 3,48 g.; 20,5 x 21,4 mm.; 6 h.; inv. n. 1651
(Obv. SALONINA AVG; Rev. PIETAS AVGG; — — —//—)

[50] RIC V.I, S. 111, Rome 35 notes 3 childern in reverse.

Antoninianus
Obv. SALONINA AVG. Diademed and draped bust of empress on crescent looking right.
Rev. VENVS VICTRIX. Venus standing left, holding apple in right hand and vertical sceptre in left hand; to left small person.
— — —//—
Lit.: MIR 36 Rom 2–4/233b; RIC 5.1, p. 194, Rome 30 var.[51]

348. AE; 3,47 g.; 17,4 x 19,1 mm.; 6 h.; inv. n. 1652
(Obv. SALONINA AVG; Rev. [VE]NVS VI[C]TRI[X]; — — —//—)

264 – 267 A.D.

Antoninianus
Obv. SALONINA AVG. Diademed and draped bust of empress on crescent looking right.
Rev. FECVNDITAS AVG. Fecunditas standing left, holding cornucopiae in left hand; at feet to left stands a small child.
— — Δ//—
Lit.: MIR 36 Rom 9[1](1)/580aa; RIC 5.1, p. 192, Rome 5

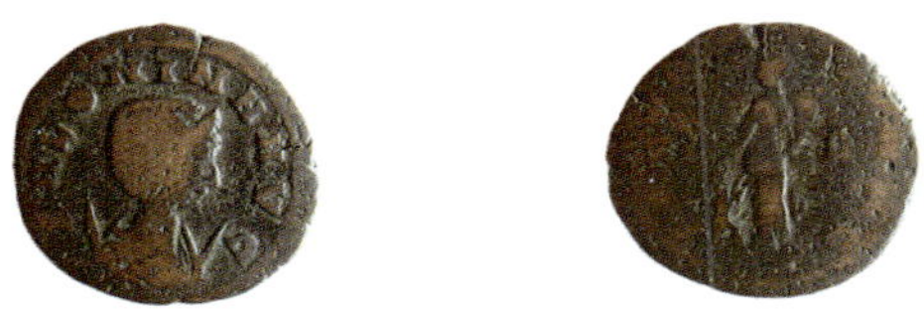

349. AE; 2,24 g.; 19,6 x 20,1 mm.; 12 h.; inv. n. 1653
(Obv. SALONINA AVG; Rev. F[ECVNDITAS AV]G; — — Δ//—)

267 – 268 A.D.

Antoninianus
Obv. COR SALONINA AVG. Diademed and draped bust of empress on crescent looking right.
Rev. IVNONI CONS AVG. Stag walking left.
— — —//Δ
Lit.: MIR 36 Rom 10/725cc; RIC 5.1, p. 193, Rome 16

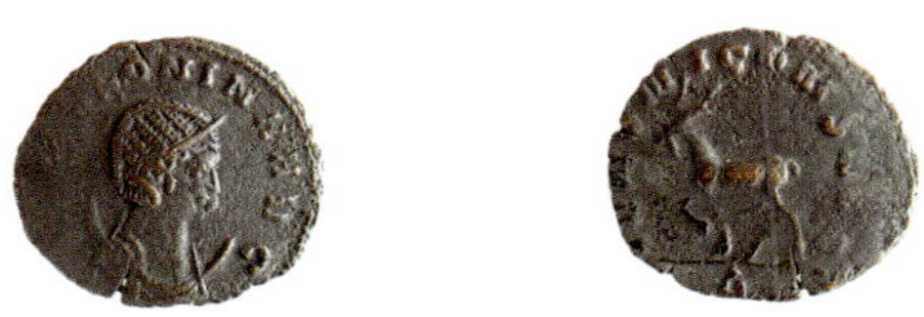

350. AE; 2,64 g.; 19,1 x 21,3 mm.; 12 h.; inv. n. 1654
(Obv. [COR SA]LONINA AVG; Rev. IVNONI CONS AVG; — — —//Δ)

[51] RIC V.I, S. 194, Rome 30 records different mint marks in the reverse field.

Siscia

267 – 268 A.D.

Antoninianus
Obv. SALONINA AVG. Diademed and draped bust of empress on crescent looking right.
Rev. PIETAS AVG. Pietas standing left, with right hand sacrificing over altar to left and holding box in left hand.
— — —//—
Lit.: MIR 36 Sis 4/1470r; RIC 5.1, p. 199, Siscia 79

351. AE; 1,88 g.; 17,8 x 17,8 mm.; 12 h.; inv. n. 1655
(Obv. SALONINA AVG; Rev. PIET-AS AVG; — — —//—)

Samosata

260 A.D.

Antoninianus
Obv. SALONINA AVG. Diademed and draped bust of empress on crescent looking right.
Rev. ROMAE AETERNAE. Emperor standing right, receiving Victory from Roma, seated on shield left, holding vertical spear in left hand.
— — —//—
Lit.: MIR 36 Sam 3b/1701i; RIC 5.1, p. 115, Mint of Asia 67

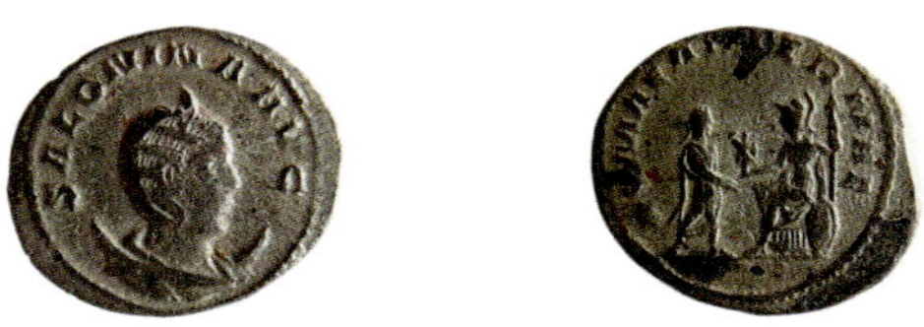

352. AE; 3,39 g.; 20,0 x 22,6 mm.; 12 h.; inv. n. 1656
(Obv. SALONINA AVG; Rev. ROMAE AETER-NAE; — — —//—)

Antoninianus
Obv. CORN SALONINA AVG. Diademed and draped bust of empress on crescent looking right.
Rev. CONCORIDIA AVGG. Emperor standing right, clasping right hand with another emperor standing left.
— * —//—
Lit.: MIR 36 Sam 3d/1706s; RIC 5.1, p. 114, Mint of Asia 63

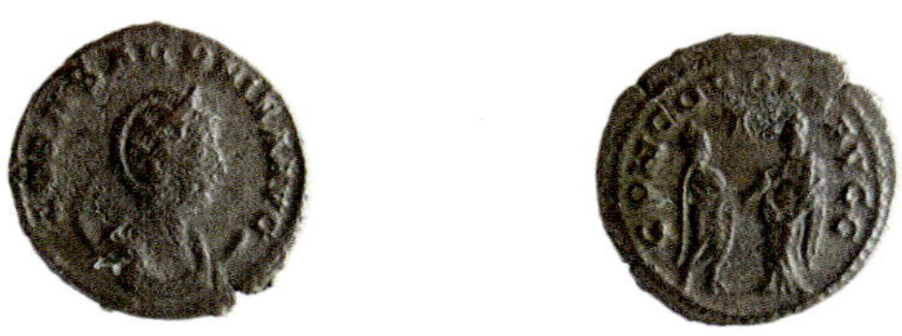

353. AE; 4,08 g.; 20,9 x 20,7 mm.; 6 h.; inv. n. 1657
(Obv. CORN SALONINA AVG; Rev. CONCORIDIA AVGG; — * —//—)

CLAUDIUS II. GOTHICUS
(268 – 270 A.D.)

Mediolanum

c. September 268 – Mid 269 A.D.

Antoninianus
Obv. IMP CLAVDIVS P F AVG. Radiated bust of emperor in cuirass and paludamentum looking right, seen from rear.
Rev. SPES PVBLICA. Spes walking left, holding flower in right hand and raising skirt with left hand.
— — —//P
Lit.: RIC temp n° 26; NOR. 1004/CUN. 2240; RIC 5.1, p. 224, Mediolanum 168 var.[52]

354. AE; 3,69 g.; 18,7 x 17,9 mm.; 12 h.; inv. n. 1658
(Obv. IMP CLA[VDIVS] P F AVG; Rev. SPES – P-VBLICA; — — —//P)

Mid of 269 – Spring 270 A.D.

Antoninianus
Obv. IMP CLAVDIVS P F AVG. Radiated bust of emperor in cuirass and paludamentum looking right, seen from rear.
Rev. VIRTVS AVG. Mars walking right, holding transverse spear in right hand and trophy over left shoulder in left hand.
— — —//P
Lit.: RIC temp n° 51; NOR. 1020/CUN. 2254; RIC 5.1, p. 225, Mediolanum 172 var.[53]

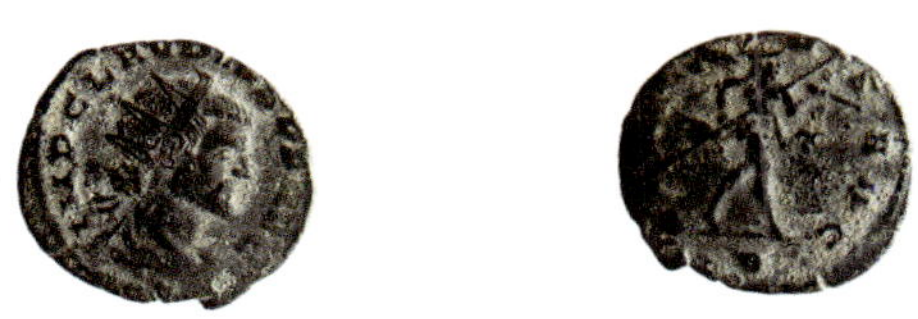

355. AE; 2,83 g.; 18,0 x 19,9 mm.; 12 h.; inv. n. 18.28
(Obv. IMP CLAVDIVS P F AVG; Rev. VIRTV-S AVG; — — —//P)

Antoninianus
Obv. IMP CLAVDIVS P F AVG. Radiated bust of emperor in cuirass and paludamentum looking right, seen from rear.
Rev. AEQVITAS AVG. Aequitas standing left, holding scales in right hand and cornucopiae in left hand.
— — —//S
Lit.: RIC temp n° 55; NOR. 1028; RIC 5.1, p. 222, Mediolanum 137 var.[54]

[52] RIC 5.1, p. 224, Mediolanum 168 notes draped bust of emperor.
[53] RIC 5.1, p. 225, Mediolanum 172 notes draped bust of emperor.
[54] RIC 5.1, p. 222, Mediolanum 137 notes draped bust of emperor.

356. AE; 3,21 g.; 18,5 x 18,0 mm.; 12 h.; inv. n. 1659
(Obv. IMP CLAVDIVS P F AVG; Rev. AEQVIT-A-S AVG; — — —//S)

Spring – c. End of August 270 A.D.

Antoninianus
Obv. IMP CLAVDIVS P F AVG. Radiated bust of emperor in cuirass and paludamentum looking right, seen from rear.
Rev. PAX AVG. Pax standing left, holding branch in right hand and vertical sceptre in left hand.
— — —//P
Lit.: RIC temp n° 80; NOR. 1039/CUN. 2265; RIC 5.1, p. 223, Mediolanum 156 var.[55]

357. AE; 3,18 g.; 17,9 x 18,4 mm.; 12 h.; inv. n. 1660
(Obv. IMP CLAVDIV[S P] F AVG; Rev. PA-X AVG; — — —//[P])

Roma

c. December 268 – Early 269 A.D.

Antoninianus
Obv. IMP C CLAVDIVS AVG. Radiated bust of emperor in cuirass looking right, seen from front.
Rev. LIBERALITAS AVG. Liberalitas standing left, holding tessera in right hand and cornucopiae in left hand.
— — —//—
Lit.: RIC temp n° 150; NOR. 0599/CUN. 1931; RIC 5.1, p. 215, Rome 57

358. AE; 2,86 g.; 18,4 x 18,7 mm.; 12 h.; inv. n. 1661
(Obv. [I]MP C CLAVDIVS AVG; Rev. LIBERALIT[AS AVG]; — — —//—)

c. September 268 – End of 269 A.D.

Antoninianus
Obv. IMP C CLAVDIVS AVG. Radiated bust of emperor in cuirass looking right, seen from front.
Rev. VICTORIA AVG. Victory standing left, holding wreath in right hand and palm in left hand.
— — —//—
Lit.: RIC temp n° 168; NOR. 0616/CUN. 1944; RIC 5.1, p. 219, Rome 104

[55] RIC 5.1, p. 223, Mediolanum 156 notes draped bust of emperor.

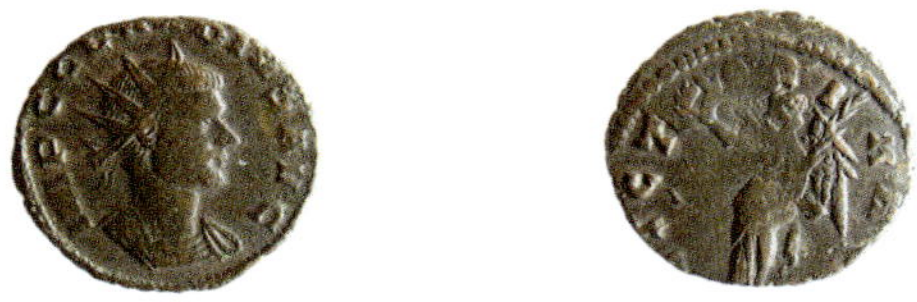

359. AE; 3,4 g.; 19,0 x 20,4 mm.; 6 h.; inv. n. 1662
(Obv. IMP C CLAVDIVS AVG; Rev. [V]ICT-ORI-A A[VG]; — — —//—)

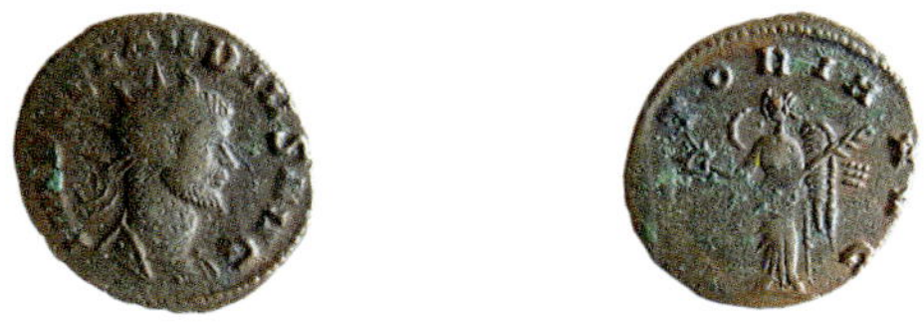

360. AE; 3,66 g.; 20,7 x 20,0 mm.; 6 h.; inv. n. 1663
(Obv. IMP C CLAVDIVS AVG; Rev. VIC-TORIA – AVG; — — —//—)

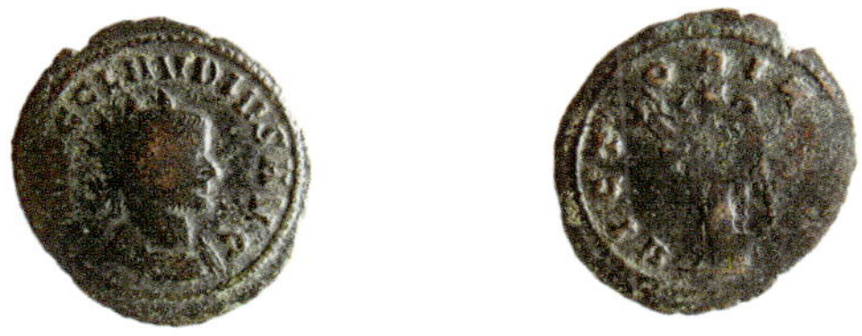

361. AE; 2,99 g.; 23,6 x 21,8 mm.; 12 h.; inv. n. 1664
(Obv. IMP C CLAVDIVS AVG; Rev. VICT-O-RIA [AVG]; — — —//—)

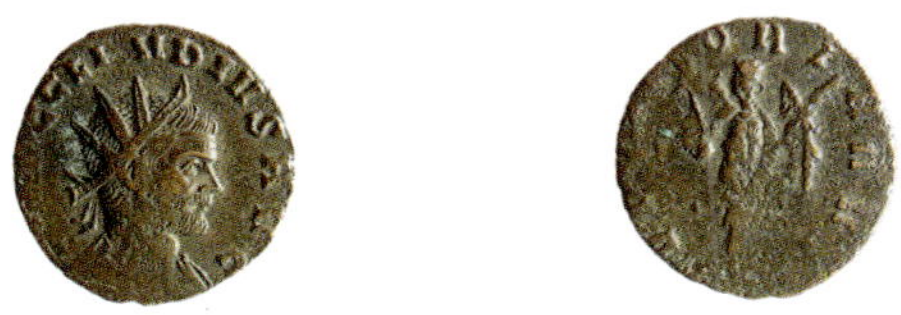

362. AE; 3,01 g.; 19,6 x 18,7 mm.; 12 h.; inv. n. 1665
(Obv. [I]MP C CLAVDIVS AVG; Rev. VIC[T]-ORI-A AV[G]; — — —//—)

Antoninianus
Obv. IMP C CLAVDIVS AVG. Radiated bust of emperor in cuirass looking right, seen from front.
Rev. VICTORIA AVG. Victory standing left, holding wreath in right hand and palm in left hand.
A — —//—
Lit.: RIC temp n° 172; NOR. 0621/CUN. 1949; RIC 5.1, p. 219, Rome 105 var.[56]

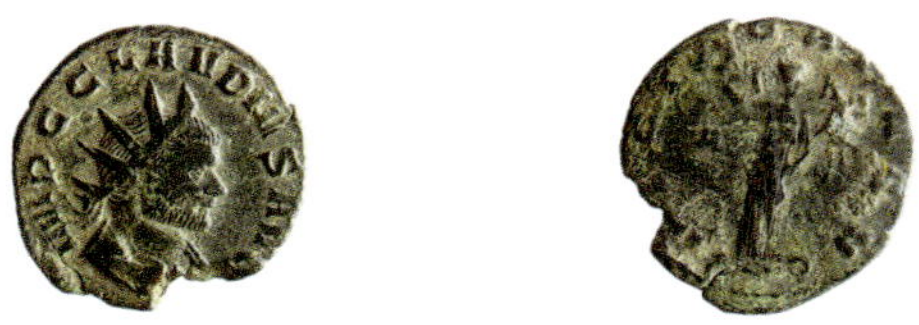

363. AE; 2,71 g.; 19,8 x 19,7 mm.; 11 h.; inv. n. 1666
(Obv. IMP C CLAVDIVS AVG; Rev. VICT-ORI-A AVG; A — —//—)

Antoninianus
Obv. IMP C CLAVDIVS AVG. Radiated bust of emperor in cuirass looking right, seen from front.
Rev. FELICITAS AVG. Felicitas standing left, holding long-handled vertical caduceus in right hand and cornucopiae in left hand.
— — —//—
Lit.: RIC temp n° 176; NOR. 0624/CUN. 1951; RIC 5.1, p. 214, Rome 32

[56] RIC 5.1, p. 219, Rome 105 notes obverse legend IMP CLAVDIVS AVG.

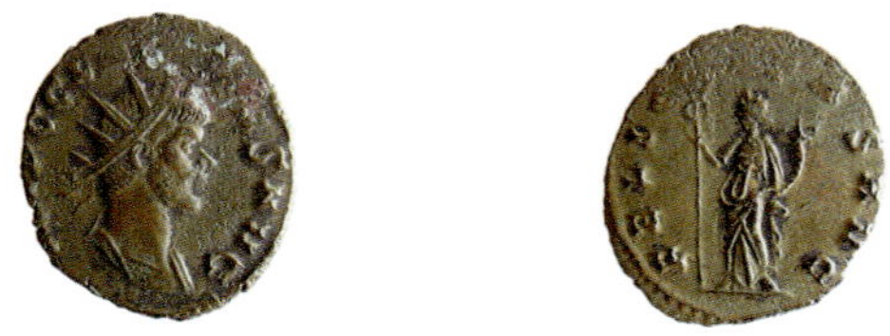

364. AE; 3,14 g.; 21,6 x 18,9 mm.; 12 h.; inv. n. 950
(Obv. [IM]P C CLA[VDI]VS AVG; Rev. FELIC[IT]AS AVG; — — —//—)

Antoninianus
Obv. IMP C CLAVDIVS AVG. Radiated bust of emperor in cuirass looking right, seen from front.
Rev. SALVS AVG. Salus standing left, holding patera in right hand, from which a snake which is rising from altar is feeding; in left hand Salus holds a long vertical sceptre.
— — —//—
Lit.: RIC temp n° 184; NOR. 0606/CUN. 1935; RIC 5.1, p. 218, Rome 98

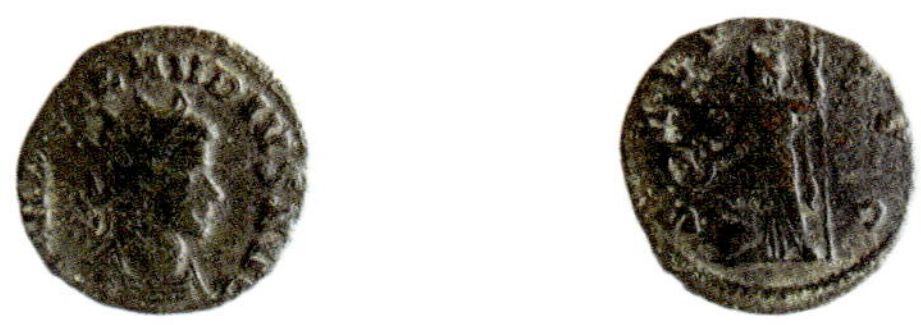

365. AE; 2,96 g.; 19,9 x 19,6 mm.; 6 h.; inv. n. 1667
(Obv. IMP C CLAVDIVS AVG; Rev. S-ALVS – AVG; — — —//—)

Antoninianus
Obv. IMP C CLAVDIVS AVG. Radiated bust of emperor in cuirass and paludamentum looking right, seen from rear.
Rev. ANNONA AVG. Annona standing left, holding corn-ears in right hand and cornucopiae in left hand; Annona's right foot is resting on prow of ship.
— — —//—
Lit.: RIC temp n° 194; NOR. 0638/CUN. 1964; RIC 5.1, p. 213, Rome 18 var.[57]

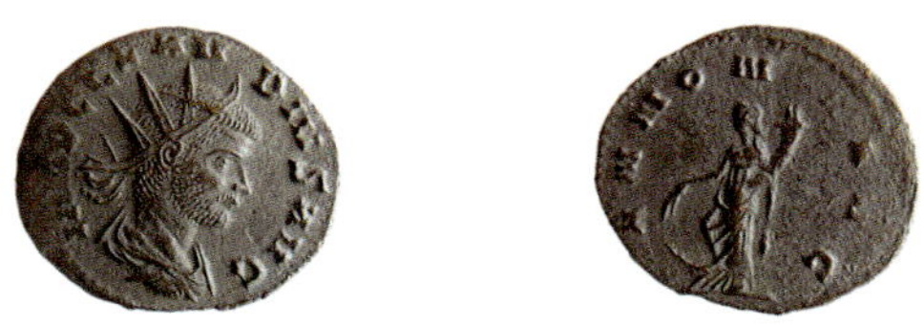

366. AE; 2,88 g.; 20,4 x 22,2 mm.; 12 h.; inv. n. 953
(Obv. IMP C CLAV-DIVS AVG; Rev. ANNONA AVG; — — —//—)

Antoninianus
Obv. IMP C CLAVDIVS AVG. Radiated bust of emperor in cuirass looking right, seen from front.
Rev. ANNONA AVG. Annona standing left, holding corn-ears in right hand and cornucopiae in left hand; Annona's right foot is resting on prow of ship.
— — —//—
Lit.: RIC temp n° 195; NOR. 0637/CUN. 1962; RIC 5.1, p. 213, Rome 18

367. AE; 1,35 g.; 16,8 x 17,2 mm.; 12 h.; inv. n. 1668
(Obv. [IM]P C CLAVDIVS AVG; Rev. [ANN]ONA AV[G]; — — —//—)

[57] RIC 5.1, p. 213, Rome 18 notes draped bust of emperor.

Antoninianus
Obv. IMP C CLAVDIVS AVG. Radiated bust of emperor in cuirass looking right, seen from front.
Rev. ANNONA AVG. Annona standing left, holding corn-ears in right hand and cornucopiae in left hand; Annona's right foot is resting on prow of ship.
— — Δ//—
Lit.: RIC temp n° 199; NOR. 0641/CUN. 1967; RIC 5.1, p. 213, Rome 18

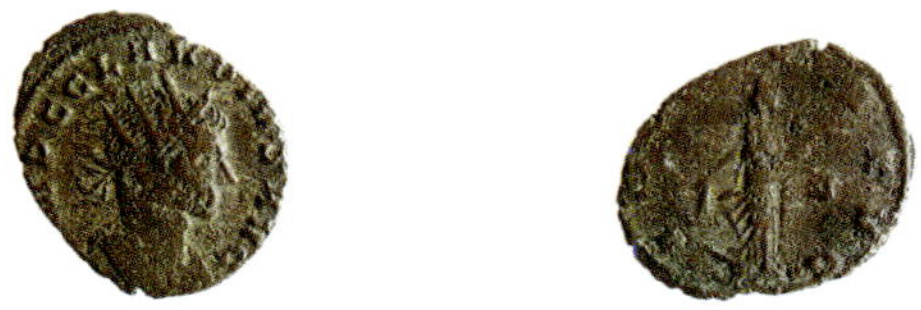

368. AE; 3,09 g.; 18,8 x 19,0 mm.; 6 h.; inv. n. 1669
(Obv. [I]MP C CLAVDIVS AVG; Rev. AN[NON]A AVG; — — Δ//—)

Antoninianus
Obv. IMP C CLAVDIVS AVG. Radiated bust of emperor in cuirass looking right, seen from front.
Rev. VIRTVS AVG. Virtus standing left, holding branch in right hand and vertical spear in left hand; shield rests against right foot.
— — —//—
Lit.: RIC temp n° 203; NOR. 0643/CUN. 1969; RIC 5.1, p. 219, Rome 109

369. AE; 2,29 g.; 18,4 x 18,6 mm.; 6 h.; inv. n. 1670
(Obv. [I]MP C CLAVDIVS AV[G]; Rev. VIRT-V[S AVG]; — — —//—)

370. AE; 3,07 g.; 18,1 x 19,5 mm.; 12 h.; inv. n. 1671
(Obv. [I]MP C CLAVDIVS AVG; Rev. VIRT-V-S AVG; — — —//—)

Antoninianus
Obv. IMP C CLAVDIVS AVG. Radiated bust of emperor looking right.
Rev. VIRTVS AVG. Virtus standing left, holding branch in right hand and vertical spear in left hand; shield rests against right foot.
inv. ε — —//—
Lit.: RIC temp n° 209; NOR. 0649/CUN. 1973; RIC 5.1, p. 219, Rome 109

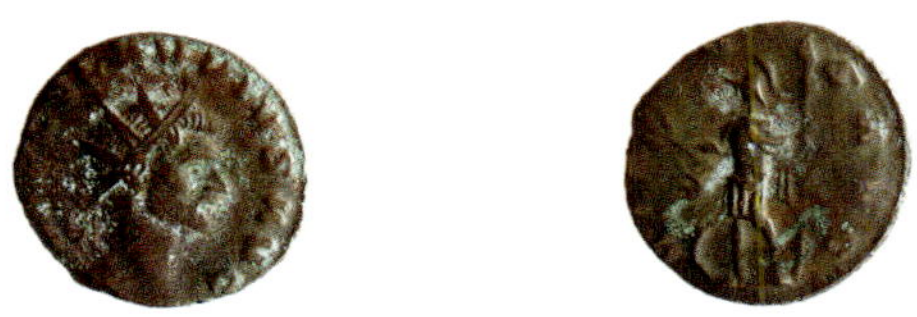

371. AE; 4,01 g.; 18,5 x 19,5 mm.; 8 h.; inv. n. 1672
(Obv. IMP C CLAVDIVS AVG; Rev. VIR-TV-S AVG; inv. ε — —//—)

Antoninianus
Obv. IMP C CLAVDIVS AVG. Radiated bust of emperor in cuirass looking right, seen from front.
Rev. SPES PVBLICA. Spes walking left, holding flower in right hand and raising skirt with left hand.
— — —//—
Lit.: RIC temp n° 213; NOR. 0611/CUN. 1938; RIC 5.1, p. 219, Rome 102

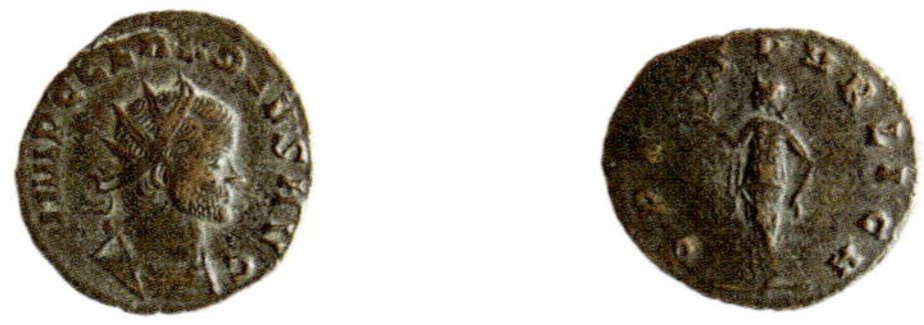

372. AE; 3,06 g.; 21,0 x 19,9 mm.; 2 h.; inv. n. 1673
(Obv. IMP C CLAVDIVS AVG; Rev. SPE-S PVBLICA; — — —//—)

Antoninianus
Obv. IMP C CLAVDIVS AVG. Radiated bust of emperor in cuirass looking right, seen from front.
Rev. AEQVITAS AVG. Aequitas standing left, holding scales in right hand and cornucopiae in left hand.
— — —//—
Lit.: RIC temp n° 219; NOR. 0652/CUN. 1976; RIC 5.1, p. 212, Rome 14

373. AE; 2,78 g.; 18,7 x 18,2 mm.; 11 h.; inv. n. 1674
(Obv. IMP [C CLAV]DIVS AVG; Rev. AE-[QVITAS AV]G; — — —//—)

Antoninianus
Obv. IMP C CLAVDIVS AVG. Radiated bust of emperor in cuirass looking right, seen from front.
Rev. GENIVS EXERCI. Genius standing left, holding patera in right hand and cornucopiae in left hand.
— — —//—
Lit.: RIC temp n° 230; NOR. 0659/CUN. 1983; RIC 5.1, p. 215, Rome 48

374. AE; 2,26 g.; 17,9 x 15,7 mm.; 3 h.; inv. n. 1675
(Obv. IMP C CLAVDI[VS AVG]; Rev. GENIVS – EXER[CI]; — — —//—)

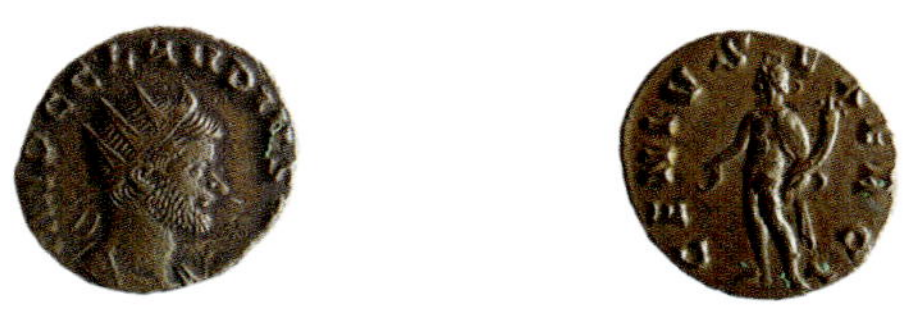

375. AE; 3,03 g.; 18,4 x 18,3 mm.; 6 h.; inv. n. 947
(Obv. IMP C CLAVDIVS [AVG]; Rev. GENIVS – EXERCI; — — —//—)

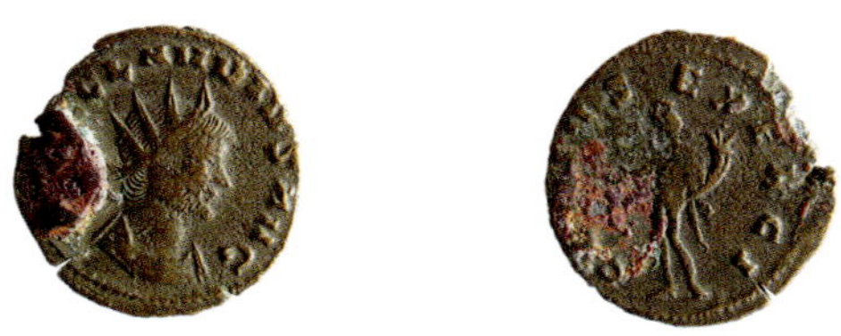

376. AE; 3,18 g.; 21,7 x 20,8 mm.; 12 h.; inv. n. 1676
(Obv. [IMP C] CLAVDIVS AVG; Rev. GENIVS – EXERCI; — — —//—)

Antoninianus
Obv. IMP C CLAVDIVS AVG. Radiated bust of emperor in cuirass looking right, seen from front.
Rev. MARS VLTOR. Mars walking right, holding transverse spear in right hand and trophy over left shoulder in left hand.
— — —//—
Lit.: RIC temp n° 243; NOR. 0668/CUN. 1989; RIC 5.1, p. 216, Rome 66

377. AE; 2,75 g.; 16,2 x 18,1 mm.; 6 h.; inv. n. 1677
(Obv. IMP C CLAVDIVS [AVG]; Rev. MARS – [VLTOR]; — — —//—)

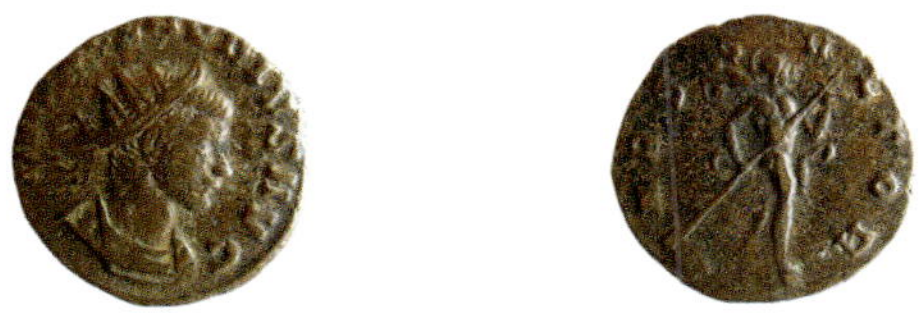

378. AE; 2,91 g.; 19,4 x 19,5 mm.; 12 h.; inv. n. 1678
(Obv. IMP C CLAVDIVS AVG; Rev. MARS – V-LTOR; — — —//—)

Antoninianus
Obv. IMP C CLAVDIVS AVG. Radiated bust of emperor in cuirass looking right, seen from front.
Rev. IOVI VICTORI. Jupiter standing front, head turned left, holding thunderbolt in right hand and vertical sceptre in left hand.
— — —//—
Lit.: RIC temp n° 252; NOR. 0676/CUN. 1998; RIC 5.1, p. 215, Rome 54

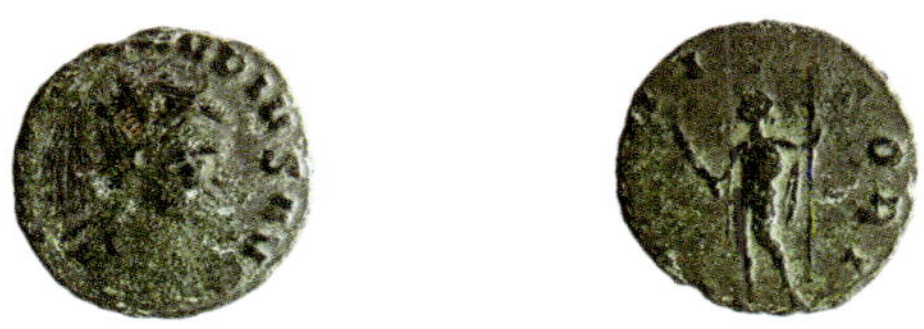

379. AE; 2,62 g.; 18,6 x 18,5 mm.; 6 h.; inv. n. 1679
(Obv. IMP C CLAVDIVS AVG; Rev. IOVI VIC-TORI; — — —//—)

Antoninianus
Obv. IMP C CLAVDIVS AVG. Radiated bust of emperor in cuirass looking right, seen from front.
Rev. IOVI VICTORI. Jupiter standing front, head turned left, holding thunderbolt in right hand and vertical sceptre in left hand.
— — N//—
Lit.: RIC temp n° 255; NOR. 0680/CUN. 2002; RIC 5.1, p. 215, Rome 54

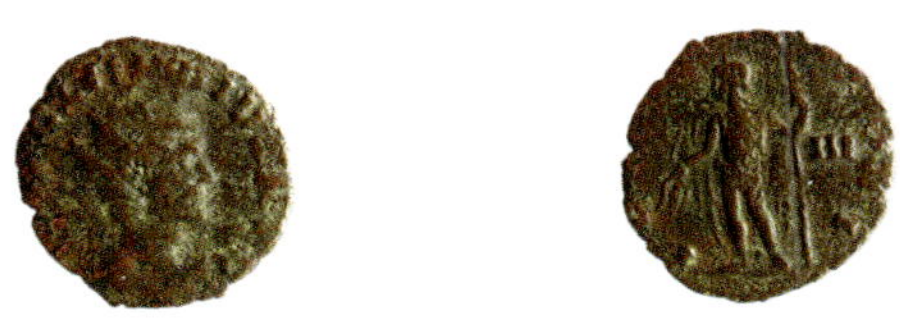

380. AE; 1,62 g.; 18,2 x 18,0 mm.; 6 h.; inv. n. 1680
(Obv. IMP C CLAVDIVS AVG; Rev. IOVI VICTORI; — — N//—)

Antoninianus
Obv. IMP C CLAVDIVS AVG. Radiated bust of emperor in cuirass looking right, seen from front.
Rev. IOVI STATORI. Jupiter standing front, head turned right, holding vertical sceptre in right hand and thunderbolt in left hand.
— — —//—
Lit.: RIC temp n° 262; NOR. 0595/CUN. 1927; RIC 5.1, p. 215, Rome 52 var.[58]

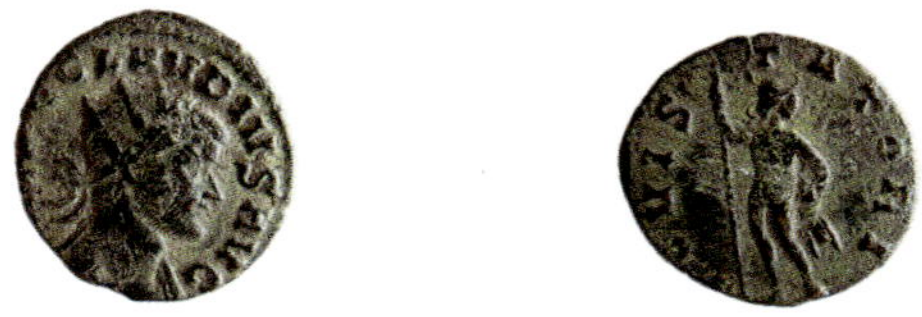

381. AE; 3,17 g.; 19,7 x 18,9 mm.; 3 h.; inv. n. 1681
(Obv. [I]MP C CLAVDIVS AVG; Rev. IOVI S-TATORI; — — —//—)

Antoninianus
Obv. IMP C CLAVDIVS AVG. Radiated bust of emperor in cuirass looking right, seen from front.
Rev. LIBERT AVG. Libertas standing left, holding pileus in right hand and long vertical sceptre in left hand.
— — X//—
Lit.: RIC temp n° 270; NOR. 0685/CUN. 2005; RIC 5.1, p. 216, Rome 62 var.[59]

382. AE; 2,43 g.; 16,1 x 18,7 mm.; 1 h.; inv. n. 1682
(Obv. IMP C C[LAVDI]VS AVG; Rev. [LIBER]T AVG; — — X//—)

Antoninianus
Obv. IMP C CLAVDIVS AVG. Radiated bust of emperor in cuirass looking right, seen from front.
Rev. FIDES EXERCI. Fides standing left, holding vertical standard in right hand and transverse standard in left hand.
— — XI//—
Lit.: RIC temp n° 282; NOR. 0701/CUN. 2009; RIC 5.1, p. 214, Rome 36

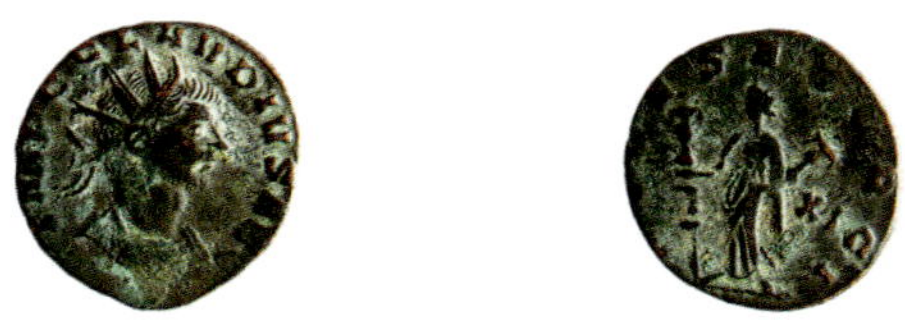

383. AE; 3,41 g.; 19,9 x 18,9 mm.; 6 h.; inv. n. 1683
(Obv. IMP C CLAVDIVS AVG; Rev. FIDES EXERCI; — — XI//—)

Antoninianus
Obv. IMP C CLAVDIVS AVG. Radiated bust of emperor in cuirass looking right, seen from front.
Rev. PROVIDENT AVG. Providentia standing left, legs crossed, holding baton in right hand, cornucopiae in left hand; left elbow leaning on column; at feet to left globe.
— — —//—
Lit.: RIC temp n° 288; NOR. 0705/CUN. 2020; RIC 5.1, p. 218, Rome 91

[58] RIC 5.1, p. 215, Rome 52 notes draped bust of emperor.
[59] RIC 5.1, p. 216, Rome 62 notes cornucopiae instead of sceptre.

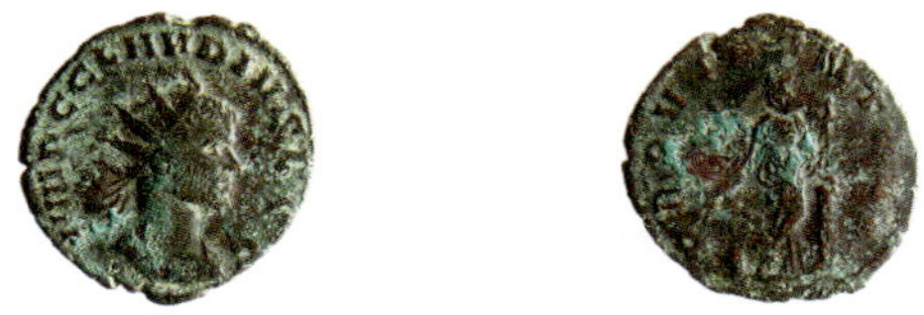

384. AE; 3,21 g.; 21,2 x 20,6 mm.; 6 h.; inv. n. 1684
(Obv. IMP C CLAVDIVS AVG; Rev. PROVIDENT AVG; — — —//—)

End of 269 A.D.

Antoninianus
Obv. IMP C CLAVDIVS AVG. Radiated bust of emperor in cuirass looking right, seen from front.
Rev. P M TR P II COS P P. Emperor standing left, holding branch in right hand and sceptre in left hand.
— — —//—
Lit.: RIC temp n° 301; NOR. 0603/CUN. 1933; RIC 5.1, p. 212, Rome 10

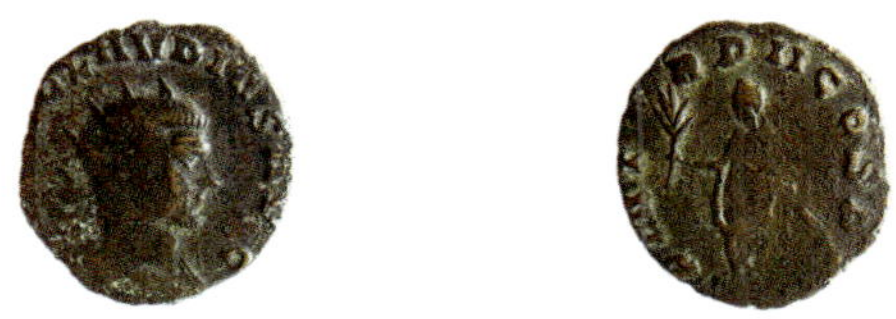

385. AE; 3,01 g.; 19,8 x 18,1 mm.; 12 h.; inv. n. 1685
(Obv. [I]MP C CLAVDIVS AVG; Rev. P M T-R P II COS P P; — — —//—)

c. Early 270 – Mid 270 A.D.

Antoninianus
Obv. IMP CLAVDIVS AVG. Radiated bust of emperor in cuirass looking right, seen from front.
Rev. VICTORIA AVG. Victory standing left, holding wreath in right hand and palm in left hand.
— — —//—
Lit.: RIC temp n° 308; NOR. 0824/CUN. 2116; RIC 5.1, p. 219, Rome 105 var.[60]

386. AE; 1,97 g.; 17,2 x 17,4 mm.; 1 h.; inv. n. 1686
(Obv. IMP CLAVD[I]VS [A]V[G]; Rev. VICTORIA AVG; — — —//—)

387. AE; 1,76 g.; 16,0 x 17,3 mm.; 5 h.; inv. n. 1687
(Obv. IMP CLAVD[IVS AVG]; Rev. [V]IC-TORI-A [AVG]; — — —//—)

[60] RIC 5.1, p. 219, Rome 105 notes mintmark A left in reverse field.

Antoninianus
Obv. IMP CLAVDIVS AVG. Radiated bust of emperor in cuirass looking right, seen from front.
Rev. GENIVS AVG. Genius standing left, holding patera over altar in right hand and cornucopiae in left hand.
— — Γ//—
Lit.: RIC temp n° 326; NOR. 0838/CUN. 2130; RIC 5.1, p. 215, Rome 46 var.[61]

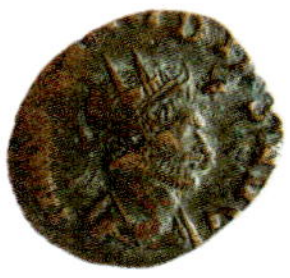
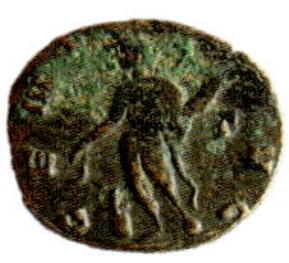

388. AE; 2,94 g.; 18,3 x 18,8 mm.; 1 h.; inv. n. 1688
(Obv. IMP C[L]AVDIVS AVG; Rev. GENI[VS A]VG; — — Γ//—)

Antoninianus
Obv. IMP CLAVDIVS AVG. Radiated bust of emperor in cuirass looking right, seen from front.
Rev. MARS VLTOR. Mars walking right, holding transverse spear in right hand and trophy over left shoulder in left hand.
— — H//—
Lit.: RIC temp n° 377; NOR. 0874; RIC 5.1, p. 216, Rome 67

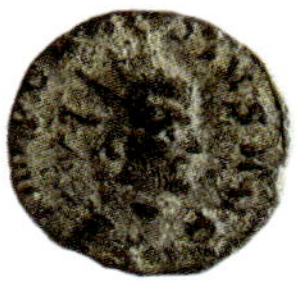
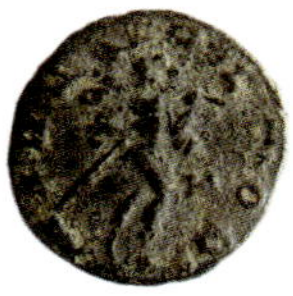

389. AE; 2,93 g.; 19,0 x 19,7 mm.; 2 h.; inv. n. 1689
(Obv. IMP CLAVDIVS AVG; Rev. MARS – V-LTOR; — — H//—)

Antoninianus
Obv. IMP CLAVDIVS AVG. Radiated bust of emperor looking right.
Rev. LIBERT AVG. Libertas standing left, holding pileus in right hand and long vertical sceptre in left hand.
— — X//—
Lit.: RIC temp n° 394; NOR. 0884/CUN. 2164; RIC 5.1, p. 216, Rome 63 var.[62]

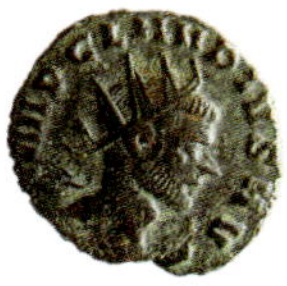
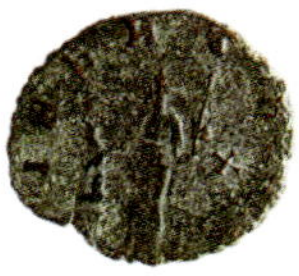

390. AE; 3,04 g.; 18,4 x 19,3 mm.; 12 h.; inv. n. 1690
(Obv. IMP CLAVDIVS AVG; Rev. [L]IBERT AVG; — — X//—)

Antoninianus
Obv. IMP CLAVDIVS AVG. Radiated bust of emperor looking right.
Rev. FIDES EXERCI. Fides standing left, holding vertical standard in right hand and transverse standard in left hand.
— — XI//—
Lit.: RIC temp n° 407; NOR. 0890/CUN. 2170; RIC 5.1, p. 214, Rome 36 var.[63]

[61] RIC 5.1, p. 215, Rome 46 notes radiated bust of emperor right.
[62] RIC 5.1, p. 216, Rome 63 notes cornucopiae instead of sceptre.
[63] RIC 5.1, p. 214, Rome 36 notes radiated cuirassed bust of emperor right and obverse legend IMP C CLAVDIVS AVG.

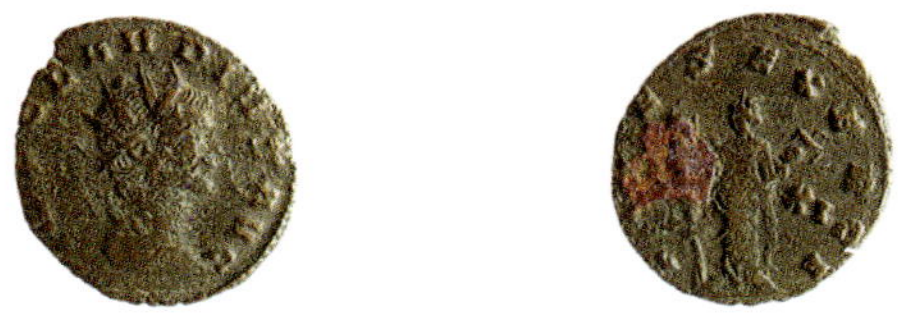

391. AE; 3,05 g.; 20,8 x 19,2 mm.; 12 h.; inv. n. 1691
(Obv. IMP CLAVDIVS AVG; Rev. FIDES EXERCI; — — XI//—)

Antoninianus
Obv. IMP CLAVDIVS AVG. Radiated bust of emperor looking right.
Rev. PROVIDENT AVG. Providentia standing left, legs crossed, holding baton in right hand, cornucopiae in left hand; left elbow leaning on column; at feet to left globe.
— — XII//—
Lit.: RIC temp n° 417; NOR. 0905/CUN. 2181; RIC 5.1, p. 218, Rome 92

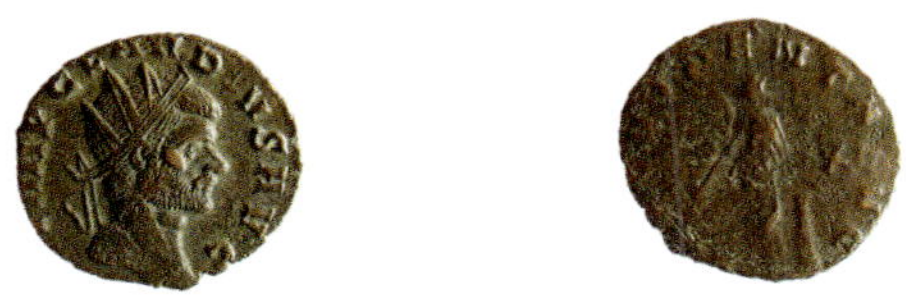

392. AE; 3 g.; 17,8 x 19,9 mm.; 11 h.; inv. n. 1692
(Obv. IMP CLAVDIVS AVG; Rev. PROVIDENT A-VG; — — XII//—)

Antoninianus
Obv. IMP CLAVDIVS AVG. Radiated bust of emperor in cuirass looking right, seen from front.
Rev. PROVID AVG. Providentia standing left, legs crossed, holding baton in right hand, cornucopiae in left hand; left elbow leaning on column; at feet to left globe.
— — —//XII
Lit.: RIC temp n° -; RIC 5.1, p. 217, Rome 86 var.[64]

393. AE; 2,5 g.; 16,8 x 17,2 mm.; 12 h.; inv. n. 1693
(Obv. IMP CLAVDIVS [AVG]; Rev. PROVID AVG; — — —//XII)

c. Mid 270 – August 270 A.D.

Antoninianus
Obv. IMP CLAVDIVS AVG. Radiated bust of emperor looking right.
Rev. PROVIDENT AVG. Providentia standing left, holding baton in right hand and vertical sceptre in left hand; at feet to left globe.
— — ς//—
Lit.: RIC temp n° 485; NOR. 0945/CUN. 2208; RIC 5.1, p. 218, Rome 94

64 RIC temp notes radiated bust of emperor right, cuirassed and draped with paludamentum (n° 431) or radiated head of emperor right (n° 433); RIC 5.1, p. 217, Rome 86 notes radiated draped bust of emperor right or radiated head of emperor right.

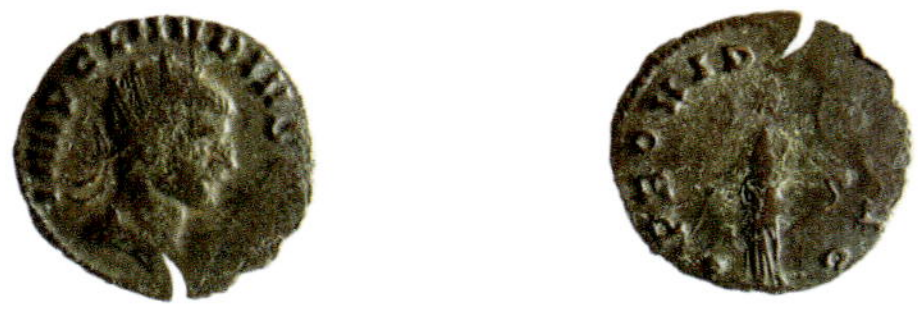

394. AE; 1,72 g.; 19,5 x 20,3 mm.; 12 h.; inv. n. 1694
(Obv. IMP CLAVDIVS [AVG]; Rev. PROVID[ENT A]VG; — — ς//—)

Siscia

End of 268 – Spring of 269 A.D.

Antoninianus
Obv. IMP CLAVDIVS AVG. Radiated bust of emperor in cuirass and paludamentum looking right, seen from rear.
Rev. FORTVNA RED. Fortuna standing left, holding rudder in right hand and cornucopiae in left hand.
— — —//—
Lit.: RIC temp n° 592; NOR. 1057/CUN. 2278; RIC 5.1, p. 226, Siscia 180 var.[65]

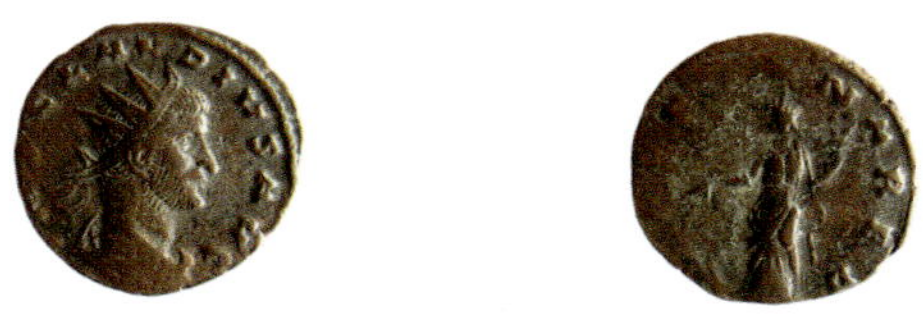

395. AE; 3,28 g.; 19,4 x 19,7 mm.; 6 h.; inv. n. 1695
(Obv. IMP CLAVDIVS AVG; Rev. FOR[T]VN-A RED; — — —//—)

Antoninianus
Obv. IMP CLAVDIVS AVG. Radiated bust of emperor in cuirass and paludamentum looking right, seen from rear.
Rev. PAX AVG. Pax standing left, holding branch in right hand and transverse sceptre in left hand.
— — —//—
Lit.: RIC temp n° 598; NOR. 1059/CUN. 2280; RIC 5.1, p. 226, Siscia 186 var.[66]

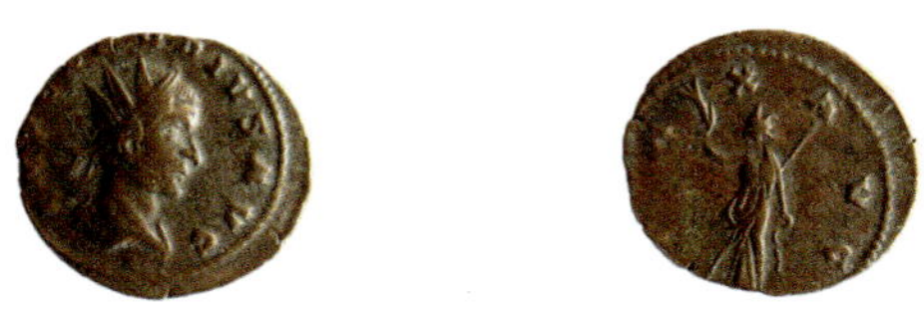

396. AE; 3,01 g.; 18,8 x 20,7 mm.; 6 h.; inv. n. 1696
(Obv. IMP CLAVDIVS AVG; Rev. PA-X AVG; — — —//—)

397. AE; 2,26 g.; 16,5 x 19,0 mm.; 12 h.; inv. n. 1697
(Obv. IMP C[LAVDIVS] AVG; Rev. P[AX A]VG; — — —//—)

[65] RIC 5.1, p. 226, Siscia 180 notes obverse legend IMP CLAVDIVS CAESAR with radiated draped bust right.
[66] RIC 5.1, p. 226, Siscia 186 notes radiated cuirassed bust of emperor right.

Antoninianus
Obv. IMP CLAVDIVS AVG. Radiated bust of emperor in cuirass and paludamentum looking right, seen from rear.
Rev. PROVIDEN AVG. Providentia standing left, holding baton in right hand and cornucopiae in left hand; at feet to left globe.
— — —//—
Lit.: RIC temp n° 601; NOR. 1060/CUN. -; RIC 5.1, p. 227, Siscia 187 var.[67]

398. AE; 1,67 g.; 16,8 x 16,7 mm.; 6 h.; inv. n. 1698
(Obv. [IMP CL]AVDIVS AVG; Rev. P[R]OVIDE-N A[VG]; — — —//—)

Antoninianus
Obv. IMP CLAVDIVS AVG. Radiated bust of emperor in cuirass and paludamentum looking right, seen from rear.
Rev. AEQVITAS AVG. Aequitas standing left, holding scales in right hand and cornucopiae in left hand.
— — I//—
Lit.: RIC temp n° 608; NOR. 1061/CUN. -; RIC 5.1, p. 226, Siscia 178 var.[68]

399. AE; 2,14 g.; 16,5 x 18,3 mm.; 12 h.; inv. n. 1699
(Obv. [I]MP CLAVD[IVS AVG]; Rev. [AE]QVITAS AVG; — — I//—)

Antoninianus
Obv. IMP CLAVDIVS AVG. Radiated bust of emperor in cuirass looking right, seen from front.
Rev. LAETITIA AVG. Laetitia standing left, holding wreath in right hand and cornucopiae in left hand.
— — I//—
Lit.: RIC temp n° 618; NOR. -/CUN. -; RIC 5.1, p. 226, Siscia 181

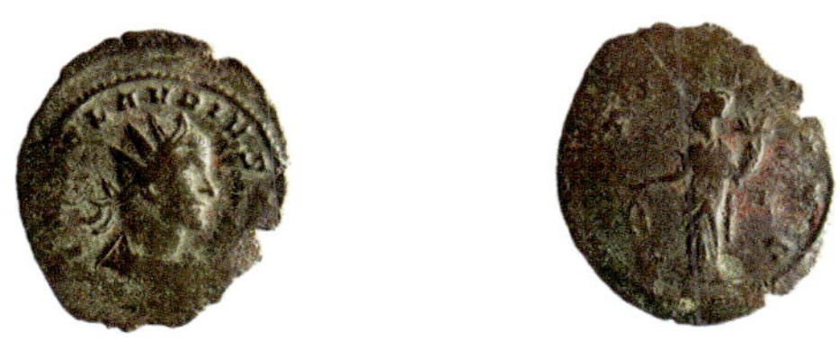

400. AE; 2,39 g.; 22,5 x 20,9 mm.; 6 h.; inv. n. 1700
(Obv. I[MP] CLAVDIVS A[VG]; Rev. [L]AETIT[IA] AVG; — — I//—)

Spring – End of 269 A.D.

Antoninianus
Obv. IMP CLAVDIVS AVG. Radiated bust of emperor in cuirass looking right, seen from front.
Rev. AEQVITAS AVG. Aequitas standing left, holding scales in right hand and cornucopiae in left hand.
— — II//—
Lit.: RIC temp n° 670; NOR. 1071/CUN. 2301; RIC 5.1, p. 226, Siscia 178 var.[69]

67 RIC 5.1, p. 227, Siscia 187 notes radiated cuirassed bust of emperor right or radiated, helmeted, cuirassed bust left holding spear and shield.
68 RIC 5.1, p. 226, Siscia 178 notes obverse legend IMP C CLAVDIVS AVG with radiated cuirassed bust of emperor right and second officina on the left side of the reverse field II — — //—.
69 RIC 5.1, p. 226, Siscia 178 notes obverse legend IMP C CLAVDIVS AVG and second officina on the left side of the reverse field II — — //—.

401. AE; 2,8 g.; 17,0 x 19,3 mm.; 12 h.; inv. n. 1701
(Obv. IMP CLAVD[IVS AVG]; Rev. [AEQV]ITAS AVG; — — II//—)

End of 269 – Early 270 A.D.

Antoninianus
Obv. IMP CLAVDIVS AVG. Radiated bust of emperor in cuirass looking right, seen from front.
Rev. LAETITIA AVG. Laetitia standing left, holding wreath in right hand and cornucopiae in left hand.
— — —//—
Lit.: RIC temp n° 740; NOR. 1092/CUN. 2304; RIC 5.1, p. 226, Siscia 181

402. AE; 3,12 g.; 18,4 x 20,7 mm.; 6 h.; inv. n. 948
(Obv. [IM]P CLAVDIVS AVG; Rev. LAETITIA AVG; — — —//—)

Antoninianus
Obv. IMP CLAVDIVS AVG. Radiated bust of emperor in cuirass looking right, seen from front.
Rev. PAX AVG. Pax standing left, holding branch in right hand and transverse sceptre in left hand.
— — —//—
Lit.: RIC temp n° 746; NOR. 1094/CUN. 2306; RIC 5.1, p. 226, Siscia 186

403. AE; 2,5 g.; 18,7 x 17,5 mm.; 12 h.; inv. n. 951
(Obv. IMP CLAVDIVS AVG; Rev. PA-X – A-VG; — — —//—)

Antoninianus
Obv. IMP CLAVDIVS AVG. Radiated bust of emperor in cuirass looking right, seen from front.
Rev. PROVIDEN AVG. Providentia standing left, holding baton in right hand and cornucopiae in left hand; at feet to left globe.
— — —//—
Lit.: RIC temp n° 749; NOR. 1095; RIC 5.1, p. 227, Siscia 187

404. AE; 2,91 g.; 18,7 x 18,6 mm.; 5 h.; inv. n. 952
(Obv. IMP CLAVDIVS [A]VG; Rev. PROVID[E]N AVG; — — —//—)

Cyzicus

c. Mid 270 – September 270 A.D.

Antoninianus
Obv. IMP CLAVDIVS P F AVG. Radiated bust of emperor in cuirass and paludamentum looking right, seen from rear.
Rev. VICTORIAE GOTHIC. Trophy between two captives.
— — —//—
Lit.: RIC temp n° 983; NOR. 1108A; RIC 5.1, p. 233, Cyzicus 252 var.[70]

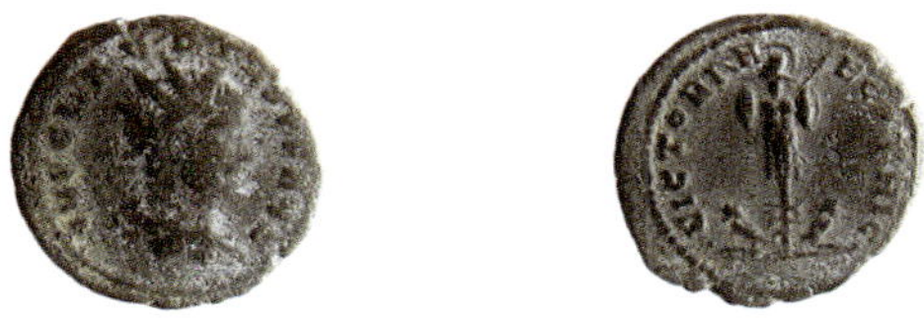

405. AE; 4,9 g.; 21,2 x 21,8 mm.; 6 h.; inv. n. 1702
(Obv. IMP CLAVDIVS P F AVG; Rev. VICTORIA-E GOTHIC; — — —//—)

POSTHUMOUS COINAGE – DIVUS CLAUDIUS

Roma

c. End of 270 – 271 A.D.

Antoninianus
Obv. DIVO CLAVDIO. Radiated bust of emperor looking right.
Rev. CONSECRATIO. Altar with flame above.
— — —//—
Lit.: RIC temp n° 1275; MIR 47 Rom 1/99m0a; RIC 5.1, p. 233, Mediolanum 261

406. AE; 2,71 g.; 19,3 x 19,8 mm.; 11 h.; inv. n. 1703
(Obv. DIVO CLAVDIO; Rev. CONSECRATIO; — — —//—)

407. AE; 1,19 g.; 14,7 x 14,7 mm.; 12 h.; inv. n. 1704
(Obv. [DIVO CLAVDIO]; Rev. [C]ONS[ECRATIO]; — — —//—; MIR 47 Rom 1/99o0a)

70 RIC 5.1, p. 233, Cyzicus 252 notes radiated draped bust of emperor right and mintmark SPQR in the reverse field — — —//SPQR.

Antoninianus
Obv. DIVO CLAVDIO. Radiated bust of emperor looking right.
Rev. CONSECRATIO. Altar with flame above and girland.
— — —//—
Lit.: RIC temp n° 1276; MIR 47 Rom 1/99L-p0b; RIC 5.1, p. 233, Mediolanum 261

408. AE; 1,83 g.; 14,5 x 16,1 mm.; 6 h.; inv. n. 1705
(Obv. [DIVO CLAVDIO]; [CONSECRATIO]; — — —//—)

409. AE; 1,62 g.; 16,5 x 16,7 mm.; 12 h.; inv. n. 1706
(Obv. [DIVO CLAVDIO]; CONSE[CRATIO]; — — —//—; MIR 47 Rom 1/99m0b)

Antoninianus
Obv. DIVO CLAVDIO. Radiated bust of emperor looking right.
Rev. CONSECRATIO. Eagle standing left, head turned right.
— — —//—
Lit.: RIC temp n° 1278; MIR 47 Rom 1/98L-p0a; RIC 5.1, p. 234, 266

410. AE; 1,53 g.; 15,4 x 16,9 mm.; 5 h.; inv. n. 1707
(Obv. [DIVO CL]AVDIO; Rev. [CONS]EC – RATIO; — — —//—)

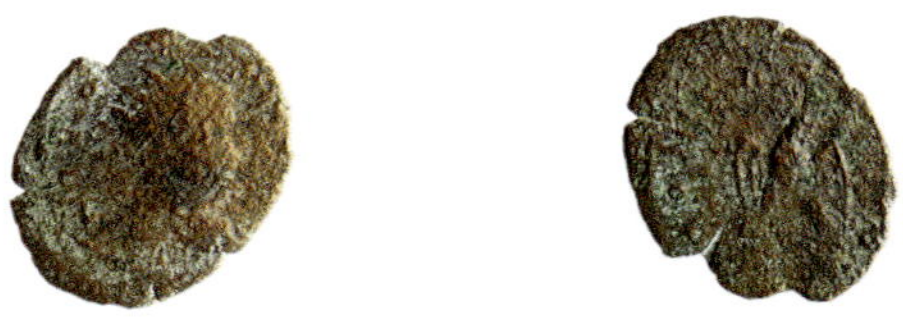

411. AE; 2,09 g.; 18,2 x 19,1 mm.; 6 h.; inv. n. 1708
(Obv. [D]IVO [CLAVDIO]; Rev. [C]ON[SECRATIO]; — — —//—)

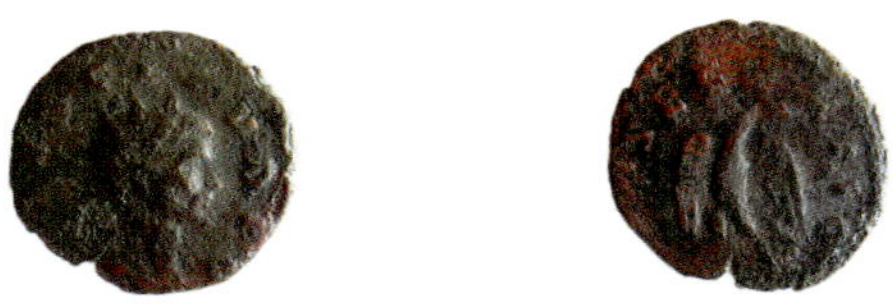

412. AE; 2,38 g.; 19,1 x 19,8 mm.; 11 h.; inv. n. 1709
(Obv. [D]IVO CLAVDIO; Rev. [CO]NSECRATIO; — — —//—; MIR 47 Rom 1/98L0a)

413. AE; 2,87 g.; 17,9 x 18,7 mm.; 5 h.; inv. n. 1710
(Obv. DIVO [CLA]VDI[O]; Rev. [C]ON[SE]CRAT[IO]; — — —//—; MIR 47 Rom 1/98o0a)

Cyzicus

c. Early 270 A.D.

Antoninianus
Obv. DIVO CLAVDIO. Radiated bust of emperor looking right; below bust ••.
Rev. CONSACRATIO. Altar with flame above.
— — —//—
Lit.: RIC temp n° 1320; MIR 47 Cyz 1/288a2; RIC 5.1, p. 234, 266 var.[71]

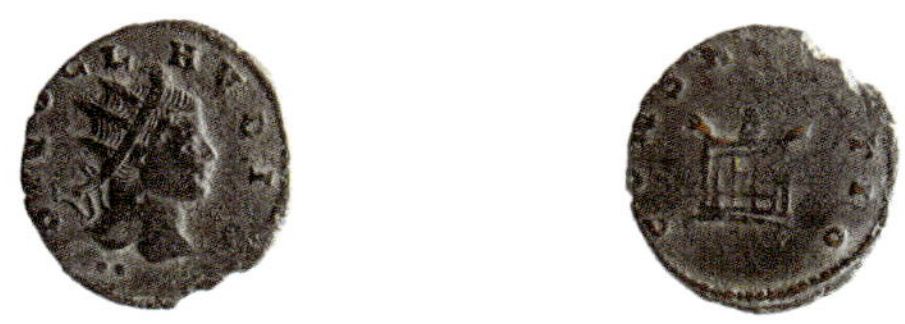

414. AE; 2,46 g.; 20,5 x 18,7 mm.; 6 h.; inv. n. 18.29
(Obv. DIVO CL-AVDIO; ••; Rev. CONSA[CRA]TIO; — — —//—)

QUINTILLUS
(270 A.D.)

Roma

270 A.D.

Antoninianus
Obv. IMP C M AVR CL QVINTILLVS AVG. Radiated bust of emperor in cuirass and paludamentum looking right, seen from rear.
Rev. VICTORIA AVG. Victory standing left, holding wreath in right hand and palm in left hand.
A — —//—
Lit.: RIC temp n° -; NOR. 1209[72]; RIC 5.1, -

415. AE; 2,68 g.; 14,6 x 15,1 mm.; 12 h.; inv. n. 1711
(Obv. [IMP C M AVR CL QVI]NTILLVS A[VG]; Rev. VICT-[ORIA AVG]; A — —//—)

[71] RIC 5.1, p. 234, 266 notes eagle in reverse field.
[72] NOR notes this coin as a mule of reverse proper to issue I – III of Claudius II. Gothicus.

THE GALLIC EMPIRE
POSTUMUS
(260 – 269 A.D.)

Augusta Treverorum

260 – 261 A.D.

Antoninianus
Obv. IMP C POSTVMVS P F AVG. Radiated bust of emperor in cuirass and paludamentum looking right, seen from front.
Rev. VICTORIA AVG. Victory walking left, holding wreath in right hand and palm in left hand; at feet to left captive.
— — —//—
Lit.: NOR. 1321/CUN. 2381; Schulzki 97a; RIC 5.2, p. 344, Lugdunum 89

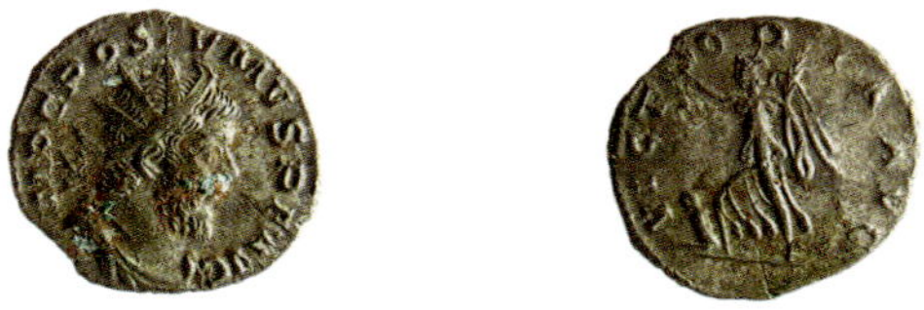

416. AR; 3,15 g.; 19,3 x 21,6 mm.; 7 h.; inv. n. 1712
(Obv. IMP C POSTVMVS P F AVG; Rev. VICT-OR-IA AVG; — — —//—)

262 A.D.

Antoninianus
Obv. IMP C POSTVMVS P F AVG. Radiated bust of emperor in cuirass and paludamentum looking right, seen from front.
Rev. MINER FAVTR. Minerva running left, holding branch in right hand and long spear and shield in left hand.
— — —//—
Lit.: NOR. 1327/CUN. 2397; Schulzki 44; RIC 5.2, p. 343, Lugdunum 74

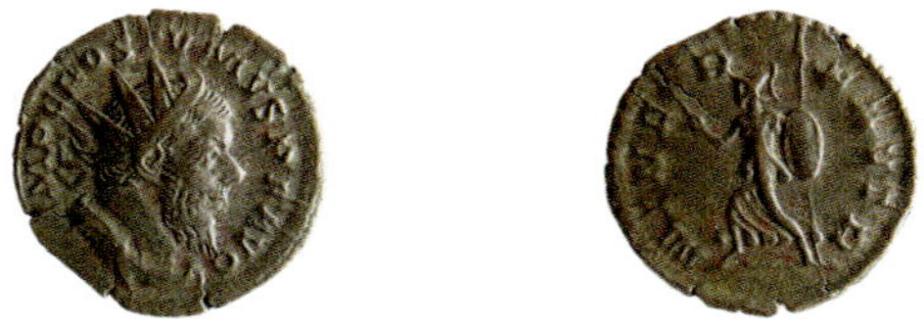

417. AR; 3,04 g.; 21,7 x 21,4 mm.; 6 h.; inv. n. 1713
(Obv. IMP C POSTVMVS P F AVG; Rev. MINE-R – FAVTR; — — —//—)

268 A.D.

Antoninianus
Obv. IMP C POSTVMVS P F AVG. Radiated bust of emperor in cuirass and paludamentum looking right, seen from front.
Rev. ORIENS AVG. Sol walking left, raising right hand, holding whip in left hand.
P — —//—
Lit.: NOR. 1341/CUN. 2454; Schulzki 49; RIC 5.2, p. 362, Cologne 316

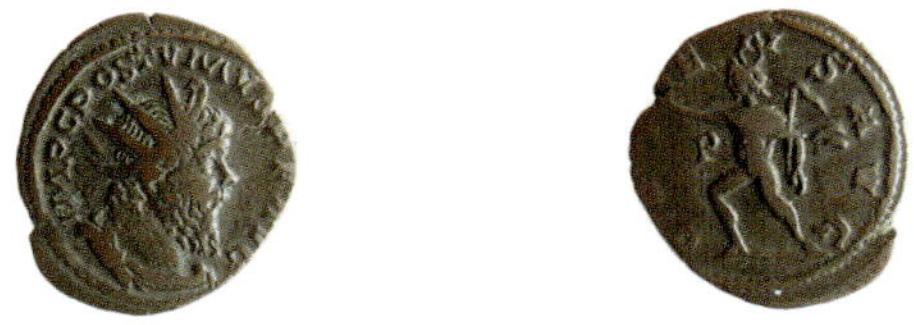

418. AE; 2,87 g.; 20,8 x 18,7 mm.; 12 h.; inv. n. 1714
(Obv. IMP C POSTVMVS P F AVG; Rev. ORI-E-N-S AVG; P — —//—)

MARIUS
(269 A.D.)

Augusta Treverorum

269 A.D.

Antoninianus
Obv. IMP C MARIVS • P • F • AVG. Radiated bust of emperor in cuirass and paludamentum looking right, seen from front.
Rev. SAEC FELICITAS. Felicitas standing left, holding long-handled vertical caduceus in right hand and cornucopiae in left hand.
— — —//—
Lit.: NOR. 1390/CUN. 2505; Schulzki 4b; RIC 5.2, p. 377, Cologne 10

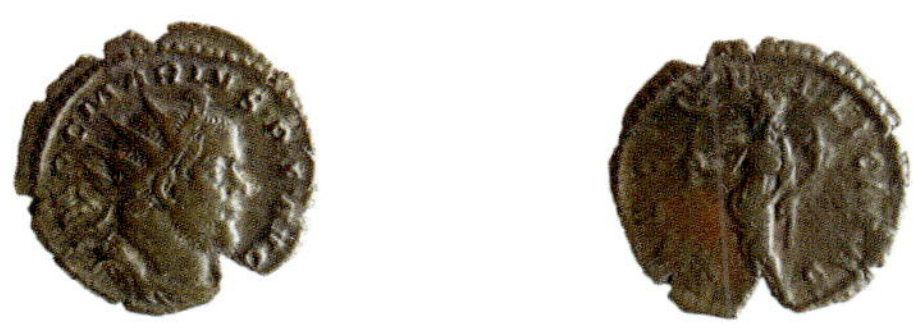

419. AE; 2,39 g.; 20,2 x 20,1 mm.; 1 h.; inv. n. 1715
(Obv. IMP C MARIVS • P • F • AVG; Rev. SAEC – F-ELICITAS; — — —//—)

VICTORINUS
(269 – 271 A.D.)

Augusta Treverorum

269 – 270 A.D.

Antoninianus
Obv. IMP C VICTORINVS P F AVG. Radiated bust of emperor in cuirass and paludamentum looking right, seen from front.
Rev. PAX AVG. Pax standing left, holding branch in right hand and transverse sceptre in left hand.
V — *//—
Lit.: NOR. 1406/CUN. 2530; Schulzki 14b; RIC 5.2, p. 397, Cologne 118

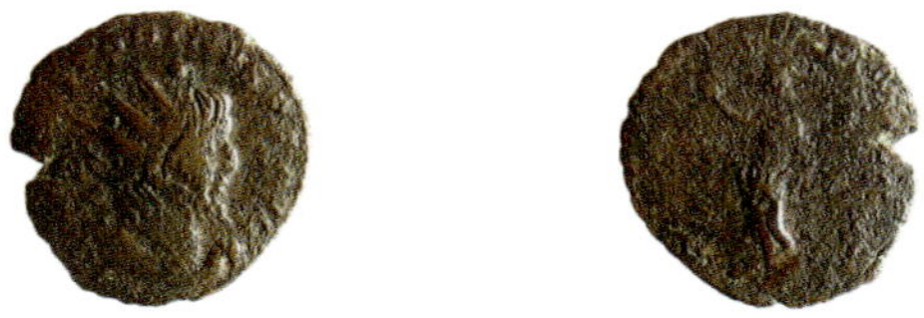

420. AE; 2,07 g.; 20,0 x 20,0 mm.; 12 h.; inv. n. 1716
(Obv. [IMP C VIC]TORINVS P F AVG; Rev. [PAX AVG]; [V] — *//—)

Colonia Agrippinensium

269 – 270 A.D.

Antoninianus
Obv. IMP C VICTORINVS P F AVG. Radiated bust of emperor in cuirass looking right, seen from front.
Rev. SALVS AVG. Salus standing right, feeding snake held in right hand from patera held in left hand.
— — —//—
Lit.: NOR. 1432/CUN. 2567; Schulzki 21c; RIC 5.2, p. 393, Southern mint 67 or RIC 5.2, p. 397, Cologne 122

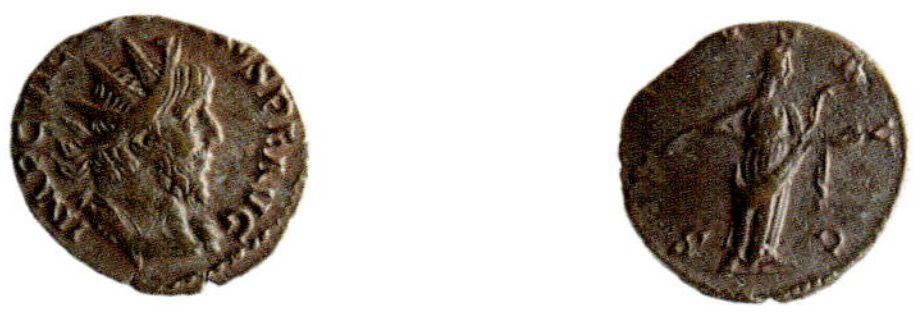

421. AE; 3,6 g.; 19,0 x 19,7 mm.; 1 h.; inv. n. 1717
(Obv. IMP C VICTO[RIN]VS P F AVG; Rev. SALVS AVG; — — —//—)

Antoninianus
Obv. IMP C VICTORINVS P F AVG. Radiated bust of emperor in cuirass looking right, seen from front.
Rev. PIETAS AVG. Pietas standing left, with right hand sacrificing over altar to left and holding box in left hand.
— — —//—
Lit.: NOR. 1441/CUN. 2572; Schulzki 16a; RIC 5.2, p. 392, Southern mint 57

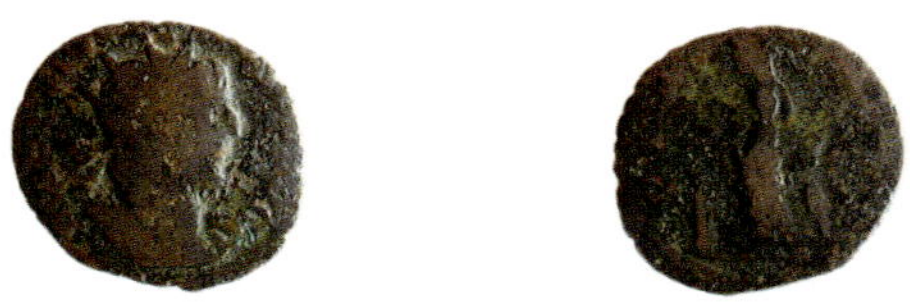

422. AE; 2,58 g.; 18,3 x 19,6 mm.; 12 h.; inv. n. 1718
(Obv. IMP C VIC[TORINVS P F A]VG; Rev. P[IETAS AVG]; — — —//—)

TETRICUS I.
(271 – 274 A.D.)

Colonia Agrippinensium

272 – 274 A.D.

Antoninianus
Obv. IMP (C) TETRICVS P F AVG. Radiated bust of emperor in cuirass looking right, seen from front.
Rev. LAETITIA AVG(G/N). Laetitia standing left, holding wreath in right hand and anchor in left hand.
— — —//—
Lit.: NOR. 1510 or 1513–6/CUN. 2639 or 2641–2 or 2645–6; Schulzki 5a or 5b, or 6a or 6b; RIC 5.2, p. 408, 86 – 88 or 90

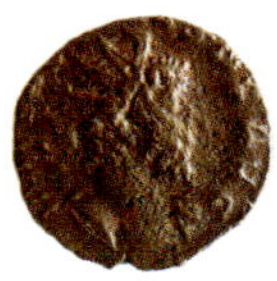

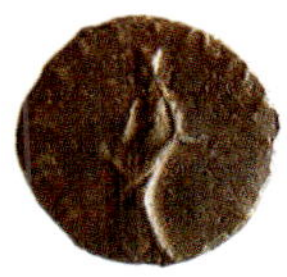

423. AE; 2,93 g.; 17,1 x 17,2 mm.; 12 h.; inv. n. 1719
(Obv. IMP [(C) TETRIC]VS P F AVG; Rev. LAETITIA AV[G(G/N)]; — — —//—)[73]

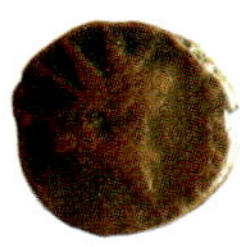

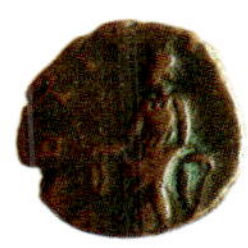

424. AE; 2,55 g.; 14,8 x 15,4 mm.; 12 h.; inv. n. 1720
(Obv. [IMP (C) TETRICV]S P F AVG; Rev. LAETIT-I[A AVG(G/N)]; — — —//—)[74]

TETRICUS II.
SON OF TETRICUS I.
(CAESAR 273 – 274 A.D.)

Augusta Treverorum

272 – 273 A.D.

Antoninianus
Obv. C PIV ESV TETRICVS CAES. Radiated bust of emperor in paludamentum looking right, seen from rear.
Rev. SPES PVBLICA. Spes walking left, holding flower in right hand and raising skirt with left hand.
— — —//—
Lit.: NOR. 1526/CUN. 2608; Schulzki 10; RIC 5.2, p. 424, 272

[73] The poor condition of the coin allows more interpretations.
[74] The poor condition of the coin allows more interpretations.

425. AE; 2,11 g.; 18,0 x 16,4 mm.; 6 h.; inv. n. 1721
(Obv. [C PIV] ESV TETRI[CVS CAES]; Rev. SPES [PVBLICA]; — — —//—)

426. AE; 1,96 g.; 20,0 x 15,9 mm.; 7 h.; inv. n. 1722
(Obv. C P[IV ESV TETRICVS CAES]; Rev. [SPES] – P-V[BLICA]; — — —//—)

427. AE; 1,12 g.; 15,4 x 14,4 mm.; 7 h.; inv. n. 1723
(Obv. C PIV ESV TETR[ICVS CAES]; Rev. [SPES P]VBL[I]C[A]; — — —//—)

273 – 274 A.D.

Antoninianus
Obv. C PIV ESV TETRICVS CAES. Radiated bust of emperor in paludamentum looking right, seen from rear.
Rev. SPES AVGG. Spes walking left, holding flower in right hand and raising skirt with left hand.
— — —//—
Lit.: NOR. 1533/CUN. 2647; Schulzki 9a; RIC 5.2, p. 424, 270

428. AE; 2,59 g.; 17,0 x 18,4 mm.; 6 h.; inv. n. 1724
(Obv. C PIV ESV TETR[ICVS C]AES; Rev. [SPE]S AVGG; — — —//—)

Contemporary imitation

273 – 274 A.D.

Antoninianus
Obv. TETRICVS CAES. Radiated bust of emperor in cuirass looking right, seen from front.
Rev. MINERVA AVG. Minerva standing left, holding patera in right hand and spear in left hand.
(*) — —//—
Lit.: NOR. -/CUN. -; Schulzki -; RIC 5.2, p. 422, 242

429. AE; 1,8 g.; 13,4 x 14,8 mm.; 7 h.; inv. n. 1725
(Obv. [TETRICV]S CAES; Rev. [MINERVA] – AVG; (*) — —//—)

THE CENTRAL EMPIRE
AURELIANUS
(270 – 275 A.D.)

Mediolanum

Summer of 271 A.D.

Antoninianus
Obv. IMP AVRELIANVS AVG. Radiated bust of emperor in cuirass and paludamentum looking right, seen from front.
Rev. CONCORDIA AVG. Emperor standing right, clasping right hand with Concordia, standing left.
— — —//S
Lit.: RIC temp n° 1431; LV 2.1 1667–1681; MIR 47 Med 4A/47a2; RIC 5.1, p. 278, Mediolanum 119

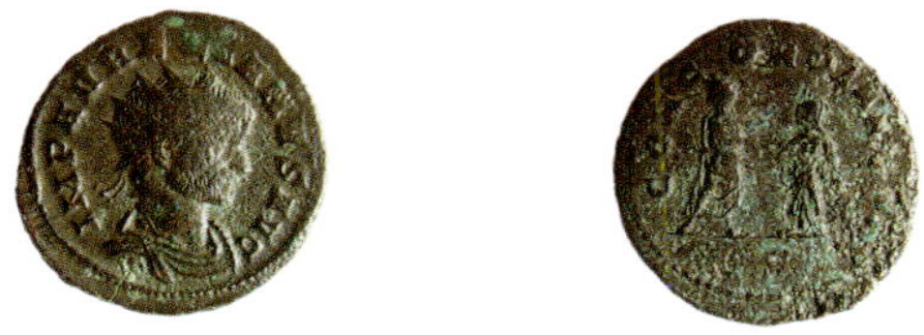

430. AE; 3,96 g.; 22,3 x 21,6 mm.; 12 h.; inv. n. 1726
(Obv. IMP AVRELIANVS AVG; Rev. CONC-ORDIA AV[G]; — — —//S)

Antoninianus
Obv. IMP AVRELIANVS AVG. Radiated bust of emperor in cuirass and paludamentum looking right, seen from front.
Rev. VICTORIA AVG. Victory walking left, holding wreath in right hand and palm in left hand.
— — —//T
Lit.: RIC temp n° 1440; LV 2.1 1774–1775; MIR 47 Med 3/40b3; RIC 5.1, p. 280, Mediolanum 144

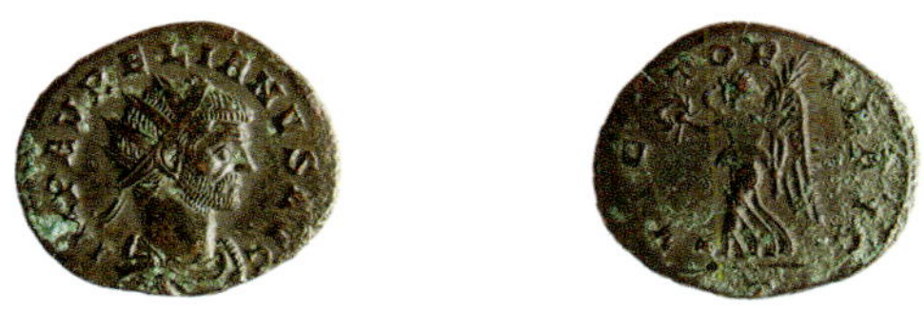

431. AE; 3,12 g.; 19,2 x 22,3 mm.; 12 h.; inv. n. 1727
(Obv. IMP AVRELIANVS AVG; Rev. VIC-TOR-IA AVG; — — —//T)

Antoninianus
Obv. IMP AVRELIANVS AVG. Radiated bust of emperor in cuirass and paludamentum looking right, seen from front.
Rev. VIRTVS AVG. Emperor standing right, holding vertical spear in right hand and globe in left hand, receiving Victory from Virtus standing left, holding transverse spear in left hand.
— — —//T
Lit.: RIC temp n° 1443; LV 2.1 1755–1773; MIR 47 Med 4A/50a3; RIC 5.1, p. 281, Mediolanum 149

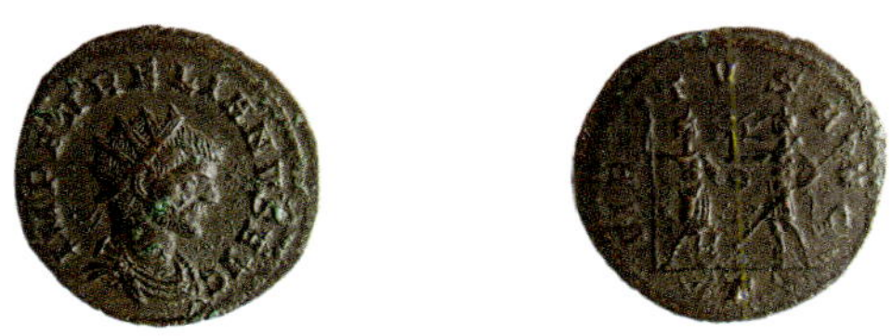

432. AE; 2,91 g.; 22,0 x 22,2 mm.; 12 h.; inv. n. 1728
(Obv. IMP AVRELIANVS AVG; Rev. VIR-TVS A-VG; — — —//T)

Autumn of 271 – Autumn of 272 A.D.

Antoninianus
Obv. IMP AVRELIANVS AVG. Radiated bust of emperor in cuirass looking right, seen from front.
Rev. FORTVNA REDVX. Fortuna seated left, holding rudder in right hand and cornucopiae in left hand; wheel beneath seatl.
— — —//P
Lit.: RIC temp n° 1456; LV 2.1 1833–1900; MIR 47 Med 4B/66b1; RIC 5.1, p. 279, Mediolanum 128

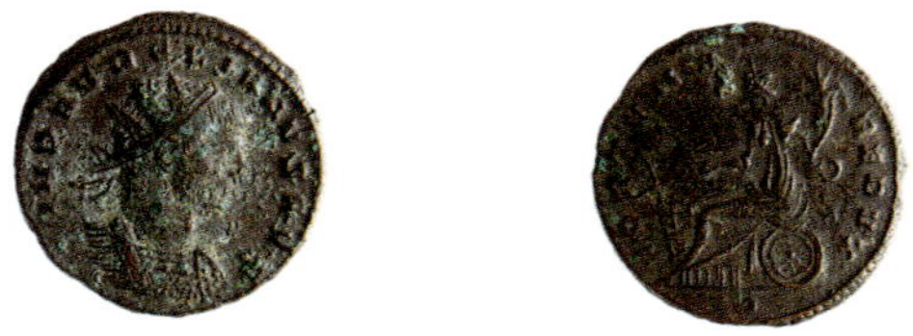

433. AE; 3,92 g.; 21,9 x 21,4 mm.; 7 h.; inv. n. 1729
(Obv. IMP AVRELIANVS AVG; Rev. FORTVNA – REDVX; — — —//P)

Antoninianus
Obv. IMP AVRELIANVS AVG. Radiated bust of emperor in cuirass looking right, seen from front.
Rev. IOVI CONSERVATORI. Emperor standing right, receiving globe from Jupiter, who is standing left, holding vertical sceptre in left hand.
— — —//P
Lit.: RIC temp n° 1457; LV 2.1 2169–2177; MIR 47 Med 4B/58b1; RIC 5.1, p. 279, Mediolanum 131 var.[75]

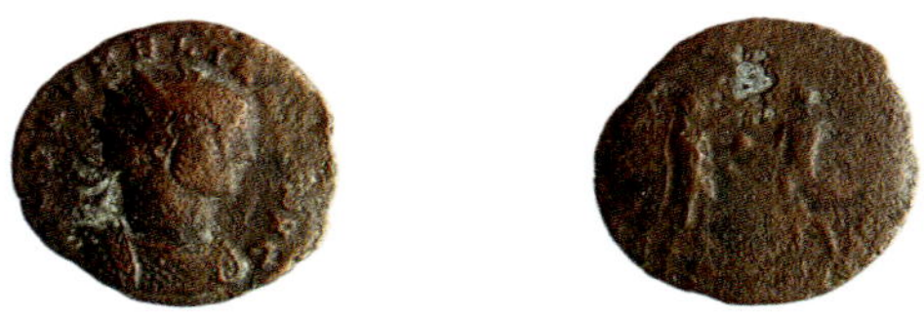

434. AE; 2,57 g.; 19,7 x 21,7 mm.; 5 h.; inv. n. 1730
(Obv. IMP AVRELIA[NVS A]VG; Rev. IOVI CO[NSERVATORI]; — — —//[P])

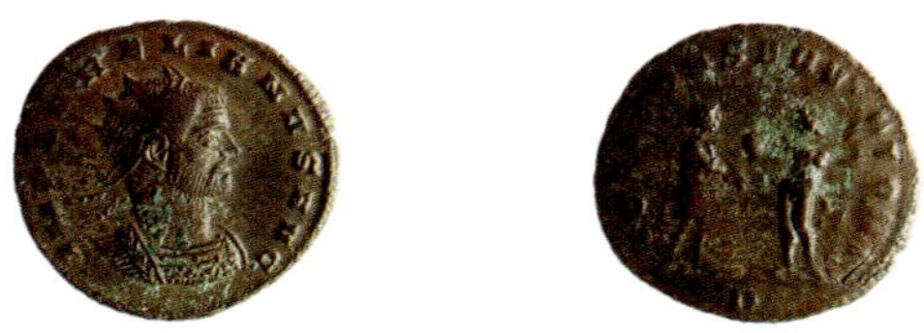

435. AE; 3,18 g.; 21,0 x 21,8 mm.; 5 h.; inv. n. 1731
(Obv. IMP AVRELIANVS AVG; Rev. IOVI CONSERV-ATORI; — — —//P)

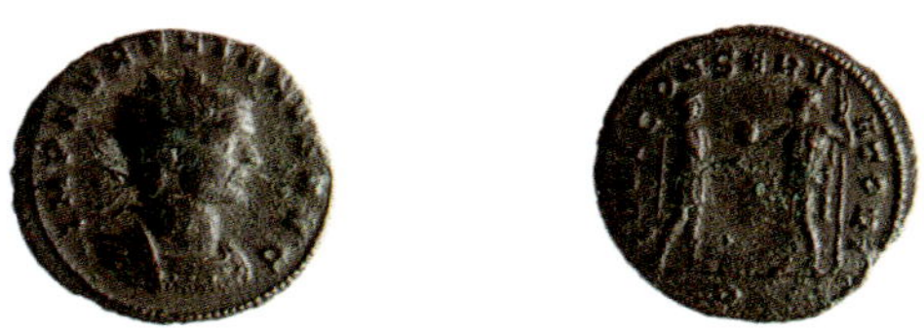

436. AE; 3,12 g.; 20,2 x 21,6 mm.; 6 h.; inv. n. 1732
(Obv. IMP AVRELIANVS AVG; Rev. IOVI CONSERV-ATORI; — — —//P)

[75] RIC 5.1, p. 279, Mediolanum 131 notes Jupiter standing right and emperor standing left.

Antoninianus

Obv. IMP AVRELIANVS AVG. Radiated bust of emperor in cuirass looking right, seen from front.

Rev. IOVI CONSER. Emperor standing right, holding transverse sceptre in left hand, receiving globe from Jupiter, who is standing left, holding vertical sceptre in left hand.

— — —//P

Lit.: RIC temp n° 1459; LV 2.1 2220–2271; MIR 47 Med 4B/59b1; RIC 5.1, p. 279, Mediolanum 129

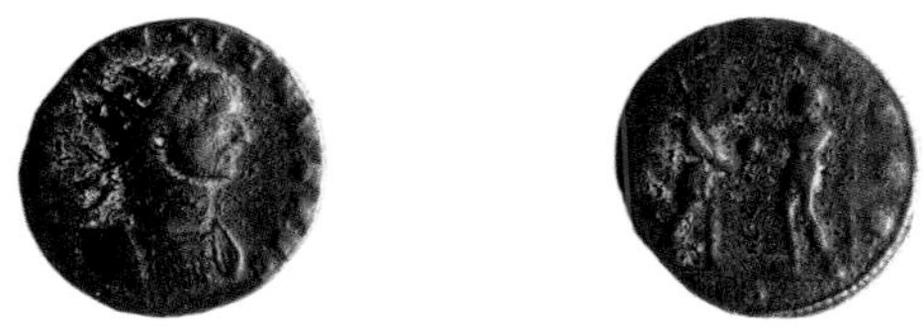

437. AE; 3,69 g.; 20,3 x 20,2 mm.; 6 h.; inv. n. 1733
(Obv. IMP AVRELIANVS AVG; Rev. [IOVI] CON-SER; — — —//P)

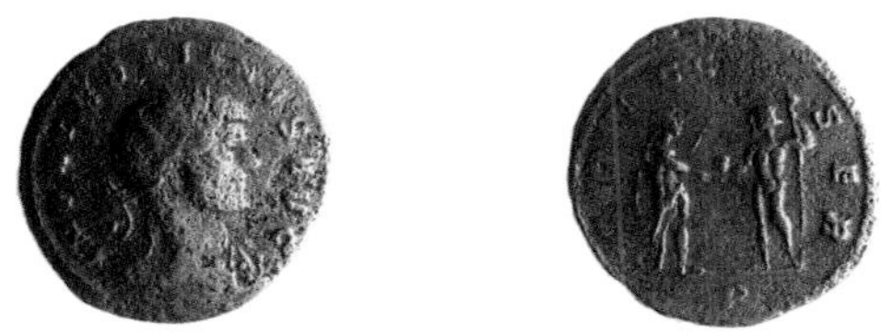

438.[76] AE; 3 g.; 22,3 x 22,4 mm.; 6 h.; inv. n. 1734
(Obv. IMP AVRELIANVS AVG; Rev. IOV CC – SER (sic!); — — —//P)

Antoninianus

Obv. IMP AVRELIANVS AVG. Radiated bust of emperor in cuirass looking right, seen from front.

Rev. RESTITVT ORIENTIS. Emperor standing left, holding vertical spear in left hand, being crowned by female figure standing right, holding wreath in right hand.

— — —//P

Lit.: RIC temp n° 1462; LV 2.1 2272–2424; MIR 47 Med 4B/55b1; RIC 5.1, p. 280, Mediolanum 140

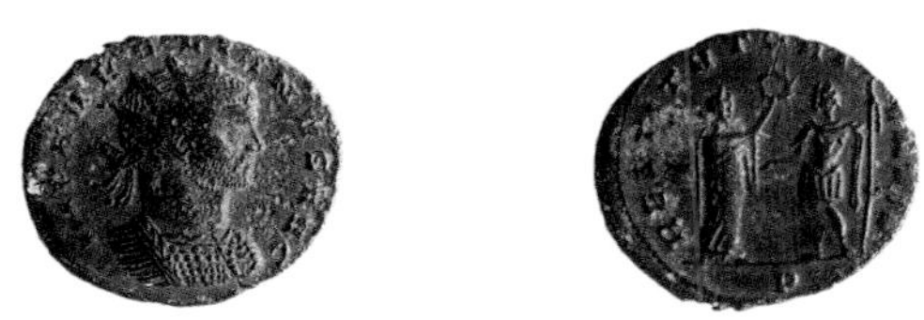

439. AE; 2,87 g.; 19,7 x 22,2 mm.; 7 h.; inv. n. 1735
(Obv. IMP AVRELIANVS AVG; Rev. RESTITVT ORI-ENTIS; — — —//P)

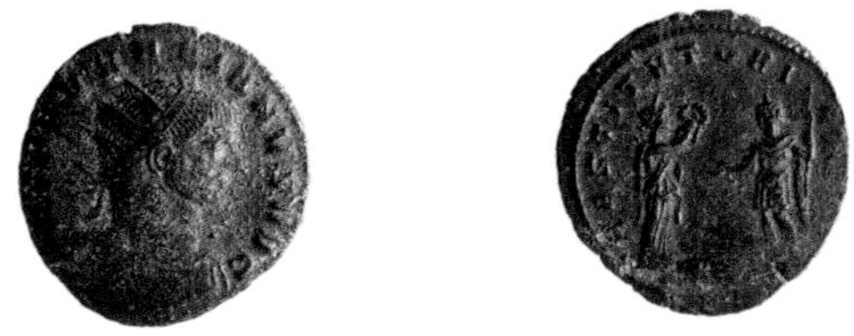

440. AE; 3,52 g.; 23,2 x 21,5 mm.; 12 h.; inv. n. 1736
(Obv. IMP AVRELIANVS AVG; Rev. RESTITVT ORI-E[NTIS]; — — —//[P])

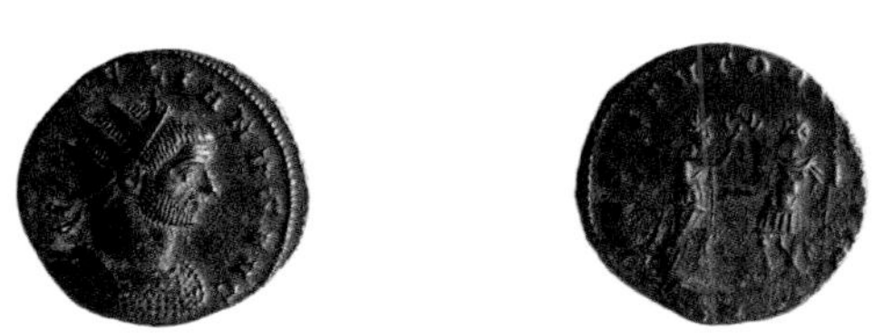

441. AE; 3,69 g.; 20,1 x 20,8 mm.; 12 h.; inv. n. 1737
(Obv. [I]MP AVRELIANVS AVG; Rev. RESTITVT ORI-ENTIS; — — —//P)

[76] The reverse transcription with double C is probably a result of a double strike from when the original IOVI CON – SER became IOV CC – SER.

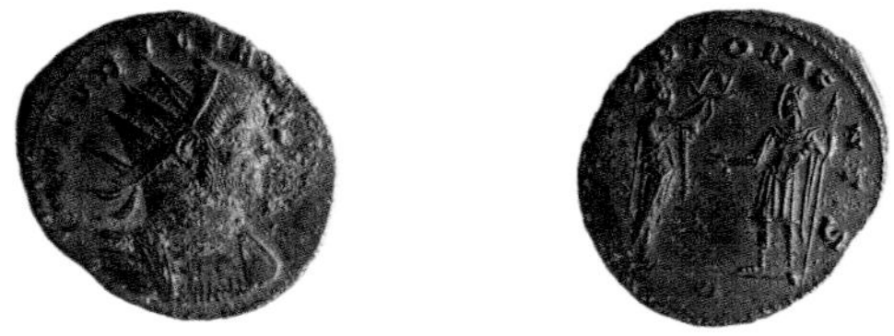

442. AE; 3,84 g.; 22,6 x 22,2 mm.; 12 h.; inv. n. 1738
(Obv. IMP AVRELIAN[VS AVG]; Rev. [REST]ITVT ORIE-NTIS; — — —//P)

Antoninianus
Obv. IMP AVRELIANVS AVG. Radiated bust of emperor in cuirass looking right, seen from front.
Rev. CONCORDIA MILITVM. Emperor standing right, clasping right hand with Concordia, standing left.
— — —//S
Lit.: RIC temp n° 1464; LV 2.1 2426–2623; MIR 47 Med 4B/60c2; RIC 5.1, p. 278, Mediolanum 120

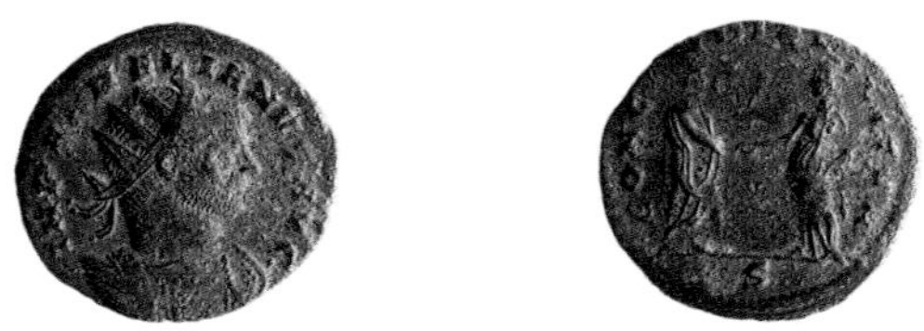

443. AE; 3,01 g.; 21,7 x 22,5 mm.; 6 h.; inv. n. 1739
(Obv. IMP AVRELIANVS AVG; Rev. CONCORDIA MILITVM; — — —//S)

Antoninianus
Obv. IMP AVRELIANVS AVG. Radiated bust of emperor in cuirass looking right, seen from front.
Rev. PIETAS AVG. Emperor standing right, sacrificing over altar with empress standing left.
— — —//S
Lit.: RIC temp n° 1468; LV 2.1 2625–2719; MIR 47 Med 4B/61b2; RIC 5.1, p. 280, Mediolanum 138

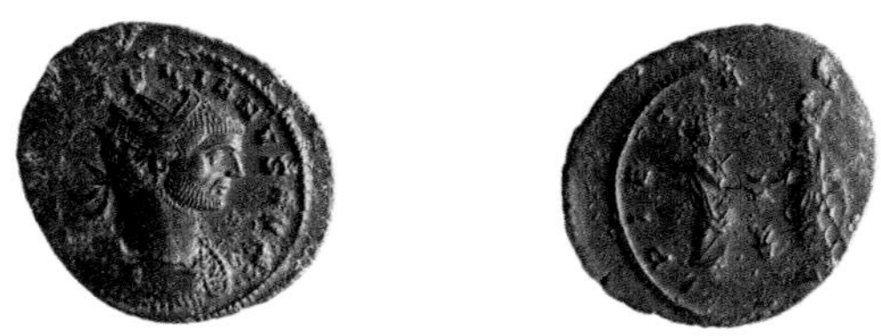

444. AE; 3,63 g.; 22,6 x 23,6 mm.; 12 h.; inv. n. 1740
(Obv. IM[P A]VRELIANVS AVG; Rev. PIE-T-A-S – [AVG]; — — —//S)

Antoninianus
Obv. IMP AVRELIANVS AVG. Radiated bust of emperor in cuirass looking right, seen from front.
Rev. FORTVNA REDVX. Fortuna seated left, holding rudder in right hand and cornucopiae in left hand; wheel beneath seat.
— — —//T
Lit.: RIC temp n° 1469; LV 2.1 1973–2060; MIR 47 Med 4B/66b3; RIC 5.1, p. 279, Mediolanum 128

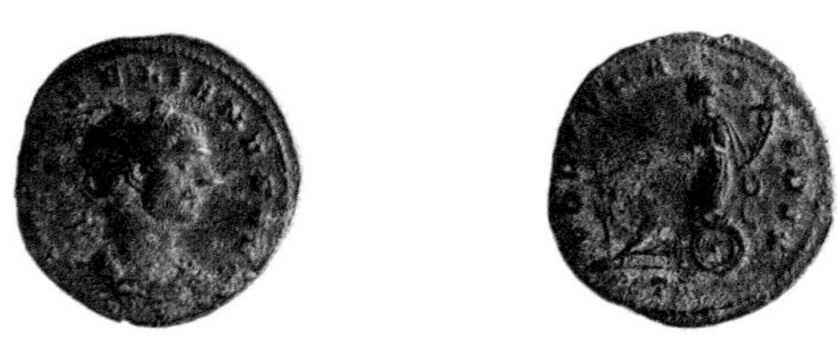

445. AE; 3,18 g.; 22,2 x 21,0 mm.; 6 h.; inv. n. 1741
(Obv. IMP AVRELIANVS AVG; Rev. FORTVNA – R-EDVX; — — —//T)

Antoninianus
Obv. IMP AVRELIANVS AVG. Radiated bust of emperor in cuirass looking right, seen from front.
Rev. VIRTVS MILITVM. Emperor standing right, holding vertical spear in right hand and globe in left hand, receiving Victory from Virtus standing left, holding transverse spear in left hand.
— — —//T
Lit.: RIC temp n° 1472; LV 2.1 2720–2940; MIR 47 Med 4B/62b3; RIC 5.1, p. 281, Mediolanum 147 var.[77]

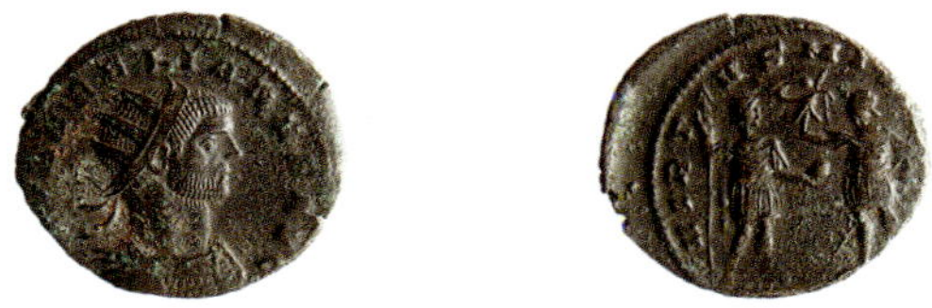

446. AE; 4,07 g.; 20,1 x 22,7 mm.; 12 h.; inv. n. 1742
(Obv. [IMP] AVRELIANVS AVG; Rev. VIRT-VS MI[LITVM]; — — —//[T])

Antoninianus
Obv. IMP AVRELIANVS AVG. Radiated bust of emperor in cuirass looking right, seen from front.
Rev. ROMAE AETERNAE. Emperor standing right, receiving Victory from Roma, seated on shield left, holding vertical sceptre in left hand.
— — —//Q
Lit.: RIC temp n° 1476; LV 2.1 2941–3081; MIR 47 Med 4B/64b4; RIC 5.1, p. 280, Mediolanum 142

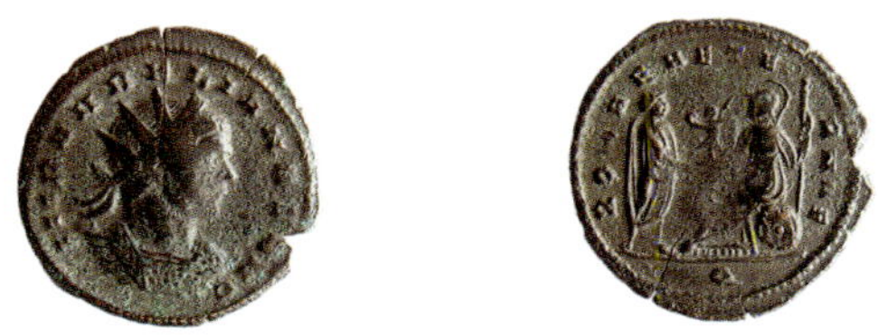

447. AE; 3,34 g.; 22,4 x 21,9 mm.; 5 h.; inv. n. 1743
(Obv. IMP AVRELIANVS AVG; Rev. ROMAE AETE-RNAE; — — —//Q)

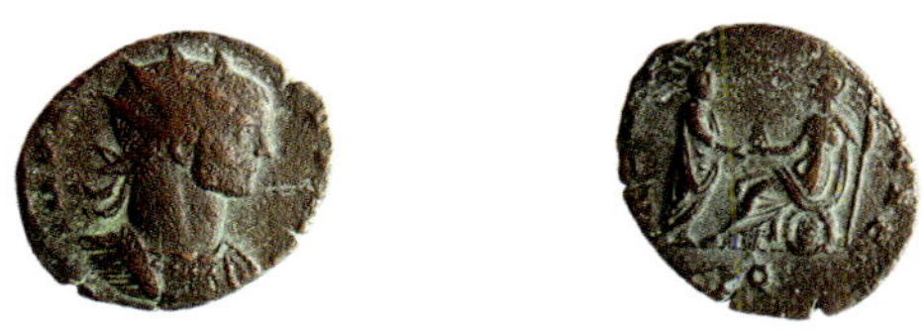

448. AE; 3,78 g.; 19,0 x 20,4 mm.; 12 h.; inv. n. 1744
(Obv. IMP AVRE[LIAN]VS [AVG]; Rev. ROMA[E AETER]NAE; — — —//Q)

End of 272 – Early 274 A.D.

Antoninianus
Obv. IMP AVRELIANVS AVG. Radiated bust of emperor in cuirass looking right, seen from front.
Rev. RESTITVT ORBIS. Emperor standing left, holding vertical spear in left hand, being crowned by female figure standing right, holding wreath in right hand.
— — —//P
Lit.: RIC temp n° 1493; LV 2.1 3705–3801; MIR 47 Med 4B/57c1; RIC 5.1, p. 280, Mediolanum 139

[77] RIC 5.1, p. 281, 147 notes Victory walking left.

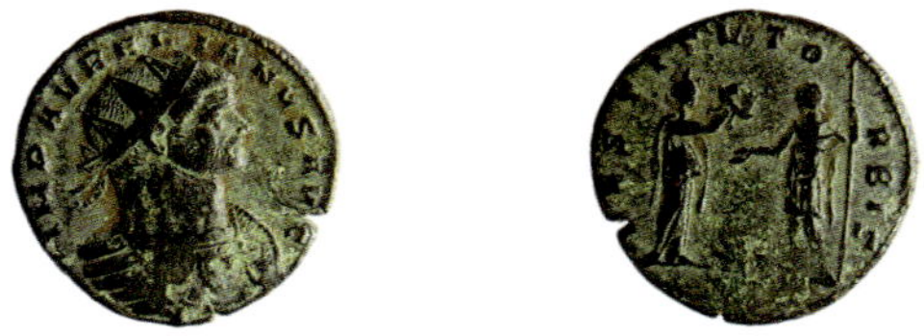

449. AE; 3,55 g.; 22,0 x 22,1 mm.; 12 h.; inv. n. 1745
(Obv. IMP AVRELIANVS AVG; Rev. RESTITVT O-RBIS; — — —//[P])

Antoninianus
Obv. IMP AVRELIANVS AVG. Radiated bust of emperor in cuirass looking right, seen from front.
Rev. CONCORDIA MILITVM. Emperor standing right, clasping right hand with Concordia, standing left.
— — —//S
Lit.: RIC temp n° 1494; LV 2.1 3815–3933; MIR 47 Med 4B/60c2; RIC 5.1, p. 278, Mediolanum 120

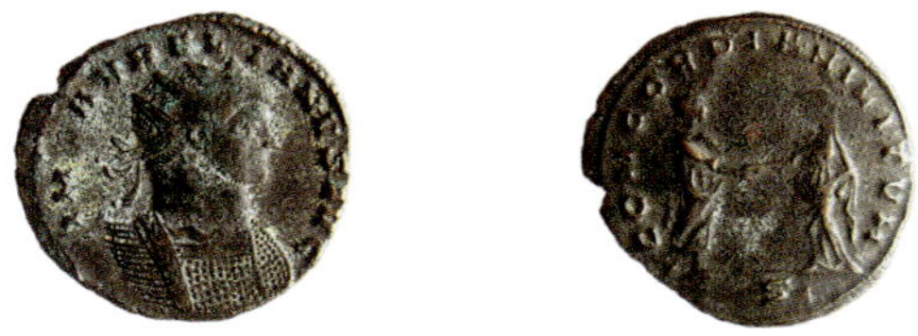

450. AE; 3,3 g.; 21,7 x 23,0 mm.; 6 h.; inv. n. 1746
(Obv. IMP AVRELIANVS AVG; Rev. CONCORDIA MILITVM; — — —//S)

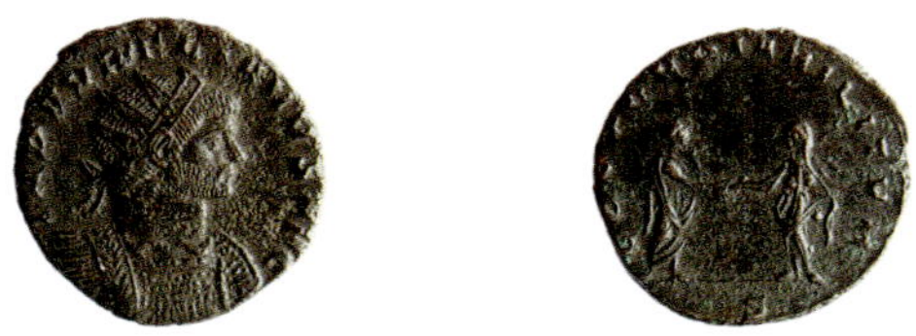

451. AE; 4,07 g.; 21,2 x 20,6 mm.; 10 h.; inv. n. 1747
(Obv. IMP AVRELIANVS AVG; Rev. CONCORDIA MILITVM; — — —//S)

Antoninianus
Obv. IMP AVRELIANVS AVG. Radiated bust of emperor in cuirass looking right, seen from front.
Rev. PIETAS AVG. Emperor standing right sacrificing over altar with empress standing left.
— — —//S
Lit.: RIC temp n° 1497; LV 2.1 3956–4116; MIR 47 Med 4B/61c2; RIC 5.1, p. 280, Mediolanum 138

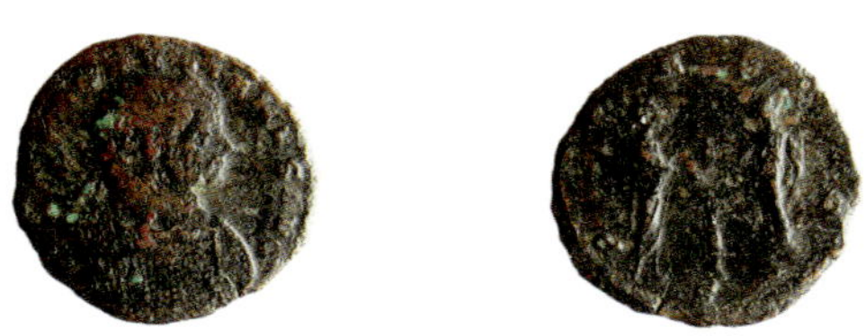

452. AE; 2,7 g.; 21,8 x 22,2 mm.; 12 h.; inv. n. 1748
(Obv. [IM]P AVRELIANVS AVG; Rev. P[I]ET-AS – [A]VG; — — —//S)

Antoninianus
Obv. IMP AVRELIANVS AVG. Radiated bust of emperor in cuirass looking right, seen from front.
Rev. FORTVNA REDVX. Fortuna seated left, holding rudder in right hand and cornucopiae in left hand; wheel beneath seat.
— — —//T
Lit.: RIC temp n° 1500; LV 2.1 3192–3263; MIR 47 Med 4B/66c3; RIC 5.1, p. 279, Mediolanum 128

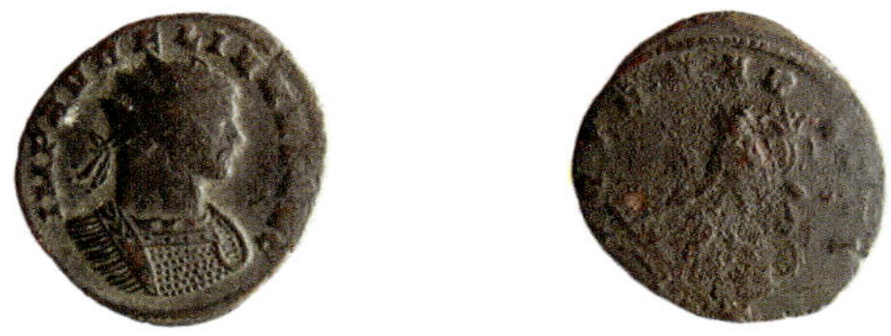

453. AE; 3,08 g.; 22,5 x 21,3 mm.; 6 h.; inv. n. 253
(Obv. IMP AVRELIANVS AVG; Rev. [F]ORTVNA R-EDVX; — — —//T)

Antoninianus
Obv. IMP AVRELIANVS AVG. Radiated bust of emperor in cuirass looking right, seen from front.
Rev. VIRT MILITVM. Emperor standing right, holding vertical spear in right hand and globe in left hand, receiving Victory from Virtus standing left, holding transverse spear in left hand.
— — —//T
Lit.: RIC temp n° 1502; LV 2.1 4121–4390; MIR 47 Med 4B/63c3; RIC 5.1, p. 281, Mediolanum 146 var.[78]

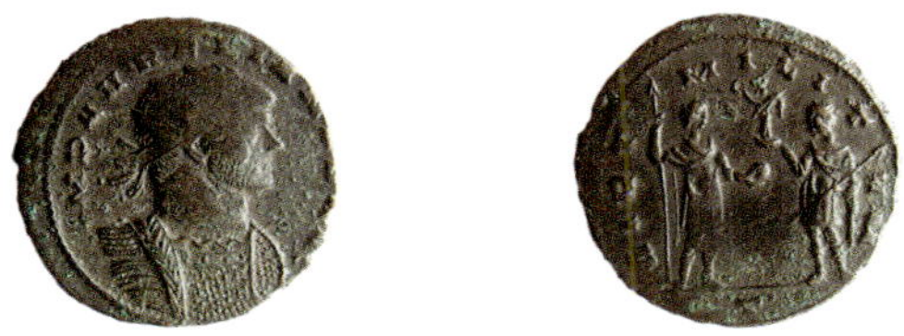

454. AE; 3,56 g.; 22,5 x 22,5 mm.; 5 h.; inv. n. 1749
(Obv. IMP AVRELIANVS AVG; Rev. VIRT – MILI-T-VM; — — —//T)

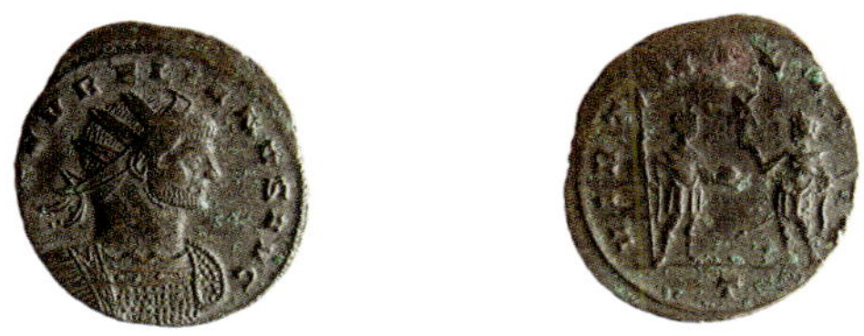

455. AE; 3,76 g.; 22,6 x 20,9 mm.; 12 h.; inv. n. 1750
(Obv. [IMP] AVRELIANVS AVG; Rev. VIRT MILIT-VM; — — —//T)

Antoninianus
Obv. IMP AVRELIANVS AVG. Radiated bust of emperor in cuirass looking right, seen from front.
Rev. ROMAE AETER. Emperor standing right, receiving Victory from Roma, seated on shield left, holding vertical sceptre in left hand.
— — —//Q
Lit.: RIC temp n° 1506; LV 2.1 4391–4579; MIR 47 Med 4B/65c4; RIC 5.1, p. 280, Mediolanum 142

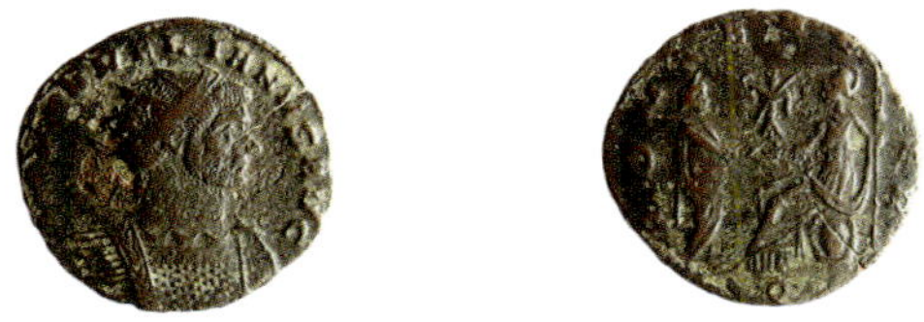

456. AE; 2,59 g.; 20,3 x 21,3 mm.; 4 h.; inv. n. 1751
(Obv. IMP AVRELIANVS AVG; Rev. ROMAE AE-TER; — — —//Q)

[78] RIC 5.1, p. 281, 146 notes Victory walking left.

Ticinum

June – September 274 A.D.

Antoninianus
Obv. IMP C AVRELIANVS AVG. Radiated bust of emperor in cuirass looking right, seen from front.
Rev. ORIENS AVG. Sol between two captives walking left, raising right hand, globe in left hand; captive under right foot.
* — —//PXXT
Lit.: RIC temp n° 1529; LV 2.1 4877–4950; MIR 47 Tic 2/72a1; RIC 5.1, p. 281, Ticinum 151

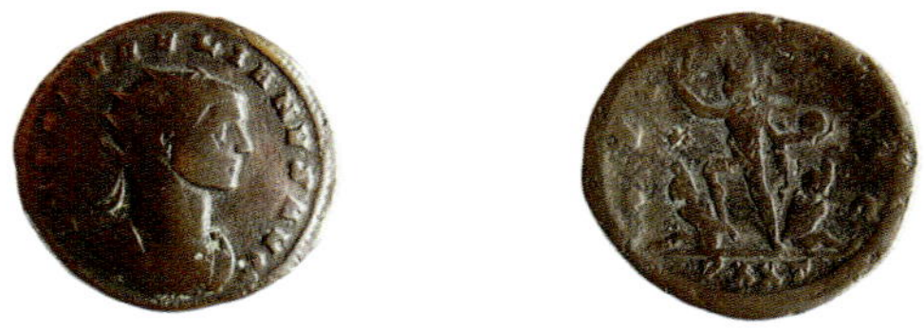

457. AE; 3,88 g.; 21,3 x 22,6 mm.; 6 h.; inv. n. 1752
(Obv. IMP C AVRELIANVS AVG; Rev. ORI-E-NS AVG; * — —//PXXT)

Roma

October – December 270 A.D.

Antoninianus
Obv. IMP C L DOM AVRELIANVS AVG. Radiated bust of emperor in cuirass and paludamentum looking right, seen from front.
Rev. FIDES MILITVM. Fides standing left, holding vertical standard in right hand and long vertical sceptre in left hand.
— — (ε)//—
Lit.: RIC temp n° 1584; LV 2.1 14–20; MIR 47 Rom 1/90a5a; RIC 5.1, p. 268, Rome 28

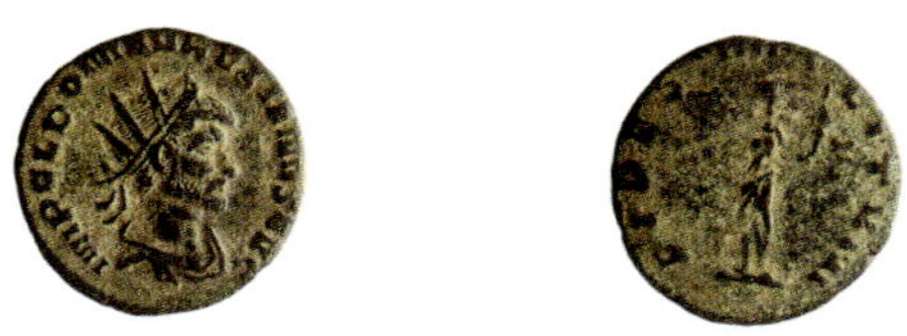

458. AE; 2,57 g.; 19,8 x 19,1 mm.; 12 h.; inv. n. 1753
(Obv. IMP C L DOM AVRELIANVS AVG; Rev. FIDES MI-LITVM; — — (ε)//—)

Summer of 273 A.D.

Antoninianus
Obv. IMP AVRELIANVS AVG. Radiated bust of emperor in cuirass looking right, seen from rear.
Rev. SOLI INVICTO. Sol standing right, head turned left, raising right hand, globe in left hand.
— — —//Δ
Lit.: RIC temp n° 1614; LV 2.1 -; MIR 47 Rom 2/113e4; RIC 5.1, p. 271, Rome 54

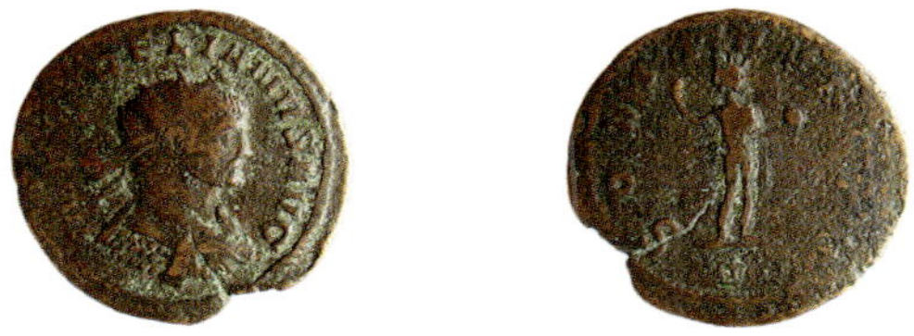

459. AE; 3,78 g.; 23,0 x 24,0 mm.; 11 h.; inv. n. 1754
(Obv. IMP [AV]RELIANVS AVG; Rev. SOLI – I-NVICTO; — — —//Δ)

Autumn of 273 A.D.

Antoninianus
Obv. IMP AVRELIANVS AVG. Radiated bust of emperor in cuirass looking right, seen from front.
Rev. ORIENS AVG. Sol walking left, raising right hand, globe in left hand; captive under right foot.
— — —//VI
Lit.: RIC temp n° 1683; LV 2.1 279–281; MIR 47 Rom 3/116e6; RIC 5.1, –

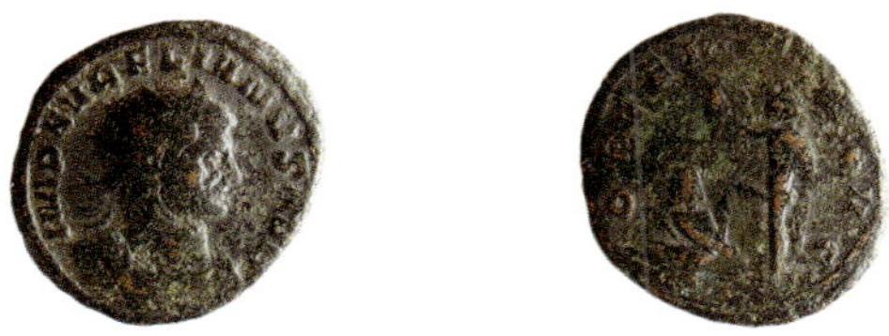

460. AE; 3,18 g.; 21,5 x 21,7 mm.; 6 h.; inv. n. 1755
(Obv. IMP AVRELIANVS AVG; Rev. ORIEN[S A-]VG; — — —//VI)

End of 273 – Early 274 A.D.

Antoninianus
Obv. AVRELIANVS AVG. Radiated bust of emperor in cuirass looking right, seen from front.
Rev. ORIENS AVG. Sol standing left, raising right hand, globe in left hand; at feet to left captive.
— — —//P
Lit.: RIC temp n° 1698; LV 2.1 361–362; MIR 47 Rom 3/115h1; RIC 5.1, -

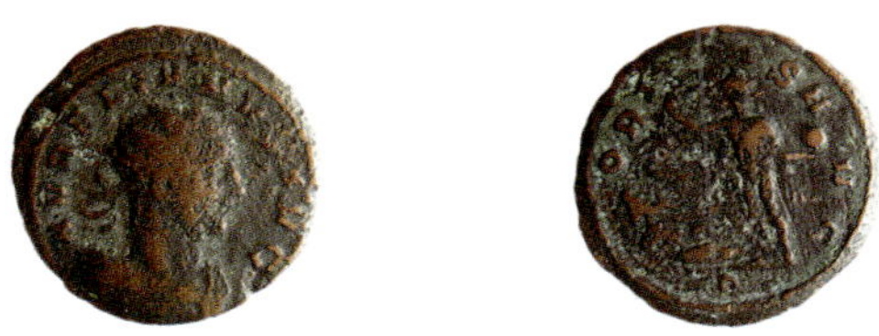

461. AE; 3,3 g.; 21,7 x 22,2 mm.; 6 h.; inv. n. 1756
(Obv. AVRELIANVS AVG; Rev. ORI[EN]S A-VG; — — —//P)

Antoninianus
Obv. AVRELIANVS AVG. Radiated bust of emperor in cuirass looking right, seen from front.
Rev. ORIENS AVG. Sol standing right, head turned left, raising right hand, globe in left hand; at feet to left captive.
— — —//T
Lit.: RIC temp n° 1702; LV 2.1 444–472; MIR 47 Rom 3/117h3; RIC 5.1, –

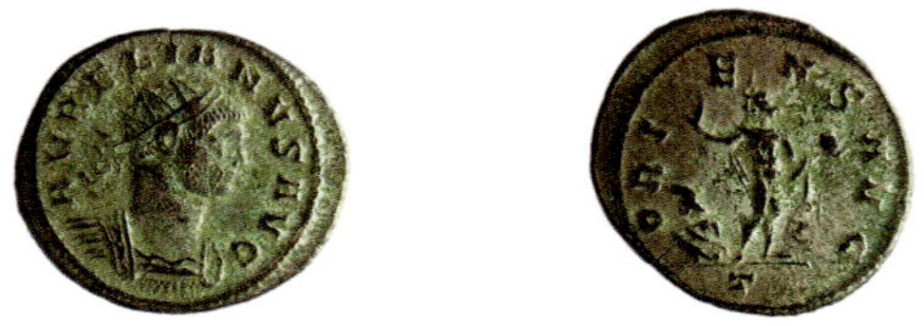

462. AE; 4,14 g.; 20,4 x 22,6 mm.; 5 h.; inv. n. 1757
(Obv. AVRELIANVS AVG; Rev. ORI-E-NS – AVG; — — —//T)

Spring – Summer of 274 A.D.

Antoninianus
Obv. IMP AVRELIANVS AVG. Radiated bust of emperor in cuirass looking right, seen from front.
Rev. ORIENS AVG. Sol between two captives walking left, raising right hand, globe in left hand; captive under right foot.
— — V//XXI
Lit.: RIC temp n° 1744; LV 2.1 807–809; MIR 47 Rom 4/119a5; RIC 5.1, p. 272, Rome 62

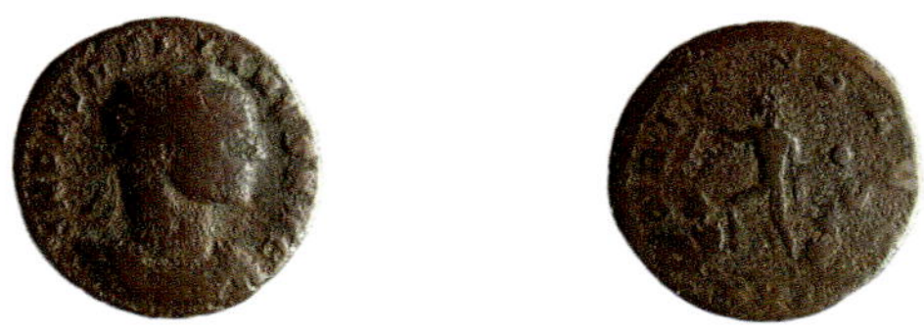

463. AE; 3 g.; 20,8 x 20,9 mm.; 6 h.; inv. n. 1758
(Obv. IMP AVRELIANVS AVG; Rev. ORI-E-NS AVG; — — V//XXI)

Antoninianus
Obv. IMP AVRELIANVS AVG. Radiated bust of emperor in cuirass looking right, seen from front.
Rev. ORIENS AVG. Sol between two captives walking left, raising right hand, globe in left hand; captive under right foot.
— — —//BXXI
Lit.: RIC temp n° 1762; LV 2.1 880–894; MIR 47 Rom 5/122b2; RIC 5.1, p. 272, Rome 62

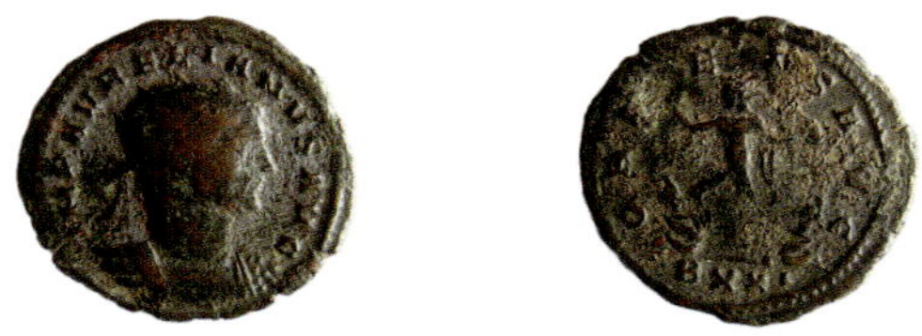

464. AE; 3,47 g.; 21,8 x 23,5 mm.; 6 h.; inv. n. 1759
(Obv. IMP AVRELIANVS AVG; Rev. ORIE-N-S AVG; — — —//BXXI)

Early – September 275 A.D.

Antoninianus
Obv. IMP AVRELIANVS AVG. Radiated bust of emperor in cuirass looking right, seen from front.
Rev. ORIENS AVG. Sol walking right, holding branch in right hand and bow in left hand; captive under left foot.
B — —//XXIR
Lit.: RIC temp n° 1815; LV 2.1 1137–1166; MIR 47 Rom 6/130h2; RIC 5.1, p. 272, Rome 64

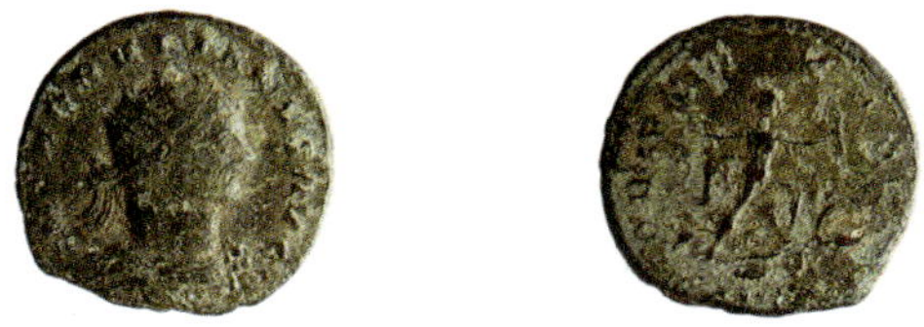

465. AE; 4,03 g.; 21,3 x 21,2 mm.; 12 h.; inv. n. 1760
(Obv. IMP AVRELIANVS AVG; Rev. ORIE-[N]-S AV[G]; B — —//[XXIR])

Antoninianus
Obv. IMP AVRELIANVS AVG. Radiated bust of emperor in cuirass looking right, seen from front.
Rev. ORIENS AVG. Sol walking right, holding branch in right hand and bow in left hand; captive under left foot.
Z — —//XXIR
Lit.: RIC temp n° 1826; LV 2.1 1267–1282; MIR 47 Rom 6/130f7; RIC 5.1, p. 272, Rome 64

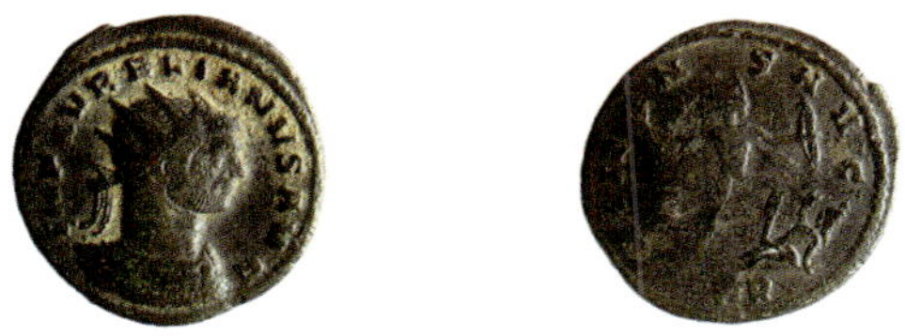

466. AE; 3,28 g.; 22,2 x 21,6 mm.; 11 h.; inv. n. 1761
(Obv. IMP AVRELIANVS AVG; Rev. ORIE-N-S AVG; Z — —//XXIR)

Denarius
Obv. IMP AVRELIANVS AVG. Laureated bust of emperor in cuirass and paludamentum looking right, seen from front.
Rev. VICTORIA AVG. Victory walking left, holding wreath in right hand and palm in left hand; at feet to left captive.
— — —//A
Lit.: RIC temp n° 1844; LV 2.1 1496; MIR 47 Rom 6/139e1; RIC 5.1, p. 273, Rome 73

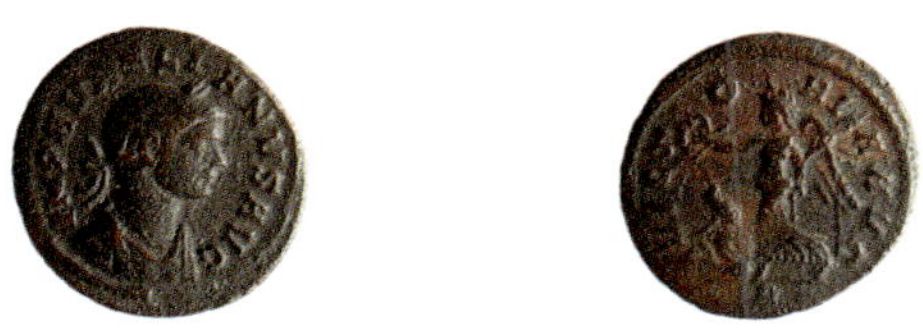

467. AE; 2,55 g.; 19,4 x 19,4 mm.; 6 h.; inv. n. 18.32
(Obv. IMP AVRELI-ANVS AVG; Rev. VICT-O-RI-A AVG; — — —//A)

As
Obv. IMP AVRELIANVS AVG. Laureated bust of emperor in cuirass looking right, seen from front.
Rev. CONCORDIA AVG. Emperor standing left, holding vertical spear in left hand, clasping right hand with empress, standing right; between them head of Sol.
— — —//Δ
Lit.: RIC temp n° 1878; LV 2.1 -; MIR 47 Rom 6/145d4; RIC 5.1, p. 275, Rome 80

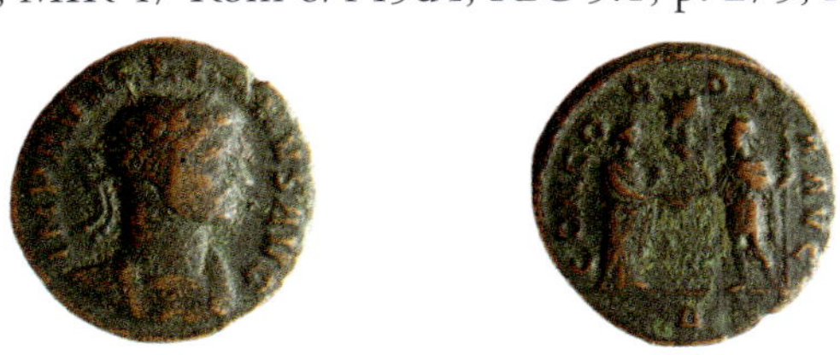

468. AE; 5,25 g.; 23,8 x 23,2 mm.; 6 h.; inv. n. 1762
(Obv. IMP AVRELIANVS AVG; Rev. CONCO-R-DI-A AVG; — — —//Δ)

Siscia

End of 271 – Autumn of 272 A.D.

Antoninianus
Obv. IMP AVRELIANVS AVG. Radiated bust of emperor in cuirass looking right, seen from front.
Rev. IOVI CONSER. Emperor standing right, holding transverse sceptre in left hand, receiving globe from Jupiter, standing left, holding vertical sceptre in left hand.
— — —//*P
Lit.: RIC temp n° 2133; LV 2.1 6448–6583; MIR 47 Sis 3B/199L1; RIC 5.1, p. 289, Siscia 225

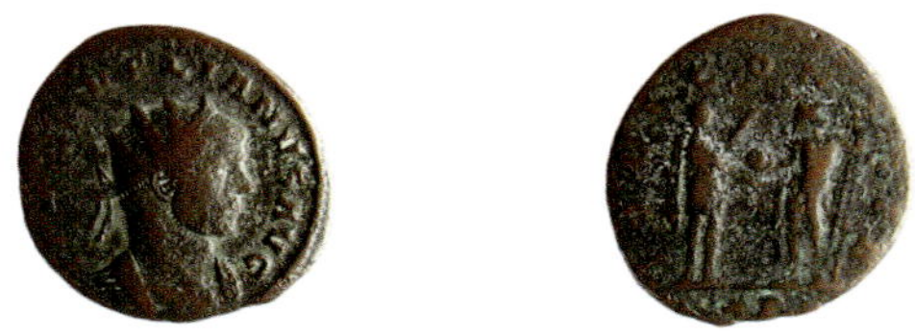

469. AE; 3,38 g.; 21,0 x 21,2 mm.; 1 h.; inv. n. 1763
(Obv. IMP [AV]RELIANVS AVG; Rev. IOVI CON-SER; — — —//*P)

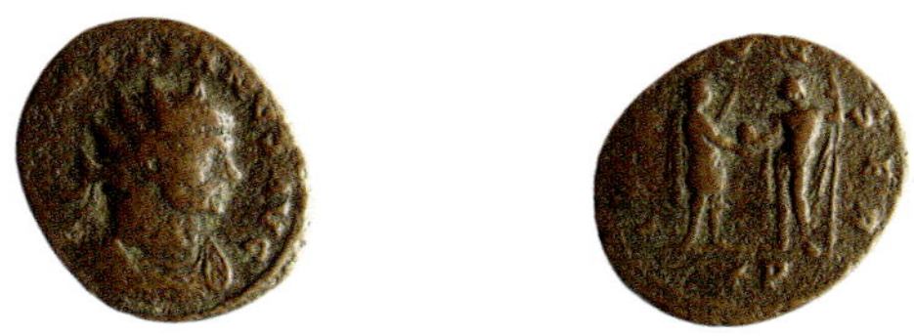

470. AE; 2,59 g.; 20,9 x 18,9 mm.; 5 h.; inv. n. 1764
(Obv. [IMP] AVRELIANVS AVG; Rev. I[OVI C]ON-SER; — — —//*P)

Antoninianus
Obv. IMP AVRELIANVS AVG. Radiated bust of emperor in cuirass looking right, seen from front.
Rev. IOVI CONSER. Emperor standing right, holding transverse sceptre in left hand, receiving globe from Jupiter, standing left, holding vertical sceptre in left hand.
— — —//*S
Lit.: RIC temp n° 2144; LV 2.1 6584–6689; MIR 47 Sis 3B/199L2; RIC 5.1, p. 289, Siscia 225

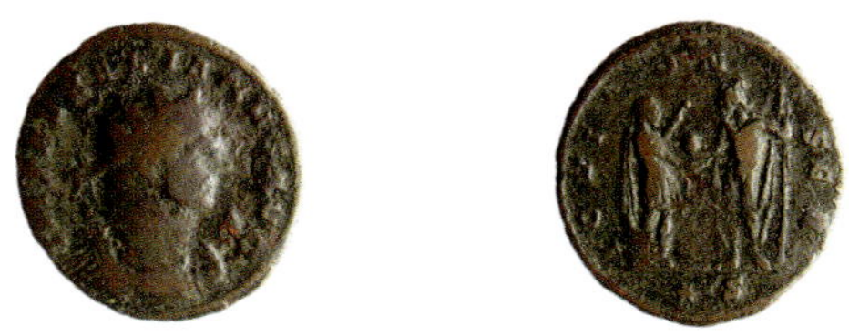

471. AE; 3,06 g.; 22,0 x 20,6 mm.; 6 h.; inv. n. 1765
(Obv. IMP AVRELIANVS AVG; Rev. IOVI C-ON-SER; — — —//*S)

Autumn of 272 – Early 274 A.D.

Antoninianus
Obv. IMP AVRELIANVS AVG. Radiated bust of emperor in cuirass looking right, seen from front.
Rev. CONCORDIA MILITVM. Emperor standing right, clasping right hand with Concordia, standing left.
— — —//*Q
Lit.: RIC temp n° 2216; LV 2.1 7526–7623; MIR 47 Sis 3B/213L4; RIC 5.1, p. 288, Siscia 216

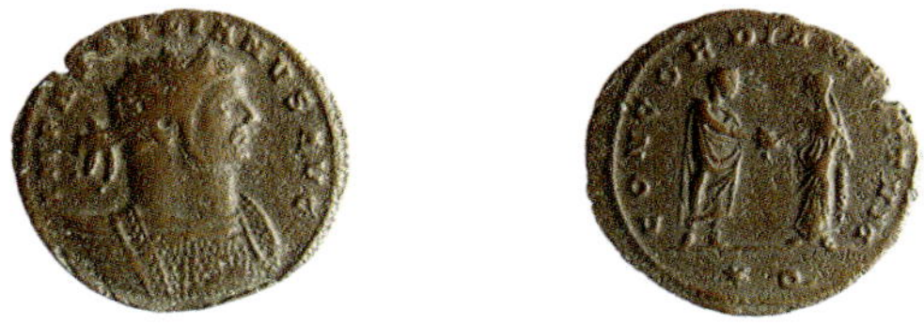

472. AE; 2,94 g.; 21,6 x 23,2 mm.; 12 h.; inv. n. 1766
(Obv. IMP AVRELIANVS AVG; Rev. CONCORDIA MI[L]ITVM; — — —//*Q)

Spring of 274 A.D.

Antoninianus
Obv. IMP C AVRELIANVS AVG. Radiated bust of emperor in cuirass looking right, seen from front.
Rev. ORIENS AVG. Sol between two captives walking left, raising right hand, globe in left hand; captive under right foot.
* — —//Q
Lit.: RIC temp n° 2272; LV 2.1 8045–8046; MIR 47 Sis 6/225c4; RIC 5.1, p. 293, Siscia 254

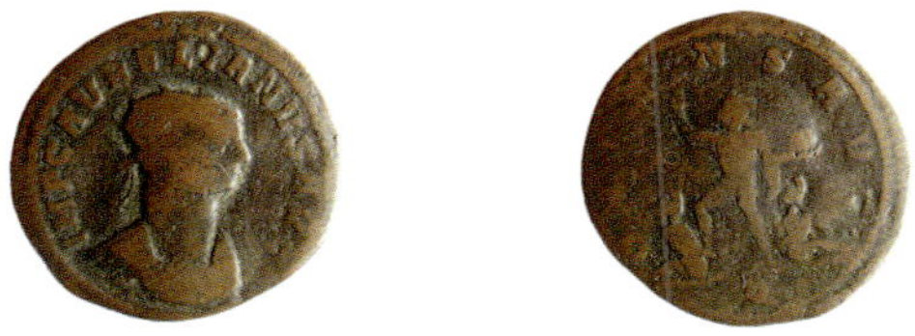

473. AE; 3,1 g.; 21,9 x 22,4 mm.; 12 h.; inv. n. 1767
(Obv. IMP C AVRELIANVS AVG; Rev. ORIE-NS AVG; * — —//Q)

Autumn of 274 – Spring of 275 A.D.

Antoninianus
Obv. IMP C AVRELIANVS AVG. Radiated bust of emperor in cuirass looking right, seen from front.
Rev. CONCORDIA MILITVM. Emperor standing right, clasping right hand with Concordia, standing left.
— — —//XXIP
Lit.: RIC temp n° 2355; LV 2.1 8304–8363; MIR 47 Sis 7/229c1; RIC 5.1, p. 292, Siscia 244

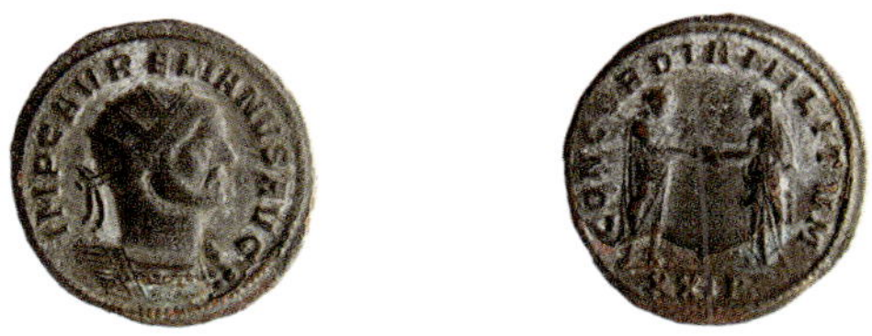

474. AE; 3,83 g.; 22,6 x 21,4 mm.; 1 h.; inv. n. 18.30
(Obv. IMP C AVRELIANVS AVG; Rev. CONCORDIA MILITVM; — — —//XXIP)

Serdica

November 274 – September 275 A.D.

Antoninianus
Obv. IMP AVRELIANVS AVG. Radiated bust of emperor in cuirass looking right, seen from rear.
Rev. RESTITVT ORBIS. Emperor standing left, holding vertical spear in left hand, being crowned by female figure standing right, holding wreath in right hand.
—*—//KAB
Lit.: RIC temp n° 2752; LV 2.1 -; MIR 47 Serdica 5/261h2; RIC 5.1, p. 297, Serdica 289 var.[79]

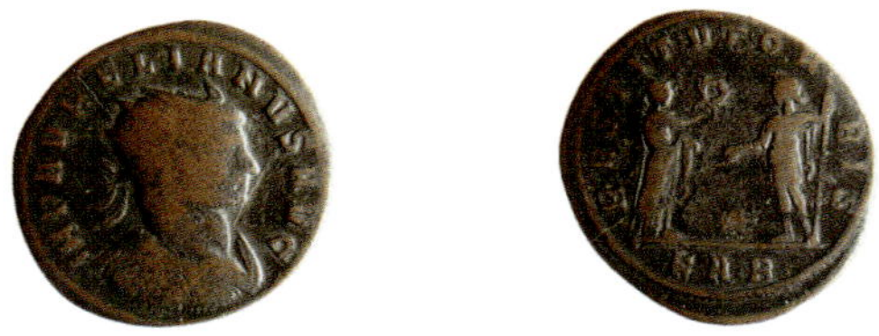

475. AE; 3,08 g.; 22,4 x 23,3 mm.; 5 h.; inv. n. 1768
(Obv. IMP AVRELIANVS AVG; Rev. RESTITVT OR-BIS; —*—//KAB)

Moneta Comitatensis – Byzantium

Autumn of 272 – Autumn of 273 A.D.

Antoninianus
Obv. IMP AVRELIANVS AVG. Radiated bust of emperor in cuirass looking right, seen from front.
Rev. IOVI CONSER. Emperor standing right, holding vertical sceptre in left hand, receiving globe from Jupiter, standing left, holding vertical sceptre in left hand.
— — —//B
Lit.: RIC temp n° 2503; LV 2.1 9098–9216; MIR 47 Moneta Comitatensis – Byzantium 2/278a2; RIC 5.1, p. 310, Tripolis 394 corr.[80]

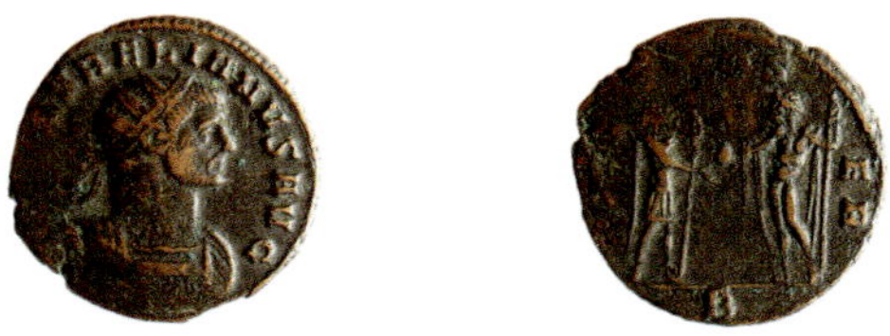

476. AE; 3,52 g.; 21,9 x 21,4 mm.; 6 h.; inv. n. 1769
(Obv. [IMP] AVRELIANVS AVG; Rev. [IOVI CO]NS-ER; — — —//B)

Antoninianus
Obv. IMP AVRELIANVS AVG. Radiated bust of emperor in cuirass looking right, seen from front.
Rev. CONCORD MILIT. Emperor standing right, holding transverse sceptre in left hand, clasping right hand with Concordia, standing left.
— — —//Γ
Lit.: RIC temp n° 2520; LV 2.1 9630–9736; MIR 47 Moneta Comitatensis – Byzantium 2/276a3; RIC 5.1, p. 309, Tripolis 391 corr.[81]

[79] RIC 5.1, p. 297, Serdica 289 does not note KAB in exergue.
[80] RIC 5.1 assigns this coin to the mint of Tripolis.
[81] RIC 5.1 assigns this coin to the mint of Tripolis.

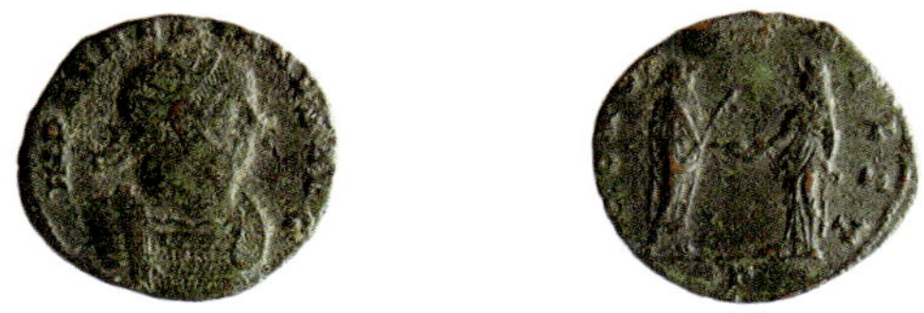

477. AE; 3,42 g.; 20,5 x 22,1 mm.; 12 h.; inv. n. 1770
(Obv. IMP AVRELIANVS AVG; Rev. CONC[ORD] MILIT; — — —//Γ)

Cyzicus

End of 271 A.D.

Antoninianus
Obv. IMP AVRELIANVS AVG. Radiated bust of emperor in cuirass looking right, seen from front.
Rev. SAECVLI FELICITAS. Emperor standing left, holding transverse spear in right hand and globe in left hand.
— — —//—
Lit.: RIC temp n° 2925; LV 2.1 10093–10105; MIR 47 Cyz 3/316a0; RIC 5.1, p. 305, Cyzicus 352

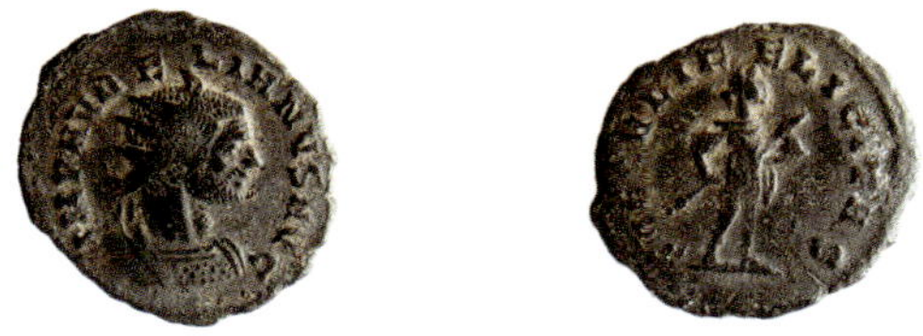

478. AE; 3,67 g.; 22,8 x 22,0 mm.; 5 h.; inv. n. 18.31
(Obv. IMP AVRE-LIANVS AVG; Rev. SAECVLI F-ELICITAS; — — —//—)

Autumn of 272 – Early 273 A.D.

Antoninianus
Obv. IMP C AVRELIANVS AVG. Radiated bust of emperor in cuirass looking right, seen from front.
Rev. RESTITVTOR ORBIS. Emperor standing left, holding vertical spear in left hand, being crowned by female figure standing right, holding wreath in right hand; captive between them.
— — —//(*A-Δ)
Lit.: RIC temp n° 2978 or 2781 or 2983 or 2984; LV 2.1 10291–10311 or 10312–10325 or 10326–10328 or 10329–10340; MIR 47 Cyz 6/337a1–4; RIC 5.1, p. 304, Cyzicus 349

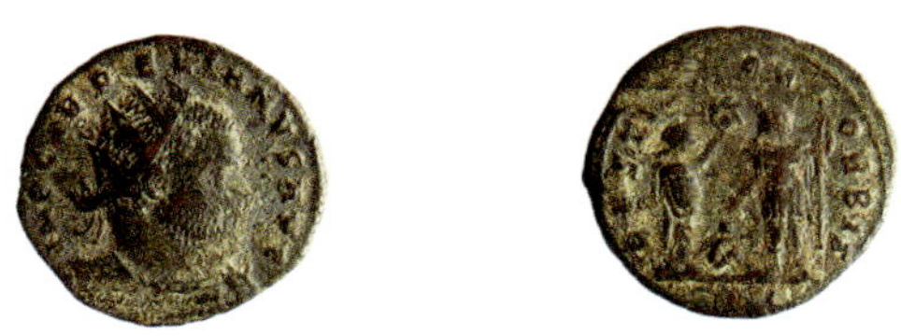

479. AE; 3,74 g.; 20,7 x 21,7 mm.; 6 h.; inv. n. 1771
(Obv. IMP C AVRELIANVS AVG; Rev. RESTI[TVT]OR – ORBIS; — — —//(*A-Δ))

Spring of 273 – Spring of 274 A.D.

Antoninianus
Obv. IMP C AVRELIANVS AVG. Radiated bust of emperor in cuirass looking right, seen from front.
Rev. RESTITVTOR ORBIS. Emperor standing left, holding vertical spear in left hand, being crowned by female figure standing right, holding wreath in right hand.
— — —//AC
Lit.: RIC temp n° 2989; LV 2.1 10347–10386; MIR 47 Cyz 7/342b1; RIC 5.1, p. 306, Cyzicus 368

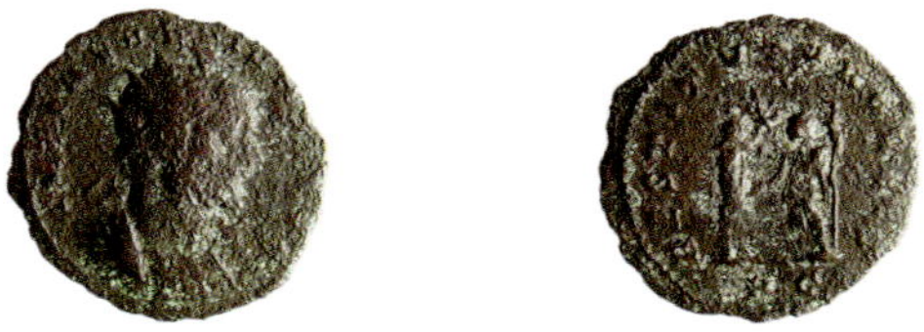

480. AE; 2,04 g.; 21,0 x 21,4 mm.; 5 h.; inv. n. 1772
(Obv. IMP C AVRELI[ANVS AVG]; Rev. RESTITVTOR ORBIS; — — —//AC)

Antoninianus
Obv. IMP C AVRELIANVS AVG. Radiated bust of emperor in cuirass looking right, seen from front.
Rev. RESTITVTOR – ORBIS. Emperor standing left, holding vertical spear in left hand, being crowned by female figure standing right, holding wreath in right hand.
— — —//BC
Lit.: RIC temp n° 2990; LV 2.1 10387–1010408; MIR 47 Cyz 7/342b2; RIC 5.1, p. 306, Cyzicus 368

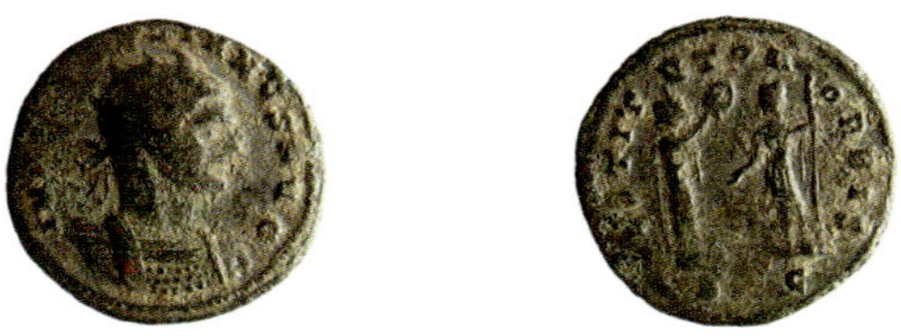

481. AE; 4,5 g.; 22,2 x 22,4 mm.; 6 h.; inv. n. 1773
(Obv. IMP [C AVRE]LIANVS AVG; Rev. [R]ESTIT-VTOR – ORBIS; — — —//BC)

SEVERINA WIFE OF AURELIANUS (AUGUSTA 274 – 275 A.D.)

Ticinum

September – November 275 A.D.

Antoninianus
Obv. SEVERINA AVG. Diademed and draped bust of empress on crescent looking right.
Rev. CONCORDIAE MILITVM. Concordia standing left, holding vertical standard in each hand.
— — —//PXXT
Lit.: RIC temp n° 1561; LV 2.1 5809–5831; MIR 47 Ticinum 5/79Aa1; RIC 5.1, p. 316, Ticinum 8

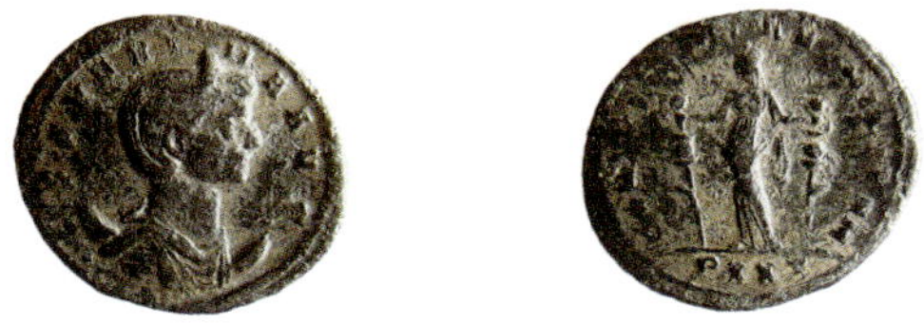

482. AE; 3,42 g.; 21,0 x 23,1 mm.; 12 h.; inv. n. 1774
(Obv. SEVERI-NA AVG; Rev. CON[C]OR-[DI]-AE – MILITVM; — — —//PXXT)

Roma

End of 274 A.D.

Antoninianus
Obv. SEVERINA AVG. Diademed and draped bust of empress on crescent looking right.
Rev. CONCORDIA AVGG. Emperor standing left, holding transverse sceptre in left hand, clasping right hand with empress, standing right.
— — —//ΓXXIR
Lit.: RIC temp n° 1792; LV 2.1 1032–1048; MIR 47 Rom 6/132s3; RIC 5.1, p. 315, Rome 3

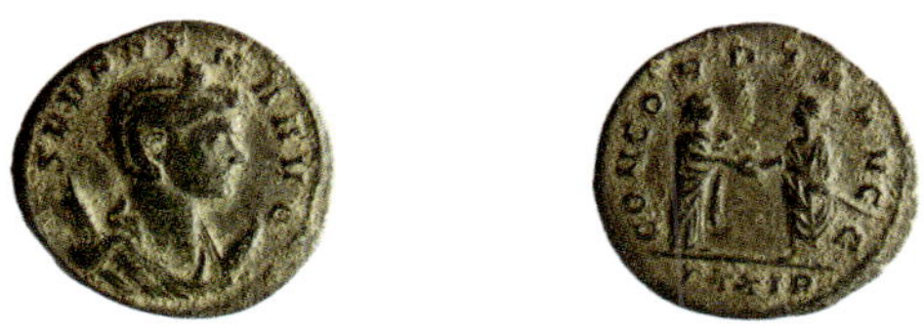

483. AE; 3,62 g.; 20,9 x 22,1 mm.; 12 h.; inv. n. 1775
(Obv. SEVERI-NA AVG; Rev. CONCO-RDIA AVG-G; — — —//ΓXXIR)

Early – September 275 A.D.

As
Obv. SEVERINA AVG. Diademed and draped bust of empress looking right.
Rev. IVNO REGINA. Juno standing left, holding patera in right hand and long vertical sceptre in left hand; at feet to left peacock.
— — —//ς
Lit.: RIC temp n° 1879; LV 2.1 -; MIR 47 Rom 6/147n6; RIC 5.1, p. 316, Rome 7

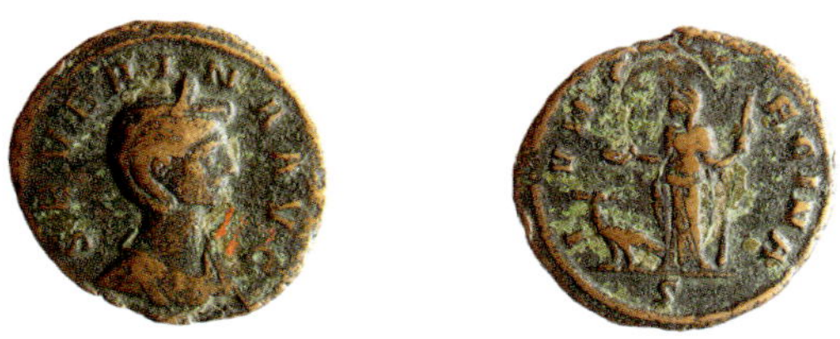

484. AE; 6,82 g.; 24,4 x 25,1 mm.; 6 h.; inv. n. 1776
(Obv. SEVERI-NA AVG; Rev. I-VNO – [R]-EGINA; — — —//ς)

Siscia

Autumn of 274 – Spring of 275 A.D.

Antoninianus
Obv. SEVERINAE AVG. Diademed and draped bust of empress on crescent looking right.
Rev. CONCORDIAE MILITVM. Concordia standing left, holding vertical standard in each hand.
— — P//XXI
Lit.: RIC temp n° 2419; LV 2.1 8913–8921; MIR 47 Sis 9/237a1; RIC 5.1, p. 317, Siscia 13

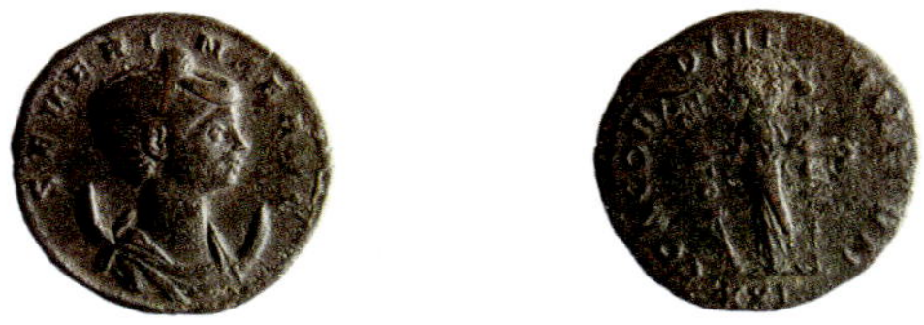

485. AE; 3,26 g.; 21,2 x 21,7 mm.; 12 h.; inv. n. 1777
(Obv. SEVERI-NAE AVG; Rev. CONCOR-DIAE MILITVM; — — P//XXI)

Antoninianus
Obv. SEVERINAE AVG. Diademed and draped bust of empress on crescent looking right.
Rev. CONCORDIAE MILITVM. Concordia standing left, holding vertical standard in each hand.
— — Q//XXI
Lit.: RIC temp n° 2430; LV 2.1 8927–8931; MIR 47 Sis 9/237a4; RIC 5.1, p. 317, Siscia 13

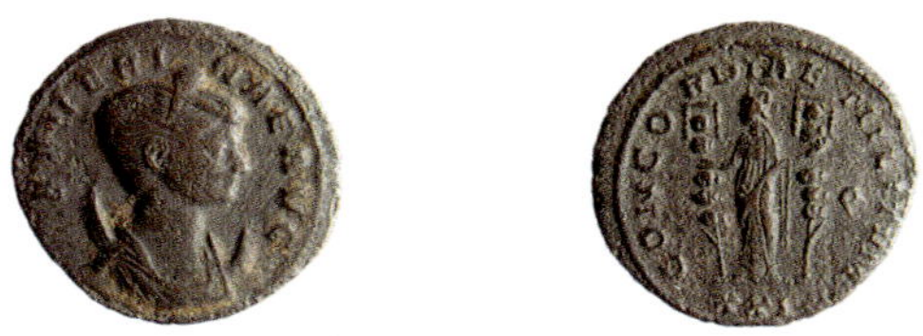

486. AE; 3,76 g.; 21,7 x 22,7 mm.; 12 h.; inv. n. 1778
(Obv. SEVERI-NAE AVG; Rev. CONCO-RDIAE – MILITVM; — — Q//XXI)

TACITUS
(275 – 276 A.D.)

Ticinum

November – December 275 A.D.

Antoninianus
Obv. IMP C M CL TACITVS AVG. Radiated bust of emperor in cuirass and paludamentum looking right, seen from front.
Rev. SALVS PVBLI. Salus standing right, feeding snake held in right hand from patera held in left hand.
— — —//T
Lit.: RIC temp n° 3370; LV 2.2 1329–1341; RIC 5.1, p. 342, Ticinum 160

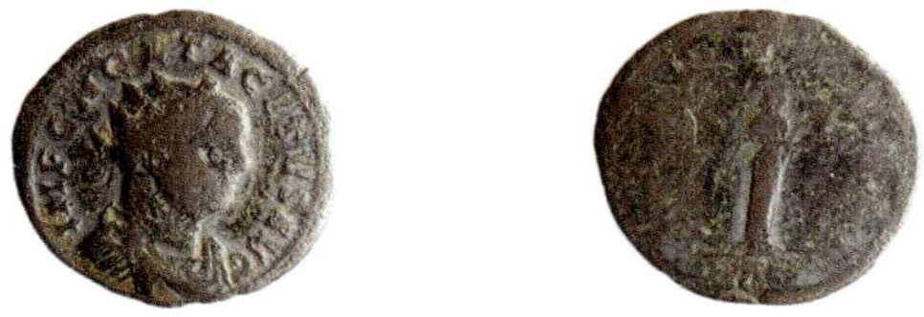

487. AE; 2,92 g.; 20,9 x 22,6 mm.; 6 h.; inv. n. 1779
(Obv. IMP C M CL TACITVS AVG; Rev. [SALV]S PVBLI; — — —//T)

Roma

November – December 275 A.D.

Antoninianus
Obv. IMP C M CL TACITVS AVG. Radiated bust of emperor in cuirass and paludamentum looking right, seen from front.
Rev. AEQVITAS AVG. Aequitas standing left, holding scales in right hand and cornucopiae in left hand.
— — —//XXIΓ
Lit.: RIC temp n° 3489; LV 2.2 89–126; RIC 5.1, p. 334, Rome 82

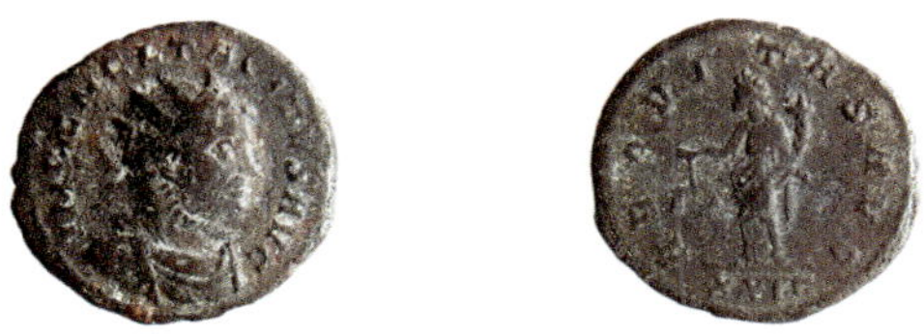

488. AE; 3,17 g.; 21,0 x 21,7 mm.; 12 h.; inv. n. 18.33
(Obv. IMP C M CL TACITVS AVG; Rev. AEQVI-TAS AVG; — — —//XXIΓ)

Siscia

November – December 275 A.D.

Antoninianus
Obv. IMP C M CLA TACITVS AVG. Radiated bust of emperor in cuirass and paludamentum looking right, seen from front.
Rev. ANNONA AVGVSTI. Annona standing left, holding corn-ears in right hand and cornucopiae in left hand; at feet to left modius.
— — —//T
Lit.: RIC temp n° 3610; LV 2.2 2123–2148; RIC 5.1, –

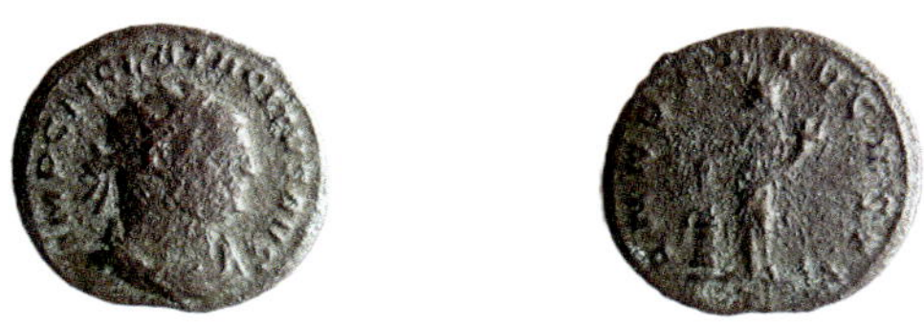

489. AE; 3,17 g.; 19,8 x 21,9 mm.; 12 h.; inv. n. 1780
(Obv. IMP C M CLA TACITVS AVG; Rev. ANNONA AVGVSTI; — — —//T)

Antoninianus
Obv. IMP C M CLA TACITVS AVG. Radiated bust of emperor in cuirass and paludamentum looking right, seen from front.
Rev. LAETITIA AVG. Laetitia standing left, holding wreath in right hand and rudder on globe in left hand.
— — —//VI
Lit.: RIC temp n° 3630; LV 2.2 2337–2354; RIC 5.1, –

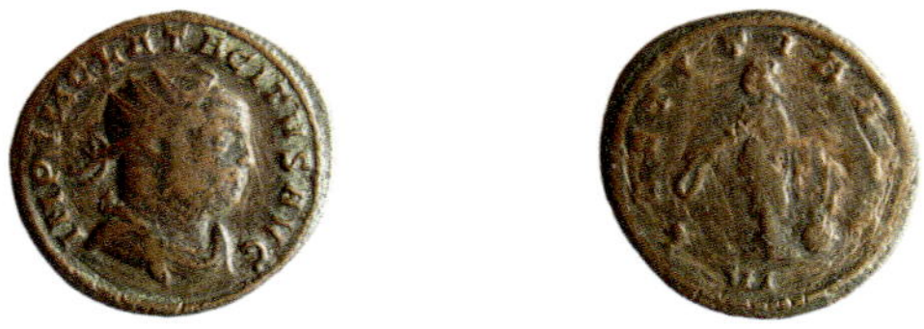

490. AE; 3,55 g.; 21,8 x 22,2 mm.; 12 h.; inv. n. 1781
(Obv. IMP [C] M CLA TACITVS AVG; Rev. LAETITIA AVG; — — —//VI)

FLORIANUS
(276 A.D.)

Roma

July – August 276 A.D.

Antoninianus
Obv. IMP C FLORIANVS AVG. Radiated bust of emperor in cuirass and paludamentum looking right, seen from rear.
Rev. CLEMENTIA TEMP. Clementia standing left, legs crossed, holding sceptre and leaning on column.
— — —//XXIZ
Lit.: RIC temp n° 4246; LV 2.2 2616–2619; RIC 5.1, p. 352, Rome 27

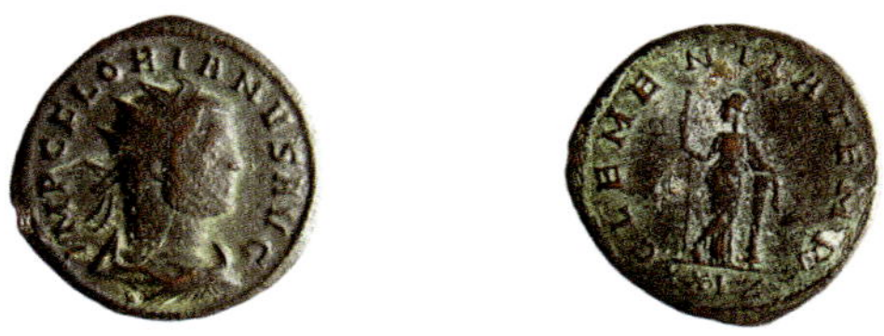

491. AE; 3,18 g.; 22,2 x 21,6 mm.; 7 h.; inv. n. 1782
(Obv. IMP C FLORIANVS AVG; Rev. CLEME-NTIA TEMP; — — —//XXIZ)

PROBUS
(276 – 282 A.D.)

Lugdunum

November – December 276 A.D.

Antoninianus
Obv. IMP C M AVR PROBVS AVG. Radiated bust of emperor in cuirass with paludamentum across left shoulder, looking right, seen from front.
Rev. ORIENS AVG. Sol between two captives walking left, raising right hand, globe in left hand; captive under right foot.
— — —//I
Lit.: Bastien I., p. 174, 164; RIC 5.2, p. 24, Lugdunum 44

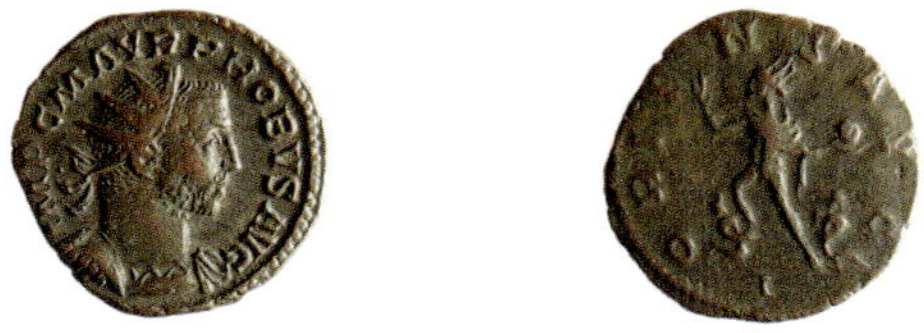

492. AE; 3,97 g.; 20,9 x 21,0 mm.; 6 h.; inv. n. 1783
(Obv. IMP C M AVR PROBVS AVG; Rev. ORIE-N-S AVG; — — —//I)

Antoninianus
Obv. IMP C M AVR PROBVS AVG. Radiated bust of emperor in cuirass with paludamentum across left shoulder, looking right, seen from front.
Rev. LAETITIA AVGVSTI. Laetitia standing left, holding wreath in right hand and anchor in left hand.
— — —//IIII
Lit.: Bastien I., p. 177, 172; RIC 5.2, p. 23, Lugdunum 31

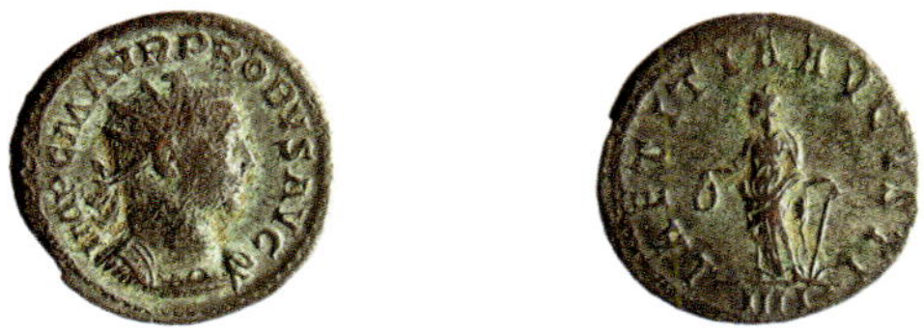

493. AE; 4,92 g.; 21,7 x 22,1 mm.; 6 h.; inv. n. 1784
(Obv. IMP C M AVR PROBVS AVG; Rev. LAETITIA AVGVSTI; — — —//IIII)

Summer of 281 A.D.

Antoninianus
Obv. IMP C PROBVS P F AVG. Radiated bust of emperor in cuirass looking right, seen from front.
Rev. SPES PROBI AVG. Spes walking left, holding flower in right hand and raising skirt with left hand.
— — —//III
Lit.: Bastien I., p. 209, 328; RIC 5.2, p. 29, Lugdunum 100

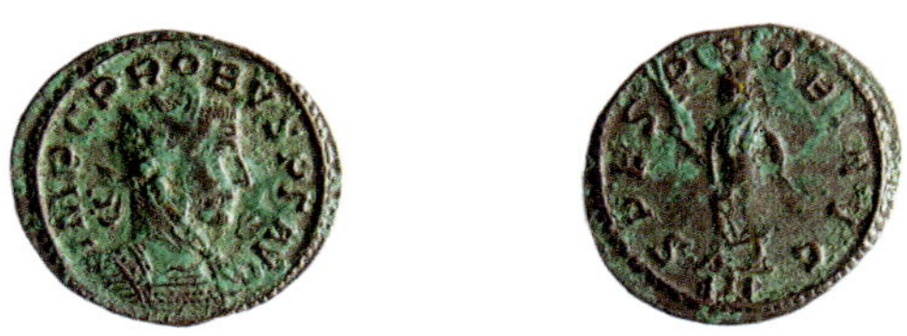

494. AE; 2,91 g.; 21,2 x 23,2 mm.; 7 h.; inv. n. 1785
(Obv. IMP C PROBVS P F AVG; Rev. SPES PROBI AVG; — — —//III)

January – August 282 A.D.

Antoninianus
Obv. IMP C M AVR PROBVS AVG. Radiated bust of emperor in cuirass and paludamentum looking right, seen from rear.
Rev. SALVS AVG. Salus standing left, holding patera in right hand, from which a snake, which is rising from altar, is feeding; in left hand Salus holds a long vertical sceptre.
— — B//—
Lit.: Bastien I., p. 222, 392; RIC 5.2, p. 30, Lugdunum 123

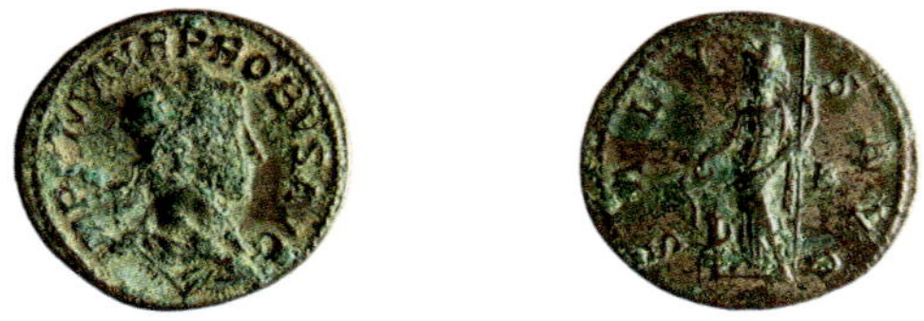

495. AE; 3,99 g.; 21,2 x 23,2 mm.; 6 h.; inv. n. 1786
(Obv. IMP [C] M AVR PROBVS AVG; Rev. SALV-S AVG; — — B//—)

Ticinum

278 A.D.

Antoninianus
Obv. IMP C PROBVS P F AVG. Radiated bust of emperor in cuirass looking right, seen from front.
Rev. HERCVLI PACIF. Hercules standing left, holding branch in right hand and club and lion's skin in left hand.
— — —//SXXT
Lit.: RIC 5.2, p. 58, Ticinum 375

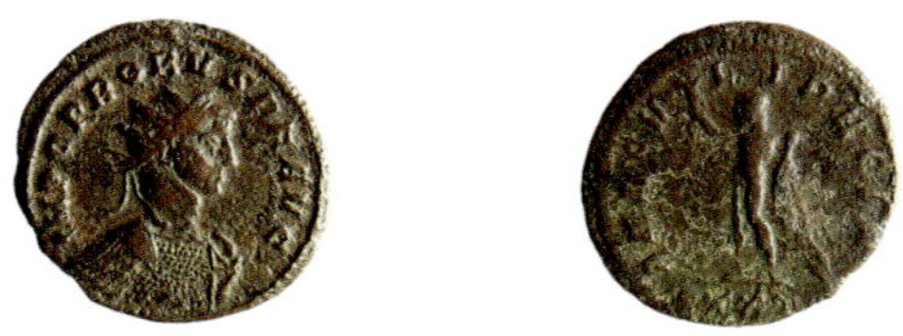

496. AE; 3,66 g.; 21,6 x 21,9 mm.; 12 h.; inv. n. 1787
(Obv. IMP C PROBVS P F AVG; Rev. HERCV-L-I PACIF; — — —//SXXT)

Antoninianus
Obv. IMP C PROBVS AVG CONS II. Radiated bust of emperor in imperial mantle looking left, holding eagle-tipped sceptre in right hand.
Rev. CONSERVAT AVG. Sol standing right, head turned left, raising right hand, globe in left hand.
— — —//TXXT
Lit.: RIC 5.2, p. 55, Ticinum 352

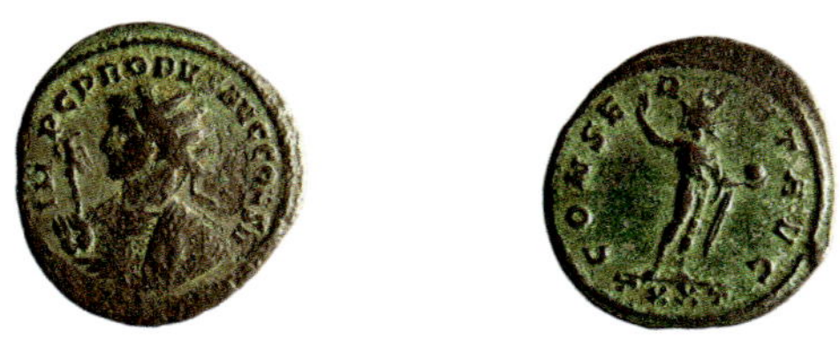

497. AE; 3,62 g.; 23,4 x 21,8 mm.; 5 h.; inv. n. 1788
(Obv. IM-P C PROBVS AVG CONS II; Rev. CONSE-R-VAT AVG; — — —//TXXT)

281 A.D.

Antoninianus
Obv. IMP C PROBVS AVG. Radiated bust of emperor in imperial mantle looking left, holding eagle-tipped sceptre in right hand.
Rev. PROVIDENT AVG. Providentia standing left, holding globe in right hand and transverse sceptre in left hand.
Q — —//SXXI
Lit.: RIC 5.2, p. 70, Ticinum 490

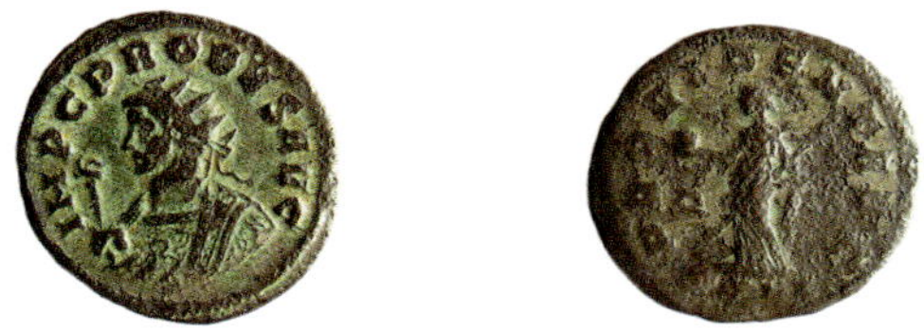

498. AE; 2,94 g.; 22,7 x 22,2 mm.; 11 h.; inv. n. 1789
(Obv. IMP C PROBVS AVG; Rev. PROVIDENT AVG; Q — —//[SXXI])

Antoninianus
Obv. IMP C PROBVS P F AVG. Radiated bust of emperor in imperial mantle looking left, holding eagle-tipped sceptre in right hand.
Rev. SECVRIT PERP. Securitas standing front, legs crossed, head left, right hand raised to head, leaning on column with left elbow.
I — —//VIXXI
Lit.: RIC 5.2, p. 73, Ticinum 524

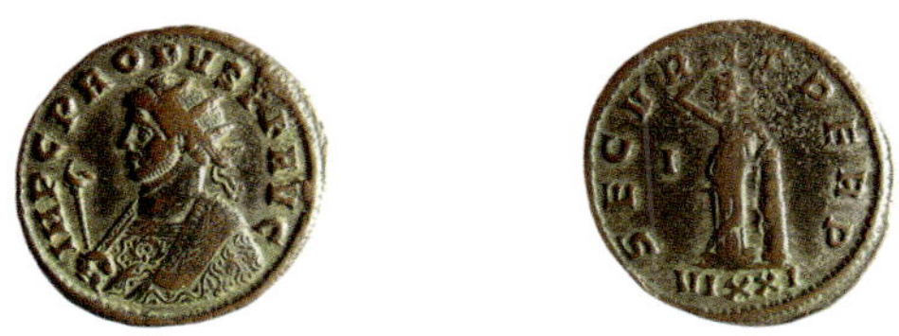

499. AE; 3,46 g.; 21,3 x 21,6 mm.; 12 h.; inv. n. 1790
(Obv. IMP C PROBVS P F AVG; Rev. SECVR-IT PERP; I — —//VIXXI)

282 A.D.

Antoninianus
Obv. IMP C PROBVS AVG. Radiated bust of emperor in imperial mantle looking left, holding eagle-tipped sceptre in right hand.
Rev. PROVIDENT AVG. Providentia standing left, holding globe in right hand and transverse sceptre in left hand.
Q — *//SXXI
Lit.: RIC 5.2, p. 70, Ticinum 490

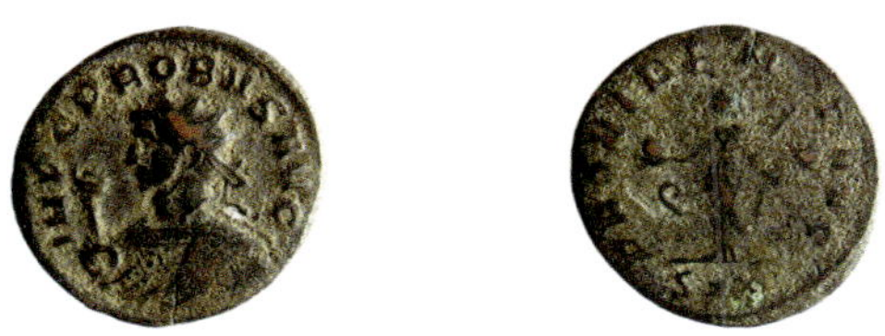

500. AE; 3,66 g.; 21,8 x 22,3 mm.; 6 h.; inv. n. 1791
(Obv. IMP C PROBVS AVG; Rev. PROVIDEN-T AVG; Q — *//SXX[I])

Antoninianus
Obv. IMP C PROBVS AVG. Radiated bust of emperor in imperial mantle looking left, holding eagle-tipped sceptre in right hand.
Rev. PAX AVGVSTI. Pax standing left, holding branch in right hand and transverse sceptre in left hand.
T — *//VXXI
Lit.: RIC 5.2, p. 72, Ticinum 516

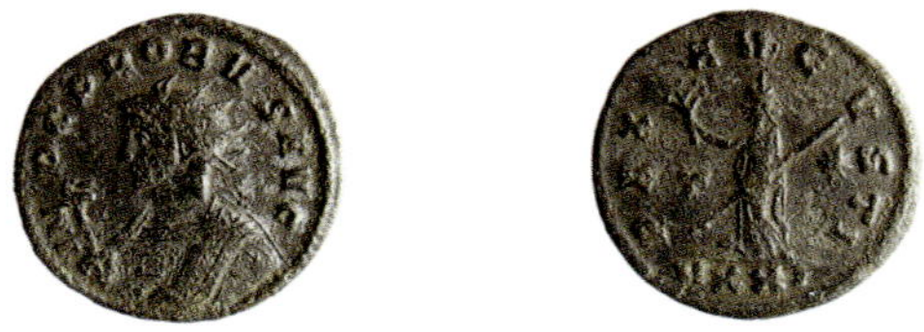

501. AE; 3,78 g.; 21,3 x 22,2 mm.; 12 h.; inv. n. 1792
(Obv. IM-P C PROBVS AVG; Rev. PAX – AVGVSTI; T — *//VXXI)

Antoninianus
Obv. VIRTVS PROBI AVG. Helmeted and radiated bust of emperor in cuirass looking left, with spear across right shoulder and with shield in his left hand, seen from front.
Rev. PAX AVGVSTI. Pax standing left, holding branch in right hand and transverse sceptre in left hand.
T — *//VXXI
Lit.: RIC 5.2, p. 72, Ticinum 517

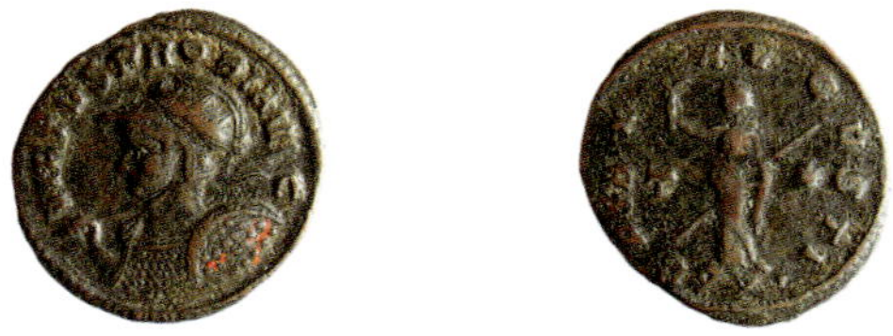

502. AE; 3,41 g.; 22,5 x 21,8 mm.; 6 h.; inv. n. 1793
(Obv. VIRTVS PROBI AV-G; Rev. PAX – AV-G-VSTI; T — *//VXXI)

Roma

October 276 – February 277 A.D.

Antoninianus
Obv. IMP C M AVR PROBVS AVG. Radiated bust of emperor in cuirass looking right, seen from front.
Rev. PROVIDENTIA AVG. Providentia standing left, holding baton in right hand and cornucopiae in left hand; at feet to left globe.
— — —//XXIA
Lit.: LV 3.1, 37–56; RIC 5.2, p. 95, Siscia 726 corr.[82]

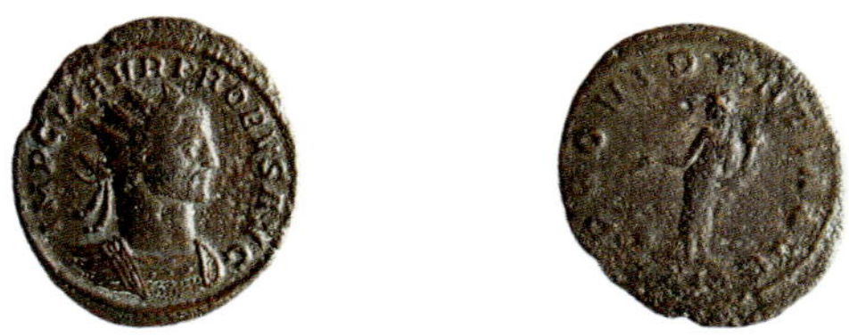

503. AE; 2,99 g.; 23,8 x 21,2 mm.; 7 h.; inv. n. 1794
(Obv. IMP C M AVR PROBVS AVG; Rev. PROVIDENTIA AVG; — — —//XXI[A])

Antoninianus
Obv. IMP C M AVR PROBVS AVG. Radiated bust of emperor in cuirass and paludamentum looking right, seen from rear.
Rev. PROVIDENTIA AVG. Providentia standing left, holding baton in right hand and cornucopiae in left hand; at feet to left globe.
— — —//XXIA
Lit.: LV 3.1, p. 154, 3; RIC 5.2, p. 95, Siscia 726 corr.[83]

[82] RIC 5.1 assigns this coin to the mint of Siscia.
[83] RIC 5.1 assigns this coin to the mint of Siscia.

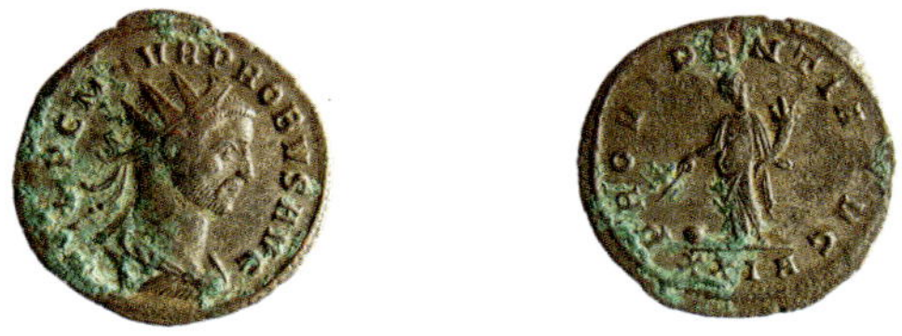

504. AE; 3,72 g.; 22,7 x 22,2 mm.; 11 h.; inv. n. 1795
(Obv. IMP C M AVR PROBVS AVG; Rev. PROVIDENTIA AVG; — — —//XXIA)

Antoninianus
Obv. IMP C M AVR PROBVS AVG. Radiated bust of emperor in cuirass looking right, seen from front.
Rev. VIRTVS AVG. Emperor standing left, holding transverse spear in right hand and globe in left hand.
— — —//XXIϛ
Lit.: LV 3.1, 343–355; RIC 5.2, p. 104, Siscia 801 corr.[84]

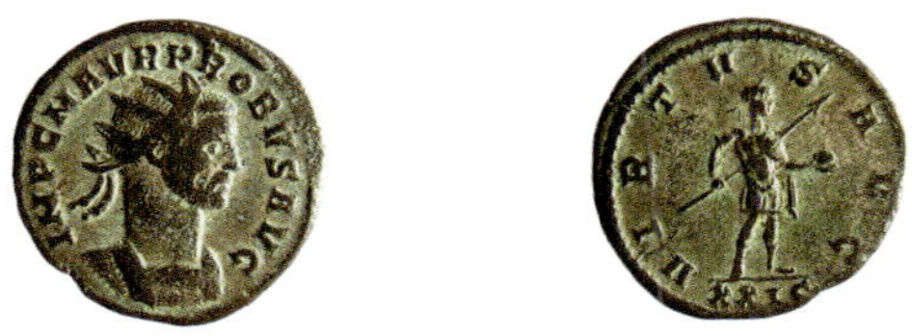

505. AE; 3,3 g.; 21,6 x 21,3 mm.; 12 h.; inv. n. 1796
(Obv. IMP C M AVR PROBVS AVG; Rev. VIRTV-S – AVG; — — —//XXIϛ)

Antoninianus
Obv. IMP C M AVR PROBVS AVG. Radiated bust of emperor in cuirass looking right, seen from front.
Rev. IOVI STATORI. Jupiter standing front, head turned right, holding vertical sceptre in right hand and thunderbolt in left hand.
— — Z//XXI
Lit.: LV 3.1, 490–527; RIC 5.2, p. 34, Rome 152

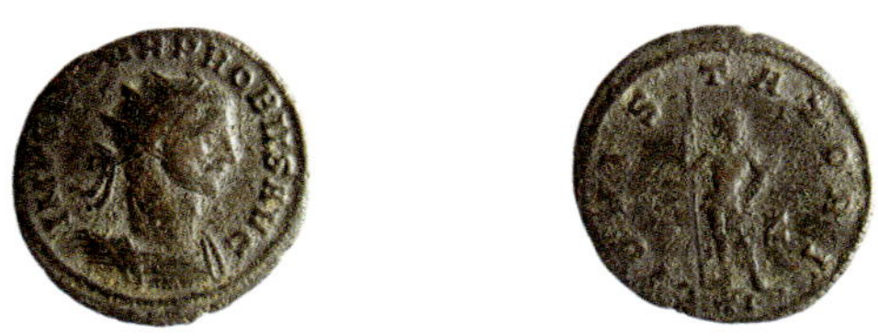

506. AE; 3,64 g.; 21,9 x 21,1 mm.; 6 h.; inv. n. 1797
(Obv. IMP C M AVR PROBVS AVG; Rev. IOVI S-TATORI; — — Z//XXI)

January 277 – February 277 A.D.

Antoninianus
Obv. IMP C M AVR PROBVS AVG. Radiated bust of emperor in cuirass and paludamentum looking right, seen from rear.
Rev. P M TR P COS P P. Emperor standing left between two standards, raising right hand, holding vertical spear in left hand.
— — —//XXIΔ
Lit.: LV 3.1, 586–592; RIC 5.2, p. 82, Siscia 607 corr.[85]

[84] RIC 5.1 assigns this coin to the mint of Siscia.
[85] RIC 5.1 assigns this coin to the mint of Siscia.

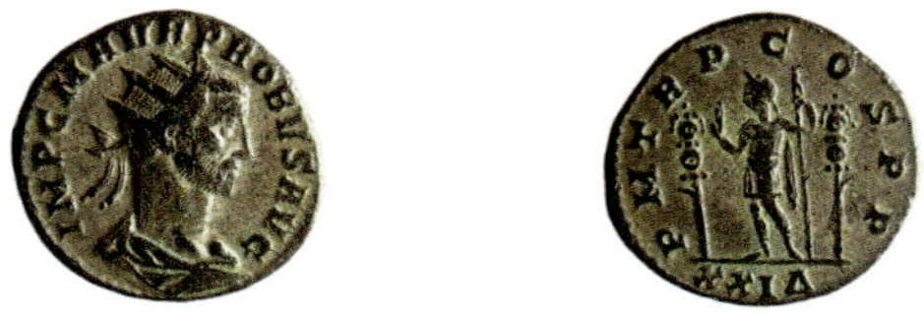

507. AE; 3,53 g.; 19,9 x 21,0 mm.; 12 h.; inv. n. 1798
(Obv. IMP C M AVR PROBVS AVG; Rev. P M TR P COS P P; — — —//XXIΔ)

Autumn of 278 A.D.

Antoninianus
Obv. IMP C M AVR PROBVS P F AVG. Radiated bust of emperor in imperial mantle looking left, holding eagle-tipped sceptre in right hand.
Rev. SOLI INVICTO. Sol in spread quadriga, raising right hand, holding whip and globe in left hand.
— — —//crescent/R*B or ε
Lit.: LV 3.1, 821–827 or 851; RIC 5.2, p. 39, Rome 204

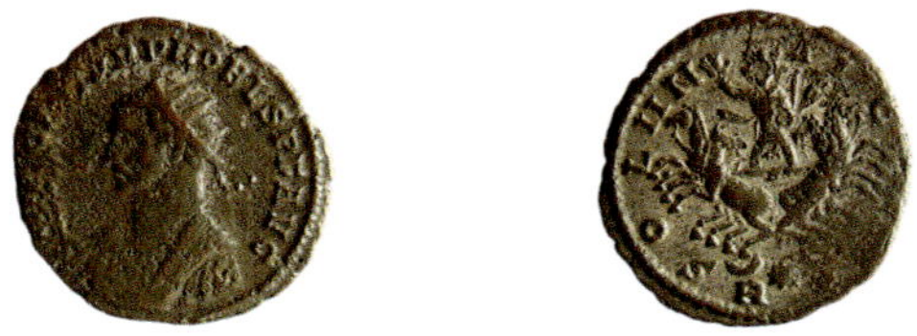

508. AE; 3,59 g.; 21,5 x 21,8 mm.; 1 h.; inv. n. 1799
(Obv. [IMP] C [M AVR] PROBVS P F AVG; Rev. S-O-LI IN-VI-C-[TO]; — — —//crescent/R*[B or ε])

End of 278 – 279 A.D.

Antoninianus
Obv. IMP PROBVS AVG. Helmeted and radiated bust of emperor in cuirass looking left, with spear across right shoulder and with shield in his left hand, seen from front.
Rev. ADVENTVS AVG. Emperor riding on horse left, raising right hand, holding transverse sceptre in left hand; to left captive.
— — —//R*Γ
Lit.: LV 3.1, 1023–1032; RIC 5.2, p. 35, Rome 157

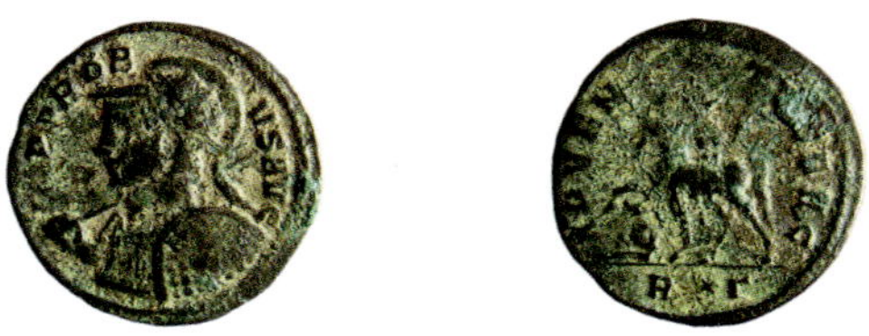

509. AE; 3,34 g.; 22,9 x 23,1 mm.; 7 h.; inv. n. 1800
(Obv. IMP PROB-VS AVG; Rev. ADVEN-TVS AVG; — — —//R*Γ)

Spring of 281 A.D.

Antoninianus
Obv. IMP PROBVS AVG. Radiated bust of emperor in cuirass looking right, seen from front.
Rev. VICTORIA GERM. Trophy between two captives.
— — —//R wreath A
Lit.: LV 3.1, 1840–1866; RIC 5.2, p. 41, Rome 222

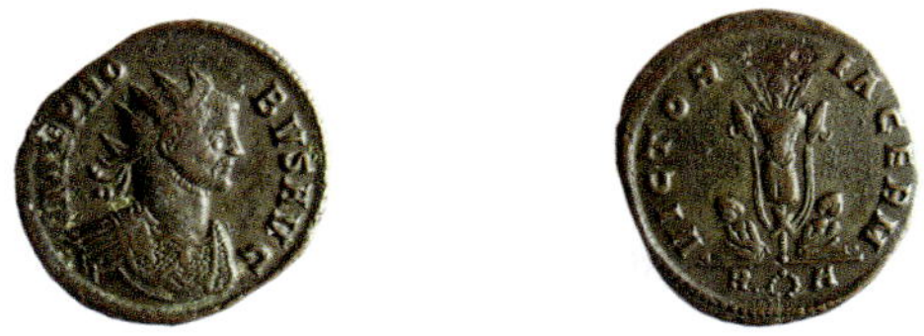

510. AE; 3,84 g.; 21,2 x 20,9 mm.; 5 h.; inv. n. 1801
(Obv. IMP PRO-BVS AVG; Rev. VICTOR-IA GERM; — — —//R wreath A)

Antoninianus
Obv. IMP PROBVS AVG. Radiated bust of emperor in imperial mantle looking left, holding eagle-tipped sceptre in right hand.
Rev. SOLI INVICTO. Sol in chariot riding left, rising right hand, holding whip and globe in left hand.
— — —//R wreath ε
Lit.: LV 3.1, 1935–1940; RIC 5.2, p. 39, Rome 202 var.[86]

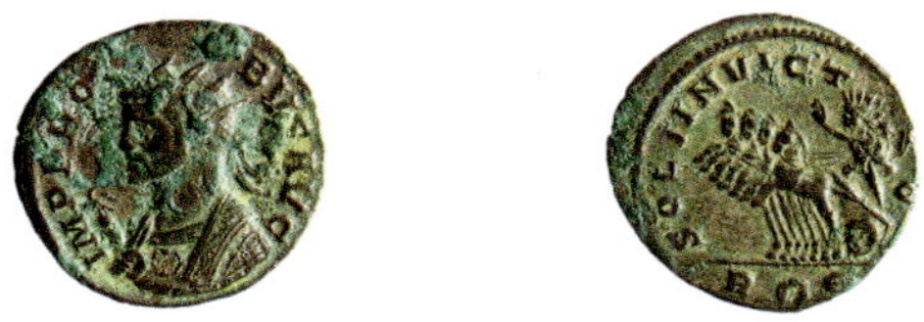

511. AE; 2,95 g.; 19,8 x 20,9 mm.; 5 h.; inv. n. 1802
(Obv. IMP PRO-BVS AVG; Rev. SOLI INVICT-O; — — —//R wreath ε)

Spring of 281 – January 282 A.D.

Antoninianus
Obv. IMP PROBVS P F AVG. Radiated bust of emperor in imperial mantle looking left, holding eagle-tipped sceptre in right hand.
Rev. ROMAE AETER. Roma seated in hexastyle temple.
— — —//R thunderbolt Δ
Lit.: LV 3.1, 2551–2695; RIC 5.2, p. 37, Rome 183 var.[87]

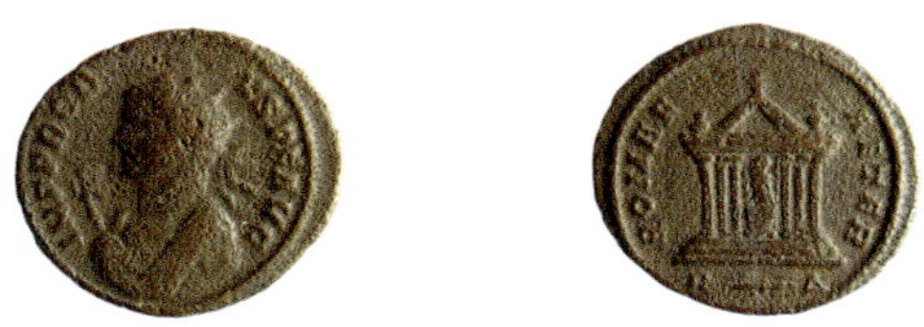

512. AE; 3,32 g.; 20,4 x 22,4 mm.; 6 h.; inv. n. 1803
(Obv. IMP PROB-VS P F AVG; Rev. ROMAE – AETER; — — —//R thunderbolt Δ)

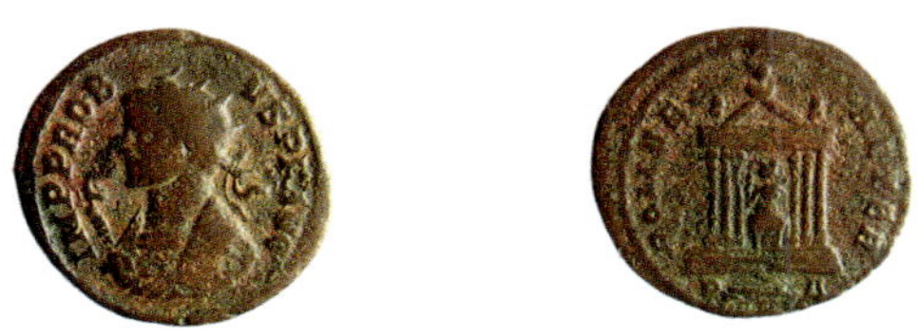

513. AE; 3,81 g.; 21,0 x 22,0 mm.; 11 h.; inv. n. 1804
(Obv. IMP PROB-VS P F AVG; Rev. ROMAE – AETER; — — —//R thunderbolt Δ)

[86] RIC 5.2, p. 39, Rome 202 notes only oficina B with wreath.
[87] RIC 5.2, p. 37, Rome 183 notes only oficina A with thunderbolt.

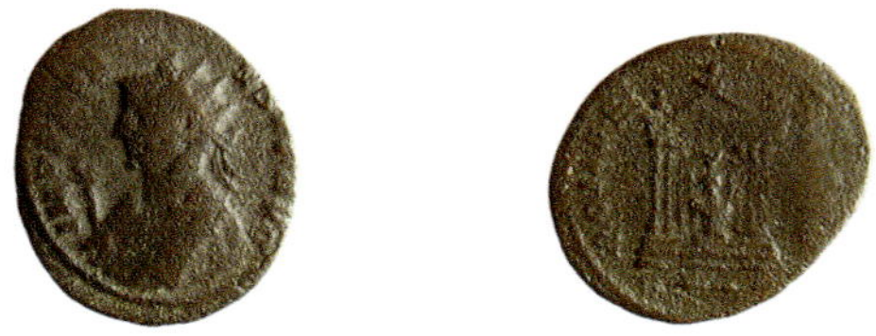

514. AE; 2,4 g.; 22,5 x 19,3 mm.; 11 h.; inv. n. 1805
(Obv. IMP PROB-VS P F AVG; Rev. ROMAE – A[ETER]; — — —//R thunderbolt [Δ])

Antoninianus
Obv. IMP PROBVS P F AVG. Radiated bust of emperor in cuirass looking right, seen from front.
Rev. FIDES MILITVM. Fides standing left holding vertical standard in each hand.
— — —//R thunderbolt ε
Lit.: LV 3.1, 2696–2806; RIC 5.2, p. 36, Rome 169

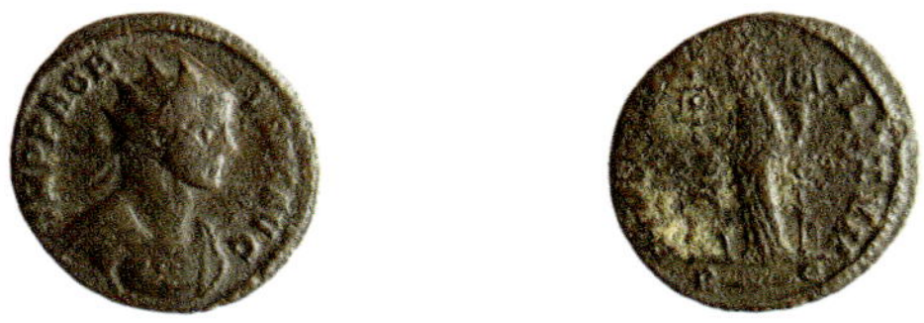

515. AE; 3,47 g.; 20,5 x 20,7 mm.; 12 h.; inv. n. 1806
(Obv. IMP PROB-VS P F AVG; Rev. FID[ES M-]ILITVM; — — —//R thunderbolt ε)

Autumn of 281 – Mid 282 A.D.

Antoninianus
Obv. PROBVS P F AVG. Radiated bust of emperor in cuirass looking right, seen from front.
Rev. VICTORIA GERM. Trophy between two captives.
— — —//R thunderbolt A
Lit.: LV 3.1, 3028–3039; RIC 5.2, p. 41, Rome 223

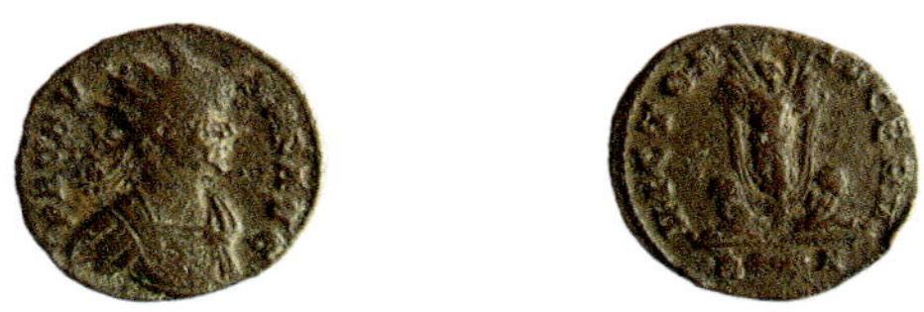

516. AE; 3,25 g.; 18,7 x 20,4 mm.; 6 h.; inv. n. 1807
(Obv. PROBV-S P F AVG; Rev. VICTOR-IA GERM; — — —//R thunderbolt A)

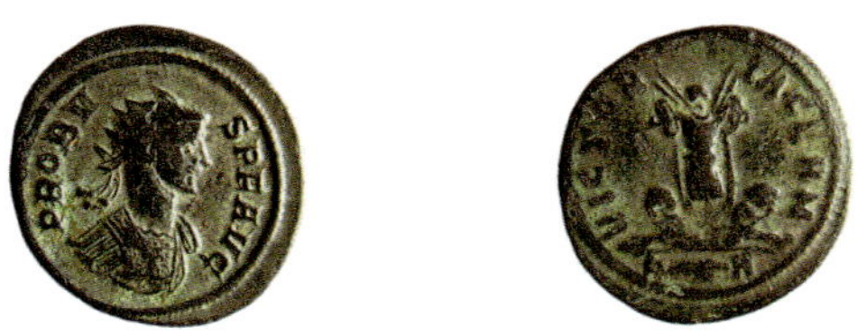

517. AE; 3,93 g.; 22,2 x 21,7 mm.; 6 h.; inv. n. 1808
(Obv. PROBV-S P F AVG; Rev. VICTOR-IA GERM; — — —//R thunderbolt A)

Antoninianus
Obv. PROBVS P F AVG. Radiated bust of emperor in cuirass looking right, seen from front.
Rev. IOVI CONS PROB AVG. Jupiter standing front, head turned left, holding thunderbolt in right hand and vertical sceptre in left hand.
— — —//R thunderbolt B
Lit.: LV 3.1, 3196–3238; RIC 5.2, p. 36, Rome 175

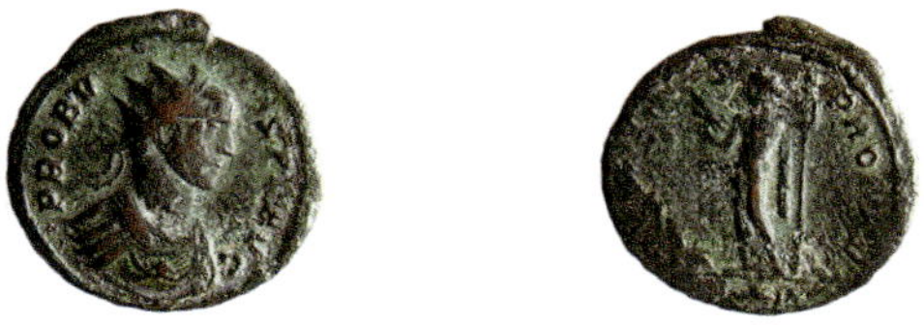

518. AE; 3,58 g.; 21,0 x 21,5 mm.; 12 h.; inv. n. 1809
(Obv. PROBVS P [F] AVG; Rev. IOVI [CON]-S – PRO[B AVG]; — — —//[R] thunderbolt B)

Antoninianus
Obv. PROBVS P F AVG. Radiated bust of emperor in imperial mantle looking left, holding eagle-tipped sceptre in right hand.
Rev. SOLI INVICTO. Sol in chariot riding left, rising right hand, holding whip and globe in left hand.
— — —//R thunderbolt Γ
Lit.: LV 3.1, 3405–3597; RIC 5.2, p. 39, Rome 203

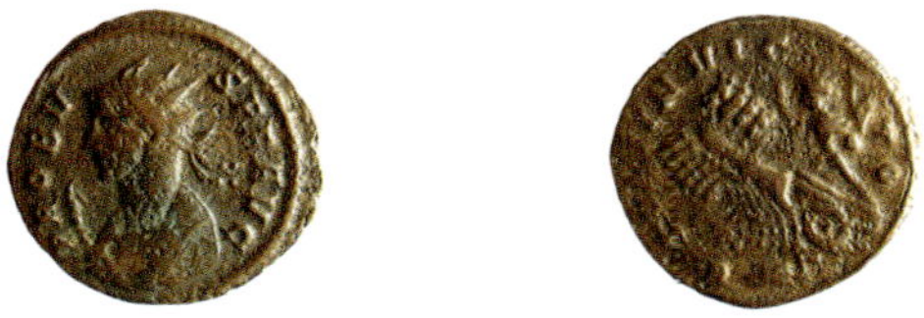

519. AE; 2,81 g.; 20,5 x 20,8 mm.; 6 h.; inv. n. 1810
(Obv. PROBV-S P F AVG; Rev. SOLI INVIC-TO; — — —//R thunderbolt Γ)

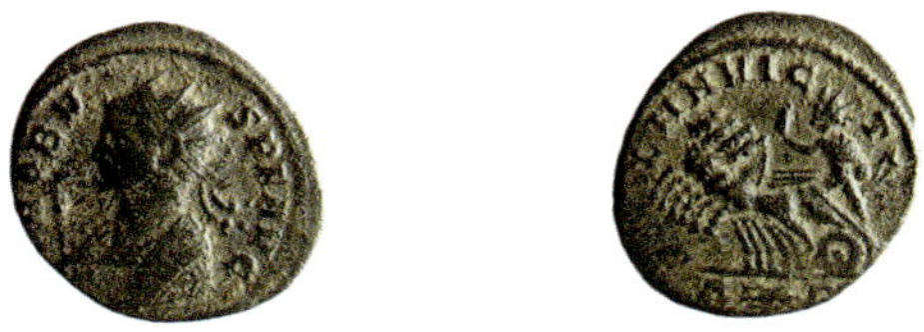

520. AE; 3,75 g.; 20,2 x 20,9 mm.; 12 h.; inv. n. 1811
(Obv. PROBV-S P F AVG; Rev. SO[L]I INVIC-TO; — — —//R thunderbolt Γ)

Antoninianus
Obv. PROBV-S P F AVG. Radiated bust of emperor in imperial mantle looking left, holding eagle-tipped sceptre in right hand.
Rev. ROMAE – AETER. Roma seated in hexastyle temple.
— — —//R thunderbolt Δ
Lit.: LV 3.1, 3598–3792; RIC 5.2, p. 37, Rome 187

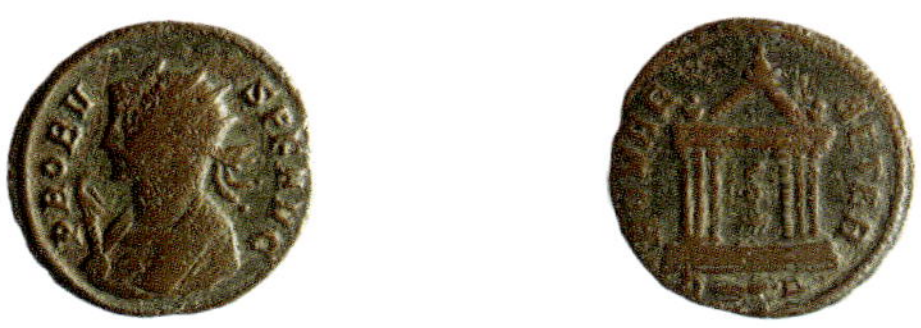

521. AE; 2,83 g.; 20,0 x 19,9 mm.; 12 h.; inv. n. 1812
(Obv. PROBV-S P F AVG; Rev. ROMAE – AETER; — — —//R thunderbolt Δ)

Antoninianus
Obv. PROBVS P F AVG. Radiated bust of emperor in cuirass looking right, seen from front.
Rev. FIDES MILITVM. Fides standing left, holding vertical standard in each hand.
— — —//R thunderbolt ε
Lit.: LV 3.1, 3819–3853; RIC 5.2, p. 36, Rome 170

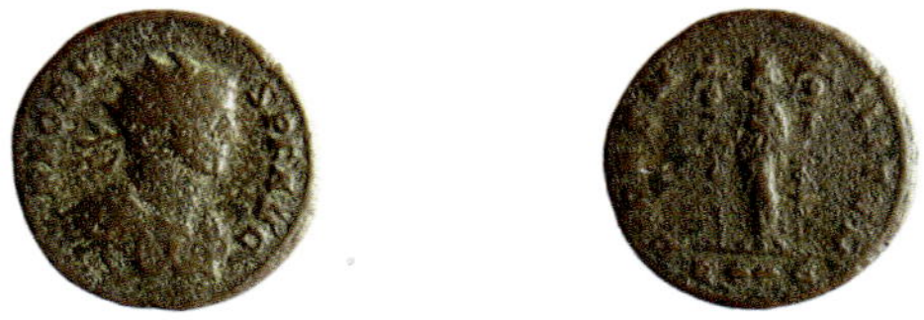

522. AE; 3,21 g.; 20,4 x 20,6 mm.; 6 h.; inv. n. 1813
(Obv. PROBV-S P F AVG; Rev. FIDES M-ILITVM; — — —//R thunderbolt ε)

Antoninianus
Obv. PROBVS P F AVG. Radiated bust of emperor in cuirass looking right, seen from front.
Rev. FIDES MILITVM. Fides standing left, holding vertical standard in each hand.
— — —//R thunderbolt ε
Lit.: LV 3.1, 3854–3966; RIC 5.2, p. 36, Rome 170

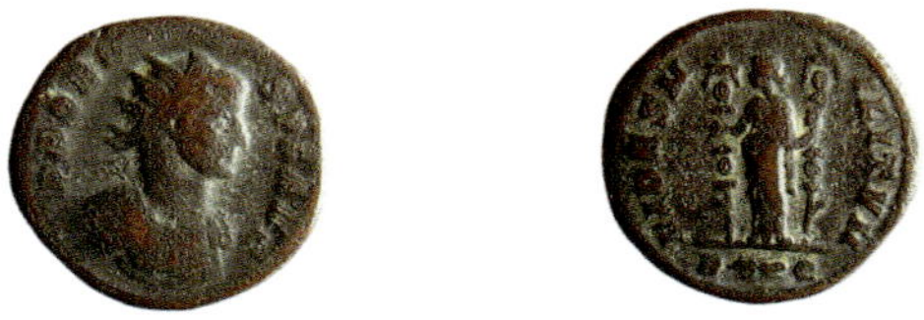

523. AE; 4,19 g.; 20,0 x 21,0 mm.; 12 h.; inv. n. 1814
(Obv. PROBV-S P F AVG; Rev. FIDES M-ILITVM; — — —//R thunderbolt ε)

Summer of 282 A.D.

Antoninianus
Obv. PROBVS P F AVG. Radiated bust of emperor in cuirass looking right, seen from front.
Rev. VICTORIA GERM. Trophy between two captives.
— — —//RAA
Lit.: LV 3.1, 4362–4374; RIC 5.2, p. 41, Rome 223

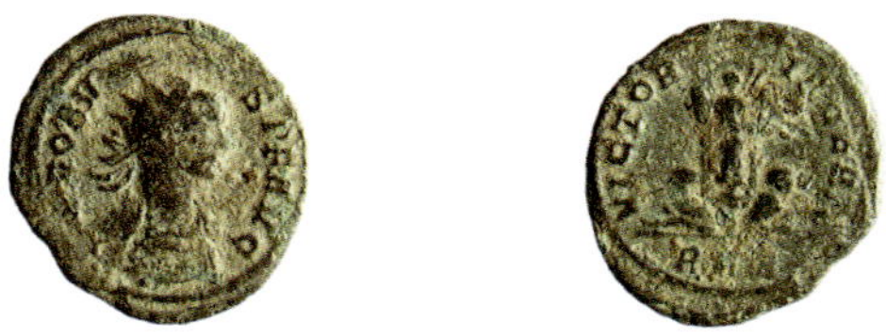

524. AE; 1,89 g.; 22,1 x 20,6 mm.; 12 h.; inv. n. 1815
(Obv. PROBV-S P F AVG; Rev. VICTOR-IA GERM; — — —//RAA)

Antoninianus
Obv. PROBVS P F AVG. Radiated bust of emperor in cuirass looking right, seen from front.
Rev. IOVI CONS PROB AVG. Jupiter standing front, head turned left, holding thunderbolt in right hand and vertical sceptre in left hand.
— — —//REB
Lit.: LV 3.1, 4408–4450; RIC 5.2, p. 36, Rome 175 var.[88]

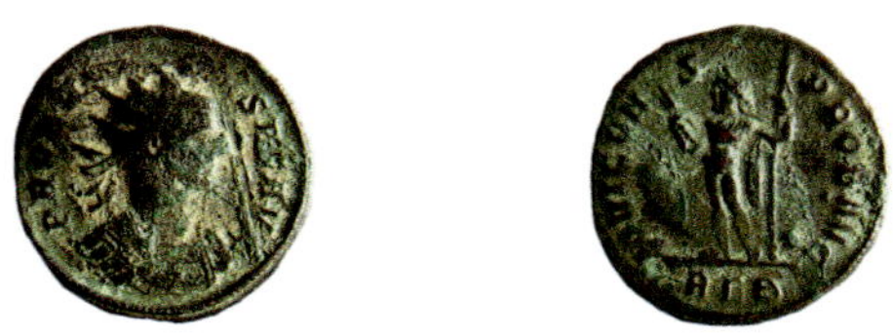

525. AE; 3,68 g.; 20,8 x 19,9 mm.; 12 h.; inv. n. 1816
(Obv. PROBV-S P F AVG; Rev. IOVI CON-S – PROB AVG; — — —//REB)

[88] RIC 5.2, p. 36, Rome 175 does not note REB in exerque.

Siscia

277 A.D.

Antoninianus
Obv. IMP C M AVR PROBVS P F AVG. Radiated bust of emperor in imperial mantle looking left, holding eagle-tipped sceptre in right hand.
Rev. VIRTVS PROBI AVG. Emperor riding on horse left, raising right hand, holding transverse sceptre in left hand; to left captive.
— — —//XXIP
Lit.: RIC 5.2, p. 106, Siscia 818

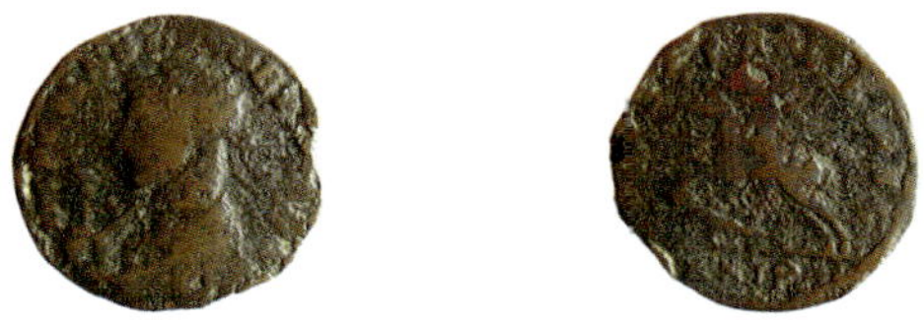

526. AE; 3,03 g.; 20,5 x 20,6 mm.; 12 h.; inv. n. 1817
(Obv. IMP C M AVR PROBVS [P F AVG]; Rev. V[IR]TVS PRO-BI AVG; — — —//XXIP)

278 A.D.

Antoninianus
Obv. IMP C M AVR PROBVS P F AVG. Radiated bust of emperor in imperial mantle looking left, holding eagle-tipped sceptre in right hand.
Rev. VIRTVS PROBI AVG. Mars walking right, holding transverse spear in right hand and trophy over left shoulder in left hand.
— — —//XXIV
Lit.: RIC 5.2, p. 105, Siscia 810

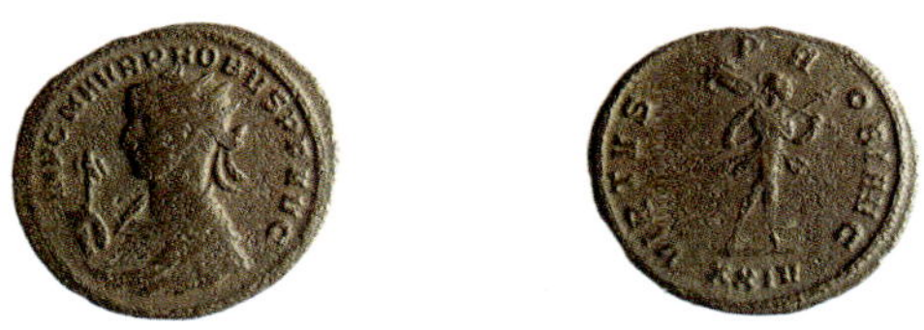

527. AE; 3,26 g.; 20,5 x 21,6 mm.; 12 h.; inv. n. 1818
(Obv. IMP C M AVR PROBVS P F AVG; Rev. VIRTVS – PR-OBI AVG; — — —//XXIV)

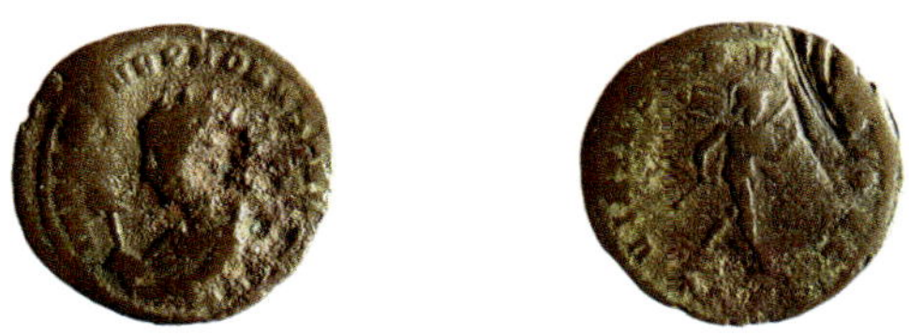

528. AE; 3,49 g.; 21,3 x 22,5 mm.; 12 h.; inv. n. 1819
(Obv. IMP C M AVR PROBVS P F A[VG]; Rev. VIRTVS – PRO-BI AVG; — — —//X[XI(T–VI)])

280 A.D.

Antoninianus
Obv. IMP C PROBVS AVG. Helmeted and radiated bust of emperor in cuirass looking left, with spear across right shoulder and with shield in his left hand, seen from front.
Rev. CONCORDIA AVG. Concordia standing left, holding patera in right hand and single cornucopiae in left hand.
— — VI//XXI
Lit.: RIC 5.2, p. 88, Siscia 662 var.[89]

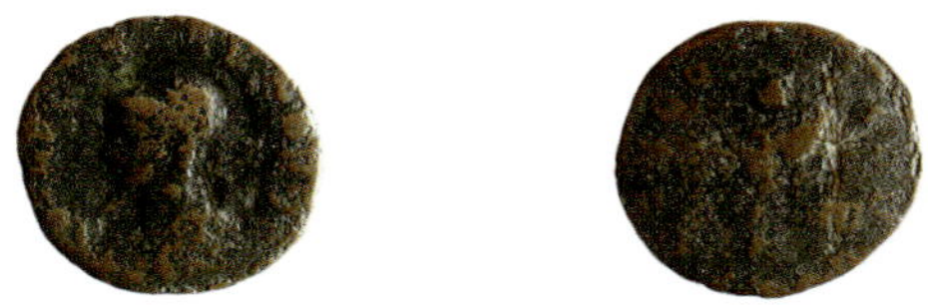

529. AE; 2,17 g.; 18,8 x 20,1 mm.; 6 h.; inv. n. 1820
(Obv. IMP C PROBVS AVG; Rev. CONCO[RDI]A AV[G]; — — VI//XXI)

Antoninianus
Obv. IMP C M AVR PROBVS AVG. Radiated bust of emperor in cuirass and paludamentum looking right, seen from rear.
Rev. CONCORD MILIT. Emperor standing right, clasping right hand with Concordia, standing left.
— S —//XXI
Lit.: RIC 5.2, p. 87, Siscia 651

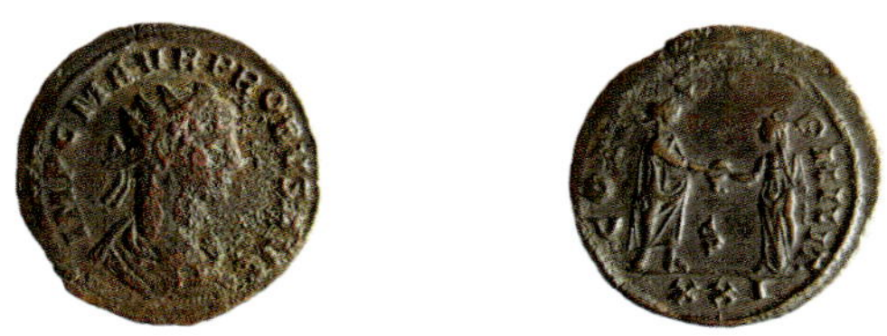

530. AE; 3,93 g.; 22,7 x 22,0 mm.; 5 h.; inv. n. 1821
(Obv. IMP C M AVR PROBVS AVG; Rev. CON-CORD MILIT; — S —//XXI)

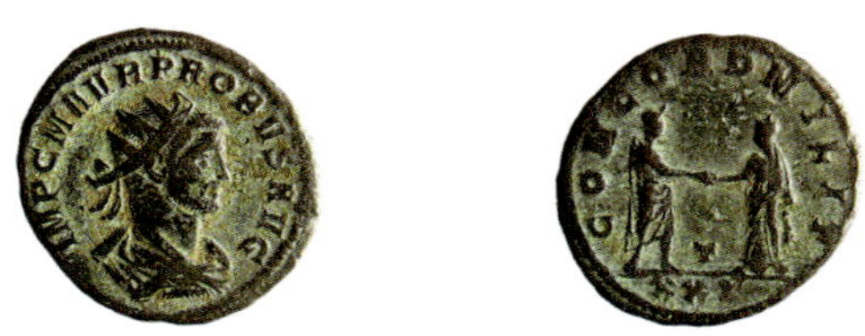

531. AE; 3,6 g.; 22,7 x 22,0 mm.; 6 h.; inv. n. 1822
(Obv. IMP C M AVR PROBVS AVG; Rev. CONCORD MILIT; — T —//XXI)

Antoninianus
Obv. IMP C M AVR PROBVS P F AVG. Radiated bust of emperor in imperial mantle looking left, holding eagle-tipped sceptre in right hand.
Rev. CONSERVAT AVG. Sol standing right, head turned left, raising right hand, globe in left hand.
— — P//XXI
Lit.: RIC 5.2, p. 89, Siscia 670

[89] RIC 5.2, p. 88, Siscia 662 notes obverse legend IMP C PROBVS P AVG.

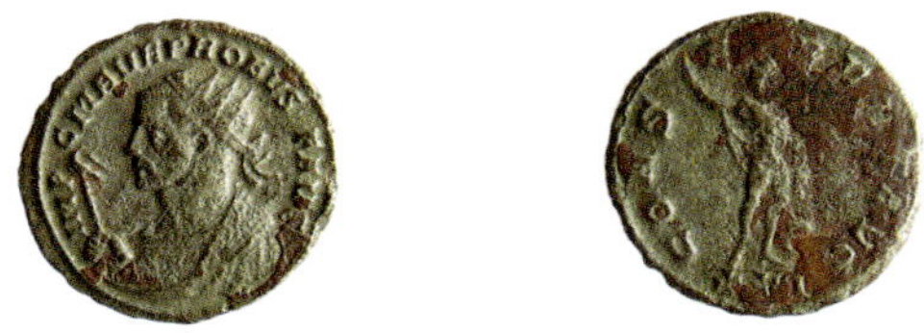

532. AE; 3,07 g.; 21,4 x 21,7 mm.; 6 h.; inv. n. 1823
(Obv. IMP – C M AVR PROBVS [P] F AVG; Rev. CONS-E-RVAT AVG; — — P//XXI)

Antoninianus
Obv. IMP PROBVS P F AVG. Helmeted and radiated bust of emperor in cuirass looking left, with spear across right shoulder and with shield in his left hand, seen from front.
Rev. SALVS AVG. Salus standing right, feeding snake held in right hand from patera held in left hand.
— — V//XXI
Lit.: RIC 5.2, p. 98, Siscia 748

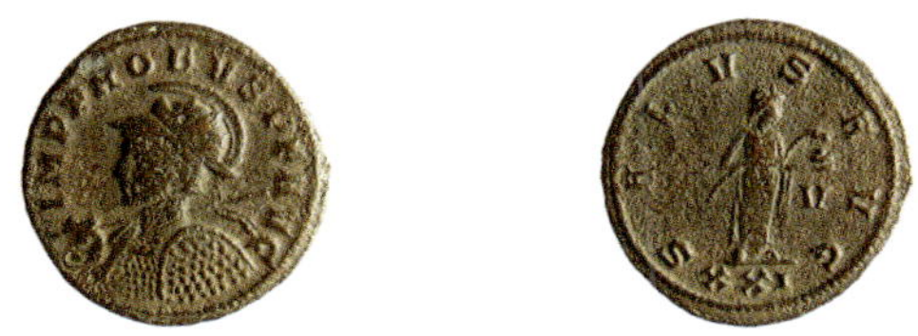

533. AE; 3,61 g.; 21,6 x 21,0 mm.; 6 h.; inv. n. 1824
(Obv. IMP PROBVS P F AVG; Rev. SALVS AVG; — — V//XXI)

Antoninianus
Obv. IMP PROBVS P F AVG. Radiated bust of emperor in imperial mantle looking left, holding eagle-tipped sceptre in right hand.
Rev. PAX AVGVSTI. Pax standing left, holding branch in right hand and transverse sceptre in left hand.
— — VI//XXI
Lit.: RIC 5.2, p. 93, Siscia 713

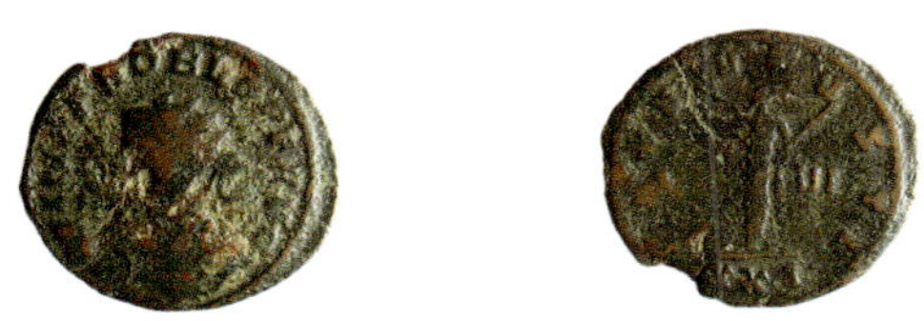

534. AE; 2,72 g.; 19,7 x 21,7 mm.; 6 h.; inv. n. 1825
(Obv. IMP PROBVS P F AVG; Rev. PAX A-VGV-STI; — — VI//XXI)

Antoninianus
Obv. IMP C M AVR PROBVS P F AVG. Helmeted and radiated bust of emperor in cuirass looking left, with spear across right shoulder and with shield in his left hand, seen from front.
Rev. VIRTVS PROBI AVG. Mars walking right, holding transverse spear in right hand and trophy over left shoulder in left hand.
— — V//XXI
Lit.: RIC 5.2, p. 105, Siscia 810

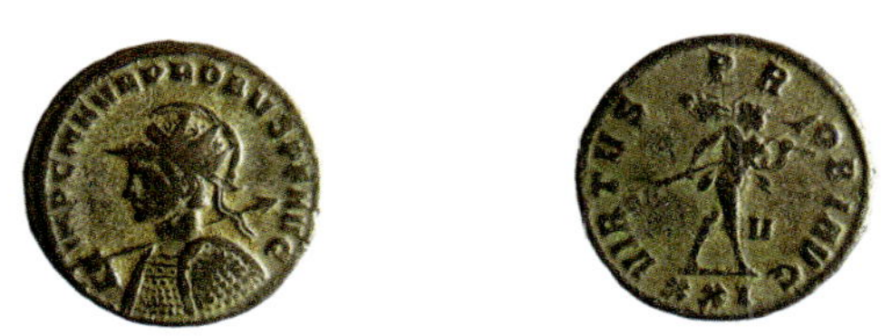

535. AE; 3,28 g.; 21,2 x 21,5 mm.; 12 h.; inv. n. 1826
(Obv. IMP C M AVR PROBVS P F AVG; Rev. VIRTVS – PR-OBI AVG; — — V//XXI)

Cyzicus

276 A.D.

Antoninianus

Obv. IMP C M AVR PROBVS AVG. Radiated bust of emperor in cuirass and paludamentum looking right, seen from rear.

Rev. CLEMENTIA TEMP. Emperor standing right, holding transverse sceptre in left hand, receiving globe from Jupiter, standing left, holding vertical sceptre in left hand.

— S —//XXI

Lit.: RIC 5.2, p. 117, Cyzicus 905

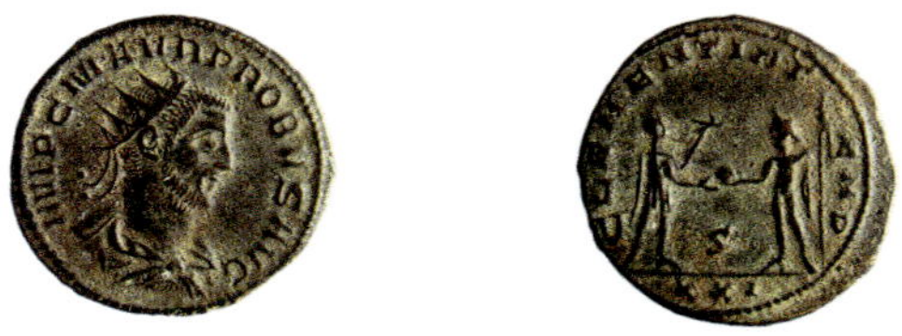

536. AE; 4,17 g.; 21,7 x 22,3 mm.; 5 h.; inv. n. 18.34
(Obv. IMP C M AVR PROBVS AVG; Rev. CLEMENTIA T-EMP; — S —//XXI)

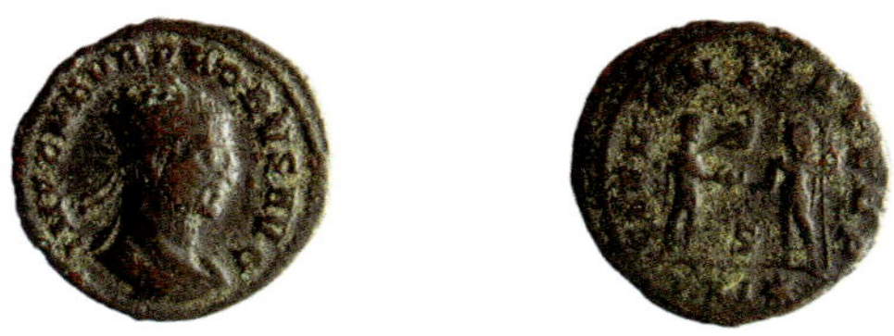

537. AE; 4,52 g.; 22,0 x 22,5 mm.; 12 h.; inv. n. 18.36
(Obv. IMP C M AVR PROBVS AVG; Rev. CLEMENTIA – TEMP; — S —//XXI*)

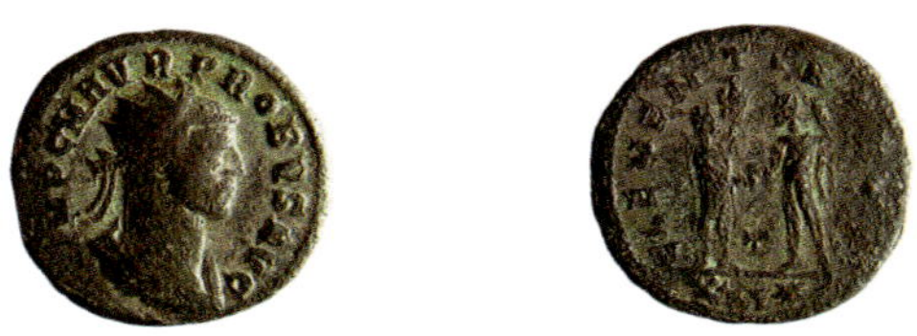

538. AE; 3,49 g.; 21,1 x 21,9 mm.; 12 h.; inv. n. 1827
(Obv. IMP C M AVR P-ROBVS AVG; Rev. CLEMENTIA TEM[P]; — T —//XXI*)

Antiochia

280 A.D.

Antoninianus

Obv. IMP C M AVR PROBVS P F AVG. Radiated bust of emperor in cuirass and paludamentum looking right, seen from rear.

Rev. CLEMENTIA TEMP. Emperor standing right, holding transverse sceptre in left hand, receiving globe from Jupiter, standing left, holding vertical sceptre in left hand.

— * —//KA

Lit.: RIC 5.2, p. 119, Antioch 920

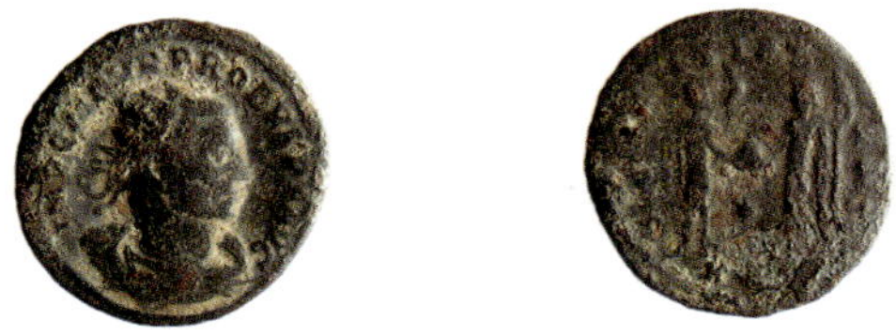

539. AE; 3,65 g.; 22,1 x 21,2 mm.; 6 h.; inv. n. 1828
(Obv. IMP C M AVR PROBVS P F AVG; Rev. [CLEME]NTIA T-[EMP]; — * —//K[A])

Antoninianus
Obv. IMP C M AVR PROBVS P F AVG. Radiated bust of emperor in cuirass and paludamentum looking right, seen from rear.
Rev. CLEMENTIA TEMP. Emperor standing right, holding transverse sceptre in left hand, receiving Victoriola from Jupiter, standing left, holding vertical sceptre in left hand.
— H —//XXI
Lit.: RIC 5.2, p. 120, Antioch 922

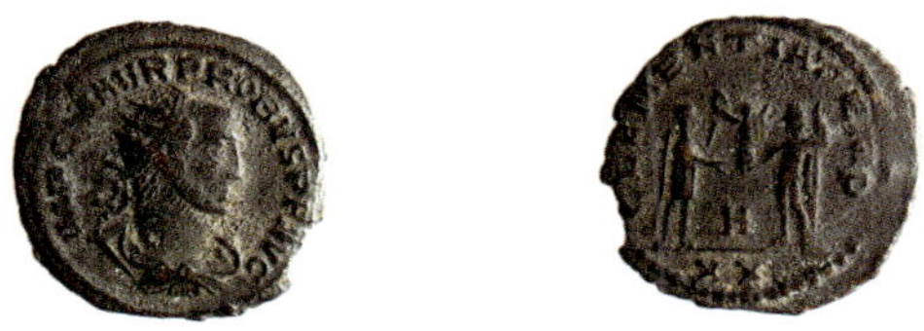

540. AE; 3,99 g.; 20,6 x 21,1 mm.; 12 h.; inv. n. 18.35
(Obv. IMP C [M] AVR PROBVS P F AVG; Rev. CLEMENTIA TEMP; — H —//XXI)

CARUS
(282 – 283 A.D)

Lugdunum

Begining of December 282 – Begining of March 283 A.D.

Antoninianus
Obv. IMP C M AVR CARVS AVG. Radiated bust of emperor in cuirass looking right, seen from front.
Rev. PAX AVGG. Pax standing left, holding branch in right hand and transverse sceptre in left hand.
B — —//—
Lit.: LV 4, 22–27; Bastien I., p. 244, 509; RIC 5.2, p. 136, Lugdunum 13

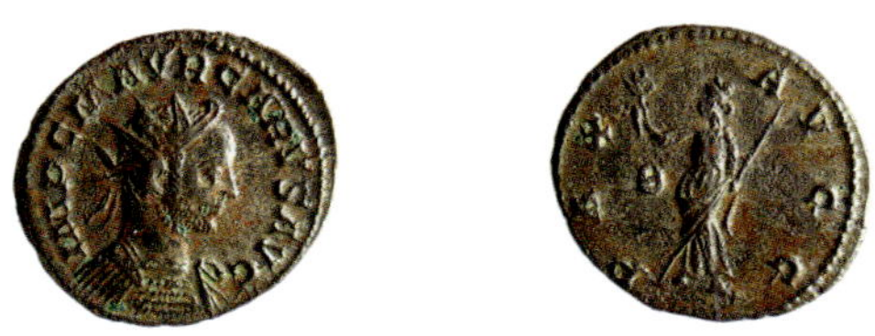

541. AE; 3,58 g.; 21,6 x 22,9 mm.; 6 h.; inv. n. 1829
(Obv. IMP C M AVR CARVS AVG; Rev. PAX – A-VGG; B — —//—)

Ticinum

March – June 283 A.D.

Antoninianus
Obv. IMP CARVS P F AVG. Radiated bust of emperor in cuirass looking right, seen from front.
Rev. SPES PVBLICA. Spes walking left, holding flower in right hand and raising skirt with left hand.
— — —//SXXI
Lit.: LV 4, 668–819; RIC 5.2, p. 144, Ticinum 82

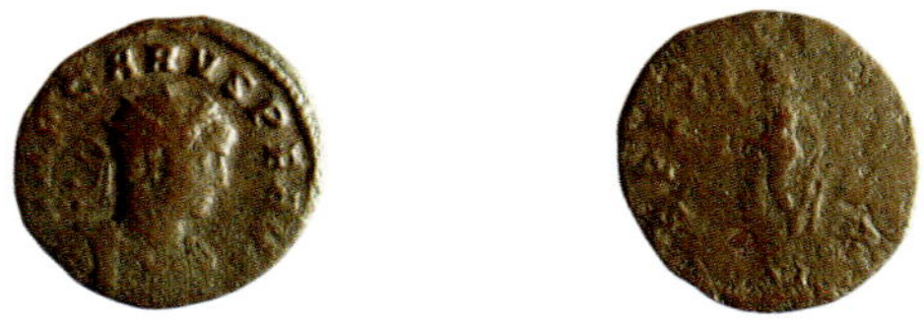

542. AE; 2,46 g.; 20,1 x 20,7 mm.; 6 h.; inv. n. 1830
(Obv. IMP CARVS P F AVG; Rev. SPES – PV[BLIC]A; — — —//[S]XXI)

Roma

c. January 283 A.D.

Antoninianus
Obv. IMP C M AVR CARVS P F AVG. Radiated bust of emperor in cuirass looking right, seen from front.
Rev. AETERNIT IMPERI. Sol walking left, raising right hand, holding whip in left hand.
— — —//KAA
Lit.: LV 4, 1950–1988; RIC 5.2, p. 139, Rome 35

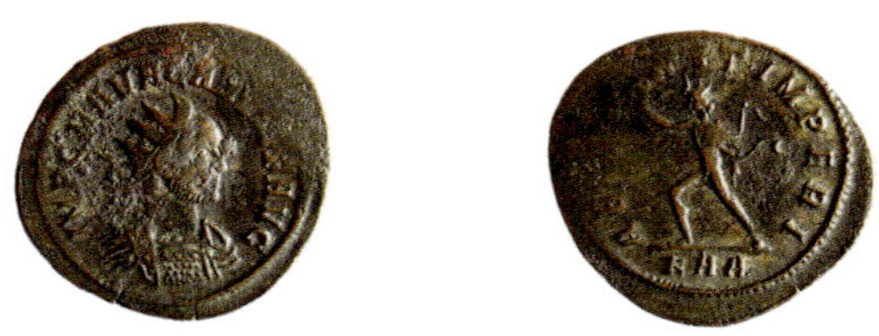

543. AE; 3,35 g.; 22,6 x 22,8 mm.; 12 h.; inv. n. 1831
(Obv. IMP C M AVR CARVS P F AVG; Rev. AE[TER]-NIT IMPERI; — — —//KAA)

NUMERIANUS SON OF CARUS (CAESAR 282 – 283 A.D., AUGUSTUS 283 – 284 A.D.)

AS CAESAR

Antiochia

Last 1/3 of February 283 A.D.

Antoninianus
Obv. IMP C M AVR NVMERIANVS NOB C. Radiated bust of emperor in cuirass and paludamentum looking right, seen from rear.

Rev. VIRTVS AVGGG. Emperor standing right, holding transverse sceptre in left hand, receiving Victoriola from another emperor standing left, holding vertical sceptre in left hand.
— * over Victoriola/A —//XXI
Lit.: RIC 5.2, p. 191, Antioch 378

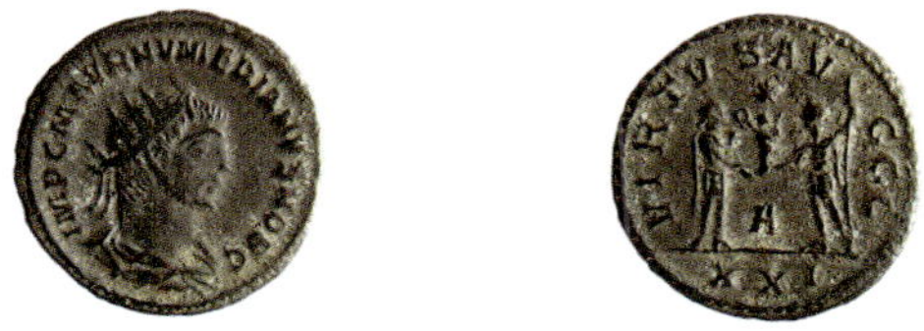

544. AE; 3,83 g.; 21,1 x 20,4 mm.; 6 h.; inv. n. 1832
(Obv. IMP C M AVR NVMERIANVS NOB C; Rev. VIRTVS AV-GGG; — * over Victoriola/A —//XXI)

AS AUGUSTUS

Lugdunum

First Half of January 284 A.D.

Antoninianus
Obv. IMP C NVMERIANVS AVG. Radiated bust of emperor in cuirass looking right, seen from front.
Rev. PAX AVGG. Pax standing left, holding branch in right hand and transverse sceptre in left hand.
B — —//—
Lit.: LV 4, 55–62; Bastien I., p. 251, 539; RIC 5.2, p. 193, Lugdunum 394

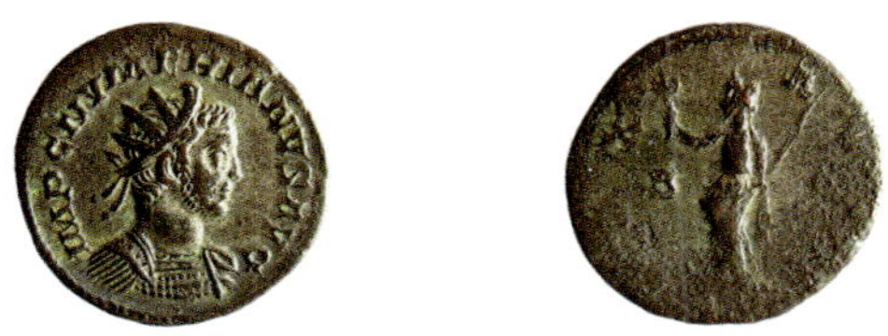

545. AE; 3,23 g.; 22,1 x 22,0 mm.; 6 h.; inv. n. 1833
(Obv. IMP C NVMERIANVS AVG; Rev. [PA]X – A-V[GG]; B — —//—)

Ticinum

March – June 283 A.D.

Antoninianus
Obv. IMP NVMERIANVS P F AVG. Radiated bust of emperor in cuirass and paludamentum looking right, seen from rear.
Rev. PROVIDENT AVGG. Providentia standing left, holding ears of corn in right hand and cornucopiae in left hand, at foot modius.
— — —//VXXI
Lit.: LV 4, 1193–1297; RIC 5.2, p. 199, Ticinum 447

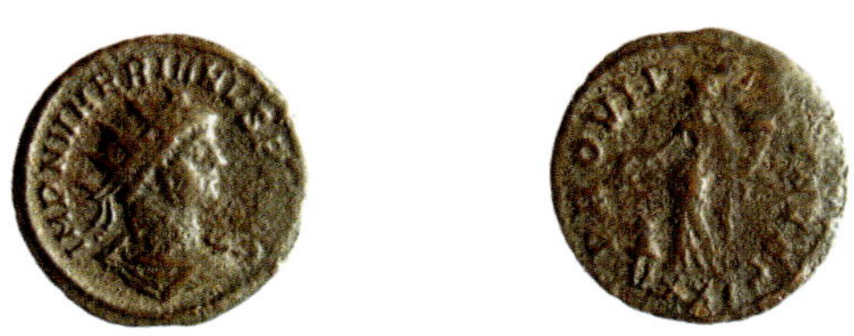

546. AE; 3,26 g.; 22,1 x 21,9 mm.; 6 h.; inv. n. 1834
(Obv. IMP NVMERIANVS P F AVG; Rev. PROVID-[E]NT AVGG; — — —//VXXI)

Antoninianus
Obv. IMP NVMERIANVS P F AVG. Radiated bust of emperor in cuirass and paludamentum looking right, seen from rear.
Rev. PROVIDENT AVGG. Providentia standing left, holding ears of corn in right hand and cornucopiae in left hand, at foot modius.
— — —//VIXXI
Lit.: LV 4, 1314–1424; RIC 5.2, p. 199, Ticinum 447

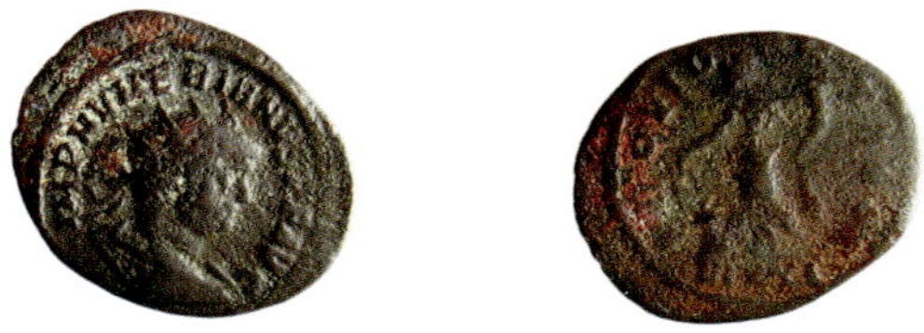

547. AE; 3,44 g.; 21,0 x 25,1 mm.; 6 h.; inv. n. 1835
(Obv. IMP NVMERIANVS P F AVG; Rev. PROVID-[EN]-T AVG[G]; — — —//VIXXI)

Roma

September 283 – January 284 A.D.

Antoninianus
Obv. IMP NVMERIANVS AVG. Radiated bust of emperor in cuirass looking right, seen from front.
Rev. PIETAS AVGG. Mercury standing left, holding purse in right hand and caduceus in left hand.
— — —//KAΔ
Lit.: LV 4, 2854–2985; RIC 5.2, p. 196, Rome 416

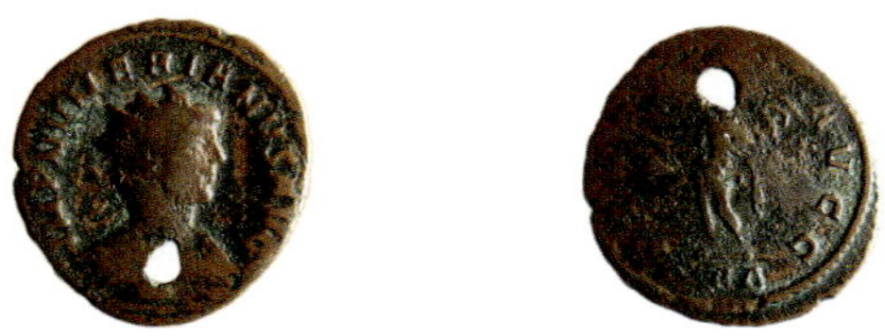

548. AE; 2,67 g.; 22,1 x 20,4 mm.; 6 h.; inv. n. 1836
(Obv. IMP NVMERIANVS AVG; Rev. PIETA[S] – AVGG; — — —//KAΔ)

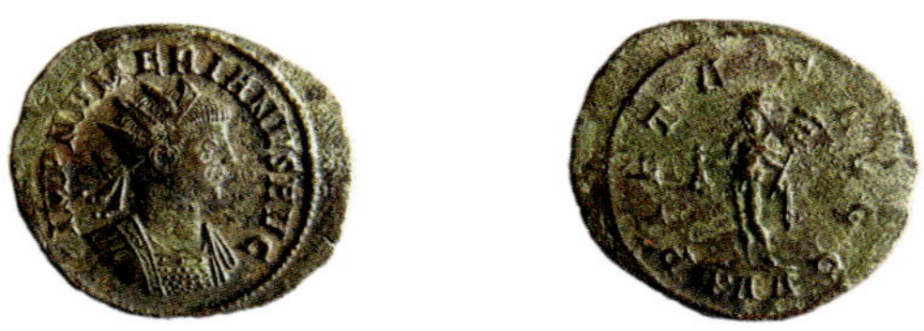

549. AE; 3,99 g.; 21,0 x 23,9 mm.; 11 h.; inv. n. 1837
(Obv. IMP NVMERIANVS AVG; Rev. PIETA-S – AVGG; — — —//KAΔ)

CARINUS
SON OF CARUS
(CAESAR 282 – 283 A.D., AUGUSTUS 283 – 285 A.D.)

AS CAESAR

Siscia

October 282 A.D.

Antoninianus
Obv. M AVR CARINVS NOB CAES. Radiated bust of emperor in cuirass looking right, seen from front.
Rev. PRINCIPI IVVENT. Emperor standing left, holding buttom in right hand and transverse spear in left hand.
— — */T//XXI
Lit.: LV 4, 4228–4239; RIC 5.2, p. 162, Siscia 197

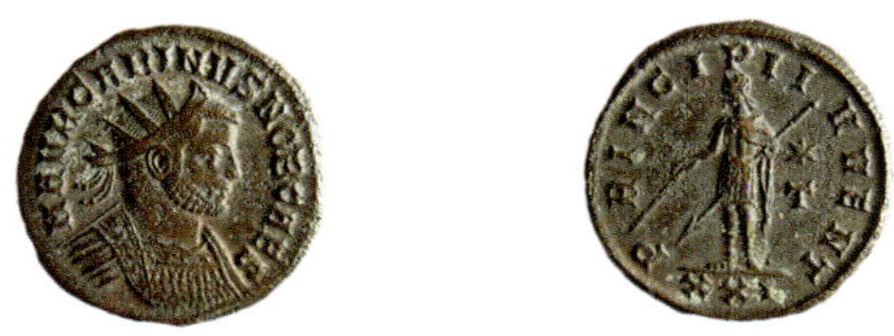

550. AE; 4,01 g.; 21,4 x 21,1 mm.; 12 h.; inv. n. 1838
(Obv. M AVR CARINVS NOB CAES; Rev. P-RINCIPI I-VVENT; — — */T//XXI)

AS AUGUSTUS

Lugdunum

January 284 A.D.

Antoninianus
Obv. IMP C M AVR CARINVS AVG. Radiated bust of emperor in cuirass and paludamentum looking right, seen from front.
Rev. SAECVLI FELICITAS. Emperor standing left, holding transverse spear in right hand and globe in left hand.
— — D//—
Lit.: LV 4, 73–79; Bastien I., p. 253, 548; RIC 5.2, p. 166, Lugdunum 214

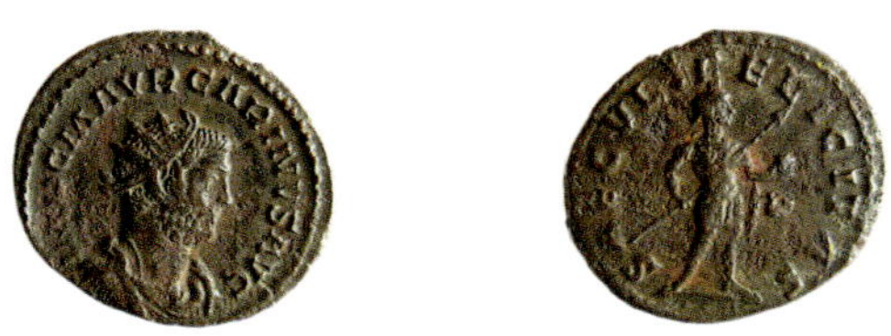

551. AE; 3,42 g.; 21,3 x 23,2 mm.; 12 h.; inv. n. 1839
(Obv. IMP C M AVR CARINVS AVG; Rev. SAECVLI FELICITAS; — — D//—)

Ticinum

March – June 283 A.D.

Antoninianus
Obv. IMP CARINVS P F AVG. Radiated bust of emperor in cuirass and paludamentum looking right, seen from front.
Rev. FELICIT PVBLICA. Felicitas standing left, legs crossed, with left elbow leaning on column, holding caduceus in right hand.
— — —//TXXI
Lit.: LV 4, 868–1015; RIC 5.2, p. 175, Ticinum 295

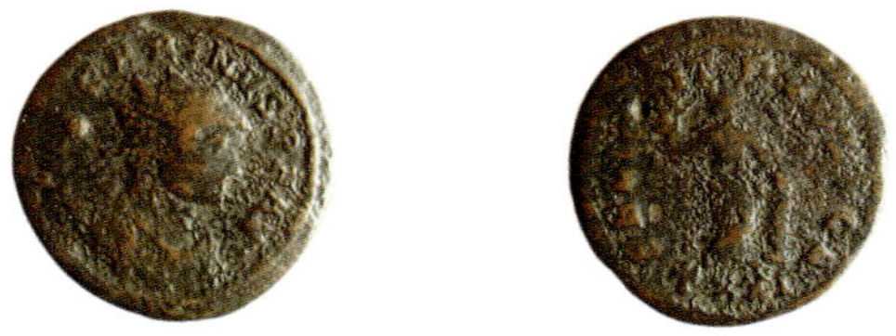

552. AE; 2,82 g.; 22,5 x 22,6 mm.; 4 h.; inv. n. 1840
(Obv. IMP CARINVS P F AVG; Rev. FELIC[I]T – PVBLICA; — — —//TXXI)

Roma

September 283 – January 284 A.D.

Antoninianus
Obv. IMP C M AVR CARINVS P F AVG. Radiated bust of emperor in cuirass and paludamentum looking right, seen from front.
Rev. AETERNIT AVGG. Aeternitas standing left, holding phoenix on globe in right hand and raising skirt with left hand.
— — —//KAΓ
Lit.: LV 4, 2683–2705; RIC 5.2, p. 170, Rome 246

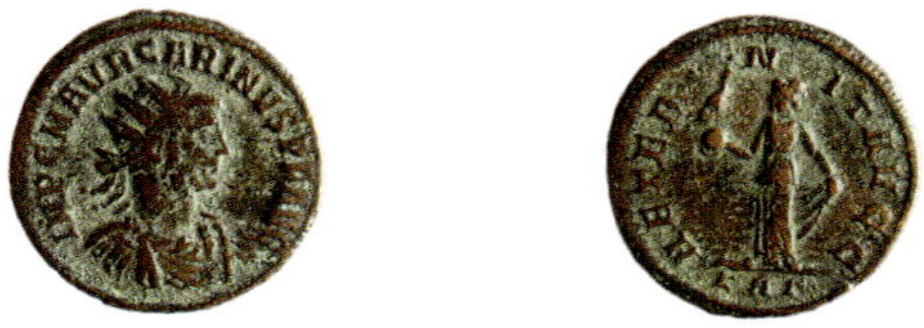

553. AE; 3,76 g.; 20,9 x 20,9 mm.; 6 h.; inv. n. 1841
(Obv. IMP C M AVR CARINVS P F AVG; Rev. AETER-N-IT AVGG; — — —//KAΓ)

Antoninianus
Obv. IMP C M AVR CARINVS AVG. Radiated bust of emperor in cuirass and paludamentum looking right, seen from front.
Rev. AETERNIT AVGG. Aeternitas standing left, holding phoenix on globe in right hand and raising skirt with left hand.
— — —//KAΓ
Lit.: LV 4, 2709–2771; RIC 5.2, p. 170, Rome 247

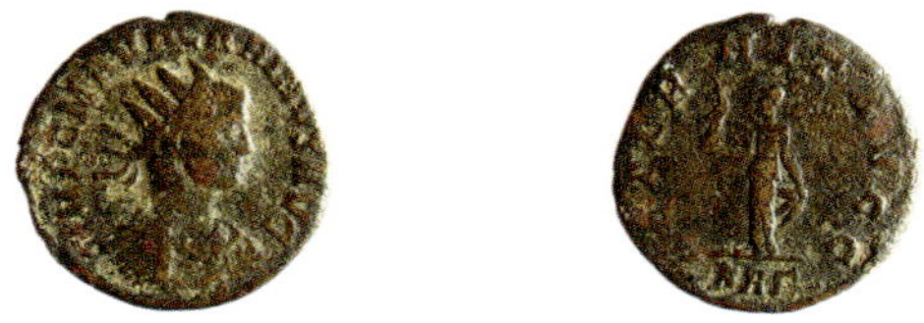

554. AE; 3,57 g.; 20,4 x 20,7 mm.; 12 h.; inv. n. 1842
(Obv. IMP C M AVR CARINVS AVG; Rev. AETE-RNIT AVGG; — — —//KAΓ)

Antoninianus
Obv. IMP CARINVS P F AVG. Radiated bust of emperor in cuirass and paludamentum looking right, seen from front.
Rev. AETERNIT AVGG. Aeternitas standing left, holding phoenix on globe in right hand and raising skirt with left hand.
— — —//KAΓ
Lit.: LV 4, 2772–2845; RIC 5.2, p. 170, Rome 248

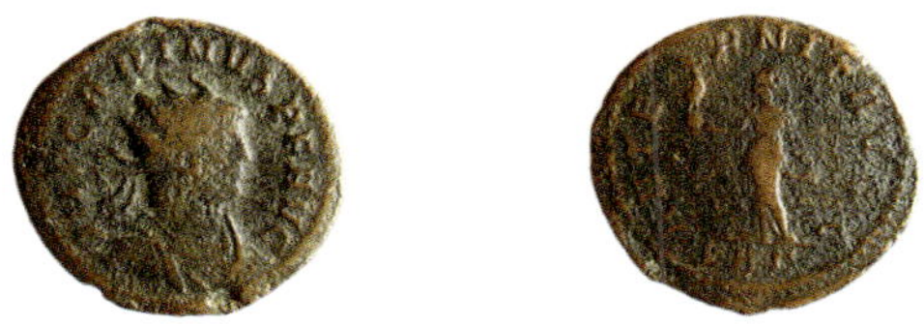

555. AE; 4,07 g.; 20,7 x 22,3 mm.; 11 h.; inv. n. 1843
(Obv. IMP CARINVS P F AVG; Rev. AETE-RNIT AVGG; — — —//KAΓ)

Antoninianus
Obv. IMP C M AVR CARINVS AVG. Radiated bust of emperor in cuirass and paludamentum looking right, seen from front.
Rev. FIDES MILITVM. Fides standing left, holding vertical standard in each hand.
— — —//KAε
Lit.: LV 4, 3012–3084; RIC 5.2, p. 170, Rome 252

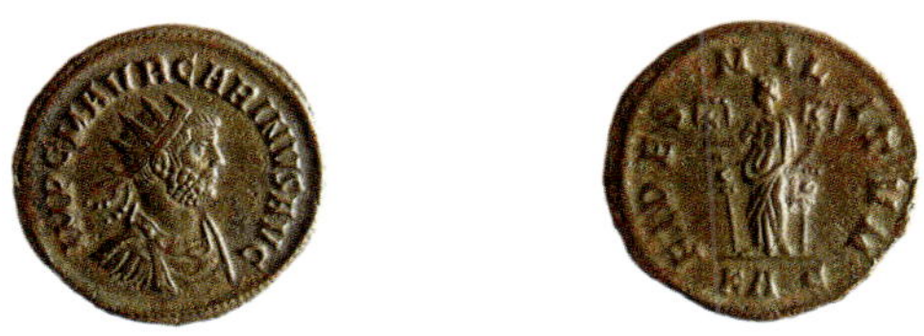

556. AE; 4,14 g.; 21,2 x 21,2 mm.; 12 h.; inv. n. 1844
(Obv. IMP C M AVR CARINVS AVG; Rev. FIDES – MIL-ITVM; — — —//KAε)

Antoninianus
Obv. IMP C M AVR CARINVS P F AVG. Radiated bust of emperor in cuirass and paludamentum looking right, seen from front.
Rev. VIRTVTI AVGG. Hercules standing right, with right hand leaning on club, holding bow in left hand and lion's skin over left arm.
— — —//KAZ
Lit.: LV 4, 3262–3282; RIC 5.2, p. 172, Rome 271

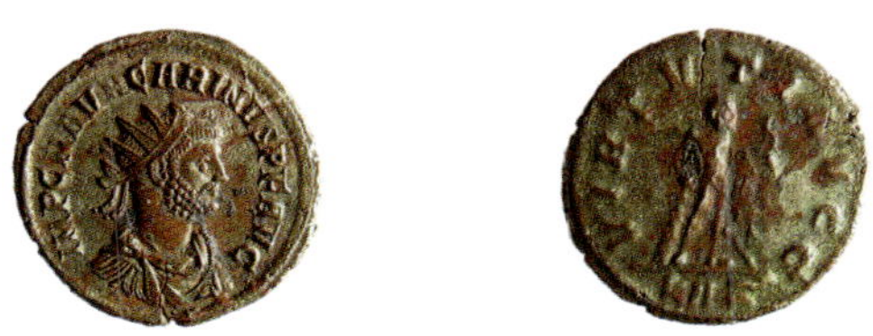

557. AE; 4,42 g.; 22,1 x 22,1 mm.; 6 h.; inv. n. 1845
(Obv. IMP C M AVR CARINVS P F AVG; Rev. VIRTV-TI AVGG; — — —//KAZ)

December 284 A.D.

Antoninianus
Obv. IMP CARINVS P F AVG. Radiated bust of emperor in cuirass looking right, seen from front.
Rev. AETERNIT AVG. Aeternitas standing left, holding phoenix on globe in right hand and raising skirt with left hand.
— — —//KAΓ
Lit.: LV 4, 3806–3846; RIC 5.2, p. 170, Rome 244

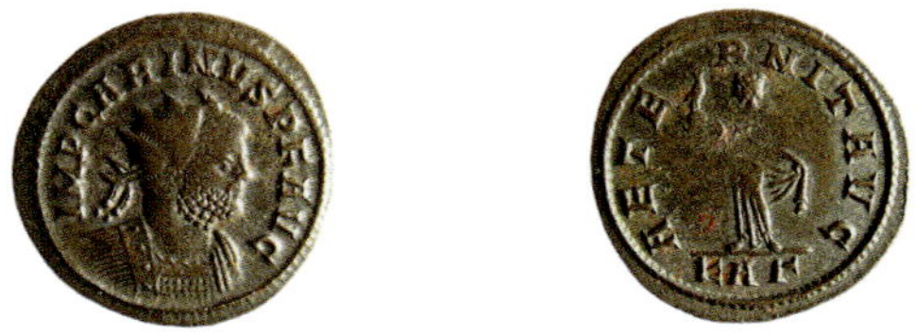

558. AE; 3,95 g.; 22,5 x 22,1 mm.; 12 h.; inv. n. 1846
(Obv. IMP CARINVS P F AVG; Rev. AETE-RNIT AVG; — — —//KAΓ)

c. January 285 A.D.

Antoninianus
Obv. IMP CARINVS P F AVG. Radiated bust of emperor in cuirass looking right, seen from front.
Rev. PIETAS AVG. Mercury standing left, holding purse in right hand and caduceus in left hand.
— — —//KA •/crescent Δ
Lit.: LV 4, 4049–4066; RIC 5.2, p. 171, Rome 264

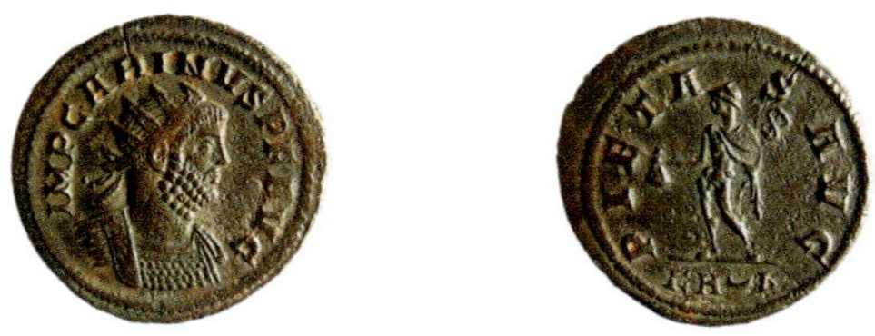

559. AE; 4,08 g.; 22,9 x 22,8 mm.; 12 h.; inv. n. 1847
(Obv. IMP CARINVS P F AVG; Rev. PIETA-S – AVG; — — —//KA •/crescent Δ)

Siscia

January 284 A.D.

Antoninianus
Obv. IMP C CARINVS P F AVG. Radiated bust of emperor in cuirass looking right, seen from front.
Rev. VIRTVS AVGG. Emperor standing right, holding transverse sceptre in left hand, receiving Victoriola from another emperor standing left, holding vertical sceptre in left hand.
—B—//XXI
Lit.: LV 4, 4323; RIC 5.2, -

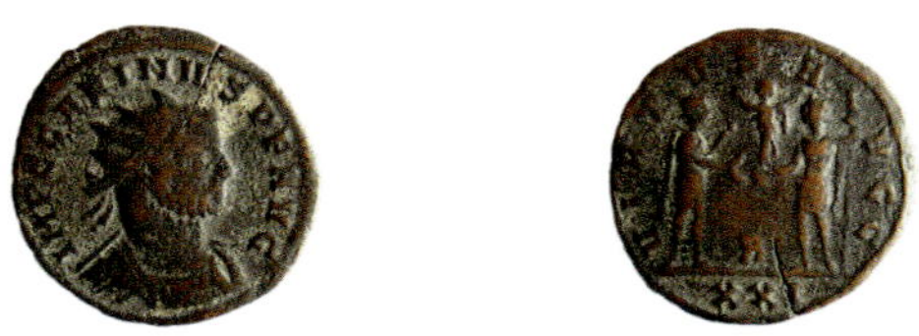

560. AE; 3,04 g.; 20,9 x 20,5 mm.; 6 h.; inv. n. 1848
(Obv. IMP C CARINVS P F AVG; Rev. VIRTVS A-VGG; —B—//XXI)

Cyzicus

July – August 284 A.D.

Antoninianus
Obv. IMP M AVR CARINVS P F AVG. Radiated bust of emperor in cuirass and paludamentum looking right, seen from rear.
Rev. CLEMENTIA (•)TEMP. Emperor standing right, holding transverse sceptre in left hand, receiving Victoriola from Jupiter, standing left, holding vertical sceptre in left hand.
— (A-ς) —//XXI
Lit.: LV 4, 4402; RIC 5.2, p. 178, Cyzicus 324

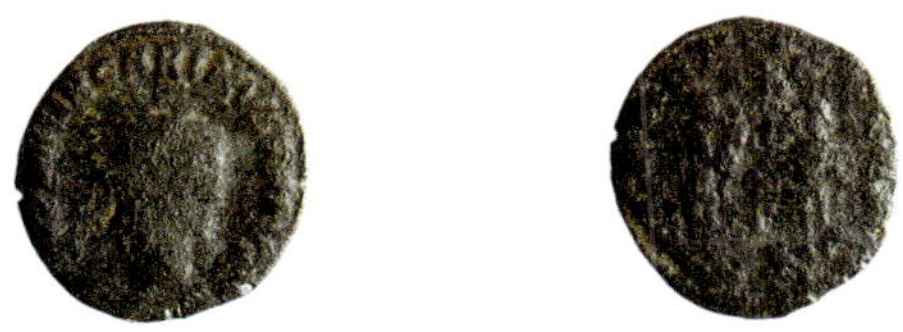

561. AE; 2,59 g.; 20,3 x 18,9 mm.; 6 h.; inv. n. 1849
(Obv. [IMP M] AVR CARINVS P F AVG; Rev. CLEMENTI[A (•)TEMP]; — (A-ς) —//[XXI])

Antiochia

May/June 284 A.D.

Antoninianus
Obv. IMP C M AVR CARINVS P F AVG. Radiated bust of emperor in cuirass looking right, seen from front.
Rev. VIRTVS AVGG. Emperor standing right, holding transverse sceptre in left hand, receiving Victoriola from another emperor standing left, holding vertical sceptre in left hand.
— B —//XXI
Lit.: RIC 5.2, p. 179, Antioch 325

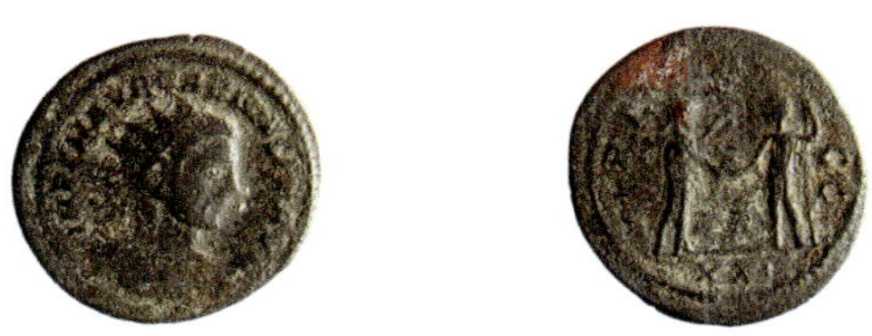

562. AE; 3,71 g.; 21,5 x 22,1 mm.; 5 h.; inv. n. 1850
(Obv. IMP C M AVR CARINVS P F AVG; Rev. VIRT[VS AV]-GG; — B —//XXI)

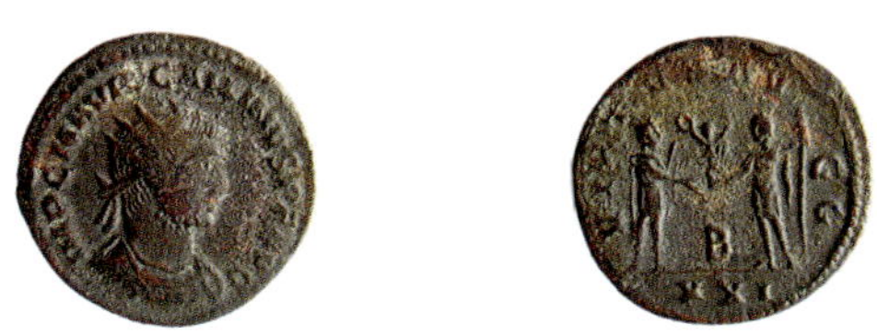

563. AE; 3,54 g.; 21,3 x 21,3 mm.; 12 h.; inv. n. 1851
(Obv. IMP C M AVR CARINVS P F AVG; Rev. VIRTVS AV-GG; — B —//XXI)

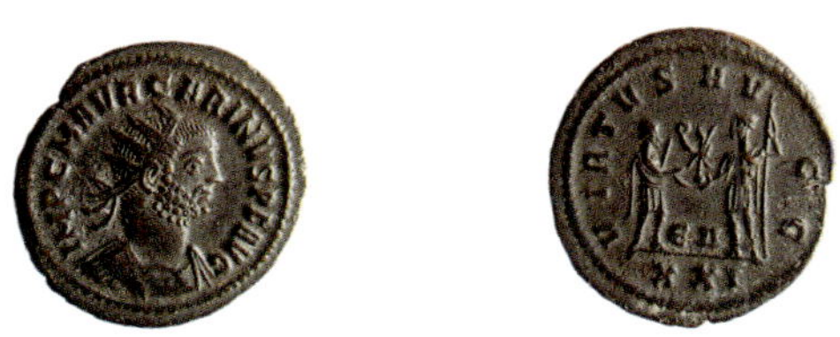

564. AE; 3,75 g.; 21,9 x 21,7 mm.; 11 h.; inv. n. 18.37
(Obv. IMP C M AVR CARINVS P F AVG; Rev. VIRTVS AV-GG; — εΔ —//XXI)

INDEXES

AUTHORITIES

MINTS

DENOMINATIONS

OBVERSE LEGEND

REVERSE LEGEND

OBVERSE TYPES

Empress

Diademed and draped bust of empress looking right. – nn. 157, 162, 164, 165, 189, 190, 484

Diademed and draped bust of empress on crescent looking right. – nn. 156, 158 – 161, 163, 166, 187, 188, 191, 231, 341 – 353, 482, 483, 485, 486

Veiled bust of empress on crescent looking right. – nn. 230, 232

Laureated bust

Laureated bust of emperor in cuirass and paludamentum looking right, seen from front. – nn. 57, 58, 467

Laureated bust of emperor in cuirass and paludamentum looking right, seen from rear. – nn. 1 – 54, 66, 67, 71 – 76, 79 – 83, 85, 89, 92, 94 – 97, 99, 101 – 104, 106, 108 – 111, 121, 122, 124, 126, 127, 131, 134, 141 – 145, 192 – 194

Laureated bust of emperor in cuirass looking right, seen from front. – nn. 214, 468

Plain head

Bust of emperor in paludamentum looking right, seen from rear. – nn. 55, 56, 146, 147, 180

Radiated bust

Helmeted and radiated bust of emperor in cuirass looking left, with spear across right shoulder and with shield in his left hand, seen from front. – nn. 502, 509, 529, 533, 535

Radiated bust of emperor in cuirass and paludamentum looking right, seen from front. – nn. 209 – 213, 215 – 221, 225 – 229, 252, 416 – 420, 430 – 432, 458, 487 – 490, 551 – 557

Radiated bust of emperor in cuirass and paludamentum looking right, seen from rear. – nn. 59 – 65, 68 – 70, 77, 78, 84, 86 – 88, 90, 91, 93, 98, 100, 105, 107, 112 – 115, 120, 123, 125, 128 – 130, 132, 133, 135 – 140, 148 – 155, 195 – 208, 222 – 224, 335, 338, 340, 354 – 357, 366, 395 – 399, 405, 415, 491, 495, 504, 507, 530, 531, 536 – 540, 544, 546, 547, 561

Radiated bust of emperor in cuirass looking left, with spear across right shoulder and with shield in his left hand, seen from front. – n. 236

Radiated bust of emperor in cuirass looking right, seen from front. – nn. 233 – 235, 237 – 239, 248 – 251, 253 – 255, 258, 259, 271, 325, 336, 337, 358 – 365, 367 – 370, 372 – 389, 393, 400 – 404, 421 – 424, 429, 433 – 457, 460 – 466, 469 – 474, 476 – 481, 494, 496, 503, 505, 506, 510, 515 – 518, 522 – 525, 541 – 543, 545, 548 – 550, 558 – 560, 562 – 564

Radiated bust of emperor in cuirass looking right, seen from rear. – nn. 116 – 119, 167 – 178, 459, 475

Radiated bust of emperor in cuirass with paludamentum across left shoulder, looking right, seen from front. – nn. 492, 493

Radiated bust of emperor in imperial mantle looking left, holding eagle-tipped sceptre in right hand. – nn. 497 – 501, 508, 511 – 514, 519 – 521, 526 – 528, 532, 534

Radiated bust of emperor in paludamentum looking right, seen from front. – n. 241

Radiated bust of emperor in paludamentum looking right, seen from rear. – nn. 179, 181 – 186, 339, 425 – 428

Radiated bust of emperor looking right with paludamentum on each shoulder. – nn. 240, 245, 326

Radiated bust of emperor looking right. – nn. 242 – 244, 246, 247, 256, 257, 260 – 270, 272 – 324, 327 – 334, 371, 390 – 392, 394, 406 – 414

REVERSE TYPES

Abundantia
Abundantia standing right, emptying cornucopiae. – nn. 264 – 267

Aequitas
Aequitas standing left, holding scales in right hand and cornucopiae in left hand. – nn. 64, 65, 67, 132 – 134, 137, 206, 258, 259, 328, 329, 356, 373, 399, 401, 488

Aeternitas
Aeternitas standing left, holding phoenix on globe in right hand and raising skirt with left hand. – nn. 553 – 555, 558

Altar
Altar with flame above and girland. – nn. 408, 409

Altar with flame above. – nn. 406, 407, 414

Annona
Annona standing left, holding corn-ears in right hand and cornucopiae in left hand; Annona's right foot is resting on prow of ship. – nn. 366 – 368

Annona standing left, holding corn-ears in right hand and cornucopiae in left hand; at feet to left modius. – n. 489

Annona standing left, holding corn-ears over prow in right had and cornucopiae in left hand. – n. 138

Antelope
Antelope walking left. – nn. 299 – 302

Apollo
Apollo seated left, holding branch in right hand and resting left elbow on lyre. – nn. 77, 89, 98, 99

Apollo standing left, holding branch in right hand and lyre which rests on rock in left hand. – n. 215

Apollo standing left, holding branch in right hand and mantle in left hand. – n. 243

Apollo standing right, aiming bow and arrow held in both hands; cloak flies out behind. – n. 216

Centaur
Centaur walking left, holding globe in right hand and rudder over left shoulder. – nn. 308, 312 – 315

Centaur walking right, aiming bow and arrow held in both hands. – nn. 309 – 311

Clementia
Clementia standing left, legs crossed, holding sceptre and leaning on column. – n. 491

Column
Low column inscribed COS/III. – nn. 143, 144

Concordia
Concordia seated left, holding patera in right hand and double cornucopiae in left hand. – nn. 68, 158, 162, 203

Concordia seated left, holding patera over altar in right hand and single cornucopiae in left hand. – n. 159

Concordia standing left, holding patera in right hand and single cornucopiae in left hand. – nn. 248, 529

Concordia standing left, holding vertical standard in each hand. – nn. 482, 485, 486

Dacia
Dacia standing left, holding long verical staff, surmounted by ass's head, in right hand. – nn. 169 – 172

Diana
Diana runnig right, with right hand drawing arrow from quiver which she has on her right shoulder and holding bow in left hand; at feet to right a small dog/stag running right. – n. 237

Doe
Doe walking right, head turned left. – nn. 304, 305

Eagle
Eagle standing left, head turned right. – nn. 410 – 413

Emperor
Emperor riding on horse left, raising right hand, holding transverse sceptre in left hand. – nn. 167, 168

Emperor riding on horse left, raising right hand, holding transverse sceptre in left hand; to left captive. – nn. 509, 526

Emperor riding on horse left, raising right hand, holding transverse spear in left hand. – n. 128

Emperor seated left on curule chair, holding globe in right hand and transverse sceptre in left hand. – n. 71

Emperor standing left between two standards, rising right hand, holding vertical spear in left hand. – nn. 6 – 8, 37 – 42, 54, 507

Emperor standing left, holding branch in right hand and sceptre in left hand. – n. 385

Emperor standing left, holding baton in right hand and transverse spear in left hand. – nn. 179, 180, 550

Emperor standing left, holding baton in right hand and transverse spear in left hand; to right two standards. – n. 56

Emperor standing left, holding globe in right hand and vertical spear in left hand, being crowned by Victory standing right, holding palm in left hand. – n. 336

Emperor standing left, holding transverse sceptre in left hand, clasping right hand with empress, standing right. – n. 483

Emperor standing left, holding transverse spear in right hand and globe in left hand. – nn. 90 – 92, 100, 101, 146, 147, 478, 505, 551

Emperor standing left, holding vertical sceptre in left hand, raising kneeling female with his right hand. – nn. 221, 233

Emperor standing left, holding vertical spear in left hand, clasping right hand with empress, standing right; between them head of Sol. – n. 468

Emperor standing left, holding vertical spear in left hand, being crowned by female figure standing right, holding wreath in right hand. – nn. 227, 229, 439 – 442, 449, 475, 480, 481

Emperor standing left, holding vertical spear in left hand, being crowned by female figure standing right, holding wreath in right hand; between them captive. – n. 479

Emperor standing right receiving globe from Jupiter, standing left, holding vertical sceptre in left hand. – nn. 434 – 436

Emperor standing right, sacrificing over altar with empress standing left. – nn. 444, 452

Emperor standing right, clasping right hand with another emperor standing left. – n. 353

Emperor standing right, clasping right hand with Concordia, standing left. – nn. 430, 443, 450, 451, 472, 474, 530, 531

Emperor standing right, holding transverse sceptre in left hand, clasping right hand with another emperor, who stands left and holds transverse sword in left hand; between them altar. – n. 338

Emperor standing right, holding transverse sceptre in left hand, clasping right hand with Concordia, standing left. – n. 477

Emperor standing right, holding transverse sceptre in left hand, receiving globe from Jupiter, standing left, holding vertical sceptre in left hand. – nn. 437, 438, 469 – 471, 536 – 539

Emperor standing right, holding transverse sceptre in left hand, receiving Victoriola from another emperor standing left, holding vertical sceptre in left hand. – nn. 544, 560, 562 – 564

Emperor standing right, holding transverse sceptre in left hand, receiving Victoriola from Jupiter, standing left, holding vertical sceptre in left hand. – nn. 540, 561

Emperor standing right, holding vertical sceptre in left hand, receiving globe from Jupiter, standing left, holding vertical sceptre in left hand. – n. 476

Emperor standing right, holding vertical spear in right hand and globe in left hand, receiving Victory from emperor standing left, holding transverse spear in left hand. – n. 228

Emperor standing right, holding vertical spear in right hand and globe in left hand, receiving Victory from Virtus standing left, holding transverse spear in left hand. – nn. 432, 446, 454, 455

Emperor standing right, receiving Victory from Roma, seated on shield left, holding vertical sceptre in left hand. – nn. 447, 448, 456

Emperor standing right, receiving Victory from Roma, seated on shield left, holding vertical spear in left hand. – n. 352

Emperor walking right, holding transverse spear in right hand and shield in left hand; captive under left foot. – n. 235

Emperor walking right, holding transverse spear in right hand and trophy in left hand. – n. 234

Emperors
Two emperors seated on curule chairs left, first of them holds vertical sceptre. – n. 152

Fecunditas
Fecunditas standing left, holding cornucopiae in left hand; at feet to left stands a small child. – n. 349

Felicitas
Felicitas standing left, holding caduceus in right hand and sceptre in left hand. – n. 192

Felicitas standing left, holding long-handled vertical caduceus in right hand and cornucopiae in left hand. – nn. 112, 126, 127, 207, 218, 226, 364, 419

Felicitas standing left, legs crossed, with left elbow leaning on column, holding caduceus in right hand. – n. 552

Fides
Fides standing left, holding vertical standard in each hand. – nn. 1, 9, 44 – 47, 121, 212, 515, 522, 523, 556

Fides standing left with head turned right, holding vertical vexilum in right hand and transverse standard in left hand. – n. 223

Fides standing left, holding vertical standard in right hand and long vertical sceptre in left hand. – nn. 285, 286, 458

Fides standing left, holding vertical standard in right hand and transverse sceptre in left hand. – n. 63

Fides standing left, holding vertical standard in right hand and transverse standard in left hand. – nn. 383, 391

Fides standing left, holding vertical vexilum in right hand and transverse standard in left hand. – n. 122

Fortuna
Fortuna seated left, holding rudder in right hand and cornucopiae in left hand. – nn. 116, 117

Fortuna seated left, holding rudder in right hand and cornucopiae in left hand; wheel beneath seat. – nn. 102, 103, 107, 136, 433, 445, 453

Fortuna standing left, holding caduceus in right hand and cornucopiae in left hand. – n. 337

Fortuna standing left, holding rudder in right hand and cornucopiae in left hand. – nn. 275 – 280, 395

Gazelle
Gazelle walking left. – nn. 324, 325

Gazelle walking right. – nn. 322, 323, 326

Genius
Genius standing left, holding patera in right hand and cornucopiae in left hand. – nn. 374 – 376

Genius standing left, holding patera in right hand and cornucopiae in left hand; in ground to right standard. – nn. 173, 178

Genius standing left, holding patera over altar in right hand and cornucopiae in left hand. – nn. 388

Goat
Goat walking left. – nn. 153, 154

Goat walking right. – nn. 306, 307

Griffin
Griffin walking left. – n. 303

Hercules
Hercules standing left, holding branch in right hand and club and lion's skin in left hand. – n. 496

Hercules standing right, hand resting on hip, left hand holding lion's skin and club which rests on rock. – nn. 86, 87

Hippocamp
Hippocamp right. – nn. 316 – 318

Juno
Juno seated front in round distyle temple; peacock at her side. – nn. 193, 194

Juno seated left, holding branch in right hand and long transverse sceptre in left hand. – n. 196

Juno standing left, holding patera in right hand and long vertical sceptre in left hand. – nn. 160, 161, 343 – 346

Juno standing left, holding patera in right hand and long vertical sceptre in left hand; at feet to left peacock. – n. 484

Jupiter

Jupiter standing front, head turned left, holding thunderbolt in right hand and vertical sceptre in left hand. – nn. 149, 290, 291, 379, 380, 518, 525

Jupiter standing front, head turned right, holding vertical sceptre in right hand and thunderbolt in left hand. – nn. 93 – 97, 289, 381, 506

Jupiter walking left, head turned right, holding thunderbolt in right hand. – nn. 255, 293

Laetitia

Laetitia standing left, holding wreath in right hand and anchor in left hand. – nn. 84, 85, 240, 241, 423, 424, 493

Laetitia standing left, holding wreath in right hand and rudder on globe in left hand. – n. 490

Laetitia standing left, foot on prow, holding patera in right hand and rudder in left hand. – nn. 123, 124

Laetitia standing left, holding wreath in right hand and cornucopiae in left hand. – nn. 400, 402

Liberalitas

Liberalitas standing left, holding tessera in right hand and cornucopiae in left hand. – nn. 62, 88, 120, 129 – 131, 217, 250, 257, 358

Libertas

Libertas standing left, holding pileus in right hand and long transverse sceptre in left hand. – nn. 197, 198

Libertas standing left, holding pileus in right hand and long vertical sceptre in left hand. – nn. 382, 390

Lion

Lion walking left. – nn. 297, 298

Mars

Mars standing left, holding branch in right hand, vertical spear and shield which rests on ground in left hand. – nn. 260 – 263

Mars standing right, holding vertical spear in right hand and shield which rests on ground in left hand. – n. 208

Mars walking right, holding transverse spear in right hand and shield in left hand. – nn. 104, 108, 186, 202

Mars walking right, holding transverse spear in right hand and trophy over left shoulder in left hand. – nn. 355, 377, 378, 389, 527, 528, 535

Mercury

Mercury standing left, holding purse in right hand and caduceus in left hand. – nn. 183, 548, 549, 559

Minerva

Minerva running left, holding branch in right hand and long spear and shiel in left hand. – n. 417

Minerva standing left, holding patera in right hand and spear in left hand. – n. 429

Obscure

Obscure. – n. 43

Pannoniae

Two Pannoniae standing facing each other, clasping right hands in front of standard in centre. – n. 175

Two Pannoniae standing front, their heads turning right and left, away from each other; each holding standard, the one on right raising right hand. – n. 174

Pax

Pax standing left, holding branch in right hand and transverse sceptre in left hand. – n. 10, 11, 48 – 50, 59, 60, 150, 151, 199, 200, 204, 256, 287, 288, 294, 330, 332, 396, 397, 403, 420, 501, 502, 534, 541, 545

Pax standing left, holding branch in right hand and vertical sceptre in left hand. – n. 357

Pax walking left, holding branch in right hand and transverse sceptre in left hand. – nn. 72 – 74, 239

Peacock

Peacock flying right, carrying Empress who is seated left, with her right hand outstretched and holding sceptre in left hand. – nn. 231, 232

Peacock facing front, head turned right. – n. 230

Pegasus

Pegasus flying right. – nn. 295, 296

Pietas

Pietas seated left, right arm outstretched to two small children who stand at Pietas's feet, to left, looking up to her; Pietas holds long vertical sceptre in left hand. – n. 347

Pietas standing left, with both hands raised, at feet to left altar. – nn. 201, 205, 246

Pietas standing left, with both hands raised. – n. 195

Pietas standing left, with right hand raised and holding box in left hand. – nn. 163 – 165

Pietas standing left, with right hand sacrificing over altar to left and holding box in left hand. – nn. 166, 351, 422

Providentia

Providentia standing left, holding baton in right hand and cornucopiae in left hand; at feet to left globe. – nn. 2 – 4, 12 – 18, 51, 57, 327, 331, 333, 398, 404, 503, 504

Providentia standing left, holding baton in right hand and vertical sceptre in left hand; at feet to left globe. – nn. 113, 394

Providentia standing left, holding ears of corn in right hand and cornucopiae in left hand, at foot modius. – nn. 546, 547

Providentia standing left, holding globe in right hand and transverse sceptre in left hand. – nn. 61, 498, 500

Providentia standing left, legs crossed, holding baton in right hand, cornucopiae in left hand; left elbow leaning on column; at feet to left globe. – nn. 384, 392, 393

Pudicitia

Veiled Pudicitia standing left, with right hand drawing veil and holding transverse sceptre in left hand. – n. 191

Veiled Pudicitia seated left, with right hand drawing veil and holding transverse sceptre in left hand. – nn. 156, 157, 187 – 190

Roma

Roma seated in hexastyle temple. – nn. 139, 140, 512 – 514, 521

Roma seated in octastyle temple. – nn. 141, 142

Roma seated on shield left, holding Victoriola in right hand and long vertical sceptre in left hand. – n. 69

Roma seated on shield left, holding Victoriola in right hand and long vertical spear in left hand. – n. 135

Sacrificial implements
Sacrificial implements, variously arranged. – nn. 55, 148, 181, 182, 339, 340

Salus
Salus seated left, feeding snake rising from altar. – nn. 19 – 31, 36

Salus standing left, holding patera in right hand, from which a snake, which is rising from altar, is feeding; in left hand Salus holds a long vertical sceptre. – n. 365, 495

Salus feeding snake rising from altar. – n. 334

Salus standing right, feeding snake held in right hand from patera held in left hand. – nn. 125, 421, 487, 533

Securitas
Securitas seated left, holding sceptre in right hand and raising left hand to head. – nn. 75, 76

Securitas standing front, legs crossed, head left, holding vertical sceptre in right hand and leaning on column with left elbow. – nn. 109, 110, 114, 247, 282 – 284

Securitas standing front, legs crossed, head left, holding vertical spear in right hand and leaning on column with left elbow. – n. 210

Securitas standing front, legs crossed, head left, right hand raised to head, leaning on column with left elbow. – n. 499

Sol
Sol between two captives walking left, raising right hand, globe in left hand; captive under right foot. – nn. 457, 463, 464, 473, 492

Sol in chariot riding left, raising right hand, holding whip and globe in left hand. – nn. 511, 519, 520

Sol in spread quadriga, raising right hand, holding whip and globe in left hand. – n. 508

Sol standing left, raising right hand, globe in left hand. – nn. 78, 80, 81, 118, 119, 211, 220, 242, 268 – 270

Sol standing left, raising right hand, globe in left hand; at feet to left captive. – n. 461

Sol standing left, raising right hand, holding whip in left hand. – nn. 219, 245

Sol standing right, head turned left, raising right hand, globe in left hand. – nn. 79, 82, 83, 459, 497, 532

Sol standing right, head turned left, raising right hand, globe in left hand; at feet to left captive. – n. 462

Sol walking left, raising right hand, globe in left hand; captive under right foot. – n. 460

Sol walking left, rising right hand, holding whip in left hand. – nn. 209, 418, 543

Sol walking right, holding branch in right hand and bow in left hand; captive under left foot. – nn. 465, 466

Spes
Spes walking left, holding flower in right hand and raising skirt with left hand. – nn. 184, 185, 244, 354, 372, 425 – 428, 494, 542

Stag
Stag walking left. – nn. 319, 320, 350

Stag walking right. – nn. 145, 321

Standard
Four standards, the second one from right side with eagle on top. – n. 155

Trophy
Trophy between two captives. – nn. 405, 510, 516, 517, 524

Uberitas
Uberitas standing left, holding purse in right hand and cornucopiae in left hand. – nn. 271 – 274

Venus
Venus seated left, holding apple in right hand and transverse sceptre in left hand; to left small person. – n. 341

Venus standing left, holding apple in right hand and vertical sceptre in left hand; to left small person. – n. 348

Vesta
Vesta standing left, holding patera in right hand and sceptre in left hand. – n. 342

Victory
Victory standing front, head turned left, holding wreath in right hand and palm in left hand. – nn. 58, 335

Victory standing left, holding wreath in right hand and palm in left hand. – nn. 213, 214, 281, 359 – 363, 386, 387, 415

Victory standing left, holding wreath in right hand and palm in left hand; at feet to left captive. – nn. 52, 53, 251

Victory standing left, right hand leaning on shield, left hand holding palm; under shield captive. – nn. 105, 106, 111, 115, 222

Victory walking left, holding wreath in right hand and palm in left hand. – nn. 176, 177, 225, 431

Victory walking left, holding wreath in right hand and palm in left hand; at feet to left captive. – nn. 416, 467

Victory walking left, holding wreath in right hand and trophy in left hand, treading down enemy. – n. 236

Victory walking right, holding wreath in right hand and palm in left hand. – nn. 5, 32 – 35

Winged Victory between two shields holding unwound diadem in both hands. – n. 238

Virtus
Virtus standing left, holding branch in right hand and vertical spear in left hand; right foot rests on helmet. – n. 292

Virtus standing left, holding branch in right hand and vertical spear in left hand; shield rests against right foot. – nn. 66, 70, 369 – 371

Virtus standing left, holding globe in right hand and vertical spear in left hand. – nn. 252 – 254

Virtus standing left, holding spear in right hand, leaning on shield set on ground. – n. 249

Virtus standing left, holding Victory in right hand, shield and vertical spear in left hand. – n. 224

CONCORDANCES

CATALOGUE NUMBER / INVENTORY NUMBER

1 – 1353
2 – 1354
3 – 1355
4 – 1356
5 – 1357
6 – 1358
7 – 1359
8 – 1360
9 – 1361
10 – 1362
11 – 1363
12 – 1364
13 – 1365
14 – 1366
15 – 1367
16 – 1368
17 – 1369
18 – 1370
19 – 1371
20 – 1372
21 – 1373
22 – 1374
23 – 1375
24 – 1376
25 – 1377
26 – 1378
27 – 1379
28 – 1380
29 – 1381
30 – 1382
31 – 1383
32 – 1384
33 – 1385
34 – 1386
35 – 1387
36 – 1388
37 – 1389
38 – 1390
39 – 1391
40 – 1392
41 – 1393
42 – 1394
43 – 1395
44 – 1396
45 – 1397
46 – 1398
47 – 1399
48 – 1400
49 – 1401
50 – 1402
51 – 1403
52 – 18.24
53 – 1404
54 – 1405
55 – 1406
56 – 1407
57 – 940
58 – 1408
59 – 1409
60 – 923
61 – 1410
62 – 1411
63 – 1412
64 – 1413
65 – 1414
66 – 18.06
67 – 1415
68 – 1416
69 – 922
70 – 1417
71 – 1418
72 – 18.25
73 – 1419
74 – 1420
75 – 1421
76 – 1422
77 – 1423
78 – 1424
79 – 1425
80 – 1426
81 – 1427
82 – 1428
83 – 1429
84 – 1430
85 – 1431
86 – 1432
87 – 1433
88 – 927
89 – 1434
90 – 1435
91 – 1436
92 – 1437
93 – 1438
94 – 344
95 – 1439
96 – 1440
97 – 1441
98 – 1442
99 – 1443
100 – 1444
101 – 1445
102 – 1446
103 – 1447
104 – 1448
105 – 926
106 – 1449
107 – 1450
108 – 1451
109 – 1452
110 – 1453
111 – 1454
112 – 927
113 – 1455
114 – 1456
115 – 921
116 – 925
117 – 1457
118 – 248
119 – 1458
120 – 1459
121 – 87
122 – 1460
123 – 1461
124 – 1462
125 – 1463
126 – 1464
127 – 1465
128 – 920
129 – 918
130 – 1466
131 – 1467
132 – 1468

133 – 1469
134 – 1470
135 – 1471
136 – 919
137 – 1472
138 – 1473
139 – 24.26
140 – 917
141 – 1474
142 – 1475
143 – 1476
144 – 1477
145 – 1478
146 – 1479
147 – 1480
148 – 1481
149 – 929
150 – 1482
151 – 1483
152 – 1484
153 – 866
154 – 928
155 – 1485
156 – 1486
157 – 1487
158 – 1488
159 – 1489
160 – 1490
161 – 24.27
162 – 48
163 – 911
164 – 1491
165 – 1492
166 – 1493
167 – 903
168 – 1494
169 – 1495
170 – 907
171 – 1496
172 – 906
173 – 1497
174 – 24.28
175 – 904
176 – 1498
177 – 1499
178 – 905
179 – 912
180 – 1500
181 – 913
182 – 1501
183 – 1502
184 – 1503
185 – 1504
186 – 1505
187 – 1506
188 – 1507
189 – 1508
190 – 1509
191 – 916
192 – 1510
193 – 1511
194 – 1512
195 – 1513
196 – 909
197 – 910
198 – 1514
199 – 908
200 – 1515
201 – 1516
202 – 1517
203 – 1518
204 – 1519
205 – 1520
206 – 1521
207 – 897
208 – 898
209 – 1522
210 – 1523
211 – 1524
212 – 1525
213 – 1526
214 – 1527
215 – 1528
216 – 1529
217 – 1530
218 – 1531
219 – 1532
220 – 1533
221 – 1534
222 – 900
223 – 901
224 – 902
225 – 381
226 – 1535
227 – 1536
228 – 1537
229 – 1538
230 – 1539
231 – 915
232 – 914
233 – 1540
234 – 1541
235 – 1542
236 – 1543
237 – 1544
238 – 1545
239 – 1546
240 – 1547
241 – 1548
242 – 1549
243 – 1550
244 – 1551
245 – 1552
246 – 1553
247 – 1554
248 – 1555
249 – 1556
250 – 1557
251 – 1558
252 – 1559
253 – 1560
254 – 1561
255 – 1562
256 – 1563
257 – 1564
258 – 1565
259 – 1566
260 – 1567
261 – 1568
262 – 1569
263 – 1570
264 – 1571
265 – 1572
266 – 1573
267 – 1574
268 – 1575
269 – 1576
270 – 15.03
271 – 1577
272 – 1578
273 – 1579
274 – 1580
275 – 1581
276 – 1582
277 – 1583
278 – 1584
279 – 1585
280 – 1586
281 – 1587
282 – 1588
283 – 1589
284 – 1590
285 – 1591
286 – 1592
287 – 1593
288 – 1594
289 – 1595
290 – 1596
291 – 1597
292 – 1598
293 – 1599
294 – 1600
295 – 1601
296 – 1602
297 – 1603
298 – 1604
299 – 1605
300 – 1606
301 – 1607
302 – 1608
303 – 1609

304 – 1610
305 – 1611
306 – 1612
307 – 1613
308 – 1614
309 – 1615
310 – 1616
311 – 1617
312 – 1618
313 – 1619
314 – 1620
315 – 1621
316 – 1622
317 – 1623
318 – 1624
319 – 1625
320 – 1626
321 – 1627
322 – 1628
323 – 1629
324 – 1630
325 – 1631
326 – 1632
327 – 1633
328 – 1634
329 – 1635
330 – 1636
331 – 1637
332 – 1638
333 – 1639
334 – 1640
335 – 1641
336 – 1642
337 – 18.26
338 – 1643
339 – 1644
340 – 1645
341 – 1646
342 – 1647
343 – 1648
344 – 1649
345 – 1650
346 – 18.27
347 – 1651
348 – 1652
349 – 1653
350 – 1654
351 – 1655
352 – 1656
353 – 1657
354 – 1658
355 – 18.28
356 – 1659
357 – 1660
358 – 1661
359 – 1662
360 – 1663
361 – 1664
362 – 1665
363 – 1666
364 – 950
365 – 1667
366 – 953
367 – 1668
368 – 1669
369 – 1670
370 – 1671
371 – 1672
372 – 1673
373 – 1674
374 – 1675
375 – 947
376 – 1676
377 – 1677
378 – 1678
379 – 1679
380 – 1680
381 – 1681
382 – 1682
383 – 1683
384 – 1684
385 – 1685
386 – 1686
387 – 1687
388 – 1688
389 – 1689
390 – 1690
391 – 1691
392 – 1692
393 – 1693
394 – 1694
395 – 1695
396 – 1696
397 – 1697
398 – 1698
399 – 1699
400 – 1700
401 – 1701
402 – 948
403 – 951
404 – 952
405 – 1702
406 – 1703
407 – 1704
408 – 1705
409 – 1706
410 – 1707
411 – 1708
412 – 1709
413 – 1710
414 – 18.29
415 – 1711
416 – 1712
417 – 1713
418 – 1714
419 – 1715
420 – 1716
421 – 1717
422 – 1718
423 – 1719
424 – 1720
425 – 1721
426 – 1722
427 – 1723
428 – 1724
429 – 1725
430 – 1726
431 – 1727
432 – 1728
433 – 1729
434 – 1730
435 – 1731
436 – 1732
437 – 1733
438 – 1734
439 – 1735
440 – 1736
441 – 1737
442 – 1738
443 – 1739
444 – 1740
445 – 1741
446 – 1742
447 – 1743
448 – 1744
449 – 1745
450 – 1746
451 – 1747
452 – 1748
453 – 253
454 – 1749
455 – 1750
456 – 1751
457 – 1752
458 – 1753
459 – 1754
460 – 1755
461 – 1756
462 – 1757
463 – 1758
464 – 1759
465 – 1760
466 – 1761
467 – 18.32
468 – 1762
469 – 1763
470 – 1764
471 – 1765
472 – 1766
473 – 1767
474 – 18.30

475 – 1768
476 – 1769
477 – 1770
478 – 18.31
479 – 1771
480 – 1772
481 – 1773
482 – 1774
483 – 1775
484 – 1776
485 – 1777
486 – 1778
487 – 1779
488 – 18.33
489 – 1780
490 – 1781
491 – 1782
492 – 1783
493 – 1784
494 – 1785
495 – 1786
496 – 1787
497 – 1788
498 – 1789
499 – 1790
500 – 1791
501 – 1792
502 – 1793
503 – 1794
504 – 1795
505 – 1796
506 – 1797
507 – 1798
508 – 1799
509 – 1800
510 – 1801
511 – 1802
512 – 1803
513 – 1804
514 – 1805
515 – 1806
516 – 1807
517 – 1808
518 – 1809
519 – 1810
520 – 1811
521 – 1812
522 – 1813
523 – 1814
524 – 1815
525 – 1816
526 – 1817
527 – 1818
528 – 1819
529 – 1820
530 – 1821
531 – 1822
532 – 1823
533 – 1824
534 – 1825
535 – 1826
536 – 18.34
537 – 18.36
538 – 1827
539 – 1828
540 – 18.35
541 – 1829
542 – 1830
543 – 1831
544 – 1832
545 – 1833
546 – 1834
547 – 1835
548 – 1836
549 – 1837
550 – 1838
551 – 1839
552 – 1840
553 – 1841
554 – 1842
555 – 1843
556 – 1844
557 – 1845
558 – 1846
559 – 1847
560 – 1848
561 – 1849
562 – 1850
563 – 1851
564 – 18.37

INVENTORY NUMBER / CATALOGUE NUMBER

15.03 – 270
18.06 – 66
18.24 – 52
18.25 – 72
18.26 – 337
18.27 – 346
18.28 – 355
18.29 – 414
18.30 – 474
18.31 – 478
18.32 – 467
18.33 – 488
18.34 – 536
18.35 – 540
18.36 – 537
18.37 – 564
24.26 – 139
24.27 – 161
24.28 – 174
48 – 162
87 – 121
248 – 118
253 – 453
344 – 94
381 – 225
866 – 153
897 – 207
898 – 208
900 – 222
901 – 223
902 – 224
903 – 167
904 – 175
905 – 178
906 – 172
907 – 170
908 – 199
909 – 196
910 – 197
911 – 163
912 – 179
913 – 181
914 – 232
915 – 231
916 – 191
917 – 140
918 – 129
919 – 136
920 – 128
921 – 115
922 – 69
923 – 60
925 – 116
926 – 105
927 – 88
927 – 112
928 – 154
929 – 149
940 – 57
947 – 375
948 – 402
950 – 364
951 – 403
952 – 404
953 – 366
1353 – 1
1354 – 2
1355 – 3
1356 – 4
1357 – 5
1358 – 6
1359 – 7
1360 – 8
1361 – 9
1362 – 10
1363 – 11
1364 – 12
1365 – 13
1366 – 14
1367 – 15
1368 – 16
1369 – 17
1370 – 18
1371 – 19
1372 – 20
1373 – 21
1374 – 22
1375 – 23
1376 – 24
1377 – 25
1378 – 26
1379 – 27
1380 – 28
1381 – 29
1382 – 30
1383 – 31
1384 – 32
1385 – 33
1386 – 34
1387 – 35
1388 – 36
1389 – 37
1390 – 38
1391 – 39
1392 – 40
1393 – 41
1394 – 42
1395 – 43
1396 – 44
1397 – 45
1398 – 46
1399 – 47
1400 – 48
1401 – 49
1402 – 50
1403 – 51
1404 – 53
1405 – 54
1406 – 55
1407 – 56
1408 – 58
1409 – 59
1410 – 61
1411 – 62
1412 – 63
1413 – 64
1414 – 65
1415 – 67
1416 – 68
1417 – 70
1418 – 71
1419 – 73

1420 – 74
1421 – 75
1422 – 76
1423 – 77
1424 – 78
1425 – 79
1426 – 80
1427 – 81
1428 – 82
1429 – 83
1430 – 84
1431 – 85
1432 – 86
1433 – 87
1434 – 89
1435 – 90
1436 – 91
1437 – 92
1438 – 93
1439 – 95
1440 – 96
1441 – 97
1442 – 98
1443 – 99
1444 – 100
1445 – 101
1446 – 102
1447 – 103
1448 – 104
1449 – 106
1450 – 107
1451 – 108
1452 – 109
1453 – 110
1454 – 111
1455 – 113
1456 – 114
1457 – 117
1458 – 119
1459 – 120
1460 – 122
1461 – 123
1462 – 124
1463 – 125
1464 – 126
1465 – 127
1466 – 130
1467 – 131
1468 – 132
1469 – 133
1470 – 134
1471 – 135
1472 – 137
1473 – 138
1474 – 141
1475 – 142
1476 – 143
1477 – 144
1478 – 145
1479 – 146
1480 – 147
1481 – 148
1482 – 150
1483 – 151
1484 – 152
1485 – 155
1486 – 156
1487 – 157
1488 – 158
1489 – 159
1490 – 160
1491 – 164
1492 – 165
1493 – 166
1494 – 168
1495 – 169
1496 – 171
1497 – 173
1498 – 176
1499 – 177
1500 – 180
1501 – 182
1502 – 183
1503 – 184
1504 – 185
1505 – 186
1506 – 187
1507 – 188
1508 – 189
1509 – 190
1510 – 192
1511 – 193
1512 – 194
1513 – 195
1514 – 198
1515 – 200
1516 – 201
1517 – 202
1518 – 203
1519 – 204
1520 – 205
1521 – 206
1522 – 209
1523 – 210
1524 – 211
1525 – 212
1526 – 213
1527 – 214
1528 – 215
1529 – 216
1530 – 217
1531 – 218
1532 – 219
1533 – 220
1534 – 221
1535 – 226
1536 – 227
1537 – 228
1538 – 229
1539 – 230
1540 – 233
1541 – 234
1542 – 235
1543 – 236
1544 – 237
1545 – 238
1546 – 239
1547 – 240
1548 – 241
1549 – 242
1550 – 243
1551 – 244
1552 – 245
1553 – 246
1554 – 247
1555 – 248
1556 – 249
1557 – 250
1558 – 251
1559 – 252
1560 – 253
1561 – 254
1562 – 255
1563 – 256
1564 – 257
1565 – 258
1566 – 259
1567 – 260
1568 – 261
1569 – 262
1570 – 263
1571 – 264
1572 – 265
1573 – 266
1574 – 267
1575 – 268
1576 – 269
1577 – 271
1578 – 272
1579 – 273
1580 – 274
1581 – 275
1582 – 276
1583 – 277
1584 – 278
1585 – 279
1586 – 280
1587 – 281
1588 – 282
1589 – 283
1590 – 284

1591 – 285
1592 – 286
1593 – 287
1594 – 288
1595 – 289
1596 – 290
1597 – 291
1598 – 292
1599 – 293
1600 – 294
1601 – 295
1602 – 296
1603 – 297
1604 – 298
1605 – 299
1606 – 300
1607 – 301
1608 – 302
1609 – 303
1610 – 304
1611 – 305
1612 – 306
1613 – 307
1614 – 308
1615 – 309
1616 – 310
1617 – 311
1618 – 312
1619 – 313
1620 – 314
1621 – 315
1622 – 316
1623 – 317
1624 – 318
1625 – 319
1626 – 320
1627 – 321
1628 – 322
1629 – 323
1630 – 324
1631 – 325
1632 – 326
1633 – 327
1634 – 328
1635 – 329
1636 – 330
1637 – 331
1638 – 332
1639 – 333
1640 – 334
1641 – 335
1642 – 336
1643 – 338
1644 – 339
1645 – 340
1646 – 341
1647 – 342
1648 – 343
1649 – 344
1650 – 345
1651 – 347
1652 – 348
1653 – 349
1654 – 350
1655 – 351
1656 – 352
1657 – 353
1658 – 354
1659 – 356
1660 – 357
1661 – 358
1662 – 359
1663 – 360
1664 – 361
1665 – 362
1666 – 363
1667 – 365
1668 – 367
1669 – 368
1670 – 369
1671 – 370
1672 – 371
1673 – 372
1674 – 373
1675 – 374
1676 – 376
1677 – 377
1678 – 378
1679 – 379
1680 – 380
1681 – 381
1682 – 382
1683 – 383
1684 – 384
1685 – 385
1686 – 386
1687 – 387
1688 – 388
1689 – 389
1690 – 390
1691 – 391
1692 – 392
1693 – 393
1694 – 394
1695 – 395
1696 – 396
1697 – 397
1698 – 398
1699 – 399
1700 – 400
1701 – 401
1702 – 405
1703 – 406
1704 – 407
1705 – 408
1706 – 409
1707 – 410
1708 – 411
1709 – 412
1710 – 413
1711 – 415
1712 – 416
1713 – 417
1714 – 418
1715 – 419
1716 – 420
1717 – 421
1718 – 422
1719 – 423
1720 – 424
1721 – 425
1722 – 426
1723 – 427
1724 – 428
1725 – 429
1726 – 430
1727 – 431
1728 – 432
1729 – 433
1730 – 434
1731 – 435
1732 – 436
1733 – 437
1734 – 438
1735 – 439
1736 – 440
1737 – 441
1738 – 442
1739 – 443
1740 – 444
1741 – 445
1742 – 446
1743 – 447
1744 – 448
1745 – 449
1746 – 450
1747 – 451
1748 – 452
1749 – 454
1750 – 455
1751 – 456
1752 – 457
1753 – 458
1754 – 459
1755 – 460
1756 – 461
1757 – 462
1758 – 463
1759 – 464
1760 – 465
1761 – 466

1762 – 468
1763 – 469
1764 – 470
1765 – 471
1766 – 472
1767 – 473
1768 – 475
1769 – 476
1770 – 477
1771 – 479
1772 – 480
1773 – 481
1774 – 482
1775 – 483
1776 – 484
1777 – 485
1778 – 486
1779 – 487
1780 – 489
1781 – 490
1782 – 491
1783 – 492
1784 – 493
1785 – 494
1786 – 495
1787 – 496
1788 – 497
1789 – 498
1790 – 499
1791 – 500
1792 – 501
1793 – 502
1794 – 503
1795 – 504
1796 – 505
1797 – 506
1798 – 507
1799 – 508
1800 – 509
1801 – 510
1802 – 511
1803 – 512
1804 – 513
1805 – 514
1806 – 515
1807 – 516
1808 – 517
1809 – 518
1810 – 519
1811 – 520
1812 – 521
1813 – 522
1814 – 523
1815 – 524
1816 – 525
1817 – 526
1818 – 527
1819 – 528
1820 – 529
1821 – 530
1822 – 531
1823 – 532
1824 – 533
1825 – 534
1826 – 535
1827 – 538
1828 – 539
1829 – 541
1830 – 542
1831 – 543
1832 – 544
1833 – 545
1834 – 546
1835 – 547
1836 – 548
1837 – 549
1838 – 550
1839 – 551
1840 – 552
1841 – 553
1842 – 554
1843 – 555
1844 – 556
1845 – 557
1846 – 558
1847 – 559
1848 – 560
1849 – 561
1850 – 562
1851 – 563

BIBLIOGRAPHY

Bastien 1976: Bastien, P.: Le monnayage de l'atelier de Lyon. De la réouverture de l'atelier par Aurélien à la mort de Carin (fin 274 – mi-285). Wetteren, 1976.

BMCRE 6: Carson, R. A. G.: Coins of the Roman Empire in the British Museum. Volume VI. Severus Alexander to Balbinus and Pupienus. London, 1962.

Carson 1978: Carson, R. A. G.: Mints in the Mid-third century. In: Scripta Nummaria Romana. Essays presented to Humphrey Sutherland. P. 65 – 74. London, 1978.

CUN = Besley et al. 1983: Besley, Edward; Bland, Roger: The Cunetio Treasure. Roman Coinage of the Third Century AD. London, 1983.

Elks 1972: Elks, K. J. J.: Reatribution of the Milan Coins of Trajan Decius to the Rome Mint. In: The Numismatic Chronicle, Seventh Series, Volume 12. 1972. P. 111–115, Pl. 14–15.

Kienast 1996: Kienast, Dietmar: Römische Kaisertabelle. Grunzüge einer römischen Kaiserchronologie. 1. Auflage. Studienausgabe (= 2. durchgesehene und erweiterte Auflage). Darmstadt, 1996.

Lužický 2007: Lužický, David: Čtyři mince vojenských císařů ze sbírky antických mincí Univerzity Karlovy v Praze. In: NS 22, 2007, 141–150.

Lužický 2008: Lužický, David: Mince římských vojenských císařů ve sbírce Univerzity Karlovy. In: NL 63.2., 2008, 49–81.

Lužický 2012: Lužický, David: Římské císařské mince ve sbírce Univerzity Karlovy a Muzea v České Lípě. In: NS 26/2, 2012, 197–200.

LV 1: Giard, Jean-Baptiste: Ripostiglio della Venèra: nuovo catalogo illustrato. 1, Gordiano III-Quintillo. L'Erma di Bretschneider. Rome, 1995.

LV 2.1: Estiot, Sylviane: Ripostiglio della Venèra : nuovo catalogo illustrato. 2.1: Aureliano. L'Erma di Bretschneider. Rome, 1995.

LV 2.2: Sylviane, Estiot: Ripostiglio della Venèra. Nuovo catalogo illustrato, 2.2: Tacito e Floriano. Museo di Castelvecchio. Verona, 1987.

LV 3.1: Giard, Jean-Baptiste, Modonesi Denise: Ripostiglio della Venèra: nuovo catalogo illustrato. 3.1: La monetazione di Probo a Roma. Rome, 2010.

LV 4: Gricourt, Daniel: Ripostiglio della Venèra: nuovo catalogo illustrato. 4: Caro-Diocleziano. Comune di Verona, Assessorato alla Cultura, Civici Musei d'Arte. Verona, 2000.

Marek 1985: Marek, Václav: The Roman Republican Coins in the Collection of the Charles University. Prague, 1985.

MIR 27: Alram, Michael: Die Münzprägung des Kaisers Maximinus I. Thrax (235/238). Verl. der Österreichischen Akademie der Wissenschaften. Vienna, 1989.

MIR 36: Göbl, Robert: Die Münzprägung der Kaiser Valerianus I., Gallienus, Saloninus (253/268), Regalianus (260) und Macrianus, Quietus (260/262). Verl. der Österreichischen Akademie der Wissenschaften. Vienna, 2000.

MIR 47: Göbl, Robert: Die Münzprägung des Kaisers Aurelianus (270/275). Verl. der Österreichischen Akademie der Wissenschaften, Vienna, 1993.

Mittag 1999: Mittag, P. F.: Alte Köpfe in neuen Händen. Urheber und Funktion der Kontorniaten. Antiquitas 38. Bonn, 1999.

Monnaies de l'Empire Romain / Roman Imperial Coinage AD 268–276: Estiot, Sylviane, and Mairat, Jérôme: Monnaies de l'Empire Romain / Roman Imperial Coinage AD 268–276. 2012. http://www.ric.mom.fr/.

NOR: Bland, Roger F. – Burnett, Andrew: The Normanby Hoard and the other Roman Coin Hoards. In: Coins Hoards from Roman Britain 8. : Brit. Mus. Publ. London, 1988.

Pfisterer 2004: Pfisterer, Matthias: Zu Robert Göbls Emissionssatierungen für Valerianus I. und Gallienus. In: Numismatische Zeitschrift 111/112, 2004, 103–106.

Pink 1935b: Pink, Karel: Der Aufbau der römischen Münzprägung in der Kaiserzeit. III. Von Alexander Severus bis Philippus. In: Numismatische Zeitschrift 28, 1935, 12–34.

Pink 1936: Pink, Karel: Der Aufbau der römischen Münzprägung in der Kaiserzeit. IV. Von Decius bis Aemilianus. In: Numismatische Zeitschrift 29, 1936, 10–28.

Pink 1949: Pink, Karel: Der Aufbau der römischen Münzprägung in der Kaiserzeit. VI/1. Probus. In: Numismatische Zeitschrift 73, 1949, 13–74.

Pink 1961: Pink, Karl: Magnia Urbica. In: Numismatische Zeitschrift 79, 1961, 5–9.

Pink 1963: Pink, Karel: Der Aufbau der römischen Münzprägung in der Kaiserzeit. VI/2. Carus und Söhne. In: Numismatische Zeitschrift 80, 1960, 5–68.

RIC 4.2: Mattingly H. – Sydenham, E. A.: The Roman Imperial Coinage. Volume IV, Part 2. Macrinus to Pupienus. London, 1938.

RIC 4.3: Sutherland, C. H. V.: The Roman Imperial Coinage. Volume IV, Part 3. Gordian III. to Uranius Antoninus. London, 1949.

RIC 5.1: Webb, P. H.: The Roman Imperial Coinage. Volume V, Part 1. London, 1927.

RIC 5.2: Webb, P. H.: The Roman Imperial Coinage. Volume V, Part 2. London, 1933.

Schulzki 1996: Schulzki, Heinz-Joachim: Die Antoninianprägung der gallischen Kaiser von Postumus bis Tetricus (AGK). Typenkatalog der regulären und nachgeprägten Münzen. Bonn, 1996.

David Lužický

CATALOGUE
OF THE ROMAN
IMPERIAL COINS
in the Charles University Collection
(235–284 A. D.)

Published by Charles University
Karolinum Press
Ovocný trh 560/5, 116 36 Prague 1, Czech Republic
Prague 2026
Edited by Karolína Klibániová
Layout by DTP Karolinum
Typeset by DTP Karolinum
Printed by Finidr, s. r. o.
First Edition

ISBN 978-80-246-6145-2
ISBN 978-80-246-6156-8 (pdf)

Author's contact address:
luzicky@gmail.com